Enduring Legacies

ANCIENT AND MEDIEVAL CULTURES

THIRD EDITION

PHILLIP C. BOARDMAN

Pearson
Custom
Publishing

PEARSON CUSTOM PUBLISHING
75 Arlington Street, Boston, MA 02116
A Pearson Education Company

COPYRIGHT ACKNOWLEDGMENTS

Contents

TIMELINES

Enduring Legacies

Introduction

Legacies, or inheritances, are mixed blessings. The treasures that are handed over to us may give us freedom, or they may bind and blind us. They may mean good fortune or bad luck. In the West our cultural legacies include influential perceptions of the nature of the divine; important habits of argument, critique, and self-examination; deep commitments to the ethical and moral grounding of human action; trust in the social efficacy of institutions; restless passion for exploration and discovery; recognition of the power of art to inspire, enslave, and subvert; and a striking faith in technological innovation. But they have also included slavery, exploitation of others, confusion of private interests and universal principles, and deeply held national and ethnic prejudices.

The pun in the title of this book lays this paradox open to view. For while the past may call up for some of us images of enduring monuments—the best of our music, art, literature, philosophy, and drama—it may also be felt as a burden to be endured (in a far deeper sense than the more obvious weight that students feel in the reading and writing assignments). The West, true to its habit of self-examination, developed myths to explore this paradox. The myth of progress values the power of education, enlightenment, and innovation to raise us above the limits and superstitions of a primitive past and promises hope for even higher achievements in the future. But the myth of the Golden Age finds in the past glimpses of lost worlds of peace, of harmony, of justice and equality, of reverence towards nature, of communion with the divine—all now gone because of a waywardness and depravity that subverts hope for the future.

The readings in this book have endured to become part of our legacy because they open up just such issues for serious reflection and discussion. My belief is that by understanding where we've been as humans, by seeing how we've changed for the better or for the worse, and by reflecting on what we mean by "better" or "worse," we will be equipped, as Henry David Thoreau said, to live deliberately, to know who we are and what we stand for.

* * *

This book contains selections chosen to supplement longer readings for a course in Western Traditions. As such, I have avoided those works which are easily and cheaply available separately and are likely to be read in their entirety—*Odyssey*, Greek tragedies, books of the *Bible*, *Beowulf*, or the *Divine Comedy*, for instance. What does appear here is a modest selection of readings likely to be useful for discovering important points about historical change, political and social institutions, literary and philosophical influence, and which make sense in excerpts. Materials from the ancient Near East and from Islam are included because of their importance in the development of the West.

The guidance and suggestions of many people went into the making of this book, especially Deborah Achtenberg, Joel Boardman, Dennis Cronan, David Fenimore, Craig Gibson, Frank Hartigan, Jack Kelly, Grant Leneaux, John Marschall, Gaye McCollum, John Pettey, Eric Rasmussen, Kevin Stevens, Frank Tobin, Judith Whitenack, and Bill Wilborn. Dennis Cronan has been particularly generous in providing a translation from *Njal's Saga*. I am grateful to our series editors, Barbara Sherry and Tom Biondi of Pearson, for their encouragement, guidance, and pressure. Finally, I want to thank Scott Casper, Dennis Dworkin, Dick Davies, and Stacy Burton for their cooperative teamwork in developing readers for our Western Traditions program, and Dean Robert Mead for his continuing support of the program.

Babylonian tablet (15th century BCE) describing the deeds of the legendary hero Gilgamesh, who sought eternal life. From Megiddo, Israel. Terracotta, fragment. Israel Museum (IDAM), Jerusalem, Israel. Erich Lessing/Art Resource, NY.

The World of the Ancient Near East

Of the many inventions that came out of the Ancient Near East—a settled agriculture, the birth of cities, a calendar combining lunar months and solar year, a mathematics based on 60 that we still use to measure time and angles, the signs of the Zodiac, the study of astronomy, the use of the "Pythagorean" rule for right triangles, monumental architecture (the *zigurrats*), and many more—none may be more profound than the invention of writing. The first writing symbols were pictures scratched in clay. At first the symbol referred to the object (*sun*, for example), then to an idea associated with the object (*heat* or *light*, perhaps), then to the pronounced word ("sun"), and then perhaps to the syllable ("sun" or "son," like our rebus games where the symbol of the bee stands for the syllable "be"). A *logographic* writing system, with a symbol for each word (like Chinese), requires thousands of different symbols; a *syllabic* system, where the symbols represent the standard syllables used to pronounce words (like Japanese or Cherokee), might require around 75 to 100 symbols. The Phoenicians went the next step, using the symbols to represent the individual sounds customarily used in speaking a language. This *alphabetic* system (from Greek "alpha" and "beta") is very efficient because of the small number of symbols to be learned, but its dependence on pronunciation for relating symbols to words means that it is far more local and less universal than *pictographic* (picture-writing) or logographic systems (think about the signs in airports or along highways that are not tied to individual languages or pronunciations). In the ancient Near East a method of writing developed which proved flexible for all of these writing systems. Scribes very early found that pressing the end of a reed carved with a wedge shape (*cuneiform* writing) into clay was faster than drawing pictorial lines in the clay. The clusters of wedge-shapes, first based on pictures, came to stand for words, then syllables, then sounds, of a great variety of languages for almost 3,000 years. The baked clay, buried in destroyed libraries and archives, has lasted very well, but has usually been broken into small pieces. The tablet at left, for instance, shows the fragmentary nature of the text that scholars must often work with. This is a Middle Babylonian text of the *Epic of Gilgamesh*, the greatest literary work of ancient Mesopotamia. The fragment here describes the death of Gilgamesh's companion, Enkidu. It was found in Megiddo, Israel, and pre-dates the writing of the Hebrew Bible.

The Epic of Gilgamesh

The Epic of Gilgamesh *is among the oldest literary works to survive into the modern world. Its hero, Gilgamesh, was actually a king in the Sumerian city of Uruk around 2700 BCE, but the epic poem about him dates from centuries later and recounts events that are clearly legendary. The best text of the poem, on twelve fragmentary cuneiform tablets in the Akkadian language, survives from the great library in Nineveh of the Assyrian king Ashurbanipal (reigned 669–627 BCE). Versions of the poem have been found in other languages, as well.*

In the poem, the gods, troubled at the harsh rule of King Gilgamesh, create a wild man named Enkidu, who lives among animals in the forest. After being initiated into civilization by a prostitute, Enkidu enters the city of Uruk, where he is bested in a trial of strength with Gilgamesh. Afterwards, as companions, the two set out to kill Humbaba, the guardian of a cedar forest. After Gilgamesh refuses an offer of marriage from Ishtar, the goddess of love, he and Enkidu kill the sacred bull sent by Ishtar to destroy him. As punishment for slaying the bull, Enkidu falls ill, troubled by dreams telling him that the gods have decided he must die. After lamenting the death of his friend and organizing an elaborate state funeral for him, Gilgamesh sets out on a solitary quest for Utnapishtim, the only man reputed to have been granted immortality by the gods. In Tablet 11, translated here, Utnapishtim tells the story of a great flood, in which he and his wife were chosen to be the only survivors. Utnapishtim then tells Gilgamesh where to find a plant that will restore his youth. When Gilgamesh has the plant, it is stolen by a serpent, and the unhappy king returns, as a mortal who must die, to his home in Uruk.

The flood story was apparently an important part of Mesopotamian lore, and several similar stories survive in Babylonian texts, such as the Enuma Elish, *as well as in the book of Genesis in the Hebrew Bible. Genesis 11:31, in fact, says that Abraham migrated to Canaan from the Mesopotamian city of Ur, and therefore it is interesting to note parallels between the Genesis story of Noah's flood and the older account in the* Gilgamesh *epic. It seems likely that the migrating Hebrew tribes carried with them the well-remembered story of the great flood which destroyed humankind. Also like the flood story in Genesis, Utnapishtim's story, especially in the speeches of the old god Ea, offers an insight into the nature of the gods and their care for humans.*

The translation, by the novelist John Gardner and John Maier (New York: Knopf, 1984), is in English verse, and it includes column headings and ellipses where the original text is missing or indecipherable—clear reminders that the original text survives only on damaged clay tablets.

TABLET XI [The Story of the Flood]

Column i

Gilgamesh said to him, to Utnapishtim the remote one:
"I look at you, Utnapishtim.
Your features are no different than mine. I'm like you.
And *you* are not different, or I from you.
Your heart burns entirely for war-making,
yet there you are, lying on your back.
Tell me, how did you stand in the Assembly of the Gods,
    asking for life?"

Utnapishtim says to him, to Gilgamesh:
"I will uncover for you, Gilgamesh, a hidden thing,
tell you the secret of the gods.

In Shurippak—you know the city, I think—
set on the bank of the Euphrates—
the city was old and close to the gods.
The great gods stirred their hearts to make the Flood.
Mama was there, and the father, Anu,
and their counsellor, the warrior Enlil;
their throne-bearer Ninurta;
their inspector of canals Ennugi;
[and] Ea, lord of the clear eye, was present with them.

Their words he, [Ea,] repeats to the wall of reeds:
'Reed-wall, reed-wall! Wall, wall!
Reed-wall, listen! Wall, pay attention!
Man of Shuruppak, son of Ubaratutu,
Tear down the house. Build an ark.
Abandon riches. Seek life.
Scorn possessions, hold onto life.
Load the seed of every living thing into your ark,
the boat that you will build.

Let her measure be measured;
let her breadth and length be equal.
Cover it with a roof as the abyss is covered.'

I understood, I said to my lord, Ea,
'My lord, what you have thus spoken
I will do in praise of you.
As for me, I will need to answer the city, the people, and
    the elders.'

Ea shaped his mouth, saying,
saying to me, his servant,
'You, you may say this to them:

Enlil hates me—me!
I cannot live in your city
or turn my face toward the land which is Enlil's.
I will go down to the Abyss, to live with Ea, my lord.
He will make richness rain down on you—
the choicest birds, the rarest fish.
The land will have its fill of harvest riches.
At dawn bread
he will pour down on you—showers of wheat.'"

Column ii

"When something of dawn appeared,
the people gathered about me,
. . .

. . .
. . . the young heroes
houses of . . . earthworks (?);
the little ones carried bitumen,
the strong brought in whatever else was needed.

On the fifth day I drew its plan.
One acre was its whole floorspace; ten dozen cubits the
  height of each wall;
ten dozen cubits its deck, square on each side.
I laid out the contours, drew it all.
I gave it six decks
and divided it, thus, into seven parts.
Its innards I divided into nine parts.
I struck water-plugs into it.
I checked the poles and laid in all that was necessary.
[For the hull] I poured 24,000 gallons of bitumen into the
  kiln;
the same amount I laid on the inside.
The basket-bearers brought on three *shars* of oil
in addition to the *shar* of oil consumed in the seed-meal
and the two *shars* of oil stowed away by the boatman.

I butchered bulls for the people
and killed sheep every day.
Drink, beer, oil, and wine
I gave the workmen to swill as if it were the water of a
  river,
so that they made festival as if it were the days of
  New Year's.
I opened the bowl of ointment and applied it to my hands.
On the seventh day the ark was completed.

The launching was not easy:

The hull had to be shifted, above and below,
until two-thirds of the structure had entered the water.
All I had I loaded into the boat:
all I had of silver I loaded,
all I had of gold I loaded,
all I had of the seed of all living creatures I loaded;
I made all my kin and family go onto the boat.
The animals of the fields, wild beasts of the fields, the
  children of all the craftsmen I drove aboard.

Shamash had set the time for me:
'When he orders *bread* at night, he will rain down *wheat*,
enter the boat and close your gate.'

The hour approached:
'When he orders *bread* at night, he will rain down *wheat*.'
I saw day coming on.
To look at that day filled me with terror.
I went into the ark and closed the gate.
For the caulking of the boat I gave to Puzur-Amuru,
  the shipbuilder,
my palace with all its goods."

Column iii

"When something of dawn appeared
a black cloud rose up from the horizon.
Adad the thunder god roared within it.
Nabû the god of despoilment and Sharru the god of
  submission rushed before it,
moving like heralds over mountains and land.
Nergal of the underworld breaks his doorposts.
Ninurta comes, making the dikes flow.
The Anunnaki lift up their torches:
the land glowed in their terrifying brightness.
The confusion of Adad sweeps the heavens
turning all that was light to blackness.
The wide land was smashed like a pot.

For one day the south wind blew:
it gathered speed, stormed, submerged the mountains.
Like a war it swept over everything:
brother could not see brother;
from heaven, the people could not be sighted.
The gods themselves were terrified by the Flood:
they shrank back, fled upward to the heavens of Anu.
Curled up like dogs, the gods lay outside [his door].

Ishtar cried out like a woman giving birth,
the sweet-voiced lady of the gods cried out,

'The days of old are turned to clay
since I spoke evil in the Assembly of the Gods.
How could I speak evil in the Assembly of the Gods?
How could I cry out for battle for the destruction of
  my people?
I myself gave birth to my people!
[Now] like the children of fish they will fill the sea!'

Even the Anunnaki wept with her;
the gods, humble now, sit weeping,
their lips drawn taut, . . . all together.

Six days and seven nights
the wind shrieked, the stormflood rolled through the land.
On the seventh day of its coming the stormflood broke
  from the battle
which had labored like a woman giving birth.
The sea grew quiet, the storm was still; the Flood stopped.
I looked out at the day. Stillness had settled in.
All of humanity was turned to clay.
The ground was like a great, flat roof.
I opened the window and light fell on my face.
I crouched, sitting, and wept.
My tears flowed over my cheeks.

I looked for a shore at the boundary of the sea,
and the twelfth time I looked, an island emerged.
The ark stood grounded on the mountain Nisir.
The mountain Nisir seized the boat; it could not rise.
A first day, a second day, the mountain Nisir seized
  the boat.
A third day, a fourth day, the mountain Nisir, *etc.*
A fifth day, a sixth day, the mountain Nisir, *etc.*
A seventh day, when it arrived,"

Column iv

"I sent out a dove, letting it fly up.
The dove went out and returned.
It could see no place to stand, and turned around.

I sent out a swallow, letting it fly.
The swallow went out and returned.
It saw no standing place, and turned around.

I sent out my crow, letting it fly.
The crow went out and, seeing that the waters had
  receded,
it ate, circled around, turned, and did not come back.

I sent them out to the four winds and offered sacrifice.

I sent out a drink offering upon the ziggurat of the
   mountain:
seven and seven cult-vessels I set up.
Beneath them I poured cane, cedar, myrtle.
The gods smelled the fragrance—
and gods smelled the sweet fragrance—
and the gods like flies gathered over the sacrificer.

From afar the lady of the gods came down.
[From the corpses] she raised up the [iridescent] fly which
   Anu made for love-making.
'Gods, let me not forget this, by the power of the lapis
   lazuli on my neck.
These [evil] days I will remember and never forget.
Gods, approach the offering.
But let Enlil not approach the offering,
for without discussion [in the Assembly of the Gods] he
   brought on the Flood,
and my people he numbered for slaughter.'

As soon as Enlil arrived
he spotted the ark. Enlil was furious.
He was filled with the wrath of the gods, the Igigi.
'Has life-breath escaped? No man was meant to live
   through the devastation!'

Ninurta shaped his mouth to speak, saying to warrior
   Enlil,
'Who but Ea can create things?
Ea knows all the Word.'

Ea shaped his mouth to speak, saying to warrior Enlil:
'You, shrewd one of the gods, warrior,
how is it—how could you—without talking it through,
   send the Flood?
Punish the one who commits the crime; punish the
   evildoer alone.
Give him play so he is not cut free; pull him in, lest he be
   lost.

Instead of your bringing on the Flood, let lions rise up
   and diminish the people.
Instead of your bringing on the Flood, let the wolf rise up
   and cut the people low.
Instead of your bringing on the Flood, let famine be set up
   to throw down the land.
Instead of your bringing on the Flood, let plague rise up
   and strike down the people.

I, I did not unhide the secret of the great gods.

[Utnapishtim] the over-wise, a vision was shown to him;
  he heard the secret of the gods.'

Think about [Ea's] words, now, [Gilgamesh].

Enlil came up to the ark.
He seized my hand and picked me up,
and he raised my wife up, making her kneel at my side.
He touched our foreheads and, standing between us, he
  blessed us.
'Before this, Utnapishtim has been human.
Now Utnapishtim and his wife are transformed, being like
  us gods.
Let Utnapishtim live far off, at the source of all
  rivers.'

They took me far away, to live at the source of the rivers.

In your case, now, who will assemble the gods for you
so that the life you seek you may discover?

Test yourself! Don't sleep for six days and seven nights."

Even as he sat there on his haunches,
sleep like a wet haze blew over him.

Utnapishtim said to his wife,
"Look at this hero who asks for life!
Sleep has blown over him like a wet haze!"
His wife answers Utnapishtim the remote:
"Touch the man, so he'll wake up.
He'll take the road, return in peace.
He'll go out through the gate, returning to his land."

Utnapishtim says to her, his wife:
"A man who is trouble will give you trouble.
Come, bake bread for him, place it near him, by his head,
and the days he sleeps score on the wall."

She baked bread for him, set it by his head,
and the days he slept she scored on the wall.
The first wafer is dried out,
the second is leathery, the third moist, the fourth turned
  white,
the fifth had gray on it, the sixth was rotten,
the seventh—
          Suddenly as he touched the man he came alive.

HAMMURABI (1792–1750 BCE)
The Law Code

The original text of Hammurabi's Law Code is a cuneiform inscription on a stone monument, now in the Louvre Museum in Paris, discovered in Persia in 1901–1902. Under a relief carving of Hammurabi praying to the god of justice, some 282 paragraphs record royal pronouncements relating to punishments, persons (social stratification), families (marriage and patriarchal control), and compensation (property and contracts). Excerpts from Hammurabi's laws have been found all over the region from many cultures and periods, attesting to the importance of this formulation of a system of justice.

Law codes always provide an interesting window into a culture. Hammurabi's laws do not, in fact, comprise a complete law code, for they assume a large body of well-known common law and custom. At first glance, Hammurabi's laws may not seem to be particularly fair or just. They enshrine the principle of lex talionis *("an eye for an eye"), as do ancient Hebrew laws. It is good first to imagine rule by arbitrary and absolute tyrants to conceive what is important about these laws: they are written down, in public, for all to see and know; they apply to all people; they prescribe, but also limit, the punishment for specified crimes; and they represent an attempt to realize ideals of justice and impartiality. Hammurabi's own writings speak of his desire "to cause justice to prevail in the land, to destroy the wicked and the evil, that the strong may not oppress the weak."*

Unlike the Ten Commandments given to Moses in the biblical book of Exodus, most of Hammurabi's laws take the form of case law: "If one does such-and-such, then this shall be done." The laws identify proper punishments for specific kinds of violations, attempting to match the penalty with the perceived severity of the crime. They carefully define relationships within the society according to an established hierarchy of rank and financial status. Intent and chance are also taken into account: one is usually not seriously liable for events that are accidental.

[Selections]

1. If a man has accused another of laying a *nêrtu* (death spell?) upon him, but has not proved it, he shall be put to death.
2. If a man has accused another of laying a *kispu* (spell) upon him, but has not proved it, the accused shall go to the sacred river, he shall plunge into the sacred river, and if the sacred river shall conquer him, he that accused him shall take possession of his house. If the sacred river shall show his innocence and he is saved, his accuser shall be put to

These excerpts from Hammurabi's law code are translated by C. H. W. Johns, *Babylonian and Assyrian Laws, Contracts and Letters* (New York: Scribner's, 1904). The numbering of the translation follows the traditional order.

death. He that plunged into the sacred river shall appropriate the house of him that accused him.

3. If a man has borne false witness in a trial, or has not established the statement that he has made, if that case be a capital trial, that man shall be put to death.

8. If a patrician has stolen ox, sheep, ass, pig, or sheep, whether from a temple, or a house, he shall pay thirtyfold. If he be a plebeian, he shall return tenfold. If the thief cannot pay, he shall be put to death.

14. If a man has stolen a child, he shall be put to death.

15. If a man has induced either a male or female slave from the house of a patrician, or plebeian, to leave the city, he shall be put to death.

16. If a man has harbored in his house a male or female slave from a patrician's or plebeian's house, and has not caused the fugitive to leave on the demand of the officer over the slaves condemned to public forced labor, that householder shall be put to death.

17. If a man has caught either a male or female runaway slave in the open field and has brought him back to his owner, the owner of the slave shall give him two shekels of silver.

18. If such a slave will not name his owner, his captor shall bring him to the palace, where he shall be examined as to his past and returned to his owner.

19. If the captor has secreted that slave in his house and afterward that slave has been caught in his possession, he shall be put to death.

20. If the slave has fled from the hands of his captor, the latter shall swear to the owner of the slave and he shall be free from blame.

21. If a man has broken into a house he shall be killed before the breach and buried there.

22. If a man has committed highway robbery and has been caught, that man shall be put to death.

23. If the highwayman has not been caught, the man that has been robbed shall state on oath what he has lost and the city or district governor in whose territory or district the robbery took place shall restore to him what he has lost.

24. If a life [has been lost], the city or district governor shall pay one mina of silver to the deceased's relatives.

25. If a fire has broken out in a man's house and one who has come to put it out has coveted the property of the householder and appropriated any of it, that man shall be cast into the self-same fire.

44. If a man has taken a piece of virgin soil to open up, on a three years' lease, but has left it alone, has not opened up the land, in the fourth year he shall break it up, hoe it, and plough it, and shall return it to the owner of the field, and shall measure out ten GUR of corn for each *GAN* of land.

45. If a man has let his field to a farmer and has received his rent for the field but afterward the field has been flooded by rain, or a storm has carried off the crop, the loss shall be the farmer's.

46. If he has not received the rent of his field, whether he let it for a half, or for a third, of the crop, the farmer and the owner of the field shall share the corn that is left in the field, according to their agreement.

47. If a tenant farmer, because he did not start farming in the early part of the year, has sublet the field, the owner of the field shall not object; his field has been cultivated; at harvest-time he shall take rent, according to his agreement.

108. If the mistress of a beer-shop has not received corn as the price of beer or has demanded silver on an excessive scale, and has made the measure of beer less than the measure of corn, that beer-seller shall be prosecuted and drowned.

109. If the mistress of a beer-shop has assembled seditious slanderers in her house and those seditious persons have not been captured and have not been haled to the palace, that beer-seller shall be put to death.

110. If a votary, who is not living in the convent, open a beer-shop, or enter a beer-shop for drink, that woman shall be put to death.

111. If the mistress of a beer-shop has given sixty *KA* of *sakani* beer in the time of thirst, at harvest, she shall take fifty *KA* of corn.

126. If a man has said that something of his is lost, which is not, or has alleged a depreciation, though nothing of his is lost, he shall estimate the depreciation on oath, and he shall pay double whatever he has estimated.

127. If a man has caused the finger to be pointed at a votary, or a man's wife, and has not justified himself, that man shall be brought before the judges, and have his forehead branded.

128. If a man has taken a wife and has not executed a marriage-contract, that woman is not a wife.

129. If a man's wife be caught lying with another, they shall be strangled and cast into the water. If the wife's husband would save his wife, the king can save his servant.

130. If a man has ravished another's betrothed wife, who is a virgin, while still living in her father's house, and has been caught in the act, that man shall be put to death; the woman shall go free.

131. If a man's wife has been accused by her husband, and has not been caught lying with another, she shall swear her innocence, and return to her house.

132. If a man's wife has the finger pointed at her on account of another, but has not been caught lying with him, for her husband's sake she shall plunge into the sacred river.

133. If a man has been taken captive, and there was maintenance in his house, but his wife has left the house and entered into another man's house; because that woman has not preserved her body, and has entered into the house of another, that woman shall be prosecuted and shall be drowned.

134. If a man has been taken captive, but there was not maintenance in his house, and his wife has entered into the house of another, that woman has no blame.

135. If a man has been taken captive, but there was no maintenance in his house for his wife, and she has entered into the house of another, and has borne him children, if in the future her [first] husband shall return and regain his city, that woman shall return to her first husband, but the children shall follow their own father.

136. If a man has left his city and fled, and, after he has gone, his wife has entered into the house of another; if the man return and seize his wife, the wife of the fugitive shall not return to her husband, because he hated his city and fled.

137. If a man has determined to divorce a concubine who has borne him children, or a votary who has granted him children, he shall return to that woman her marriage-portion, and shall give her the usufruct of field, garden, and goods, to bring up her children. After her children have grown up, out of whatever is given to her children, they shall give her one son's share, and the husband of her choice shall marry her.

138. If a man has divorced his wife, who has not borne him children, he shall pay over to her as much money as was given for her bride-price and the marriage-portion which she brought from her father's house, and so shall divorce her.
139. If there was no bride-price, he shall give her one mina of silver, as a price of divorce.
140. If he be a plebeian, he shall give her one-third of a mina of silver.
141. If a man's wife, living in her husband's house, has persisted in going out, has acted the fool, has wasted her house, has belittled her husband, he shall prosecute her. If her husband has said, "I divorce her," she shall go her way; he shall give her nothing as her price of divorce. If her husband has said, "I will not divorce her," he may take another woman to wife; the wife shall live as a slave in her husband's house.
142. If a woman has hated her husband and has said, "You shall not possess me," her past shall be inquired into as to what she lacks. If she has been discreet, and has no vice, and her husband has gone out, and has greatly belittled her, that woman has no blame, she shall take her marriage-portion and go off to her father's house.
143. If she has not been discreet, has gone out, ruined her house, belittled her husband, she shall be drowned.
152. From the time that woman entered into the man's house they together shall be liable for all debts subsequently incurred.
153. If a man's wife, for the sake of another, has caused her husband to be killed, that woman shall be impaled.
154. If a man has committed incest with his daughter, that man shall be banished from the city.
155. If a man has betrothed a maiden to his son and his son has known her, and afterward the man has lain in her bosom, and been caught, that man shall be strangled and she shall be cast into the water.
156. If a man has betrothed a maiden to his son, and his son has not known her, and that man has lain in her bosom, he shall pay her half a mina of silver, and shall pay over to her whatever she brought from her father's house, and the husband of her choice shall marry her.
157. If a man, after his father's death, be caught in the bosom of his mother, they shall both of them be burnt together.
158. If a man, after his father's death be caught in the bosom of his step-mother who has borne children, that man shall be cut off from his father's house.
159. If a man, who has presented a gift to the house of his prospective father-in-law and has given the bride-price, has afterward looked upon another woman and has said to his father-in-law, "I will not marry your daughter"; the father of the girl shall keep whatever he has brought as a present.
160. If a man has presented a gift to the house of his prospective father-in-law, and has given the bride-price, but his comrade has slandered him and his father-in-law has said to the suitor, "You shall not marry my daughter," [the father] shall return double all that was presented to him. Further, the comrade shall not marry the girl.
162. If a man has married a wife, and she has borne him children, and that woman has gone to her fate, her father shall lay no claim to her marriage-portion. Her marriage-portion is her children's only.
165. If a man has presented field, garden, or house to his son, the first in his eyes, and has written him a deed of gift; after the father has gone to his fate when the brothers share,

he shall keep the present his father gave him, and over and above shall share equally with them in the goods of his father's estate.

166. If a man has taken wives for the other sons he had, but has not taken a wife for his young son, after the father has gone to his fate, when the brothers share, they shall set aside from the goods of their father's estate money, as a bride-price, for their young brother, who has not married a wife, over and above his share, and they shall cause him to take a wife.

167. If a man has taken a wife, and she has borne him children and that woman has gone to her fate, and he has taken a second wife, and she also has borne children; after the father has gone to his fate, the sons shall not share according to mothers, but each family shall take the marriage-portion of its mother, and all shall share the goods of their father's estate equally.

168. If a man has determined to disinherit his son and has declared before the judge, "I cut off my son," the judge shall inquire into the son's past, and, if the son has not committed a grave misdemeanor such as should cut him off from sonship, the father shall not disinherit his son.

169. If he has committed a grave crime against his father, which cuts off from sonship, for the first offence he shall pardon him. If he has committed a grave crime a second time, the father shall cut off his son from sonship.

170. If a man has had children borne to him by his wife, and also by a maid, if the father in his lifetime has said, "My sons," to the children whom his maid bore him, and has reckoned them with the sons of his wife; then after the father has gone to his fate, the children of the wife and of the maid shall share equally. The children of the wife shall apportion the shares and make their own selections.

175. If either a slave of a patrician, or of a plebeian, has married the daughter of a free man, and she has borne children, the owner of the slave shall have no claim for service on the children, of a free woman. And if a slave, either of a patrician or of a plebeian, has married a free woman and when he married her she entered the slave's house with a marriage-portion from her father's estate, be he slave of a patrician or of a plebeian, and from the time they started to keep house, they have acquired property; after the slave, whether of a patrician or of a plebeian, has gone to his fate, the free woman shall take her marriage-portion, and whatever her husband and she acquired, since they started house-keeping. She shall divide it into two portions. The master of the slave shall take one half, the other half the free woman shall take for her children.

176. If the free woman had no marriage-portion, whatever her husband and she acquired since they started house-keeping he shall divide into two portions. The owner of the slave shall take one half, the other half the free woman shall take for her children.

177. If a widow, whose children are young, had determined to marry again, she shall not marry without consent of the judge. When she is allowed to remarry, the judge shall inquire as to what remains of the property of her former husband and shall intrust the property of her former husband to that woman and her second husband. He shall give them an inventory. They shall watch over the property, and bring up the children. Not a utensil shall they sell. A buyer of any utensil belonging to the widow's children shall lose his money and shall return the article to its owners.

181. If a father has vowed his daughter to a god, as a temple maid, or a virgin, and has given her no portion; after the father has gone to his fate, she shall share in the property of her

father's estate, taking one-third of a child's share. She shall enjoy her share, as long as she lives. After her, it belongs to her brothers.

185. If a man had taken a young child, a natural son of his, to be his son, and has brought him up, no one shall make a claim against that foster child.

186. If a man has taken a young child to be his son, and after he has taken him, the child discover his own parents, he shall return to his father's house.

187. The son of a royal favorite, of one that stands in the palace, or the son of a votary shall not be reclaimed.

188, 189. If a craftsman has taken a child to bring up and has taught him his handicraft, he shall not be reclaimed. If he has not taught him his handicraft, that foster child shall return to his father's house.

192. If the son of a palace favorite or the son of a vowed woman has said to the father that brought him up, "You are not my father," or to the mother that brought him up, "You are not my mother," his tongue shall be cut out.

193. If the son of a palace favorite or the son of a vowed woman has come to know his father's house and has hated his father that brought him up, or his mother that brought him up, and shall go off to his father's house, his eyes shall be torn out.

194. If a man has given his son to a wet-nurse to suckle, and that son has died in the hands of the nurse, and the nurse, without consent of the child's father or mother, has nursed another child, they shall prosecute her; because she has nursed another child, without consent of the father or mother, her breasts shall be cut off.

195. If a son has struck his father, his hands shall be cut off.

Woman or Goddess with Snakes, from the palace complex, Knossos, Crete c. 1700–1550 BCE. Faience, height 11 5/8" (29.5 cm). Archeological Museum, Iraklion, Crete. Giraudon/Art Resource, NY.

The Greek World

Introduction

In 1871, the wealthy German businessman Heinrich Schliemann began his life's work—the discovery of ancient Troy. Fascinated from his boyhood with the stories of Agamemnon, Odysseus, Priam, and Achilles, Schliemann set out to make a fortune to finance his quest. In the course of his business dealings, he learned nearly a dozen languages, became an American citizen, traveled around the world, and studied archeology. Attracted to a mound at Hissarlik, on the Turkish coast, he dug and discovered a cache of gold jewelry, which he called "Priam's treasure." Although he dug through what might have been Homer's Troy to a much older city beneath it, Schliemann's discovery effectively changed the way people thought about Homer's poems. Not simply imaginative fantasies, they now seemed to have a kernel of historical reality at their centers. This view was bolstered somewhat by Schliemann's next dig, at Mycenae in Greece. Once again digging to a level deeper and older than he sought, Schliemann found the graves of ancient Mycenian kings, along with gold funerary objects. Seeing a striking golden mask, Schliemann declared, "I have looked on the face of Agamemnon!" Schliemann also hoped to find the fabled palace of King Minos of Crete, central to the story of Theseus and the Minotaur. It was finally the British archeologist Sir Arthur Evans who located the great palace at Knossos in 1900. Evans found the impressive remains of an advanced civilization, called Minoan after the legendary king. The people lived in an unfortified palace so large and complex its name—*Labyrinth*, "Palace of the Double-Axes"—became the word for a maze. The discovery of many female figurines with snake motifs, like the so-called *snake goddess* shown here, has led to the suggestion that the Minoans of Crete were a peace-loving, goddess-worshiping people whose high culture, art, and literacy stood in tragic contrast with the male-centered, sky-god-worshiping Mycenians and then Dorian Greeks who succeeded them as powers in the Aegean.

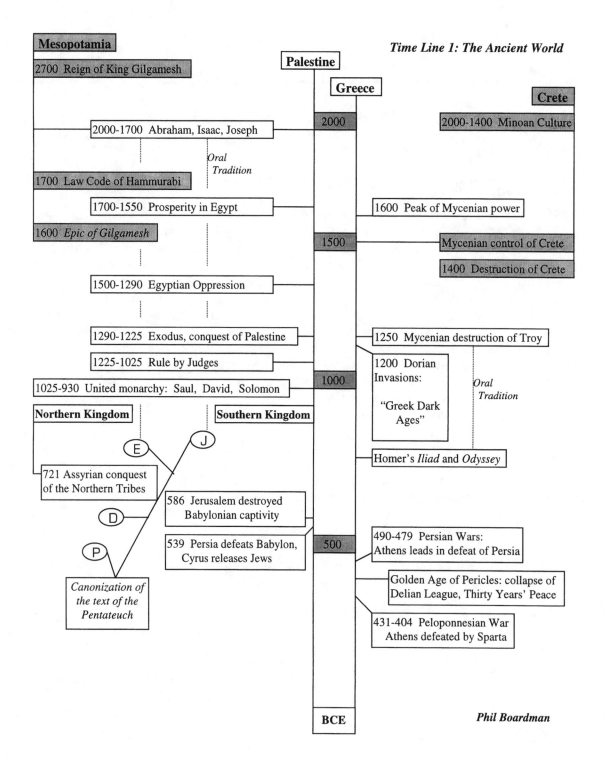

Time Line 1: The Ancient World

Mesopotamia

2700 Reign of King Gilgamesh

Palestine

Greece

Crete

2000

2000-1400 Minoan Culture

2000-1700 Abraham, Isaac, Joseph

Oral Tradition

1700 Law Code of Hammurabi

1700-1550 Prosperity in Egypt

1600 Peak of Mycenian power

1600 *Epic of Gilgamesh*

1500

Mycenian control of Crete

1400 Destruction of Crete

1500-1290 Egyptian Oppression

1290-1225 Exodus, conquest of Palestine

1250 Mycenian destruction of Troy

1225-1025 Rule by Judges

1200 Dorian Invasions:

"Greek Dark Ages"

Oral Tradition

1025-930 United monarchy: Saul, David, Solomon

1000

Northern Kingdom

Southern Kingdom

E   J

Homer's *Iliad* and *Odyssey*

721 Assyrian conquest of the Northern Tribes

586 Jerusalem destroyed Babylonian captivity

D

539 Persia defeats Babylon, Cyrus releases Jews

500

490-479 Persian Wars: Athens leads in defeat of Persia

P

Canonization of the text of the Pentateuch

Golden Age of Pericles: collapse of Delian League, Thirty Years' Peace

431-404 Peloponnesian War Athens defeated by Sparta

BCE

Phil Boardman

HESIOD (8TH CENTURY BCE)
The Theogony [The Creation of the Gods]

We know very little of Hesiod other than what he tells us in his later epic, Works and Days, *a didactic poem based on his personal experiences as a farmer. In that poem he rails against his brother, who, according to Hesiod, stole his inheritance and bribed public officials for support. Hesiod, a shepherd who lived near Mt. Helicon in central Greece, began writing poems when he heard the Muses instructing him to "sing of the race of the blessed gods immortal." The song which he sang about these blessed gods is the* Theogony, *an account of the generations of the gods. Along with the epic poems of his near contemporary, Homer, Hesiod's poems came almost to have the status of religious texts to later Greeks.*

Theogony is a difficult work because of the great procession of names and events identified but not elaborated in a work that seems to have no plot. In some ways it is this procession which is most important in the work, for it is the key to Hesiod's themes—the endless pattern of crime and rebellion and the supreme power of Zeus—and it provides an insight into the deeper ways of Greek myth. The poem shows us three generations of gods: the (1) **elemental generation** *of Void (Chaos), Earth (Gaea), and Eros. After the birth of Darkness and Night, Earth herself gives birth to Sky (or Heaven, Uranus), who then breeds upon her the generation (2) of* **Titans**, *including gods representing Ocean, the Sun (Hyperion), Law, Memory, and Time (Cronus). These gods, whose very names evoke aspects of nature, lay in place the backdrop of natural forces against which humans construct their lives and with which they inevitably contend.*

The Titans seize power when Cronus, at the urging of Mother Earth, castrates his father Sky. Then he sleeps with his sister Rhea, who gives birth to the generation (3) of the **Olympian gods**, *so named because they eventually reside on Mount Olympus. A central episode of the* Theogony *is the so-called "Titanomachia," the battle by which the Olympians, led by the clever Zeus, defeat the Titans, who support Cronus. In the course of the battle we see yet another struggle emerging, this time between humans and the Olympians, who often show themselves to be fickle, petty, and dangerous. In* Theogony, *humans are treated to two models: the god Prometheus, who fights against Zeus on behalf of humans, and the first woman, later called Pandora, who is sent by Zeus as a curse to plague mankind.*

[Selections]

Daughters of Zeus, I greet you; add passion to my song, and tell of the sacred race of gods who are forever, descended from Earth and starry Sky, from dark Night, and from salty Sea. Tell how in the beginning the gods and the earth came into being, as well as the rivers, the

---

The selection is translated by Norman O. Brown and taken from Hesiod's *Theogony* (New York: Macmillan/Library of Liberal Arts, 1953).

limitless sea with its raging surges, the shining stars, and the broad sky above—also how they divided the estate and distributed privileges among themselves, and how they first established themselves in the folds of Mount Olympus. Relate these things to me, Muses whose home is Olympus, from the beginning; tell me which of them first came into being.

II. First of all, the Void came into being, next broad-bosomed Earth, the solid and eternal home of all, and Eros [Desire], the most beautiful of the immortal gods, who in every man and every god softens the sinews and overpowers the prudent purpose of the mind. Out of Void came Darkness and black Night, and out of Night came Light and Day, her children conceived after union in love with Darkness. Earth first produced starry Sky, equal in size with herself, to cover her on all sides. Next she produced the tall mountains, the pleasant haunts of the gods, and also gave birth to the barren waters, sea with its raging surges—all this without the passion of love. Thereafter she lay with Sky and gave birth to Ocean with its deep current, Coeus and Crius and Hyperion and Iapetus; Thea and Rhea and Themis [Law] and Mnemosyne [Memory]; also golden-crowned Phoebe and lovely Tethys. After these came cunning Cronus, the youngest and boldest of her children; and he grew to hate the father who had begotten him.

Earth also gave birth to the violent Cyclopes—Thunderer, Lightner, and bold Flash—who made and gave to Zeus the thunder and the lightning-bolt. They were like the gods in all respects except that a single eye stood in the middle of their foreheads, and their strength and power and skill were in their hands.

There were also born to Earth and Sky three more children, big, strong, and horrible, Cottus and Briareus and Gyes. This unruly brood had a hundred monstrous hands sprouting from their shoulders, and fifty heads on top of their shoulders growing from their sturdy bodies. They had monstrous strength to match their huge size.

III. Of all the children born of Earth and Sky these were the boldest, and their father hated them from the beginning. As each of them was about to be born, Sky would not let them reach the light of day; instead he hid them all away in the bowels of Mother Earth. Sky took pleasure in doing this evil thing. In spite of her enormous size, Earth felt the strain within her and groaned. Finally she thought of an evil and cunning stratagem. She instantly produced a new metal, gray steel, and made a huge sickle. Then she laid the matter before her children; the anguish in her heart made her speak boldly: "My children, you have a savage father; if you will listen to me, we may be able to take vengeance for his evil outrage: he was the one who started using violence."

This was what she said; but all the children were gripped by fear, and not one of them spoke a word. Then great Cronus, the cunning trickster, took courage and answered his good mother with these words: "Mother, I am willing to undertake and carry through your plan. I have no respect for our infamous father, since he was the one who started using violence."

This was what he said, and enormous Earth was very pleased. She hid him in ambush and put in his hands the sickle with jagged teeth, and instructed him fully in her plot. Huge Sky came drawing night behind him and desiring to make love; he lay on top of Earth stretched all over her. Then from his ambush his son reached out with his left hand and with his right took the huge sickle with its long jagged teeth and quickly sheared the organs from his own father and threw them away, backward over his shoulder. But that was not the end of them. The drops of blood that spurted from them were all taken in by Mother Earth, and in the course of the revolving years she gave birth to the powerful Erinyes [Spirits of Vengeance] and the huge Giants with shining armor and long spears. As for the organs themselves, for a long time they drifted round the sea just as they were when Cronus cut them off with the steel edge and threw them from the land into the waves of the ocean; then white foam issued from the divine flesh, and in the foam a girl began to grow. First she came near to holy Cythera, then reached Cyprus, the land surrounded by sea. There she stepped out, a goddess, tender and beautiful, and round her slender feet the green grass shot up. She is called Aphrodite by gods and men, because she grew in the *froth*, and also Cytherea, because she came near to Cythera, and the Cyprian, because she was born in watery Cyprus. Eros [Desire] and beautiful Passion were her attendants both at her birth and at her first going to join the family of the gods. The rights and privileges assigned to her from the beginning and recognized by men and gods are these: to preside over the whispers and smiles and tricks which girls employ, and the sweet delight and tenderness of love.

Great Father Sky called his children the Titans, because of his feud with them: he said that they blindly had *tightened* the noose and had done a savage thing for which they would have to pay in time to come.

VIII. Rhea submitted to the embraces of Cronus and bore him children with a glorious destiny: Hestia, Demeter, and Hera, who walks on golden sandals; Hades, the powerful god whose home is underground and whose heart is pitiless; Poseidon, the god whose great blows make the earth quake; and Zeus the lord of wisdom, the father of gods and men, whose thunder makes the broad earth tremble. As each of these children came out of their mother's holy womb onto her knees, great Cronus swallowed them. His purpose was to prevent the kingship of the gods from passing to another one of the august descendants of Sky; he had been told by Earth and starry Sky that he was destined to be overcome by his own son. For that reason he kept a sleepless watch and waited for his own children to be born and then swallowed them. Rhea had no rest from grief; so, when she was about to give birth to Zeus, the father of gods and men, she begged her own dear parents, Earth and starry Sky, to help her contrive a plan whereby she might bear her child without Cronus' knowing it, and make amends to the vengeful spirits of her father Sky. Earth and Sky listened to their daughter and granted her request; they told her what was destined to happen to King Cronus and to his bold son. When she was about to give birth to great Zeus, her youngest child, they sent her to the rich Cretan town of Lyctus. Huge Mother Earth undertook to nurse and raise the infant in the broad land of Crete. Dark night was rushing on as Earth arrived there carrying him, and Lyctus was the first place where she stopped. She took him and hid him in an inaccessible cave, deep in the bowels of holy earth, in the dense woods of Mount Aegeum. Then she wrapped a huge stone in baby blankets and handed it to the royal son of Sky, who then was king of the gods. He took the stone and swallowed it into his belly—the fool! He did not know that a stone had replaced his son, who survived, unconquered and untroubled, and who was going to overcome him by force and drive him from his office and reign over the gods in his place.

The young prince grew quickly in strength and stature. After years had passed Cronus the great trickster fell victim to the cunning suggestions of Mother Earth and threw up his own children again. The first thing he vomited was the stone, the last thing he had swallowed; Zeus set it up on the highways of the earth in holy Pytho under the slopes of Parnassus, to be a sign and a wonder to mankind thereafter.

Zeus also set free his father's brothers from the cruel chains in which their father Sky had in foolish frenzy bound them. They gratefully remembered his kindness and gave him the thunder and the lightning-bolt and flash, which huge Earth had kept hidden till then. In these weapons Zeus trusts; they make him master over gods and men.

IX. Iapetus took Clymene, the shapely daughter of Ocean, as his wife and entered her bed. She gave birth to a violent-spirited son called Atlas; she also bore a proud-spirited Menoetius, and Prometheus the cunning trickster, and the half-wit Epimetheus, who brought bad luck on men who earn their bread by work: he first accepted the artificial woman sent by Zeus. Lawless Menoetius, because of his savage insolence and overbearing boldness, was struck by the smoking thunderbolt of Zeus and sent down to the lower darkness. Atlas was condemned to hold up the broad sky at the end of the earth, facing the place where the Hesperian nymphs raise their thrilling voices; there he stands and holds the sky up with head and hands that never tire. Such was the fate wise Zeus decreed for him. Cunning Prometheus he bound with unbreakable and painful chains and drove a stake through his middle.

And he turned on him a long-winged eagle, which ate his immortal liver; by night the liver grew as much again as the long-winged bird had eaten in the whole day. The bird was killed by shapely Alcmene's heroic son Heracles, who delivered the son of Iapetus from his evil plight and released him from his sufferings, with the consent of Olympian Zeus the heavenly king, who wanted to raise even higher than before the fame of Theban-born Heracles over all the populous earth. This was his purpose; he exalted his son with honor, and angry though he was he laid aside his former feud with Prometheus.

Such was Prometheus' punishment for having quarreled with the purposes of the all-powerful son of Cronus. For when gods and men came to Mecone to settle their dispute, Prometheus placed before them a huge ox, which he had carefully divided, intending to play a trick on Zeus. He served the men with meat and entrails rich in fat placed inside the skin and covered with the stomach of the ox, while he served Zeus with the bare bones of the ox dressed with a covering of white fat: this was his cunning trick. Zeus the father of gods and men spoke to him and said: "Son of Iapetus, second to none in this noble company, how unfairly you have divided the portions, my friend." With these words Zeus, full of immortal wisdom, rebuked him. Cunning Prometheus had not forgotten his skill at trickery and replied, smiling slightly, "Zeus, noblest and greatest of the gods who are forever, choose whichever of these portions your heart prefers." He said this with intent to deceive: but Zeus, whose wisdom is invincible, saw and did not fail to see the deception; in his heart he was already planning bad luck for mankind, and his plan was about to be fulfilled. With both hands Zeus took up the white fat. Anger filled his mind and fury pierced his heart when he saw the white bones cunningly concealed underneath. (That is why the race of men on earth burn the white bones of animals as a savory offering on the altars of the gods.) But as for Prometheus, Zeus, the master of the clouds, indignantly addressed him saying, "Son of Iapetus, your mind was always the deepest, my friend, and it now appears that you have lost none of your cunning."

Zeus was angry, and his wisdom is invincible. He never forgot this trick, and in return for it he withheld from the race of men who live and die on earth the all-consuming power of fire. But the bold son of Iapetus tricked him again: he stole the radiant light of all-consuming fire in a hollow stalk. This bit deeper into the heart of Zeus the thunder-god: he was enraged when he saw mankind enjoying the radiant light of fire. In return for the theft of fire he instantly produced a curse to plague mankind. At the orders of the son of Cronus, the famous lame smith-god [Hephaestus] shaped some clay in the image of a tender girl. The bright-eyed goddess Athena dressed and decked her in silvery clothes. A marvelous embroidered veil fell from her head and was held in her hands. Round her head the goddess tied a golden diadem on which the smith-god himself had exercised his skill, to please his father Zeus. When Zeus had completed this beautiful curse to go with the blessing of fire, he displayed the girl in an assembly of the gods and men, all decked out in the finery supplied by the bright-eyed daughter of the lord of hosts. Gods and men were speechless when they say how deadly and how irresistible was the trick with which Zeus was going to catch mankind.

This was the origin of the damnable race of women—a plague which men must live with. They have no place where the curse of poverty is; they belong with luxury. Just as bees in their hollow hives support mischievous drones—the bees work busily all day till sunset making the white wax, while the drones sit at home in the shade of the hive and harvest into their bellies the fruits of another's labor—so Zeus the thunder-god made women mischievous in their ways and a curse for men: he dispensed a curse to go with a blessing.

Whoever seeks to avoid marriage and the troublesome ways of women, and therefore refuses to marry, finds old age a curse without anyone to tend his years; though he does not lack livelihood while he lives, on his death his kinsmen divide up his estate. As for the man fated to marry, even if he get a good wife well suited to his temper, evil is continually balanced with good in his life; if he should get pestilent children, the grief in his heart and soul is unremitting throughout life: this evil has no cure.

Thus it is not possible to deceive the mind of Zeus or escape his judgment. Even the trickster Prometheus, Iapetus' son, was not able to escape the heavy consequences of his anger. In spite of all his cleverness he lies helplessly bound by a great chain.

X. The Hundred-Arms—Briareus, Cottus, and Gyes—had been bound fast in chains by their father Sky when he turned against them in fear of their size and shape and overbearing boldness. He made them live underneath the highways of the earth. For a long time they lay in their subterranean dungeon far away at the distant ends of the earth, suffering pain and anguish and grief. But now they were restored to the light by Zeus and the other gods born of the loves of Cronus and fair-haired Rhea. The gods were following the advice of Mother Earth, who revealed all the future to them, prophesying that with the aid of the Hundred-Arms they would win the glorious triumph which they prayed for. For there had been a long war with much suffering on both sides and many bloody battles between the Titan generation of gods and the children of Cronus. The mighty Titans fought from the top of Mount Othrys, while the Olympian gods, from whom all blessings flow, the children of Cronus and fair-haired Rhea, fought from Mount Olympus. For ten full years they had fought without ceasing, so bitterly did they hate each other: there was no truce in the hard-fought struggle, no decision for either side; the fortunes of war were equally balanced. Then the Olympians provided the Hundred-Arms with full equipment, with nectar and ambrosia, the gods' own food, and restored their fighting spirit. Zeus the father of gods and men chose this moment to address his new allies, saying: "You fine sons of Earth and Sky, listen while I tell you what is in my mind. For a long time now there has been warfare every day between the Titan generation of gods and the children of Cronus, to decide which shall be the victors and have the supreme power. Your duty is to employ the great strength of your invincible arms in the stress of battle on our side against the Titans; remember that we have been your good friends, and that you are indebted to our action for your release from the agony of imprisonment and for your return from the dark underworld to the light of day."

That was what Zeus said, and good Cottus replied to him saying: "Sir, you tell us nothing that we did not know. We know that you are first in wisdom, first in knowledge; and you have shown yourself able to save immortal beings from a chilling fate. Son of Cronus, you are our master. Thanks to your decision we have returned to this world from that forlorn dungeon in the dark underworld where we had abandoned all hope. For these reasons we will join the bloody battle against the Titans and strengthen your side in the fierce struggle with unflagging energy and loyal hearts."

When they had heard Cottus' speech, the Olympian gods, from whom all blessings flow, applauded. They became even more eager for war than before: so on that same day a dismal battle started in which all the gods, male and female, joined—the Titans on the one side and on the other the children of Cronus together with the terrible monsters with their enormous strength, whom Zeus had brought from the lower darkness to the light. Each of them had a hundred arms growing from their shoulders and fifty heads on top of their shoulders growing from their sturdy bodies. They grasped massive rocks in their sturdy hands and took their place in the bitter battle against the Titans.

On the other side the Titans prudently strengthened their ranks. Both sides employed all the strength in their hands. The limitless expanse of the sea echoed terribly; the earth rumbled loudly, and the broad area of the sky shook and groaned. Mount Olympus trembled from base to summit as the immortal beings clashed, and a heavy quaking penetrated to the gloomy depths of Tartarus—the sharp vibration of innumerable feet running and missiles thrown. While the weapons discharged at each other whistled through the air, both sides shouted loud battle cries as they came together, till the noise reached the starry sky.

Then Zeus decided to restrain his own power no longer. A sudden surge of energy filled his spirit, and he exerted all the strength he had. He advanced through the sky from Olympus sending flash upon flash of continuous lightning. The bolts of lightning and thunder flew thick and fast from his powerful arm, forming a solid roll of sacred fire. Fertile tracts of land all around crackled as they burned, and immense forests roared in the fire. The whole earth and the Ocean-streams and the barren sea began to boil. An immense flame shot up into the atmosphere, so that the hot air enveloped the Titans, while their eyes, powerful as they were, were blinded by the brilliant flash of the lightning-bolt. The prodigious heat filled the Void. The sight there was to see, and the noise there was to hear, made it seem as if Earth and vast Sky above were colliding. If Earth were being smashed and if Sky were smashing down upon her, the noise would be as great as the noise that arose when the gods met in battle. The winds added to the confusion, whirling dust around together with great Zeus' volleys of thunder and lightning-bolts, and carrying the battle cries and shouts from one side to the other, so that the uproar was deafening. It was a terrible conflict, which revealed the utmost power of the contestants. After many heavy engagements, in which both sides obstinately resisted each other, the battle was finally decided.

Throughout the bitter battle Cottus and Briareus and Gyes were in the forefront. They attacked relentlessly, throwing showers of three hundred stones one after another with all the force of their enormous hands, till they darkened the Titans with a cloud of missiles. Their brute force was stronger than all the valiant efforts of the Titans. They then conducted them under the highways of the earth as far below the ground as the ground is below the sky, and tied them with cruel chains. So far down below the ground is gloomy Tartarus: a bronze anvil falling from the sky would fall nine days and nights, and reach earth on the tenth; a bronze anvil falling from the earth would fall nine days and nights and reach Tartarus on the tenth. Tartarus is surrounded by a bronze moat; three thicknesses of night are spread round its bottleneck, above which the roots of earth and barren sea are planted. In that gloomy underground region the Titans were imprisoned by the decree of Zeus, the master of the clouds. The dismal place lies at the end of the monstrous earth. No exit is open to them: Poseidon made gates of bronze to secure the place; a wall runs all the way round; and the three strong brothers, Gyes, Cottus, and Briareus, now live there—guards on whose loyalty Zeus the lord of the aegis can rely.

SAPPHO (FL. C.600 BCE)
Poems

We know very little of Sappho's life, and even that little is encrusted with legend and fancy. Born in the mid- to late-seventh century, she grew up on the island of Lesbos. She possibly had a husband and a daughter. The poems suggest that she had responsibility for training young girls before their marriages. When they left her to get married, she composed bridal odes in their honor. Whatever her occupation, later references to her recognize her only as a poet and a singer of songs, and the vase paintings of her that survive usually show her playing a lyre. Because of her praise of Aphrodite and her references to rites, some think she was a priestess of that goddess.

Although widely known, Sappho's poetry survived only in quotations by others until papyruses of her poems were found in Egypt in this century. Today nearly 200 of her poems have surfaced, only one of them surely complete (Poem #1, the "Hymn to Aphrodite"). The rest are fragments, several containing complete lines and stanzas, but most scattered phrases, and many only a few words. Many of her works have suffered mistranslation, either to give a false sense of greater completeness, or to hide the clear references to Sappho's passion for other women or girls. While there is little in the surviving poems to prove that her relationships with other women were sexual, the tradition that Sappho was a lesbian was current among the ancient Greeks who presumably were familiar with many more poems than we have. Her position as the first woman poet and as a passionate lyric voice in an age dominated by the Iliad *and the* Odyssey *have in recent years made her poetry the focus of much attention and praise.*

Sappho's poetry is notable especially for its energetic portrayal of feelings and passions, as in Poem #4. There the voyeur-poet who "must endure all this" suffers a startlingly physical reaction as part of her feelings of love or of jealousy. This strong emotion is heightened for the reader by the uncertainty about the object of those feelings: which of the two does she admire and which does she envy? Her poems also exploit a striking use of images. Poem #3, for instance, draws from Homer's world of horses, armor, chariots, and ships in order to use Helen as an example of the power of love.

[1]

Eternal Aphrodite, rainbow-throned,
you cunning, wily child of Zeus, I beg you,
do not break me, Lady,
with the pains and raging ills of love.

The translations are by Suzy Q. Groden, in *The Poems of Sappho* (Indianapolis: Bobbs-Merrill, 1966). Because there are several competing ways of numbering the poems of Sappho, the seven poems included here are simply numbered in order.

But come to me, if ever in the past
you heard my far-off cries
and heeding, came,
leaving the golden home of Zeus
in your bridled chariot.
Beautiful swift sparrows bore you,
eddying through the mid-air, their wings a-whirr,
from heaven to the dark earth,
and there they were. And you, blessed Lady,
smiling your immortal smile,
asked me what ailed me now,
and why I called again,
and what my mad heart most craved:

"Whom, Sappho,
shall I lead to be your love
this time?
Who wrongs you now?
Even if she flees you, soon she'll chase,
and if she scorns your gifts, why, she will offer hers.
And if she does not love you,
soon she'll love, although she does not want to."

Now come to me once again, and free me
from these aching sorrows. Do for my heart
what it desires, and be yourself my help and ally

[2]

Come to me here, from Crete,
to this sacred temple of the lovely apple grove.
Your altars are fragrant here with offerings of frankincense,
and cool water rustles through the apple shoots.
All the place is shadowed with roses
and deep sleep slips down through the shimmering leaves.
In here is a meadow, with horses grazing, alive
with spring blossoms and breezes
that blow redolent.
And here may you, Cypris, pour,
with graceful charm,
your nectar, mixed with our own festive rites,
into these golden cups.

[3]

There are those who say
an array of horsemen,
and others of marching men,
and others of ships, is

the most beautiful thing on the dark earth.
But I say it is whatever one loves.

It is very easy
to show this to all:
for Helen,
by far the most beautiful of mortals,
left her husband
and sailed to Troy
giving no thought at all
to her child nor dear parents,
but was led. . .
[by her love alone.]

Now, far away, Anactoria
comes to my mind.
For I would rather watch her
moving in her lovely way,
and see her face, flashing radiant,
than all the force of Lydian chariots,
and their infantry in full display of arms.

[4]

An equal to the gods, he seems to me,
the man who, with his face toward yours,
sits close and listens to the whispers of
your sweet voice and enticing laugh.
To watch has made my heart a pounding hammer in my
  breast.
For as I look at you, if only for an instant,
my voice no longer comes to me.
My silent tongue is broken,
and a quick and subtle flame
runs up beneath my skin.
I lose my sense of sight, hear only drumming in my ears.
I drip cold sweat,
and a trembling chases all through me.
I am greener than the pale grass
and it seems to me that I am close to death.
Still, I must endure all this

[5]

To have beauty is to have only that,
but to have goodness
is to be beautiful
too.

[6]

Happy bridegroom!
Now your wedding has come true,
as you have prayed, and you have
the girl for whom you prayed.
You are a joy to look at,
with your gentle eyes,

and love showers down about
your handsome face. . .
Aphrodite has honored you
above all others. . .

[7]

These are the ashes of Timas
who died before she could wed,
whom the blue-dark room of Persephone
took in instead.
And when she was dead
every girl her own age
cut, with a fresh-sharpened blade,
a beautiful lock from her head
[to lay on the grave]

PINDAR (518–438 BCE)

Odes

Pindar was an aristocrat from the city of Thebes. It is believed he wrote seventeen volumes of lyric poetry of virtually every kind during his lifetime, but only his epinicia, *choral odes in honor of the winners of the great athletic games, survive. The four volumes of* epinicia *that do survive were probably saved by being used in the second century CE as school textbooks. One volume was devoted to each of the most important of the ancient games: Olympian odes for the winners of the Olympic events held at Olympia every four years, Pythian odes for the winners of the games held at Delphi every four years, Nemean odes celebrating victories in the northeastern Peloponnese every two years, and the Isthmian odes for the games held near Corinth every two years. Pindar was the last and greatest master of the choral ode, a form that during his lifetime was being swallowed up into the immensely popular tragic drama. We thus have no idea how the odes were performed: Was the chorus static or did it move around? What was the range of voices used? What kind of music accompanied the poetry? What is clear is that Pindar was an innovative voice within a very formal poetic structure. No two of his odes have the same metrical form, and he uses these celebrations of athletic prowess to praise cities and families, to draw out deep religious connections with the past through stories from myth, to offer personal reflections, and to extol the enduring importance of leadership and competition—everything, in fact, but the grubby details of the competition itself. In place of the sweaty athlete, Pindar raised a vision of the hero as representative of his family, city, and aristocratic values.*

These values were apparently very important to Pindar, whose conservative attitudes seem to have changed very little in his eighty years. Although he must have traveled to many of the cities whose victorious athletes he celebrated in his poems, he remained loyal all his life to his home city of Thebes. He maintained this staunch patriotism even though Thebes was an ally of Persia in the Persian Wars, against the cities of Athens and Sparta that were giving the Greeks a proud new identity. Throughout this period of dangerous political turmoil, Pindar was admired for the quality and strength of his poetry. His voice gave powerful expression to the Greek admiration for physical beauty and competitive striving.

The two odes here have been translated from Greek into English verse by C. M. Bowra (Penguin, 1969).

Olympian XI

For Hagesidamos of Western Lokroi, winner in the boys' boxing

There is a time when men's strongest need
Is for the winds, and a time for the sky's water,
The clouds' showery children.
If anyone toils and succeeds,
Sweet voices of song
Are paid on account for words to come
And a faithful pledge to surpassing actions.

Beyond grudging, this praise
Is laid up for Olympian victors. Such themes
My tongue loves to tend,
But it is God who makes a man
To flower as his wise mind wishes.
Know now, son of Archestratos,
Hagesidamos, because of your boxing

I shall sing a sweet song
To be a jewel in your crown of golden olive,
And honour the Western Lokrians' race.
Join there in the revel! I shall give my word,
Muses, that he will not come
To a host that puts strangers to flight
Or knows not beautiful things;
They stand on wisdom's height and are soldiers.
—Its inborn ways neither the tawny fox
Shall change, nor loud-bellowing lions.

PYTHIAN VII

For Megakles of Athens, winner in the chariot-race

Athens the mighty city!
For the strong house of the Alkmaionidai
This is the finest prelude
To lay as foundation-stone
Of my chariot-song.
For in what country, what clan, would you dwell
And have more magnificent renown
For Hellas to hear?

For in every city the story runs
Of the citizens of Erechtheus,
Who built in shining Pytho
Thy porch, Apollo, marvelous to behold.
There call to me also
Five victories at the Isthmos
And one paramount at God's Olympia
And two by Krisa,

Megakles, yours and your fathers'!
And in this last happy fortune
Some pleasure I have; but sorrow as well
At envy requiting your fine deeds.
—Thus always, they say,
Happiness, flowering and constant,
Brings after it
One thing with another.

HERODOTUS (C.484–C.430 BCE)
The Persian Wars

Herodotus (484–425 BCE) was exiled from his native Asia Minor (modern Turkey, then under Persian rule), traveled widely throughout Egypt and the Persian Empire, lived for a time in Athens, and settled in Italy before he began his groundbreaking Histories. *For Herodotus, "histories" meant, simply, "investigations." And investigations they were: through extensive travel, research, and interviews, Herodotus attempted to understand the truth of the events he wrote about. His writing is infused with an inquiring and skeptical attitude toward what happened. He works carefully to reconstruct events, using a historical method that we might call scientific, for he checks varying sources and interviews participants and observers. He speaks openly with the reader about problems with these sources, as in his "Introduction," where he says, "Which of these two accounts is true I shall not trouble to decide."*

The first part of his book is a review of the cultures and customs of the people inhabiting the Mediterranean world. The rest is devoted to his detailed account of the Persian Wars, which he saw as capping a great struggle between East and West. Though he clearly saw that the wars marked the rise of Greece as a power in the eastern Mediterranean, and the ascendancy of Athens (over Sparta) within Greece, he did not in his writings show a bias toward Athens or the Greeks. He emphasizes always the character of individual humans, and discounts the intervention of the gods as agents in historical events. This approach brings to the fore the fundamental irony which became the magnetic center of the Greek view of history: the yawning gap between what humans intend or plan, on the one hand, and what their actions lead to, on the other.

The two selections here suggest interesting comparisons with other Greek stories. "Helen and Alexander" casts light on the differences in method between epic and history, for Herodotus offers an account of the events leading to the Trojan War which is different from Homer's. The Odyssey suggests that Menelaus delayed his return from Troy for seven years because he was trading with the Egyptians, according to Nestor; Menelaus, for his part, attributes the delay to a god's anger at a failure in sacrifice. In Herodotus, Menelaus travels to Egypt after the war to redeem his wife, Helen, who actually resided there and not in Troy as the Greeks had thought. Leaving from Egypt, Menelaus sacrifices two Egyptian children to gain favorable winds; in the Homeric tradition, Menelaus's brother Agamemnon sacrificed his own daughter Iphigenia on the way to Troy (a partial motive for Clytemnestra's slaughter of her husband). Herodotus's view is the rational one: "If Helen had been at Troy, the inhabitants would, I think, have given her up to the Greeks."

"The Story of Adrastus," for its part, can fruitfully be compared with Sophocles's tragedy of Oedipus. In both stories we see men marked out for misfortune; oracles in both stories show that

---

The translation used here is by George Rawlinson, first published 1858–60, and often reprinted.

Oedipus and Adrastus are simply acting out the will of some god. Yet in spite of their moral innocence, each is repelled by the horror of what he has done and acts to remove himself from human society.

[Introduction]

These are the researches of Herodotus of Halicarnassus, which he publishes, in the hope of thereby preserving from decay the remembrance of what men have done, and of preventing the great and wonderful actions of the Greeks and the Barbarians from losing their due meed of glory; and withal to put on record what were their grounds of feud.

1. According to the Persians best informed in history, the Phoenicians began the quarrel. This people, who had formerly dwelt on the shores of the Red Sea, having migrated to the Mediterranean and settled in the parts which they now inhabit, began at once, they say, to adventure on long voyages, freighting their vessels with the wares of Egypt and Assyria. They landed at many places on the coast, and among the rest at Argos, which was then pre-eminent above all the states included now under the common name of Hellas. Here they exposed their merchandise, and traded with the natives for five or six days; at the end of which time, when almost everything was sold, there came down to the beach a number of women, and among them the daughter of the king, who was, they say, agreeing in this with the Greeks, Io, the child of Inachus. The women were standing by the stern of the ship intent upon their purchases, when the Phoenicians, with a general shout, rushed upon them. The greater part made their escape, but some were seized and carried off. Io herself was among the captives. The Phoenicians put the women on board their vessel, and set sail for Egypt. Thus did Io pass into Egypt, according to the Persian story, which differs widely from the Phoenician: and thus commenced, according to their authors, the series of outrages.

2. At a later period, certain Greeks, with whose name they are unacquainted, but who would probably be the Cretans, made a landing at Tyre, on the Phoenician coast, and bore off the king's daughter, Europe. In this they only retaliated; but afterwards the Greeks, they say, were guilty of a second violence. They manned a ship of war, and sailed to Aea, a city of Colchis, on the river Phasis; from whence, after despatching the rest of the business on which they had come, they carried off Medea, the daughter of the king of the land. The monarch sent a herald into Greece to demand reparation of the wrong, and the restitution of his child; but the Greeks made answer, that having received no reparation of the wrong done them in the seizure of Io the Argive, they should give none in this instance.

3. In the next generation afterwards, according to the same authorities, Alexander the son of Priam, bearing these events in mind, resolved to procure himself a wife out of Greece by violence, fully persuaded, that as the Greeks had not given satisfaction for their outrages, so neither would he be forced to make any for his. Accordingly he made prize of Helen; upon which the Greeks decided that, before resorting to other measures, they would send envoys to reclaim the princess and require reparation of the wrong. Their demands were met by a reference to the violence which had been offered to Medea, and they were asked with what face they could now require satisfaction, when they had formerly rejected all demands for either reparation or restitution addressed to them.

4. Hitherto the injuries on either side had been mere acts of common violence; but in what followed the Persians consider that the Greeks were greatly to blame, since before any attack had been made on Europe, they led an army into Asia. Now as for the carrying off of women, it is the deed, they say, of a rogue; but to make a stir about such as are carried off, argues a

man a fool. Men of sense care nothing for such women, since it is plain that without their own consent they would never be forced away. The Asiatics, when the Greeks ran off with their women, never troubled themselves about the matter; but the Greeks, for the sake of a single Lacedaemonian girl, collected a vast armament, invaded Asia, and destroyed the kingdom of Priam. Henceforth they ever looked upon the Greeks as their open enemies. For Asia, with all the various tribes of barbarians that inhabit it, is regarded by the Persians as their own; but Europe and the Greek race they look on as distinct and separate.

5. Such is the account which the Persians give of these matters. They trace to the attack upon Troy their ancient enmity towards the Greeks. The Phoenicians, however, as regards Io, vary from the Persian statements. They deny that they used any violence to remove her into Egypt; she herself, they say, having formed an intimacy with the captain, while his vessel lay at Argos, and suspecting herself to be with child, of her own free will accompanied the Phoenicians on their leaving the shore, to escape the shame of detection and the reproaches of her parents. Which of these two accounts is true I shall not trouble to decide. I shall proceed at once to point out the person who first within my own knowledge commenced aggressions on the Greeks, after which I shall go forward with my history, describing equally the greater and the lesser cities. For the cities which were formerly great, have most of them become insignificant; and such as are at present powerful, were weak in the olden time. I shall therefore discourse equally of both, convinced that human happiness never continues long in one stay.

[The Story of Helen and Alexander (Paris)]

113. The priests, in answer to my inquiries on the subject of Helen, informed me of the following particulars. When Alexander had carried off Helen from Sparta, he took ship and sailed homewards. On his way across the Aegean a gale arose, which drove him from his course and took him down to the sea of Egypt; hence, as the wind did not abate, he was carried on to the coast, when he went ashore, landing at the Salt-Pans, in that mouth of the Nile which is now called the Canobic. At this place there stood upon the shore a temple, which still exists, dedicated to Heracles. If a slave runs away from his master, and taking sanctuary at this shrine gives himself up to the god, and receives certain sacred marks upon his person, whosoever his master may be, he cannot lay hand on him. This law still remained unchanged to my time. Hearing, therefore, of the custom of the place, the attendants of Alexander deserted him, and fled to the temple where they sat as suppliants. While there, wishing to damage their master, they accused him to the Egyptians, narrating all the circumstances of the rape of Helen and the wrong done to Menelaus. These charges they brought, not only before the priests, but also before the warden of that mouth of the river, whose name was Thonis.

114. As soon as he received the intelligence, Thonis sent a message to Proteus, who was at Memphis, to this effect, "A stranger is arrived from Greece; his is by race a Teucrian, and has done a wicked deed in the country from which he is come. Having beguiled the wife of the man whose guest he was, he carried her away with him, and much treasure also. Compelled by stress of weather, he has now put in here. Are we to let him depart as he came, or shall we seize what he has brought?" Proteus replied, "Seize the man, be he who he may, that has dealt thus wickedly with his friend, and bring him before me, that I may hear what he will say for himself."

115.   Thonis, on receiving these orders, arrested Alexander, and stopped the departure of his ships; then, taking with him Alexander, Helen, the treasures, and also the fugitive slaves, he went up to Memphis. When all were arrived, Proteus asked Alexander, "Who he was, and whence he had come?" Alexander replied by giving his descent, the name of his country, and a true account of his late voyage. Then Proteus questioned him as to how he got possession of Helen. In his reply Alexander became confused, and diverged from the truth, whereon the slaves interposed, confuted his statements, and told the whole history of the crime. Finally, Proteus delivered judgment as follows, "Did I not regard it as a matter of the utmost consequence that no stranger driven to my country by adverse winds should ever be put to death, I would certainly have avenged the Greek by slaying you, basest of men, after accepting hospitality, to do so wicked a deed! First, you did seduce the wife of your own host—then, not content therewith, you must violently excite her mind, and steal her away from her husband. Nay, even so you were not satisfied, but on leaving, you plundered the house in which you had been a guest. Now then, as I think it of the greatest importance to put no stranger to death, I suffer you to depart; but the woman and the treasures I shall not permit to be carried away. Here they must stay, till the Greek stranger comes in person and takes them back with him. For yourself and your companions, I command you to leave my land within the space of three days—and I warn you, that otherwise at the end of that time you will be treated as enemies."

116.   Such was the tale told me by the priests concerning the arrival of Helen at the court of Proteus. It seems to me that Homer was acquainted with this story, and while discarding it, because he thought it less adapted for epic poetry than the version which he followed, showed that it was not unknown to him. This is evident from the travels which he assigns to Alexander in the *Iliad*—and let it be borne in mind that he has nowhere else contradicted himself—making him be carried out of his course on his return with Helen, and after divers wanderings come at last to Sidon in Phoenicia. The passage is in the Bravery of Diomede, and the words are as follows:

> There were the robes, many coloured, the work of Sidonian
>   women:
> They from Sidon had come, what time god-shaped
> Alexander
> Over the broad sea brought, that way, the high-born Helen.

In the *Odyssey* also the same fact is alluded to, in these words:

> Such, so wisely prepared, were the drugs that her stores
>   afforded,
> Excellent; gift which one Polydamna, partner of Thonis,
> Gave her in Egypt, where many the simples that grow in
>   the meadows,
> Potent to cure in part, in part as potent to injure.

Menelaus too, in the same poem, thus addresses Telemachus:

> Much did I long to return, but the gods still kept me in Egypt—
> Angry because I had failed to pay them their hecatombs duly.

In these places Homer shows himself acquainted with the voyage of Alexander to Egypt, for Syria borders on Egypt, and the Phoenicians, to whom Sidon belongs, dwell in Syria.

117. From these various passages, and from that about Sidon especially, it is clear that Homer did not write the *Cypria*. For there it is said that Alexander arrived at Ilium with Helen on the third day after he left Sparta, the wind having been favourable, and the sea smooth; whereas in the *Iliad*, the poet makes him wander before he brings her home. Enough, however, for the present of Homer and the *Cypria*.

118.   I made inquiry of the priests, whether the story which the Greeks tell about Ilium is a fable, or no. In reply they related the following particulars, of which they declared that Menelaus had himself informed them. After the rape of Helen, a vast army of Greeks, wishing to render help to Menelaus, set sail for the Teucrian territory; on their arrival they disembarked, and formed their camp, after which they sent ambassadors to Ilium, of whom Menelaus was one. The embassy was received within the walls, and demanded the restoration of Helen with the treasures which Alexander had carried off, and likewise required satisfaction for the wrong done. The Teucrians gave at once the answer in which they persisted ever afterwards, backing their assertions sometimes even with oaths, to wit, that neither Helen, nor the treasures claimed, were in their possession, both the one and the other had remained, they said, in Egypt; and it was not just to come upon them for what Proteus, king of Egypt, was detaining. The Greeks, imagining that the Teucrians were merely laughing at them, laid siege to the town, and never rested until they finally took it. As, however, no Helen was found, and they were still told the same story, they at length believed in its truth, and despatched Menelaus to the court of Proteus.

119. So Menelaus travelled to Egypt, and on his arrival sailed up the river as far as Memphis, and related all that had happened. He met with the utmost hospitality, received Helen back unharmed, and recovered all his treasures. After this friendly treatment Menelaus, they said, behaved most unjustly towards the Egyptians; for as it happened that at the time when he wanted to take his departure, he was detained by the wind being contrary, and as he found this obstruction continue, he had recourse to a most wicked expedient. He seized, they said, two children of the people of the country, and offered them up in sacrifice. When this became known, the indignation of the people was stirred, and they went in pursuit of Menelaus, who, however, escaped with his ships to Libya, after which the Egyptians could not say whither he went. The rest they knew full well, partly by the inquiries which they had made, and partly from the circumstances having taken place in their own land, and therefore not admitting of doubt.

120. Such is the account given by the Egyptian priests, and I am myself inclined to regard as true all that they say of Helen from the following considerations: If Helen had been at Troy, the inhabitants would, I think, have given her up to the Greeks, whether Alexander consented to it or no. For surely neither Priam, nor his family, could have been so infatuated as to endanger their own persons, their children, and their city, merely that Alexander might possess Helen. At any rate, if they determined to refuse at first, yet afterwards when so many of the Trojans fell on every encounter with the Greeks, and Priam too in each battle lost a son, or sometimes two, or three, or even more, if we may credit the epic poets, I do not believe that even if Priam himself had been married to her he would have declined to deliver her up, with the view of bringing the series of calamities to a close. Nor was it as if Alexander had been heir to the crown, in which case he might have had the chief management of affairs, since Priam was already old. Hector, who was his elder brother, and a far braver man, stood before him, and was the heir to the kingdom on the death of their father Priam. And it could not be Hector's interest to uphold his brother in his wrong, when it brought such dire calamities

upon himself and the other Trojans. But the fact was that they had no Helen to deliver, and so they told the Greeks, but the Greeks would not believe what they said—Divine Providence, as I think, so willing, that by their utter destruction it might be made evident to all men that when great wrongs are done, the gods will surely visit them with great punishments. Such, at least, is my view of the matter.

[The Story of Adrastus]

34. After Solon had gone away a dreadful vengeance, sent of God, came upon Croesus, to punish him, it is likely, for deeming himself the happiest of men. First he had a dream in the night, which foreshowed him truly the evils that were about to befall him in the person of his son. For Croesus had two sons, one blasted by a natural defect, being deaf and dumb; the other distinguished far above all his co-mates in every pursuit. The name of the last was Atys. It was this son concerning whom he dreamt a dream, that he would die by the blow of an iron weapon. When he woke, he considered earnestly with himself, and, greatly alarmed at the dream, instantly made his son take a wife, and whereas in former years the youth had been wont to command the Lydian forces in the field, he now would not suffer him to accompany them. All the spears and javelins, and weapons used in the wars, he removed out of the male apartments, and laid them in heaps in the chambers of the women, fearing lest perhaps one of the weapons that hung against the wall might fall and strike him.

35. Now it chanced that while he was making arrangements for the wedding, there came to Sardis a man under a misfortune who had upon him the stain of blood. He was by race a Phrygian, and belonged to the family of the king. Presenting himself at the palace of Croesus, he prayed to be admitted to purification according to the customs of the country. . . . Croesus granted the request, and went through all the customary rites, after which he asked the suppliant of his birth and country, addressing him as follows:—"Who are you, stranger, and from what part of Phrygia did you flee to take refuge at my hearth? And, whom, moreover, what man or what woman, have you slain?" "Oh! king," replied the Phrygian, "I am the son of Gordias, son of Midas. I am named Adrastus. The man I unintentionally slew was my own brother. For this my father drove me from the land, and I lost all. Then fled I here to you." "You are the offspring," Croesus rejoined, "of a house friendly to mine, and you have come to friends. You shall want for nothing so long as you abide in my dominions. Bear your misfortune as easily as you may, so will it go best with you." Thenceforth Adrastus lived in the palace of the king.

36. It chanced that at this very same time there was in the Mysian Olympus a huge monster of a boar, which went forth often from this mountain-country, and wasted the corn-fields of the Mysians. Many a time had the Mysians collected to hunt the beast, but instead of doing him any hurt, they came off always with some loss to themselves. At length they sent ambassadors to Croesus, who delivered their message to him in these words: "Oh! king, a mighty monster of a boar has appeared in our parts, and destroys the labour of our hands. We do our best to take him, but in vain. Now, therefore, we beseech you to let your son accompany us back, with some chosen youths and hounds, that we may rid our country of the animal." Such was the tenor of their prayer.

But Croesus thought about his dream, and answered, "Say no more of my son going with you; that may not be in any wise. He is but just joined in wedlock, and is busy enough with that. I will grant you a picked band of Lydians, and all my hunting army, and I will charge those whom I send to use all zeal in aiding you to rid your country of this brute."

37. With this reply the Mysians were content; but the king's son, hearing what the prayer of the Mysians was, came suddenly in, and on the refusal of Croesus to let him go with them, thus addressed his father: "Formerly, my father, it was deemed the noblest and most suitable thing for me to frequent the wars and hunting parties, and win myself glory in them; but now you keep me away from both, although you have never beheld in me either cowardice or lack of spirit. What face meanwhile must I wear as I walk to the forum or return from it? What must the citizens, what must my young bride think of me? What sort of man will she suppose her husband to be? Either, therefore, let me go to the chase of this boar, or give me a reason why it is best for me to do according to your wishes."

38. Then Croesus answered, "My son, it is not because I have seen in you either cowardice or aught else which has displeased me that I keep you back; but because a vision, which came before me in a dream as I slept, warned me that you were doomed to die young, pierced by an iron weapon. It was this which first led me to hasten on your wedding, and now it hinders me from sending you upon this enterprise. I would rather keep watch over you, if by any means I may cheat fate of you during my own lifetime. For you are the one and only son that I possess; the other, whose hearing is destroyed, I regard as if he were not."

39. "Ah! father," returned the youth, "I blame you not for keeping watch over me after a dream so terrible; but if you are mistaken, if you do not apprehend the dream aright, it is no blame for me to show you wherein you are wrong. Now the dream, you said yourself, foretold that I should die stricken by an iron weapon. But what hands has a boar to strike with? What iron weapon does he wield? Yet, this is what you fear for me. Had the dream said that I should die pierced by a tusk, then you had done well to keep me away; but it said a weapon. Now here we do not combat men, but a wild animal. I pray you, therefore, let me go with them."

40. "There you have me, my son," said Croesus, "your interpretation is better than mine. I yield to it, and change my mind, and consent to let you go."

41. The king sent for Adrastus the Phrygian, and said to him, "Adrastus, when you were struck with the rod of affliction—no reproach, my friend—I purified you and have taken you to live with me in my palace, and have been at every charge. Now, therefore, it behoves you to repay the good offices which you have received at my hands by consenting to go with my son on this hunting-party, and to watch over him, if perchance you should be attacked upon the road by some band of daring robbers. Even apart from this, it were right for you to go where you may make yourself famous by noble deeds. They are the heritage of your family, and you too are so stalwart and strong."

42. Adrastus answered, "Except for your request, Oh! king, I would rather have kept away from this hunt, for I think it ill becomes a man under a misfortune such as mine to consort with his happier compeers, and besides, I have no heart for it. On many grounds I would rather stay behind, but, as you urge it, and I am bound to please you (for truly it does behove me to repay your good offices), I am content to do as you wish. For your son, whom you give into my charge, be sure you shall receive him back safe and sound, so far as depends upon a guardian's carefulness."

43. Thus assured, Croesus let them depart, accompanied by a band of picked youths, and well provided with dogs of chase. When they reached Olympus, they scattered in quest of the animal; he was soon found, and the hunters, drawing round him in a circle, hurled their weapons at him. Then the stranger, the man who had been purified of blood, whose name was Adrastus, he also hurled his spear at the boar, but missed his aim, and struck Atys. Thus was

the son of Croesus slain by the point of an iron weapon, and the warning of the vision was fulfilled. Then one ran to Sardis to bear the tidings to the king, and he came and informed him of the combat, and of the fate that had befallen his son.

44. If it was a heavy blow to the father to learn that his child was dead, it yet more strongly affected him to think that the very man whom he himself once purified had done the deed. In the violence of his grief, he called aloud on Zeus, to be a witness of what he had suffered at the stranger's hand, . . . because he had unwittingly harboured in his house the man who had now slain his son; and because the stranger, who had been sent as his child's guardian, had turned out his most cruel enemy.

45. Presently the Lydians arrived, bearing the body of the youth, and behind them followed the murderer. He took his stand in front of the corpse, and, stretching forth his hands to Croesus, delivered himself into his power with earnest entreaties that he would sacrifice him upon the body of his son—"his former misfortune was burden enough; now that he had added to it a second, and had brought ruin on the man who purified him, he could not bear to live." Then Croesus, when he heard these words, was moved with pity towards Adrastus, notwithstanding the bitterness of his own calamity; and so he answered, "Enough, my friend; I have all the revenge that I require, since you give sentence of death against yourself. But in truth, it is not you who have injured me, except so far as you have unwittingly dealt the blow. Some god is the author of my misfortune, and I was forewarned of it a long time ago." Croesus after this buried the body of his son, with such honours as befitted the occasion. Adrastus, son of Gordias, son of Midas, the destroyer of his brother in time past, the destroyer now of his purifier, regarding himself as the most unfortunate wretch whom he had ever known, so soon as all was quiet about the place, slew himself upon the tomb. Croesus, bereft of his son, gave himself up to mourning for two full years.

Thucydides (c.460–400 bce)
The Peloponnesian War

Most of what we know about Thucydides comes from the history he wrote, a detailed account of the Peloponnesian War in which Athens and Sparta fought. During the first part of the war, as an Athenian citizen, he was directly involved in events. He was in Athens when the plague struck in 430 BCE, and he caught the disease himself, but recovered. In 424 he was named one of the ten strategoi *for the year and was put in command of the fleet responsible for defending Amphipolis. When the Spartans suddenly attacked and took the city, Thucydides was recalled in disgrace. A trial resulted in his exile, which ended only when Athens finally fell twenty years later. He took advantage of his exile to continue to do research on the Spartan side of the ongoing struggle, but when he died sometime shortly after the end of the war, his history was left incomplete.*

As a participant in events, Thucydides drew upon his great store of personal observation. But he was also very aware of the great bane of historians, that people recall and interpret events in very different ways. Thucydides is frank about weighing conflicting accounts in order to arrive at the most accurate historical picture possible. At the same time, it is a trademark of his method to utter, through the mouths of his subjects, great speeches of his own devising, always based on what he could first determine about the original speech. The funeral oration of Pericles is the best example of this practice and one of the most famous prose passages in Greek literature.

In this speech, Thucydides's Pericles both defines and models the ideal Athenian, in an exercise that provides a textbook study of rhetorical techniques. Over and over Pericles praises the virtues of freedom, excellence in body and mind, open discussion, versatility, and the pursuit of beauty and grace. But in spite of these ringing idealisms—perhaps because of them—the "Funeral Oration" is also a good place to find traces of deeper social customs in Greek society. Because men are writing the histories, for instance, it is hard to find solid evidence of the conditions of women in Greek society. In the "Funeral Oration," in fact, Pericles tells the women of Athens that their greatest glory would be to be least talked about by men. This makes a virtue of what we know to be the case with Greek women, that they lived in virtual seclusion, managing household duties and child-rearing, while their husbands alone had recourse to the agora, *the public forum for politics, discussion, and exchange. It is therefore one of the motive forces of Greek literature to show women threatening these boundaries, as in* Antigone *by Sophocles or* Lysistrata *by Aristophanes.*

The plague, which broke out in Athens during the first year of the war and killed countless Athenians, provides a good example of the kind of irony that the Greeks saw as infesting human action and therefore historical narrative. Athens had prepared for war carefully by fortifying itself, even build-

---

This translation is a famous one by the Victorian professor of Greek at Oxford, Benjamin Jowett (1881).

ing long walls all the way to its port at the sea. After they retreated to the safety of the walled city, Athenians were made more vulnerable to disease by the crowded conditions and the difficulty of protecting their water supply. The loss of a third of the Athenian population in three years of plague, without significant victories over Sparta and her allies, was destructive of the Athenian spirit. Thucydides therefore exploits a double irony: the tremendous loss of life that resulted from the Athenian strategy of safe retreat, and the loss of heart among the Athenians almost before the noble echoes of the "Funeral Oration" have died down.

[Introduction]

1. Thucydides, an Athenian, wrote the history of the war in which the Peloponnesians and the Athenians fought against one another. He began to write when they first took up arms, believing that it would be great and memorable above any previous war. For he argued that both states were then at the full height of their military power, and he saw the rest of the Hellenes either siding or intending to side with one or other of them. No movement ever stirred Hellas more deeply than this; it was shared by many of the Barbarians, and might be said even to affect the world at large. The character of the events which preceded, whether immediately or in more remote antiquity, owing to the lapse of time cannot be made out with certainty. But, judging from the evidence which I am able to trust after most careful enquiry, I should imagine that former ages were not great either in their wars or in anything else.

2. The country which is now called Hellas was not regularly settled in ancient times. The people were migratory, and readily left their homes whenever they were overpowered by numbers. There was no commerce, and they could not safely hold intercourse with one another either by land or sea. The several tribes cultivated their own soil just enough to obtain a maintenance from it. But they had no accumulations of wealth, and did not plant the ground; for, being without walls, they were never sure that an invader might not come and despoil them. Living in this manner and knowing that they could anywhere obtain a bare subsistence, they were always ready to migrate; so that they had neither great cities nor any considerable resources. The richest districts were most constantly changing their inhabitants; for example, the countries which are now called Thessaly and Boeotia, the greater part of the Peloponnesus with the exception of Arcadia, and all the best parts of Hellas. For the productiveness of the land increased the power of individuals; this in turn was a source of quarrels by which communities were ruined, while at the same time they were more exposed to attacks from without. Certainly Attica, of which the soil was poor and thin, enjoyed a long freedom from civil strife, and therefore retained its original inhabitants. And a striking confirmation of my argument is afforded by the fact that Attica through immigration increased in population more than any other region. For the leading men of Hellas, when driven out of their own country by war or revolution, sought an asylum at Athens; and from the very earliest times, being admitted to rights of citizenship, so greatly increased the number of inhabitants that Attica became incapable of containing them, and was at last obliged to send out colonies to Ionia.

3. The feebleness of antiquity is further proved to me by the circumstance that there appears to have been no common action in Hellas before the Trojan War. And I am inclined to think that the very name was not as yet given to the whole country, and in fact did not exist at all before the time of Hellen, the son of Deucalion; the different tribes, of which the Pelasgian was the most widely spread, gave their own names to different districts. But when Hellen and his sons became powerful in Phthiotis, their aid was invoked by other cities, and

those who associated with them gradually began to be called Hellenes, though a long time elapsed before the name prevailed over the whole country. Of this Homer affords the best evidence; for he, although he lived long after the Trojan War, nowhere uses this name collectively, but confines it to the followers of Achilles from Phthiotis, who were the original Hellenes; when speaking of the entire host he calls them Danaans, or Argives, or Achaeans. Neither is there any mention of Barbarians in his poems, clearly because there were as yet no Hellenes opposed to them by a common distinctive name. Thus the several Hellenic tribes (and I mean by the term Hellenes those who, while forming separate communities, had a common language, and were afterwards called by a common name), owing to their weakness and isolation, were never united in any great enterprise before the Trojan War. And they only made the expedition against Troy after they had gained considerable experience of the sea.

[Pericles' Funeral Oration]

34. During the same winter, in accordance with an ancestral custom, the funeral of those who first fell in this war was celebrated by the Athenians at the public charge. The ceremony is as follows: Three days before the celebration they erect a tent in which the bones of the dead are laid out, and every one brings to his own dead any offering which he pleases. At the time of the funeral the bones are placed in chests of cypress wood, which are conveyed on waggons; there is one chest for each tribe. They also carry a single empty litter decked with a pall for all whose bodies are missing, and cannot be recovered after the battle. The procession is accompanied by any one who chooses, whether citizen or stranger, and the female relatives of the deceased are present at the place of interment and make lamentation. The public sepulchre is situated in the most beautiful spot outside the walls; there they always bury those who fall in war; only after the battle of Marathon the dead, in recognition of their pre-eminent valour, were interred on the field. When the remains have been laid in the earth, some man of known ability and high reputation, chosen by the city, delivers a suitable oration over them; after which the people depart. Such is the manner of interment; and the ceremony was repeated from time to time throughout the war. Over those who were the first buried Pericles was chosen to speak. At the fitting moment he advanced from the sepulchre to a lofty platform, which had been erected in order that he might be heard as far as possible by the multitude, and spoke as follows:

35. "Most of those who have spoken here before me have commended the lawgiver who added this oration to our other funeral customs; it seemed to them a worthy thing that such an honour should be given at their burial to the dead who have fallen on the field of battle. But I should have preferred that, when men's deeds have been brave, they should be honoured in deed only, and with such an honour as this public funeral, which you are now witnessing. Then the reputation of many would not have been imperilled on the eloquence or want of eloquence of one, and their virtues believed or not as he spoke well or ill. For it is difficult to say neither too little nor too much; and even moderation is apt not to give the impression of truthfulness. The friend of the dead who knows the facts is likely to think that the words of the speaker fall short of his knowledge and of his wishes; another who is not so well informed, when he hears of anything which surpasses his own powers, will be envious and will suspect exaggeration. Mankind are tolerant of the praises of others so long as each hearer thinks that he can do as well or nearly as well himself, but, when the deed is beyond him, jealousy is aroused and he begins to be incredulous. However, since our ancestors have set the

seal of their approval upon the practice, I must obey, and to the utmost of my power shall endeavour to satisfy the wishes and beliefs of all who hear me.

36. "I will speak first of our ancestors, for it is right and becoming that now, when we are lamenting the dead, a tribute should be paid to their memory. There has never been a time when they did not inhabit this land, which by their valour they have handed down from generation to generation, and we have received from them a free state. But if they were worthy of praise, still more were our fathers, who added to their inheritance, and after many a struggle transmitted to us their sons this great empire. And we ourselves assembled here to-day, who are still most of us in the vigour of life, have chiefly done the work of improvement, and have richly endowed our city with all things, so that she is sufficient for herself both in peace and war. Of the military exploits by which our various possessions were acquired, or of the energy with which we or our fathers drove back the tide of war, Hellenic or barbarian, I will not speak; for the tale would be long and is familiar to you. But before I praise the dead, I should like to point out by what principles of action we rose to power, and under what institutions and through what manner of life our empire became great. For I conceive that such thoughts are not unsuited to the occasion, and that this numerous assembly of citizens and strangers may profitably listen to them.

37. "Our form of government does not enter into rivalry with the institutions of others. We do not copy our neighbours, but are an example to them. It is true that we are called a democracy, for the administration is in the hands of the many and not of the few. But while the law secures equal justice to all alike in their private disputes, the claim of excellence is also recognised; and when a citizen is in any way distinguished, he is preferred to the public service, not as a matter of privilege, but as the reward of merit. Neither is poverty a bar, but a man may benefit his country whatever be the obscurity of his condition. There is no exclusiveness in our public life, and in our private intercourse we are not suspicious of one another, nor angry with our neighbour if he does what he likes; we do not put on sour looks at him which, though harmless, are not pleasant. While we are thus unconstrained in our private intercourse, a spirit of reverence pervades our public acts; we are prevented from doing wrong by respect for authority and for the laws, having an especial regard to those which are ordained for the protection of the injured as well as to those unwritten laws which bring upon the transgressor of them the reprobation of the general sentiment.

38. "And we have not forgotten to provide for our weary spirits many relaxations from toil; we have regular games and sacrifices throughout the year; at home the style of our life is refined; and the delight which we daily feel in all these things helps to banish melancholy. Because of the greatness of our city the fruits of the whole earth flow in upon us; so that we enjoy the goods of other countries as freely as our own.

39. "Then, again, our military training is in many respects superior to that of our adversaries. Our city is thrown open to the world, and we never expel a foreigner or prevent him from seeing or learning anything of which the secret if revealed to an enemy might profit him. We rely not upon management or trickery, but upon our own hearts and hands. And in the matter of education, whereas they from early youth are always undergoing laborious exercises which are to make them brave, we live at ease, and yet are equally ready to face the perils which they face. And here is the proof. The Lacedaemonians come into Attica not by themselves, but with their whole confederacy following; we go alone into a neighbour's country; and although our opponents are fighting for their homes and we on a foreign soil, we have seldom any difficulty in overcoming them. Our enemies have never yet felt our united

strength; the care of a navy divides our attention, and on land we are obliged to send our own citizens everywhere. But they, if they meet and defeat a part of our army, are as proud as if they had routed us all, and when defeated they pretend to have been vanquished by us all.

"If then we prefer to meet danger with a light heart but without laborious training, and with a courage which is gained by habit and not enforced by law, are we not greatly the gainers? Since we do not anticipate the pain, although, when the hour comes, we can be as brave as those who never allow themselves to rest; and thus too our city is equally admirable in peace and in war.

40. "For we are lovers of the beautiful, yet with economy, and we cultivate the mind without the loss of manliness. Wealth we employ, not for talk and ostentation, but when there is a real use for it. To avow poverty with us is no disgrace; the true disgrace is in doing nothing to avoid it. An Athenian citizen does not neglect the state because he takes care of his own household; and even those of us who are engaged in business have a very fair idea of politics. We alone regard a man who takes no interest in public affairs, not as a harmless, but as a useless character; and if few of us are originators, we are all sound judges of a policy. The great impediment to action is, in our opinion, not discussion, but the want of that knowledge which is gained by discussion preparatory to action. For we have a peculiar power of thinking before we act and of acting too, whereas other men are courageous from ignorance but hesitate upon reflection. And they are surely to be esteemed the bravest spirits who, having the clearest sense both of the pains and pleasures of life, do not on that account shrink from danger. In doing good, again, we are unlike others; we make our friends by conferring, not by receiving favours. Now he who confers a favour is the firmer friend, because he would fain by kindness keep alive the memory of an obligation; but the recipient is colder in his feelings, because he knows that in requiting another's generosity he will not be winning gratitude but only paying a debt. We alone do good to our neighbours not upon a calculation of interest, but in the confidence of freedom and in a frank and fearless spirit.

41. "To sum up: I say that Athens is the school of Hellas, and that the individual Athenian in his own person seems to have the power of adapting himself to the most varied forms of action with the utmost versatility and grace. This is no passing and idle word, but truth and fact; and the assertion is verified by the position to which these qualities have raised the state. For in the hour of trial Athens alone among her contemporaries is superior to the report of her. No enemy who comes against her is indignant at the reverses which he sustains at the hands of such a city; no subject complains that his masters are unworthy of him. And we shall assuredly not be without witnesses; there are mighty monuments of our power which will make us the wonder of this and of succeeding ages; we shall not need the praises of Homer or of any other panegyrist whose poetry may please for the moment, although his representation of the facts will not bear the light of day. For we have compelled every land and every sea to open a path for our valour, and have everywhere planted eternal memorials of our friendship and of our enmity. Such is the city for whose sake these men nobly fought and died; they could not bear the thought that she might be taken from them; and every one of us who survive should gladly toil on her behalf.

42. "I have dwelt upon the greatness of Athens because I want to show you that we are contending for a higher prize than those who enjoy none of these privileges, and to establish by manifest proof the merit of these men whom I am now commemorating. Their loftiest praise has been already spoken. For in magnifying the city I have magnified them, and men like them whose virtues made her glorious. And of how few Hellenes can it be said as of them,

that their deeds when weighed in the balance have been found equal to their fame! It seems to me that a death such as theirs has been given the true measure of a man's worth; it may be the first revelation of his virtues, but is at any rate their final seal. For even those who come short in other ways may justly plead the valour with which they have fought for their country; they have blotted out the evil with the good, and have benefited the state more by their public services than they have injured her by their private actions. None of these men were enervated by wealth or hesitated to resign the pleasures of life; none of them put off the evil day in the hope, natural to poverty, that a man, though poor, may one day become rich. But, deeming that the punishment of their enemies was sweeter than any of these things, and that they could fall in no nobler cause, they determined at the hazard of their lives to be honourably avenged, and to leave the rest. They resigned to hope their unknown chance of happiness; but in the face of death they resolved to rely upon themselves alone. And when the moment came they were minded to resist and suffer, rather than to fly and save their lives; they ran away from the word of dishonour, but on the battle-field their feet stood fast, and in an instant, at the height of their fortune, they passed away from the scene, not of their fear, but of their glory.

43. "Such was the end of these men; they were worthy of Athens, and the living need not desire to have a more heroic spirit, although they may pray for a less fatal issue. The value of such a spirit is not to be expressed in words. Any one can discourse to you for ever about the advantages of a brave defence which you know already. But instead of listening to him I would have you day by day fix your eyes upon the greatness of Athens, until you become filled with the love of her; and when you are impressed by the spectacle of her glory, reflect that this empire has been acquired by men who knew their duty and had the courage to do it, who in the hour of conflict had the fear of dishonour always present to them, and who, if ever they failed in an enterprize, would not allow their virtues to be lost to their country, but freely gave their lives to her as the fairest offering which they could present at her feast. The sacrifice which they collectively made was individually repaid to them; for they received again each one for himself a praise which grows not old, and the noblest of all sepulchres—I speak not of that in which their remains are laid, but of that in which their glory survives, and is proclaimed always and on every fitting occasion both in word and deed. For the whole earth is the sepulchre of famous men; not only are they commemorated by columns and inscriptions in their own country, but in foreign lands there dwells also an unwritten memorial of them, graven not on stone but in the hearts of men. Make them your examples, and esteeming courage to be freedom and freedom to be happiness, do not weigh too nicely the perils of war. The unfortunate who has no hope of a change for the better has less reason to throw away his life than the prosperous who, if he survive, is always liable to a change for the worse, and to whom any accidental fall makes the most serious difference. To a man of spirit, cowardice and disaster coming together are far more bitter than death striking him unperceived at a time when he is full of courage and animated by the general hope.

44. "Wherefore I do not now commiserate the parents of the dead who stand here; I would rather comfort them. You know that your life has been passed amid manifold vicissitudes; and that they may be deemed fortunate who have gained most honour, whether an honourable death like theirs, or an honourable sorrow like yours, and whose days have been so ordered that the term of their happiness is likewise the term of their life. I know how hard it is to make you feel this, when the good fortune of others will too often remind you of the gladness which once lightened your hearts. And sorrow is felt at the want of those blessings,

not which a man never knew, but which were a part of his life before they were taken from him. Some of you are of an age at which they may hope to have other children, and they ought to bear their sorrow better; not only will the children who may hereafter be born make them forget their own lost ones, but the city will be doubly a gainer. She will not be left desolate, and she will be safer. For a man's counsel cannot have equal weight or worth, when he alone has no children to risk in the general danger. To those of you who have passed their prime, I say, 'Congratulate yourselves that you have been happy during the greater part of your days; remember that your life of sorrow will not last long, and be comforted by the glory of those who are gone. For the love of honour alone is ever young, and not riches, as some say, but honour is the delight of men when they are old and useless.'

45. "To you who are the sons and brothers of the departed, I see that the struggle to emulate them will be an arduous one. For all men praise the dead, and, however pre-eminent your virtue may be, hardly will you be thought, I do not say to equal, but even to approach them. The living have their rivals and detractors, but when a man is out of the way, the honour and good-will which he receives is unalloyed. And, if I am to speak of womanly virtues to those of you who will henceforth be widows, let me sum them up in one short admonition: To a woman not to show more weakness than is natural to her sex is a great glory, and not to be talked about for good or for evil among men.

46. "I have paid the required tribute, in obedience to the law, making use of such fitting words as I had. The tribute of deeds has been paid in part; for the dead have been honourably interred, and it remains only that their children should be maintained at the public charge until they are grown up: this is the solid prize with which, as with a garland, Athens crowns her sons living and dead, after a struggle like theirs. For where the rewards of virtue are greatest, there the noblest of citizens are enlisted in the service of the state. And now, when you have duly lamented, every one his own dead, you may depart."

[The Plague in Athens]

47. Such was the order of the funeral celebrated in this winter, with the end of which ended the first year of the Peloponnesian War. As soon as summer returned, the Peloponnesian army, comprising as before two-thirds of the force of each confederate state, under the command of the Lacedaemonian king Archidamus, the son of Zeuxidamus, invaded Attica, where they established themselves and ravaged the country. They had not been there many days when the plague broke out at Athens for the first time. A similar disorder is said to have previously smitten many places, particularly Lemnos, but there is no record of such a pestilence occurring elsewhere, or of so great a destruction of human life. For a while physicians, in ignorance of the nature of the disease, sought to apply remedies; but it was in vain, and they themselves were among the first victims, because they oftenest came into contact with it. No human art was of any avail, and as to supplications in temples, enquiries of oracles, and the like, they were utterly useless, and at last men were overpowered by the calamity and gave them all up.

48. The disease is said to have begun south of Egypt in Aethiopia; thence it descended into Egypt and Libya, and after spreading over the greater part of the Persian empire, suddenly fell upon Athens. It first attacked the inhabitants of the Piraeus, and it was supposed that the Peloponnesians had poisoned the cisterns, no conduits having as yet been made there. It afterwards reached the upper city, and then the mortality became far greater. As to its probable origin or the causes which might or could have produced such a disturbance of

nature, every man, whether a physician or not, will give his own opinion. But I shall describe its actual course, and the symptoms by which any one who knows them beforehand may recognise the disorder should it ever reappear. For I was myself attacked, and witnessed the sufferings of others.

49. The season was admitted to have been remarkably free from ordinary sickness; and if anybody was already ill of any other disease, it was absorbed in this. Many who were in perfect health, all in a moment, and without any apparent reason, were seized with violent heats in the head and with redness and inflammation of the eyes. Internally the throat and the tongue were quickly suffused with blood, and the breath became unnatural and fetid. There followed sneezing and hoarseness; in a short time the disorder, accompanied by a violent cough, reached the chest; then fastening lower down, it would move the stomach and bring on all the vomits of bile to which physicians have ever given names; and they were very distressing. An ineffectual retching producing violent convulsions attacked most of the sufferers; some as soon as the previous symptoms had abated, others not until long afterwards. The body externally was not so very hot to the touch, nor yet pale; it was of a livid colour inclining to red, and breaking out in pustules and ulcers. But the internal fever was intense; the sufferers could not bear to have on them even the finest linen garment; they insisted on being naked, and there was nothing which they longed for more eagerly than to throw themselves into cold water. And many of those who had no one to look after them actually plunged into the cisterns, for they were tormented by unceasing thirst, which was not in the least assuaged whether they drank little or much. They could not sleep; a restlessness which was intolerable never left them. While the disease was at its height the body, instead of wasting away, held out amid these sufferings in a marvellous manner, and either they died on the seventh or ninth day, not of weakness, for their strength was not exhausted, but of internal fever, which was the end of most; or, if they survived, then the disease descended into the bowels and there produced violent ulceration; severe diarrhoea at the same time set in, and at a later stage caused exhaustion, which finally with few exceptions carried them off. For the disorder which had originally settled in the head passed gradually through the whole body, and, if a person got over the worst, would often seize the extremities and leave its mark, attacking the genitals and the fingers and the toes; and some escaped with the loss of these, some with the loss of their eyes. Some again had no sooner recovered than they were seized with a forgetfulness of all things and knew neither themselves nor their friends.

50. The malady took a form not to be described, and the fury with which it fastened upon each sufferer was too much for human nature to endure. There was one circumstance in particular which distinguished it from ordinary diseases. The birds and animals which feed on human flesh, although so many bodies were lying unburied, either never came near them, or died if they touched them. This was proved by a remarkable disappearance of the birds of prey, who were not to be seen either about the bodies or anywhere else; while in the case of the dogs the fact was even more obvious, because they live with man.

51. Such was the general nature of the disease; I omit many strange peculiarities which characterised individual cases. None of the ordinary sicknesses attacked any one while it lasted, or, if they did, they ended in the plague. Some of the sufferers died from want of care, others equally who were receiving the greatest attention. No single remedy could be deemed a specific; for that which did good to one did harm to another. No constitution was of itself strong enough to resist or weak enough to escape the attacks; the disease carried off all alike and defied every mode of treatment. Most appalling was the despondency which seized upon

any one who felt himself sickening; for he instantly abandoned his mind to despair and, instead of holding out, absolutely threw away his chance of life. Appalling too was the rapidity with which men caught the infection; dying like sheep if they attended on one another; and this was the principal cause of mortality. When they were afraid to visit one another, the sufferers died in their solitude, so that many houses were empty because there had been no one left to take care of the sick; or if they ventured they perished, especially those who aspired to heroism. For they went to see their friends without thought of themselves and were ashamed to leave them, even at a time when the very relations of the dying were at last growing weary and ceased to make lamentations, overwhelmed by the vastness of the calamity. But whatever instances there may have been of such devotion, more often the sick and the dying were tended by the pitying care of those who had recovered, because they knew the course of the disease and were themselves free from apprehension. For no one was ever attacked a second time, or not with a fatal result. All men congratulated them, and they themselves, in the excess of their joy at the moment, had an innocent fancy that they could not die of any other sickness.

52. The crowding of the people out of the country into the city aggravated the misery; and the newly arrived suffered most. For, having no houses of their own, but inhabiting in the height of summer stifling huts, the mortality among them was dreadful, and they perished in wild disorder. The dead lay as they had died, one upon another, while others hardly alive wallowed in the streets and crawled about every fountain craving for water. The temples in which they lodged were full of the corpses of those who died in them; for the violence of the calamity was such that man, not knowing where to turn, grew reckless of all law, human and divine. The customs which had hitherto been observed at funerals were universally violated, and they buried their dead each one as best he could. Many, having no proper appliances, because the deaths in their household had been so frequent, made no scruple of using the burial-place of others. When one man had raised a funeral pile, others would come, and throwing on their dead first, set fire to it; or when some other corpse was already burning, before they could be stopped would throw their own dead upon it and depart.

53. There were other and worse forms of lawlessness which the plague introduced at Athens. Men who had hitherto concealed their indulgence in pleasure now grew bolder. For, seeing the sudden change, how the rich died in a moment, and those who had nothing immediately inherited their property, they reflected that life and riches were alike transitory, and they resolved to enjoy themselves while they could, and to think only of pleasure. Who would be willing to sacrifice himself to the law of honour when he knew not whether he would ever live to be held in honour? The pleasure of the moment and any sort of thing which conduced to it took the place both of honour and of expediency. No fear of God or law of man deterred a criminal. Those who saw all perishing alike, thought that the worship or neglect of the gods made no difference. For offences against human law no punishment was to be feared; no one would live long enough to be called to account. Already a far heavier sentence had been passed and was hanging over a man's head; before that fell, why should he not take a little pleasure?

54. Such was the grievous calamity which now afflicted the Athenians; within the walls their people were dying, and without, their country was being ravaged. In their troubles they naturally called to mind a verse which the elder men among them declared to have been current long ago:

A Dorian war will come and a plague with it.

There was a dispute about the precise expression; some saying that *limos*, a famine, and not *loimos*, a plague, was the original word. Nevertheless, as might have been expected, for men's memories reflected their sufferings, the argument in favour of *loimos* prevailed at the time. But if ever in future years another Dorian war arises which happens to be accompanied by a famine, they will probably repeat the verse in the other form. The answer of the oracle to the Lacedaemonians when the god was asked whether they should go to war or not, and he replied that if they fought with all their might, they would conquer, and that he himself would take their part, was not forgotten by those who had heard of it, and they quite imagined that they were witnessing the fulfilment of his words. The disease certainly did set in immediately after the invasion of the Peloponnesians, and did not spread into Peloponnesus in any degree worth speaking of, while Athens felt its ravages most severely, and next to Athens the places which were most populous. Such was the history of the plague.

Greek Philosophy and Science

The first Greek thinkers were what we would call scientists. They examined the world around them and speculated about physical reality. Three kinds of investigation preoccupied them: terrestrial measurement, astronomy, and the analysis of physical matter. They developed a science that sought logical answers to questions that had previously been answered by mythic stories that were the basis of religious belief. Soon this logical inquiry into the things of the world embraced the human realm as well, and the famous motto of the Delphic Oracle—"Know Thyself"—became the central concern of thinkers like Heraclitus and Socrates.

Thales of Miletus (624–546 BCE)

Thales was the founder of the Milesian school of philosophy. Tradition has him traveling widely, introducing Egyptian geometry to Greece, working as an engineer and astronomer, meanwhile making a fortune in olive oil. He is popularly credited with determining the height of the pyramids by measuring their shadows at the time when his own shadow equaled his height. Although none of his writings survives, he was so widely admired by later generations that he was always placed among the Seven Sages and his ideas were repeated and challenged by later philosophers. Aristotle, for instance, credited him with four main ideas: that water is the first principle and basic ingredient of all things; that the earth, which is flat, floats upon water; that all things are full of gods; and that a magnetic stone has soul because it can cause iron to move.

Anaximander (fl. 560 BCE)
from *On Nature*

Anaximander, probably a student of Thales, did not agree that water was the basis of all things. Instead he sought the unity that lay behind the division of the natural world into properties like wet and dry, hot and cold. In his view, the essential substance of the natural world was what he called "the unlimited." He was the first western philosopher to write treatises, but only one sentence of his own writing survives: the principles he believed in were preserved by his followers and later writers. He was a geog-

---

The translations come mainly from Arthur Fairbanks' *The First Philosophers of Greece* (London: Kegan Paul, 1898). Xenophanes's poem is translated by Willis Barnstone (New York: Bantam, 1962). The works of Hippocrates are translated by Francis Adams (1849), Archimedes by T. L. Heath (London: Clay, 1897), and Ptolemy by G. J. Toomer (London: Duckworth, 1984).

rapher and astronomer. He made a map of the world, and introduced geometry into the mapping of the heavens. He invented the sundial and believed the earth was at rest in the center of the universe.

1. "Immortal and indestructible," surrounds all and directs all.

2. The first principle is older than water and is eternal motion; in this all things come into being, and all things perish.

3. The first principle and element of all things is infinite. . . . It is neither water nor any other one of the things called elements, but the infinite is something of a different nature, from which came all the heavens and the worlds in them; and from what source things arise, to that they return of necessity when they are destroyed.

4. There are no other causes besides the infinite (such as mind, or friendship), but . . . it itself is divine; for it is immortal and indestructible.

5. Things come into being [not] by change in the nature of the element, but by the separation of the opposites which the eternal motion causes.

6. Existing opposites are separated from the unity.

7. Motion is eternal, and as a result of it the heavens arise. The earth is a heavenly body, controlled by no other power, and keeping its position because it is the same distance from all things; the form of it is curved, cylindrical like a stone column; it has two faces, one of these is the ground beneath our feet, and the other is opposite to it. The stars are a circle of fire, separated from the fire about the world, and surrounded by air. There are certain breathing-holes like the holes of a flute through which we see the stars; so that when the holes are stopped up, there are eclipses. The moon is sometimes full and sometimes in other phases as these holes are stopped up or open. The circle of the sun is twenty-seven times that of the moon, and the sun is higher than the moon, but the circles of the fixed stars are lower.

8. Animals come into being through vapours raised by the sun. Man, however, came into being from another animal, namely the fish, for at first he was like a fish.

9. An infinite number of worlds have been generated and have perished again and returned to their source.

Anaximenes (fl. c.545 BCE)
from *Air*

Anaximenes, the pupil of Anaximander, was the third of the Milesian philosophers and he too sought the basic substance that informed all of nature. His observations led him to believe that air formed the underlying principle of creation, and that apparently different substances simply reflected different quantities of air. Invisible air condensed into visible mist, then water, then solid ice, earth, or stone. The constant movement of air meant that it was alive, and thus, in its divine form, the cause of the divine gods as well as the souls of humans. After two centuries, Anaximenes' works disappeared and were preserved only as quotations in other writers.

1. Air is the one, moveable, infinite, first principle of all things.

2. Air is the nearest to an immaterial thing; for since we are generated in the flow of air, it is necessary that it should be infinite and abundant, because it is never exhausted.

3. The earth was wet, and when it dried it broke apart, and . . . earthquakes are due to the breaking and falling of hills; accordingly earthquakes occur in droughts, and in rainy seasons

also; they occur in drought, as has been said, because the earth dries and breaks apart, and it also crumbles when it is wet through with waters.

4. Air differs in rarity and in density as the nature of things is different; when very attenuated it becomes fire, when more condensed wind, and then cloud, and when still more condensed water and earth and stone, and all other things are composed of these. . . . Motion is eternal and by this changes are produced.

5. The form of air is as follows: When it is of very even consistency, it is imperceptible to vision, but it becomes evident as the result of cold or heat or moisture, or when it is moved. It is always in motion; for things would not change as they do unless it were in motion. It has a different appearance when it is made more dense or thinner; when it is expanded into a thinner state it becomes fire, and again winds are condensed air, and air becomes cloud by compression, and water when it is compressed farther, and earth and finally stones as it is more condensed. So that generation is controlled by the opposites, heat and cold.

6. The broad earth is supported on air; similarly the sun and the moon and all the rest of the stars, being fiery bodies, are supported on the air by their breadth.

7. The stars do not give forth heat because they are so far away. Winds are produced when the air that has been attenuated is set in motion; and when it comes together and is yet farther condensed, clouds are produced, and so it changes into water. And hail is formed when the water descending from the clouds is frozen; and snow, when these being yet more filled with moisture become frozen; and lightning, when clouds are separated by violence of the winds; for when they are separated, the flash is bright and like fire. And a rainbow is produced when the sun's rays fall on compressed air; and earthquakes are produced when the earth is changed yet more by heating and cooling.

8. Air is god, and . . . it is boundless and infinite and always in motion.

9. As our soul which is air holds us together, so wind [i.e., breath] and air encompass the whole world.

Xenophanes (c.570–c.455 BCE)

Xenophanes was less a natural philosopher than a poet, but in his poetry and other works he spoke of the unity he saw underlying everything. He was especially scornful of the popular religious views—based on Homer and Hesiod—that saw the gods as being like immoral humans in character and behavior. This is characteristic of his method, which is to examine popular beliefs from a rational viewpoint rather than to examine nature itself. In the poem included here, he makes fun of the notion of reincarnation popular among the followers of Pythagoras, the mystical philosopher who first used the word "cosmos" to describe the world and who saw the cosmos as generated from numbers and ordered mathematically.

"Pythagoras and the Transmigrated Soul"

One day a dog was being thrashed in the street,
and behold, Pythagoras, philosopher of spirits,
was walking by.
His heart was in his mouth
for the poor pup.

"Stop! Stop!" he cried.
"Don't beat him any more.
This is my dear friend's soul.
I recognize the voice when I hear him bark."

from *On Nature*

1. God is one, supreme among gods and men, and not like mortals in body or in mind.
2. The whole [of god] sees, the whole perceives, the whole hears.
3. But without effort he sets in motion all things by mind and thought.
4. It [i.e. being] always abides in the same place, not moved at all, nor is it fitting that it should move from one place to another.
5. But mortals suppose that the gods are born (as they themselves are), and that they wear man's clothing and have human voice and body.
6. But if cattle or lions had hands, so as to paint with their hands and produce works of art as men do, they would paint their gods and give them bodies in form like their own—horses like horses, cattle like cattle.
7. Homer and Hesiod attributed to the gods all things which are disreputable and worthy of blame when done by men; and they told of them many lawless deeds, stealing, adultery, and deception of each other.
8. For all things come from earth, and all things end by becoming earth.
9. All things that come into being and grow are earth and water.
10. This upper limit of earth at our feet is visible and touches the air, but below it reaches to infinity.
11. Accordingly there has not been a man, nor will there be, who knows distinctly what I say about the gods or in regard to all things, for even if one chances for the most part to say what is true, still he would not know; but every one thinks he knows.
12. In the beginning the gods did not at all reveal all things clearly to mortals, but by searching men in the course of time find them out better.
13. But if one wins a victory by swiftness of foot, or in the pentathlon, where the grove of Zeus lies by Pisas' stream at Olympia, or as a wrestler, or in painful boxing, or in that severe contest called the pancration, he would be more glorious in the eyes of the citizens, he would win a front seat at assemblies, and would be entertained by the city at the public table, and he would receive a gift which would be a keepsake for him. If he won by means of horses he would get all these things although he did not deserve them, as I deserve them, for our wisdom is better than the strength of men or of horses. This is indeed a very wrong custom, nor is it right to prefer strength to excellent wisdom. For if there should be in the city a man good at boxing, or in the pentathlon, or in wrestling, or in swiftness of foot, which is honoured more than strength (among the contests men enter into at the games), the city would not on that account be any better governed. Small joy would it be to any city in this case if a citizen conquers at the games on the banks of the Pisas, for this does not fill with wealth its secret chambers.

Heraclitus (fl. c.500 BCE)
from *On Nature*

Like most of the other early philosophers, Heraclitus exists for us in the record provided by other writers. His one book is lost, but the several fragments that survive show that he was controversial in his own time, and amazingly "modern" in anticipating ideas that have become central in our own time, like relativism, entropy, and the balance of opposing forces. Heraclitus saw that both stability and change were illusory, covering a huge system in which fire was the basic element and movement or flow the basic principle. Change is generated by the pull of opposites, by Strife, and the result is actually harmony and order. A river is for Heraclitus the perfect analogy: it is always the same, and yet it is forever moving and changing.

---

1. Not on my authority, but on that of truth, it is wise for you to accept the fact that all things are one.

2. Eyes and ears are bad witnesses for men, since their souls lack understanding.

3. Seekers for gold dig much earth, and find little gold.

4. Eyes are more exact witnesses than ears.

5. Wisdom is one thing: it is willing and it is unwilling to be called by the name Zeus.

6. This order, the same for all things, no one of gods or men has made, but it always was, and is, and ever shall be, an ever-living fire, kindling according to fixed measure, and extinguished according to fixed measure.

7. All things are exchanged for fire, and fire for all things; as wares are exchanged for gold, and gold for wares.

8. Hesiod is the teacher of most men; they suppose that his knowledge was very extensive, when in fact he did not know night and day, for they are one.

9. God is day and night, winter and summer, war and peace, satiety and hunger; but he assumes different forms, just as when incense is mingled with incense; every one gives him the name he pleases.

10. Cool things become warm, and warm grows cool; the wet dries, the parched becomes wet.

11. You could not step twice in the same rivers; for other and yet other waters are ever flowing on.

12. War is father of all and king of all; and some he made gods and some men, some slaves and some free.

13. Opposition unites. From what draws apart results the most beautiful harmony. All things take place by strife.

14. Good and bad are the same.

15. The limits of the soul you could not discover, though traversing every path.

16. Life and death, and waking and sleeping, and youth and old age, are the same; for the latter change and are the former, and the former change back to the latter.

17. Even a potion separates into its ingredients when it is not stirred.

18. Though reason is common, most people live as though they had an understanding peculiar to themselves.

19. It is hard to contend with passion; for whatever it desires to get it buys at the cost of soul.

20. It is better to conceal stupidity, but it is an effort in time of relaxation and over the wine.

21. There awaits men at death what they do not expect or think.

Parmenides (fl. 470 BCE)
from *On Nature*

Tradition has it that, at age 65, Parmenides visited Athens and discussed philosophy with Socrates. A student of Xenophanes, Parmenides also wrote poetry and brought philosophical inquiry to the study of metaphysics. He felt that change and multiplicity were appearances that masked the true reality, that of Being.

1. Come now I will tell you—and hear my word and heed it—what are the only ways of enquiry that lead to knowledge. The one way, assuming that being is and that it is impossible for it not to be, is the trustworthy path, for truth attends it. The other, that not-being is and that it necessarily is, I call a wholly incredible course, since you cannot recognize not-being (for this is impossible), nor could you speak of it, for thought and being are the same thing.

2. It is necessary both to say and to think that being is; for it is possible that being is, and it is impossible that not-being is; this is what I bid you ponder. I restrain you from this first course of investigation; and from that course also along which mortals knowing nothing wander aimlessly, since helplessness directs the roaming thought in their bosoms, and they are borne on deaf and likewise blind, amazed, headstrong races, they who consider being and not-being as the same and not the same; and that all things follow a back-turning course.

3. There is left but this single path to tell you of: namely, that being is. And on this path there are many proofs that being is without beginning and indestructible; it is universal, existing alone, immovable and without end; nor ever was it nor will it be, since it now is, all together, one, and continuous. . . . From what did it grow and how? I will not permit you to say or to think or to say that it came from non-being; for it is impossible to think or to say that not-being is. . . . So it is necessary that being either is absolute or is not. Nor will the force of the argument permit that anything spring from being except being itself.

4. Therefore thinking and that by reason of which thought exists are one and the same thing, for you will not find thinking without the being from which it receives its name. Nor is there nor will there be anything apart from being; for fate has linked it together, so that it is a whole and immovable. Wherefore all these things will be but a name, all these things which mortals determined in the belief that they were true, namely, that things arise and perish, that they are and are not, that they change their position and vary in colour.

Anaxagoras (c.500–c.428 BCE)
from *On Nature*

Born in what is today Turkey, Anaxagoras moved to Athens in 480 and brought with him the Ionian habits of scientific inquiry. During his time in Athens, he had Pericles as his principal supporter, even when he was tried for impiety for claiming that the sun was a fiery stone a bit larger than the Peloponnese. Besides discovering the cause of eclipses, Anaxagoras is remembered for two key ideas. He held, first, that everything was made up not of one or of four elements, but of an infinite number of different spermata *("seeds of things"); within each individual thing the seeds of all things are present, but the individual takes on the character of those elemental seeds which exist in greatest number. Second, and more importantly, Anaxagoras believed that the motive force of creation is* nous, *or "mind," which spins out material opposites and which, in each individual, directs its energies. Both Plato and Aristotle adopted Anaxagoras's concept of mind, developing it further by giving it an ethical motion: for them mind does not simply seek nourishment and satisfaction, but actively works toward the Good. After his trial for impiety, Anaxagoras left Athens and founded a school at Lampsacus.*

---

1. In all things there is a portion of everything except mind; and there are things in which there is mind also.

2. Other things include a portion of everything, but mind is infinite and self-powerful and mixed with nothing, but it exists alone itself by itself. For if it were not by itself, but were mixed with anything else, it would include parts of all things. . . . For it is the most rarified of all things and the purest, and it has all knowledge in regard to everything and the greatest power; over all that has life, both greater and less, mind rules. And mind ruled the rotation of the whole, so that it set it in rotation in the beginning. . . . And whatever things were to be, and whatever things were, as many as are now, and whatever things shall be, all these mind arranged in order; and it arranged that rotation, according to which now rotate stars and sun and moon and air and ether, now that they are separated.

3. And when mind began to set things in motion, there was separation from everything that was in motion, and however much mind set in motion, all this was made distinct. The rotation of the things that were moved and made distinct caused them to be yet more distinct.

4. Earth is condensed out of these things that are separated. For water is separated from the clouds, and earth from the water; and from the earth stones are condensed by cold; and these are separated farther from water.

5. But mind, as it always has been, especially now also is where all other things are, in the surrounding mass, and in the things that were separated, and in the things that are being separated.

6. For neither is there a least of what is small, but there is always a less. For being is not non-being. But there is always a greater than what is great. And it is equal to the small in number; but with reference to itself each thing is both small and great.

7. The Greeks do not rightly use the terms "coming into being" and "perishing." For nothing comes into being nor yet does anything perish, but there is mixture and separation of things that are. So they would do right in calling the coming into being "mixture," and the perishing "separation."

Protagoras (c.485–c.415 BCE)

*Protagoras, unlike many of the other early philosophers, gave his attention to moral and political questions. In fact, he disliked science and mathematics and developed views of knowledge which emphasized subjectivity and relativity. He was the first professional sophist, and he made a fortune lecturing on grammar and rhetoric. He wrote books (*On Truth *and* On the Gods*) which were eventually lost, but he is well remembered through Plato's treating him as the Athenian rival of Socrates and through two fragments of his thought that do survive. "Man is the measure of all things," he said; "of things that are, that they are, and of things that are not, that they are not." While this sounds like the battle cry of*

Renaissance-style humanism, it is first a statement about subjectivity—that the world is filtered through human perceptions. The other fragment was equally upsetting of Athenian values: "Of the gods I know nothing, whether they exist or do not exist: nor what they are like in form." Because of his views about the gods, Protagoras was exiled from Athens and his books burnt.

Hippocrates (469–399 BCE)

Hippocrates has a great reputation, ancient and modern, but very little is known about him. Biographies written about him a few centuries after he lived contained lots of stories and legends, but little reliable information. The writings attributed to him constitute a medical library—about 70 works—and the books probably became part of the great library at Alexandria and were copied and re-copied. Thus Hippocrates' fate is very different from that of most Greek thinkers: about sixty of his works survive, and a version of his famous oath still is part of the initiation rite of physicians. Scholars believe that he did not write all of the works attributed to him (including the Oath itself), but the writings as a group show a willingness to look at the whole body as an organism and to treat diseases as having discoverable, physical causes. The treatise on epilepsy, for instance, argues that this "Sacred Disease" is like other diseases and can be treated as other diseases are. He then analyzes the functioning of the brain as part of the human body, a part with its own structure of strengths and weaknesses.

[The Oath]

I swear by Apollo the physician, and Aesculapius, and Health, and All-heal, and all the gods and goddesses, that, according to my ability and judgment, I will keep this Oath and this stipulation—to reckon him who taught me this Art equally dear to me as my parents, to share my substance with him, and relieve his necessities if required; to look upon his offspring in the same footing as my own brothers, and to teach them this art, if they shall wish to learn it, without fee or stipulation; and that by precept, lecture, and every other mode of instruction, I will impart a knowledge of the Art to my own sons, and those of my teachers, and to disciples bound by a stipulation and oath according to the law of medicine, but to none others. I will follow that system of regimen which, according to my ability and judgment, I consider for the benefit of my patients, and abstain from whatever is deleterious and mischievous. I will give no deadly medicine to any one if asked, nor suggest any such counsel; and in like manner I will not give to a woman a pessary to produce abortion. With purity and with holiness I will pass my life and practice my Art. I will not cut persons laboring under the stone, but will leave this to be done by men who are practitioners of this work. Into whatever houses I enter, I will go into them for the benefit of the sick, and will abstain from every voluntary act of mischief and corruption; and, further from the seduction of females or males, of freemen and slaves. Whatever, in connection with my professional practice or not, in connection with it, I see or hear, in the life of men, which ought not to be spoken of abroad, I will not divulge, as reckoning that all such should be kept secret. While I continue to keep this Oath unviolated, may it be granted to me to enjoy life and the practice of the art, respected by all men, in all times! But should I trespass and violate this Oath, may the reverse be my lot!

[The Sacred Disease]

It is thus with regard to the disease called Sacred: it appears to me to be nowise more divine nor more sacred than other diseases, but has a natural cause from the originates like other affections. Men regard its nature and cause as divine from ignorance and wonder, because it is not at all like to other diseases. And this notion of its divinity is kept up by their inability to comprehend it, and the simplicity of the mode by which it is cured, for men are freed from it by purifications and incantations. But if it is reckoned divine because it is wonderful, instead of one there are many diseases which would be sacred; for, as I will show, there are others no less wonderful and prodigious, which nobody imagines to be sacred. The quotidian, tertian, and quartan fevers, seem to me no less sacred and divine in their origin than this disease, although they are not reckoned so wonderful. And I see men become mad and demented from no manifest cause, and at the same time doing many things out of place; and I have known many persons in sleep groaning and crying out, some in a state of suffocation, some jumping up and fleeing out of doors, and deprived of their reason until they awaken, and afterward becoming well and rational as before, although they be pale and weak; and this will happen not once but frequently. And there are many and various things of the like kind, which it would be tedious to state particularly.

They who first referred this malady to the gods appear to me to have been just such persons as the conjurors, purificators, mountebanks, and charlatans now are, who give themselves out for being excessively religious, and as knowing more than other people. Such persons, then, using the divinity as a pretext and screen of their own inability to afford any assistance, have given out that the disease is sacred, adding suitable reasons for this opinion, and they have instituted a mode of treatment which is safe for themselves, namely, by applying purifications and incantations, and enforcing abstinence from baths and many articles of food which are unwholesome to men in diseases. . . . And they forbid to have a black robe, because black is expressive of death; and to sleep on a goat's skin, or to wear it, and to put one foot upon another, or one hand upon another; for all these things are held to be hindrances to the cure. All these they enjoin with reference to its divinity, as if possessed of more knowledge, and announcing beforehand other causes so that if the person should recover, theirs would be the honor and credit; and if he should die, they would have a certain defense, as if the gods, and not they, were to blame, seeing they had administered nothing either to eat or drink as medicines, nor had overheated him with baths, so as to prove the cause of what had happened. But I am of opinion that (if this were true) none of the Libyans, who live in the interior, would be free from this disease, since they all sleep on goats' skins, and live upon goats' flesh; neither have they couch, robe, nor shoe that is not made of goat's skin, for they have no other herds but goats and oxen. But if these things, when administered in food, aggravate the disease, and if it be cured by abstinence from them, godhead is not the cause at all; nor will purifications be of any avail, but it is the food which is beneficial and prejudicial, and the influence of the divinity vanishes.

Thus, they who try to cure these maladies in this way, appear to me neither to reckon them sacred nor divine. For when they are removed by such purifications, and this method of cure, what is to prevent them from being brought upon men and induced by other devices similar to these? So that the cause is no longer divine, but human. . . .

This disease seems to me to be no more divine than others; but it has its nature such as other diseases have, and a cause whence it originates, and its nature and cause are divine only just as much as all others are, and it is curable no less than the others, unless . . . it is confirmed, and has became stronger than the remedies applied. Its origin is hereditary, like that of other diseases. . . .

But the brain is the cause of this affection, as it is of other very great diseases, and in what manner and from what cause it is formed, I will now plainly declare. The brain of man, as in all other animals, is double, and a thin membrane divides it through the middle, and therefore the pain is not always in the same part of the head; for sometimes it is situated on either side, and sometimes the whole is affected; and veins run toward it from all parts of the body, many of which are small, but two are thick, the one from the liver, and the other from the spleen. . . .

Of little children who are seized with this disease, the greater part die, provided the defluxion be copious and humid, for the veins being slender cannot admit the phlegm, owing to its thickness and abundance; but the blood is cooled and congealed, and the child immediately dies. But if the phlegm be in small quantity, and make a defluxion into both the veins, or to those on either side, the children survive, but exhibit notable marks of the disorder; for either the mouth is drawn aside, or an eye, the neck, or a hand, wherever a vein being filled with phlegm loses its tone, and is attenuated, and the part of the body connected with this vein is necessarily rendered weaker and defective. . . .

To persons of a more advanced age, it neither proves fatal, nor produces distortions. For their veins are capacious and are filled with hot blood; and therefore the phlegm can neither prevail nor cool the blood, so as to coagulate it, but it is quickly overpowered and mixed with the blood, and thus the veins receive the air, and sensibility remains; and, owing to their strength, the aforesaid symptoms are less likely to seize them. But when this disease attacks very old people, it therefore proves fatal, or induces paraplegia, because the veins are empty, and the blood scanty, thin, and watery.

Men ought to know that from nothing else but the brain come joys, delights, laughter and sports, and sorrows, griefs, despondency, and lamentations. And by this, in an especial manner, we acquire wisdom and knowledge, and see and hear, and know what are foul and what are fair, what are bad and what are good, what are sweet, and what unsavory; some we discriminate by habit, and some we perceive by their utility. By this we distinguish objects of relish and disrelish, according to the seasons; and the same things do not always please us. And by the same organ we become mad and delirious, and fears and terrors assail us, some by night, and some by day, and dreams and untimely wanderings, and cares that are not suitable, and ignorance of present circumstances, desuetude, and unskillfulness. All these things we endure from the brain, when it is not healthy. . . .

And the disease called the Sacred arises from causes as the others, namely, those things which enter and quit the body, such as cold, the sun, and the winds, which are ever changing and are never at rest. And these things are divine, so that there is no necessity for making a distinction, and holding this disease to be more divine than the others, but all are divine, and all human. And each has its own peculiar nature and power, and none is of an ambiguous nature, or irremediable. And the most of them are curable by the same means as those by which any other thing is food to one, and injurious to another.

Archimedes (287–212 BCE)
from *The Sand Reckoner*

More is known about Archimedes than about any other ancient scientist, but many of the stories are popular anecdotes and perhaps fictions. During the Roman siege of Syracuse, where Archimedes spent most of his life, he is supposed to have set the Roman ships afire by placing large mirrors above the harbor. When he discovered how to determine the proportions of gold and silver in a wreath by weighing it in water, he is supposed to have leapt from his bath and run naked through the streets shouting

"Eureka! I have found it!" Impressed by the mechanical power of pulleys and levers, he is supposed to have said, "Give me a place to stand and I can move the earth." Whether the appealing human part of these stories is true or not, the scientific part certainly is. Archimedes was a leading mathematician, with interests in mechanics, optics, and astronomy. Educated at Alexandria, Archimedes did not take much credit for his inventions, preferring instead to write theoretical treatises on mechanics, hydrostatics, spheres and cylinders, measurement of spirals, parabolas, and the circle (he calculated the value of π), centers of gravity, statics, and levers. His Sand-Reckoner *is fascinating for several reasons. He argues that the number of grains of sand in the universe is countable and then invents a place-value system for calculating large numbers to make up for weaknesses in the existing Greek notation. But he also describes and accounts for in his calculations, with an entirely open and searching mind, the system of the universe proposed by Aristarchus, with the sun at the center rather than the earth.*

There are some, king Gelon, who think that the number of the sand is infinite in multitude; and I mean by the sand not only that which exists about Syracuse and the rest of Sicily but also that which is found in every region whether inhabited or uninhabited. Again there are some who, without regarding it as infinite, yet think that no number has been named which is great enough to exceed its multitude. And it is clear that they who hold this view, if they imagined a mass made up of sand in other respects as large as the mass of the earth, including in it all the seas and the hollows of the earth filled up to a height equal to that of the highest of the mountains, would be many times further still from recognizing that any number could be expressed which exceeded the multitude of the sand so taken. But I will try to show you by means of geometrical proofs, which you will be able to follow, that, of the numbers named by me and given in the work which I sent to Zeuxippus, some exceed not only the number of the mass of sand equal in magnitude to the earth filled up in the way described, but also that of a mass equal in magnitude to the universe. Now you are aware that 'universe' is the name given by most astronomers to the sphere whose centre is the centre of the earth and whose radius is equal to the straight line between the centre of the sun and the centre of the earth. This is the common account . . . as you have heard from astronomers. But Aristarchus of Samos brought out a book consisting of some hypotheses, in which the premises lead to the result that the universe is many times greater than that now so called. His hypotheses are that the fixed stars and the sun remain unmoved, that the earth revolves about the sun in the circumference of a circle, the sun lying in the middle of the orbit, and that the sphere of the fixed stars situated about the same centre as the sun, is so great that the circle in which he supposes the earth to revolve bears such a proportion to the distance of the fixed stars as the centre of the sphere bears to its surface. Now it is easy to see that this is impossible; for, since the centre of the sphere has no magnitude, we cannot conceive it to bear any ratio whatever to the surface of the sphere. We must however take Aristarchus to mean this: since we conceive the earth to be, as it were, the centre of the universe, the ratio which the earth bears to what we describe as the "universe' is the same as the ratio which the sphere containing the circle in which he supposes the earth to revolve bears to the sphere of the fixed stars. For he adapts the proofs of his results to a hypothesis of this kind, and in particular he appears to suppose the magnitude of the sphere in which he represents the earth as moving to be equal to what we call the 'universe.'

I say then that, even if a sphere were made up of the sand, as great as Aristarchus supposes the sphere of the fixed stars to be, I shall still prove that, of the numbers named in the

Principles, some exceed in multitude the number of the sand which is equal in magnitude to the sphere referred to, provided that the following assumptions be made.

1. *The perimeter of the earth is about 3,000,000 stadia and not greater. . . .*
2. *The diameter of the earth is greater than the diameter of the moon, and the diameter of the sun is greater than the diameter of the earth. . . .*
3. *The diameter of the sun is about 30 times the diameter of he moon and not greater. . . .*

Application to the number of the sand.

By Assumption 5

(diam. of poppy-seed) $\not<$ 1/40 (finger-breadth);

and, since spheres are to one another in the triplicate ratio of their diameters, it follows that

(sphere of diam. 1 finger-breadth $\not<$ 64,000 poppy-seeds
$>$ 64,000 x 10,000
$>$ 640,000,000
$>$ 6 units of *second order* + 40,000,000 units of *first order*
(*a fortiori*) $<$ 10 units of *second order* of numbers.
$\Big\}$ grains of sand.

We now gradually increase the diameter of the supposed sphere, multiplying it by 100 each time. Thus, remembering that the sphere is thereby multiplied by 100^3 or 1,000,000, the number of grains of sand which would be contained in a sphere with each successive diameter may be arrived at as follows.

[Archimedes here goes through a series of multiplications that he prepared for earlier in the work by introducing and explaining a place-value system of notation for very large numbers. His calculations, figuring 1 stadium <10,000 finger-breadths, yield the number of grains of sand that would fill either an earth-centered or a sun-centered universe.]

Hence *the number of grains of sand which could be contained in a sphere of the size of our 'universe' is less than 1,000 units of the seventh order of numbers* [or 10^{51}].

From this we can prove further that *a sphere of the size attributed by Aristarchus to the sphere of the fixed stars would contain a number of grains of sand less than 10,000,000 units of the eighth order of numbers* [or $10^{56+7} = 10^{63}$].

For, by hypothesis,

(earth) : ('universe') = ('universe') : (sphere of fixed stars).

And

(diameter of 'universe') < 10,000 (diam. of earth);

whence

(diam. of sphere of fixed stars) < 10,000 (diam. of 'universe').

Therefore

(sphere of fixed stars) < $(10,000)^3$ ('universe').

It follows that the number of grains of sand which would be contained in a sphere equal to the sphere of the fixed stars

< $(10,000)^3$ x 1,000 units of *seventh order*

< (13th term of series) x (52nd term of series)

< 64th term of series   [i.e. 10^{63}]

< [10^7 or] 10,000,000 units of *eighth order* of numbers.

Conclusion.

I conceive that these things, king Gelon, will appear incredible to the great majority of people who have not studied mathematics, but that to those who are conversant therewith and have given thought to the question of the distances and sizes of the earth the sun and moon and the whole universe the proof will carry conviction. And it was for this reason that I thought the subject would be not inappropriate for your consideration.

Ptolemy (fl. 121–151 CE)
from *The Almagest*

Although we know practically nothing about his life, Claudius Ptolemaeus gained a reputation as a geographer and an astronomer. His treatise, The Mathematical Collection, *influential among medieval Arab thinkers, became known by its Arabic name and is still called by that today,* Almagest. *A study of the stars and planets, the* Almagest *became an encyclopedia for later astronomers, especially since it offered a catalog of 1,022 stars. He also argued passionately that the earth is round and that it lies at the center of the universe, a view that leads us to call the belief in an earth-centered universe* Ptolemaic, *as opposed to the sun-centered* Copernican *view that later won out. The Ptolemaic universe is depicted inside the back cover of this book.*

4. (THAT THE EARTH TOO, TAKEN AS A WHOLE, IS SENSIBLY SPHERICAL)

That the earth, too, taken as a whole, is sensibly spherical can best be grasped from the following considerations. We can see, again, that the sun, moon, and other stars do not rise and set simultaneously for everyone on earth, but do so earlier for those more toward the east, later for those toward the west. For we find that the phenomena at eclipses, especially lunar eclipses, which take place at the same time [for all observers], are nevertheless not recorded as occurring at the same hour (that is at an equal distance from noon) by all observers. Rather, the hour recorded by the more easterly observers is always later than that recorded by the more westerly. We find that the differences in the hour are proportional to the distances between the places [of observation]. Hence one can reasonably conclude that the earth's surface is spherical, because its evenly curving surface (for so it is when considered as a whole) cuts off [the heavenly bodies] for each set of observers in turn in a regular fashion.

If the earth's shape were any other, this would not happen, as one can see from the following arguments. If it were concave, the stars would be seen rising first by those more toward the west; if it were plane, they would rise and set simultaneously for everyone on earth; if it were triangular or square or any other polygonal shape, by a similar argument, they would rise and set simultaneously for all those living on the same plane surface. Yet it is apparent that nothing like this takes place. Nor could it be cylindrical, with the curved surface in the east-west direction, and the flat sides towards the poles of the universe, which some might suppose more plausible. This is clear from the following: For those living on the curved surface none of the stars would be ever-visible, but either all stars would rise and set for all observers, or the same stars, for an equal [celestial] distance from each of the poles, would always be invisible for all observers. In fact, the farther we travel toward the north, the more of the southern stars disappear and the more of the northern stars appear. Hence it is clear that here too the curvature of the earth cuts off [the heavenly bodies] in a regular fashion in a north-south direction, and proves the sphericity [of the earth] in all directions.

There is the further consideration that if we sail toward mountains or elevated places from and to any direction whatever, they are observed to increase gradually in size as if rising up from the sea itself in which they had previously been submerged: this is due to the curvature of the surface of the water.

5. (THAT THE EARTH IS IN THE MIDDLE OF THE HEAVENS)

Once one has grasped this, if one next considers the position of the earth, one will find that the phenomena associated with it could take place only if we assume that it is in the middle of the heavens, like the center of a sphere. . . .

To sum up, if the earth did not lie in the middle [of the universe], the whole order of things which we observe in the increase and decrease of the length of daylight would be fundamentally upset. Furthermore, eclipses of the moon would not be restricted to situations where the moon is diametrically opposite the sun (whatever part of the heaven [the luminaries are in]), since the earth would often come between them when they were not diametrically opposite, but at intervals of less than a semicircle.

6. (THAT THE EARTH HAS THE RATIO OF A POINT TO THE HEAVENS)

Moreover, the earth has, to the senses, the ratio of a point to the distance of the sphere of the so-called fixed stars. A strong indication of this is the fact that the sizes and distances of the stars, at any given time, appear equal and the same from all parts of the earth everywhere, as observations of the same [celestial] objects from different latitudes are found to have not the least discrepancy from each other. . . .

Another clear indication that this is so is that the planes drawn through the observer's lines of sight at any point [on earth], which we call "horizons," always bisect the whole heavenly sphere. This would not happen if the earth were of perceptible size in relation to the distance of the heavenly bodies; in that case only the plane drawn through the center of the earth could bisect the sphere, while a plane through any point on the surface of the earth would always make the section [of the heavens] below the earth greater than the section above it.

7. (THAT THE EARTH DOES NOT HAVE ANY MOTION FROM PLACE TO PLACE, EITHER)

One can show by the same arguments as the preceding that the earth cannot have any motion in the aforementioned directions, or indeed ever move at all from its position at the center. For the same phenomena would result as would if it had any position other than the central one. Hence I think it is idle to seek for causes for the motion of objects towards the center, once it has been so clearly established from the actual phenomena that the earth occupies the middle place in the universe, and that all heavy objects are carried toward the earth. The following fact alone would most readily lead one to this notion [that all objects fall towards the center]. In absolutely all parts of the earth, which, as we said, has been shown to be spherical and in the middle of the universe, the direction and path of the motion (I mean the proper, [natural] motion) of all bodies possessing weight is always and everywhere at right angles to the rigid plane drawn tangent to the point of impact. It is clear from this fact that, if [these falling objects] were not arrested by the surface of the earth, they would certainly reach the center of the earth itself, since the straight line to the center is also always at right angles to the plane tangent to the sphere at the point of intersection [of that radius] and the tangent.

Those who think it paradoxical that the earth, having such a great weight, is not supported by anything and yet does not move, seem to me to be making the mistake of judging on the basis of their own experience instead of taking into account the peculiar nature of the universe. They would not, I think, consider such a thing strange once they realized that this great bulk of the earth, when compared with the whole surrounding mass [of the universe], has the ratio of a point to it. For when one looks at it in that way, it will seem quite possible that that which is relatively smallest should be overpowered and pressed in equally from all directions to a position of equilibrium by that which is the greatest of all and of uniform nature. For there is no up and down in the universe with respect to itself, any more than one could imagine such a thing in a sphere; instead the proper and natural motion of the compound bodies in it is as follows: Light and rarefied bodies drift outward towards the circumference, but seem to move in the direction which is "up" for each observer, since the overhead direction for all of us, which is also called "up" points toward the surrounding surface; heavy and dense bodies, on the other hand, are carried toward the middle and the center, but seem to fall downward, because, again, the direction which is for all of us toward our feet, called "down," also points towards the center of the earth. These heavy bodies, as one would expect, settle about the center because of their mutual pressure and resistance, which is equal and uniform from all directions. Hence, too, one can see that it is plausible that the earth, since its total mass is so great compared with the bodies which fall toward it, can remain motionless under the impact of these very small weights (for they strike it from all sides), and receive, as it were, the objects falling on it. If the earth had a single motion in common with other heavy objects, it is obvious that it would be carried down faster than all of them because of its much greater size: Living things and individual heavy objects would be left behind, riding on the air, and the earth itself would very soon have fallen completely out of the heavens. But such things are utterly ridiculous merely to think of.

But certain people . . . think that there could be no evidence to oppose their view if, for instance, they supposed the heavens to remain motionless, and the earth to revolve from west to east about the same axis [as the heavens], making approximately one revolution each day. . . . They do not realize that, although there is perhaps nothing in the celestial phenomena which would count against that hypothesis, at least from simpler considerations, nevertheless from what would occur here on earth and in the air, one can see that such a notion is quite ridiculous. . . . Nevertheless, they would have to admit that the revolving motion of the earth must be the most violent of all motions associated with it, seeing that it makes one revolution in such a short time; the result would be that all objects not actually standing on the earth would appear to have the same motion, opposite to that of the earth: Neither clouds nor other flying or thrown objects would ever be seen moving toward the east, since the earth's motion toward the east would always outrun and overtake them, so that all other objects would seem to move in the direction of the west and the rear. But if they said that the air is carried around in the same direction and with the same speed as the earth, the compound objects in the air would nonetheless always seem to be left behind by the motion of both [earth and air]; or if those objects too were carried around, fused, as it were, to the air, then they would never appear to have any motion either in advance or rearwards: they would always appear still, neither wandering about nor changing position, whether they were flying or thrown objects. Yet we quite plainly see that they do undergo all these kinds of motion, in such a way that they are not even slowed down or speeded up at all by any motion of the earth. . . .

Plato (c.427–347 bce)

Plato has the distinction of being perhaps the most influential philosopher in history and the attraction of being the most readable. This is due both to the form he developed to explore ideas, the dialogue, and to the fascinating hero of most of the dialogues, his teacher Socrates. Plato may have wanted to become a playwright, and the dialogue form exploits his dramatic and rhetorical strengths. It also recreates the question-and-answer method associated with Socrates, whose ideas survive only in the writings of his students. Plato's school in Athens, the Academy, became known as the best in Greece and it survived for centuries. During the fourth century BCE, the most important mathematical discoveries (solid geometry, conic sections, the doctrine of proportion, the astronomical model of concentric spheres) were made by friends and students of Plato at his Academy. His most famous student, and later rival, was Aristotle.

Plato's interests were very broad and his philosophical investigations into questions of the good life, proper education, the best form of the state, the nature of good, and the standards of judgment, draw on his knowledge of geometry, cosmology, science, and the law. His ideas became part of the fabric of Western thinking in later centuries, even during the Middle Ages when his writings could no longer be read because of the loss of Greek. Christianity, formed in the Hellenistic Greek milieu of first-century CE Palestine, is thoroughly Platonic in its perception of God as all goodness, truth, and love; the triumph of Christianity in Europe ensured the survival of the Platonic heritage until the Renaissance. Then the Platonic dialogues were "rediscovered" (they had been alive the whole time in the hands of Arabic scholars) and Plato became the rage: neo-Platonic academies were set up in Italy and France, and English poets wrote love poems steeped in Platonic ideas.

The Republic

Plato is called an idealist, which means that he felt that the realm of ideas, of principles—the World of Forms—existed prior to and is more real than the material world we inhabit. He shows this in a figurative parable in the Republic, Plato's evocation of the ideal state, ruled by a philosopher-king. Our life is likened to that of prisoners living in a cave whose knowledge of the outside world comes from reflected shadows on the wall. The world of the senses is darkness compared to the blazing sunlight of the knowledge apprehended by our souls in the real world we came from and to which we will return. One scholar suggests that students might think of a movie theater as an apt equivalent of the cave in Plato's figure.

The translation is by H. D. P. Lee (Baltimore: Penguin, 1955).

'I want you to go on to picture the enlightenment or ignorance of our human conditions somewhat as follows. Imagine an underground chamber, like a cave with an entrance open to the daylight and running a long way underground. In this chamber are men who have been prisoners there since they were children, their legs and necks being so fastened that they can only look straight ahead of them and cannot turn their heads. Behind them and above them a fire is burning, and between the fire and the prisoners runs a road, in front of which a curtain-wall has been built, like the screen at puppet shows between the operators and their audience, above which they show their puppets.'

'I see.'

'Imagine further that there are men carrying all sorts of gear along behind the curtain-wall, including figures of men and animals made of wood and stone and other materials, and that some of these men, as is natural, are talking and some not.'

'An odd picture and an odd sort of prisoner.'

'They are drawn from life,' I replied. 'For, tell me, do you think our prisoners could see anything of themselves or their fellows except the shadows thrown by the fire on the wall of the cave opposite them?'

'How could they see anything else if they were prevented from moving their heads all their lives?'

'And would they see anything more of the objects carried along the road?'

'Of course not.'

'Then if they were able to talk to each other, would they not assume that the shadows they saw were real things?'

'Inevitably.'

'And if the wall of their prison opposite them reflected sound, don't you think that they would suppose, whenever one of the passers-by on the road spoke, that the voice belonged to the shadow passing before them?'

'They would be bound to think so.'

'And so they would believe that the shadows of the objects we mentioned were in all respects real.'

'Yes, inevitably.'

'Then think what would naturally happen to them if they were released from their bonds and cured of their delusions. Suppose one of them were let loose, and suddenly compelled to stand up and turn his head and look and walk towards the fire; all these actions would be painful and he would be too dazzled to see properly the objects of which he used to see the shadows. So if he was told that what he used to see was mere illusion and that he was now nearer reality and seeing more correctly, because he was turned towards objects that were more real, and if on top of that he were compelled to say what each of the passing objects was when it was pointed out to him, don't you think he would be at a loss, and think that what he used to see was more real than the objects now being pointed out to him?'

'Much more real.'

'And if he were made to look directly at the light of the fire, it would hurt his eyes and he would turn back and take refuge in the things which he could see, which he would think really far clearer than the things being shown him.'

'Yes.'

'And if,' I went on, 'he were forcibly dragged up the steep and rocky ascent and not let go till he had been dragged out into the sunlight, the process would be a painful one, to which he would much object, and when he emerged into the light his eyes would be so over-whelmed by the brightness of it that he wouldn't be able to see a single one of the things he was now told were real.'

'Certainly not at first,' he agreed.

'Because he would need to grow accustomed to the light before he could see things in the world outside the cave. First he would find it easiest to look at shadows, next at the reflections of men and other objects in water, and later on at the objects themselves. After that he would find it easier to observe the heavenly bodies and the sky at night than by day, and to look at the light of the moon and stars, rather than at the sun and its light!'

'Of course!'

'The thing he would be able to do last would be to look directly at the sun, and observe its nature without using reflections in water or any other medium, but just as it is.'

'That must come last.'

'Later on he would come to the conclusion that it is the sun that produces the changing seasons and years and controls everything in the visible world, and is in a sense responsible for everything that he and his fellow-prisoners used to see.'

'That is the conclusion which he would obviously reach.'

'And when he thought of his first home and what passed for wisdom there, and of his fel-low-prisoners, don't you think he would congratulate himself on his good fortune and be sorry for them?'

'Very much so.'

'There was probably a certain amount of honour and glory to be won among the prison-ers, and prizes for keen-sightedness for anyone who could remember the order of sequence among the passing shadows and so be best able to predict their future appearances. Will our released prisoner hanker after these prizes or envy this power or honour? Won't he be more likely to feel, as Homer says, that he would far rather be "a serf in the house of some landless man" or indeed anything else in the world, than live and think as they do?'

'Yes,' he replied, 'he would prefer anything to a life like theirs!'

'Then what do you think would happen,' I asked, 'if he went back to sit in his old seat in the cave? Wouldn't his eyes be blinded by the darkness, because he had come in suddenly out of the daylight?'

'Certainly.'

'And if he had to discriminate between the shadows, in competition with the other pris-oners, while he was still blinded and before his eyes got used to the darkness—a process that might take some time—wouldn't he be likely to make a fool of himself? And they would say that his visit to the upper world had ruined his sight, and that the ascent was not worth even attempting. And if anyone tried to release them and lead them up, they would kill him if they could lay hands on him.'

'They certainly would!

'Now, my dear Glaucon,' I went on, 'this simile must be connected, throughout, with what preceded it.' The visible realm corresponds to the prison, and the light of the fire in the prison to the power of the sun. And you won't go wrong if you connect the ascent into the upper world and the sight of the objects there with the upward progress of the mind into the intel-ligible realm—that's my guess, which is what you are anxious to hear. The truth of the matter is, after all, known only to God. But in my opinion, for what it is worth, the final thing to be perceived in the intelligible realm, and perceived only with difficulty, is the absolute form of

Good; once seen, it is inferred to be responsible for everything right and good, producing in the visible realm light and the source of light, and being, in the intelligible realm itself, controlling source of reality and intelligence. And anyone who is going to act rationally either in public or private must perceive it.'

'I agree,' he said, 'so far as I am able to understand you.'

'Then you will perhaps also agree with me that it won't be surprising if those who get so far are unwilling to return to mundane affairs, and if their minds long to remain among higher things. That's what we should expect if our simile is to be trusted.'

'Yes, that's to be expected!'

'Nor will you think it strange that anyone who descends from contemplation of the divine to the imperfections of human life should blunder and make a fool of himself, if, while still blinded and unaccustomed to the surrounding darkness, he's forcibly put on trial in the lawcourts or elsewhere about the images of justice or their shadows, and made to dispute about the conceptions of justice held by men who have never seen absolute justice.'

'There's nothing strange in that.'

'But anyone with any sense,' I said, 'will remember that the eyes may be unsighted in two ways, by a transition either from light to darkness or from darkness to light, and that the same distinction applies to the mind. So when he sees a mind confused and unable to see clearly he will not laugh without thinking, but will ask himself whether it has come from a clearer world and is confused by the unaccustomed darkness, or whether it is dazzled by the stronger light of the clearer world to which it has escaped from its previous ignorance. The first state is a reason for congratulation, the second for sympathy, though if one wants to laugh at it one can do so with less absurdity than at the mind that has descended from the daylight of the upper world.'

'You put it very reasonably.'

'If this is true,' I continued, 'we must reject the conception of education professed by those who say that they can put into the mind knowledge that was not there before—rather as if they could put sight into blind eyes.'

'It is a claim that is certainly made,' he said.

'But our argument indicates that this is a capacity which is innate in each man's mind, and that the faculty by which he learns is like an eye which cannot be turned from darkness to light unless the whole body is turned; in the same way the mind as a whole must be turned away from the world of change until its eye can bear to look straight at reality, and at the brightest of all realities which is what we call the Good. Isn't that so?'

'Yes.'

'Then this business of turning the mind round might be made a subject of professional skill, which would effect the conversion as easily and effectively as possible. It would not be concerned to implant sight, but to ensure that some one who had it already was turned in the right direction and looking the right way.'

'That may well be so.'

'The rest, therefore, of what are commonly called qualities of the mind perhaps resemble those of the body, in that they are not innate, but are implanted by training and practice; but the power of knowing, it seems, belongs to some diviner faculty, which never loses its power, but whose effects are good or bad according to the direction in which it is turned. Have you never noticed how shrewd is the glance of the type of men commonly called bad but clever? Their intelligence is limited, but their sight is sharp enough in matters that concern them; it's not that their sight is weak, but that they put it to bad use, so that the keener it is the worse its effects.'

'That's true.'

'But suppose,' I said, 'that such natures were cut loose, when they were still children, from the dead weight of worldliness, fastened on them by sensual indulgences like gluttony, which distorts their minds' vision to lower things, and suppose that when so freed they were turned towards the truth, then the same faculty in them would have as keen a vision of truth as it has of the objects on which it is at present turned.'

'Very likely.'

'And is it not also likely, and indeed a necessary consequence of that we have said, that society will never be properly governed either by the uneducated, who have no knowledge of the truth, or by those who are allowed to spend all their lives in purely intellectual pursuits? The uneducated have no single aim in life to which all their actions, public and private, are directed, the intellectuals will take no practical action of their own accord, fancying themselves to be no longer of this world.'

'True.'

'Then our job as Lawgivers is to compel the best minds to attain what we have called the highest form of knowledge, and to ascend to the vision of the Good as we have described, and when they have achieved this and seen enough, prevent them behaving as they now do.'

'What do you mean by that?'

'Remaining in the upper world, and refusing to return again to the prisoners in the cave below and share their labours and rewards, whether they are worth having or not.'

'But surely,' he protested, 'that will not be fair. We shall be compelling them to live a poorer life than they might live.'

'The object of our legislation,' I reminded him again, 'is not the welfare of any particular class, but of the whole community. It uses persuasion or force to unite all citizens and make them share together the benefits which each individually can confer on the community; and its purpose in fostering this attitude is not to enable everyone to please himself, but to make each man a link in the unity of the whole.'

'You are right; I had forgotten,' he said.

'You see, then, Glaucon,' I went on, 'we shan't be unfair to our philosophers, but shall be quite justified in compelling them to have some care and responsibility for others. We shall tell them that philosophers in other states can reasonably refuse to take part in the hard work of politics; for society produces them quite involuntarily and unintentionally, and it is only just that anything that grows up on its own should feel it has nothing to repay for an upbringing which it owes to no one. "But you," we shall say, "have been bred to rule to your own advantage and that of the whole community, like kingbees in a hive; you are better educated than the rest and better qualified to combine the practice of philosophy and politics. You must therefore each descend in turn and live with your fellows in the cave and get used to seeing in the dark; once you get used to it you will see a thousand times better than they do and will recognize the various shadows, and know what they are shadows of, because you have seen the truth about things right and just and good. And so our state and yours will be really awake, and not merely dreaming like most societies to-day, with their shadow battles and their struggles for political power, which they treat as some great prize. The truth is quite different: the state whose rulers come to their duties with least enthusiasm is bound to have the best and most tranquil government, and the state whose rulers are eager to rule the worst."

'I quite agree.'

'Then will our pupils, when they hear what we say, refuse to take their share of the hard work of government, though spending the greater part of their time together in the pure air of philosophy?'

'They cannot refuse, for we are making a just demand of just men. But of course, unlike present rulers, they will approach the business of government as an unavoidable necessity.'

'Yes, of course,' I agreed. 'The truth is that if you want it well-governed state you must find for your future rulers some career they like better than government; for only then will you have government by the truly rich, those, that is, whose riches consist not of money, but of the happiness of a right and rational life. If you get, in public affairs, men who are so morally impoverished that they have nothing they can contribute themselves, but who hope to snatch some compensation for their own inadequacy from a political career, there can never be good government. They start fighting for power, and the consequent internal and domestic conflicts ruin both them and society!

'True indeed.'

'Is there any other life except that of true philosophy which looks down on political power?'

'None that I know of.'

'And yet the only men to get power should be men who do not love it, otherwise we shall have rivals' quarrels.'

'That is certain.'

'Who else, then, are we to compel to undertake the responsibilities of ruling, if it is not to be those who know most about good government and who yet value other things more highly than politics and its rewards?

'There is no one else.'

Timaeus

The Timaeus, *one of Plato's later dialogues, is not often read by students because its subject is science and cosmology, not metaphysics. In it, Plato introduces God as the intelligent cause of order and structure in a universe in the process of becoming. But the rule of reason is hemmed in and limited by the power of material necessity (ananke). In this discussion of natural science, Plato introduces a myth that many people know and love but don't associate with Plato—the story of Atlantis, the lost continent for which the ocean is named.*

[The Story of Atlantis]

Critias. Then listen, Socrates, to a tale which, though strange, is certainly true, having been attested by Solon, who was the wisest of the seven sages. He was a relative and a dear friend of my great-grandfather, Dropides, as he himself says in many passages of his poems, and he told the story to Critias, my grandfather, who remembered and repeated it to us. There were of old, he said, great and marvelous actions of the Athenian city, which have passed into

---

The translation is an old classic (1871) by Benjamin Jowett.

oblivion through lapse of time and the destruction of mankind, and one in particular, greater than all the rest. . . .

Critias, at the time of telling it, was as he said, nearly ninety years of age, and I was about ten. Now the day was that day of the Apaturia which is called the Registration of Youth, at which, according to custom, our parents gave prizes for recitations, and the poems of several poets were recited by us boys, and many of us sang the poems of Solon, which at that time had not gone out of fashion. One of our tribe, either because he thought so or to please Critias, said that in his judgment Solon was not only the wisest of men, but also the noblest of poets. The old man, as I very well remember, brightened up at hearing this and said, smiling: Yes, Amynander, if Solon had only, like other poets, made poetry the business of his life, and had completed the tale which he brought with him from Egypt, and had not been compelled, by reason of the factions and troubles which he found stirring in his own country when he came home, to attend to other matters, in my opinion he would have been as famous as Homer or Hesiod, or any poet.

And what was the tale about, Critias? said Amynander.

About the greatest action which the Athenians ever did, and which ought to have been the most famous, but, through the lapse of time and the destruction of the actors, it has not come down to us.

Tell us, said the other, the whole story, and how and from whom Solon heard this veritable tradition.

He replied: In the Egyptian Delta, at the head of which the river Nile divides, there is a certain district which is called the district of Sais, and the great city of the district is also called Sais, and is the city from which King Amasis came. The citizens have a deity for their foundress; she is called in the Egyptian tongue Neith, and is asserted by them to be the same whom the Hellenes call Athene; they are great lovers of the Athenians, and say that they are in some way related to them. To this city came Solon, and was received there with great honour; he asked the priests who were most skilful in such matters, about antiquity, and made the discovery that neither he nor any other Hellene knew anything worth mentioning about the times of old. On one occasion, wishing to draw them on to speak of antiquity, he began to tell about the most ancient things in our part of the world—about Phoroneus, who is called "the first man," and about Niobe; and after the Deluge, of the survival of Deucalion and Pyrrha; and he traced the genealogy of their descendants, and reckoning up the dates, tried to compute how many years ago the events of which he was speaking happened. Thereupon one of the priests, who was of a very great age, said: O Solon, Solon, you Hellenes are never anything but children, and there is not an old man among you. Solon in return asked him what he meant. I mean to say, he replied, that in mind you are all young; there is no old opinion handed down among you by ancient tradition, nor any science which is hoary with age. And I will tell you why. There have been, and will be again, many destructions of mankind arising out of many causes; the greatest have been brought about by the agencies of fire and water, and other lesser ones by innumerable other causes. There is a story, which even you have preserved, that once upon a time Phaethon, the son of Helios, having yoked the steeds in his father's chariot, because he was not able to drive them in the path of his father, burnt up all that was upon the earth, and was himself destroyed by a thunderbolt. Now this has the form of a myth but really signifies a declination of the bodies moving in the heavens around the earth, and a great conflagration of things upon the earth, which recurs after long intervals; at such times those who live upon the mountains and in dry and lofty places are more liable to destruction than those who dwell by rivers or on the seashore. And from this calamity the Nile, who is our never-failing saviour, delivers and preserves us. When, on the other hand, the gods purge the earth with a deluge of water, the survivors in your country are herdsmen and shepherds who dwell on the mountains, but those who, like you, live in cities are carried by the rivers into the sea. Whereas in this land, neither then nor at any other time, does the water come down from above on the fields, having always a tendency to come up from below; for which reason the traditions preserved here are the most ancient.

The fact is, that wherever the extremity of winter frost or of summer does not prevent, mankind exist, sometimes in greater, sometimes in lesser numbers. And whatever happened either in your country or in ours, or in any other region of which we are informed—if there were any actions noble or great or in any other way remarkable, they have all been written down by us of old, and are preserved in our temples. Whereas just when you and other nations are beginning to be provided with letters and the other requisites of civilized life, after the usual interval, the stream from heaven, like a pestilence, comes pouring down, and leaves only those of you who are destitute of letters and education; and so you have to begin all over again like children, and know nothing of what happened in ancient times, either among us or among yourselves. As for those genealogies of yours which you just now recounted to us, Solon, they are no better than the tales of children. In the first place you remember a single deluge only, but there were many previous ones; in the next place, you do not know that there formerly dwelt in your land the fairest and noblest race of men which ever lived, and that you and your whole city are descended from a small seed or remnant of them which survived. And this was unknown to you, because, for many generations, the survivors of that destruction died, leaving no written word. For there was a time, Solon, before the greatest deluge of all, when the city which now is Athens was first in war and in every way the best governed of all cities; it is said to have performed the noblest deeds and to have had the fairest constitution of any of which tradition tells, under the face of heaven.

Solon marvelled at his words and earnestly requested the priests to inform him exactly and in order about these former citizens. You are welcome to hear about them, Solon, said the priest, both for your own sake and for that of your city, and above all, for the sake of the goddess who is the common patron and parent and educator of both our cities. She founded your city a thousand years before ours, receiving from the Earth and Hephaestus the seed of your race, and afterwards she founded ours, of which the constitution is recorded in our sacred registers to be eight thousand years old. As touching your citizens of nine thousand years ago, I will briefly inform you of their laws and of their most famous action; the exact particulars of the whole we will hereafter go through at our leisure in the sacred registers themselves. If you compare these very laws with ours you will find that many of ours are the counterpart of yours as they were in the olden time. In the first place, there is the caste of priests, which is separated from all the others; next, there are the artificers, who ply their several crafts by themselves and do not intermix; and also there is the class of shepherds and of hunters, as well as that of husbandmen; and you will observe, too, that the warriors in Egypt are distinct from all the other classes, and are commanded by the law to devote themselves solely to military pursuits; moreover, the weapons which they carry are shields and spears, a style of equipment which the goddess taught of Asiatics first to us, as in your part of the world first to you. Then as to wisdom, do you observe how our law from the very first made a study of the whole order of things, extending even to prophecy and medicine which gives health, out of these divine elements deriving what was needful for human life, and adding every sort of

knowledge which was akin to them. All this order and arrangement the goddess first impart-
ed to you when establishing your city; and she chose the spot of earth in which you were born,
because she saw that the happy temperament of the seasons in that land would produce the
wisest of men. Wherefore the goddess, who was a lover both of war and of wisdom, selected
and first of all settled that spot which was the most likely to produce men likest herself. And
there you dwelt, having such laws as these and still better ones, and excelled all mankind in
all virtue, as became the children and disciples of the gods.

Many great and wonderful deeds are recorded of your state in our histories. But one of
them exceeds all the rest in greatness and valour. For these histories tell of a mighty power
which unprovoked made an expedition against the whole of Europe and Asia, and to which
your city put an end. This power came forth out of the Atlantic Ocean, for in those days the
Atlantic was navigable; and there was an island situated in front of the straits which are by
you called the Pillars of Heracles; the island was larger than Libya and Asia put together, and,
was the way to other islands, and from these you might pass to the whole of the opposite continent which surrounded the true ocean; for this sea which is within the Straits of Heracles is
only a harbour, having a narrow entrance, but that other is a real sea, and the surrounding
land may be most truly called a boundless continent. Now in this island of Atlantis there was
a great and wonderful empire which had rule over the whole island and several others, and
over parts of the continent, and, furthermore, the men of Atlantis had subjected the parts of
Libya within the columns of Heracles as far as Egypt, and of Europe as far as Tyrrhenia. This
vast power, gathered into one, endeavoured to subdue at a blow our country and yours and
the whole of the region within the straits; and then, Solon, your country shone forth, in the
excellence of her virtue and strength, among all mankind. She was pre-eminent in courage
and military skill, and was the leader of the Hellenes. And when the rest fell off from her,
being compelled to stand alone, after having undergone the very extremity of danger, she
defeated and triumphed over the invaders, and preserved from slavery those who were not
yet subjugated, and generously liberated all the rest of us who dwell within the pillars. But
afterwards there occurred violent earthquakes and floods; and in a single day and night of
misfortune all your warlike men in a body sank into the earth, and the island of Atlantis in
like manner disappeared in the depths of the sea. For which reason the sea in those parts is
impassable and impenetrable, because there is a shoal of mud in the way; and this was caused
by the subsidence of the island.

I have told you briefly, Socrates, what the aged Critias heard from Solon and related to us.

ARISTOTLE (384–322 BCE)

If to Plato what is truly real lies outside the world of our senses, to Aristotle all knowledge is grounded in the things we perceive. Although he was perhaps Plato's greatest pupil, Aristotle finally rejected Plato's otherworldliness and wrote treatises examining almost every aspect of the world we know and live in. Everything, from rhetoric and ethics to physics and music, came under scrutiny in works which survive mainly in the form of lecture notes collected by his followers. His studies in biology helped him to see everything in terms of growth and movement from potentiality toward actuality. A great organizer, he saw the world arranged in categories and hierarchies, and he applied the same habits of thought to less tangible things, like tragedy, which he analyzes in his treatise on Poetics. *Even there, he starts from what is and not from what ought to be. Aristotle's most famous student was the son of King Philip of Macedon, Alexander, who later set out to conquer the world before his early death. Aristotle's notions of logic were central to the study of logic into our own century; his way of talking about God became part of Christianity in the medieval treatises of Thomas Aquinas, and his way of examining and classifying the world around him became the basis of our "modern" scientific method and our model of taxonomy.*

Poetics

It is hard to exaggerate the importance of Sophocles's play Oedipus the King, *since—besides being a powerful and terrifying play—it also suggested to Freud his "Oedipus Complex" and to Aristotle the outlines of a theory of tragedy. It is important to recognize, however, that this theory is as descriptive as it is prescriptive: when he characterizes tragedy, Aristotle is, in the main, describing the way* Oedipus *works, and not all tragedies. And even then it is possible to be misled by what he says. For centuries, literary critics have been looking for a tragic flaw in each of Shakespeare's tragic heroes, based on Aristotle's identification of the source of tragic action in the hero's* hamartia, *"error in judgment." While Shakespeare's heroes can sometimes be said to have moral flaws (Shakespeare, too, had misread his Aristotle!), Greek tragedies are quite varied in their evocation of a cause of the tragic action. In* Antigone, *for instance, both Antigone and Creon hold staunchly to views that are right, although in conflict. Hamartia, then, might properly be thought of as "mistake," elevated in the plays by necessity, chance, and cosmic perversity into true catastrophe. The translation which follows may imply both views in the use of the words "error" and "frailty."*

The Poetics *contains discussions of both tragedy and epic. A companion work on comedy was lost early on. Some readers may remember that the appearance of a manuscript of Aristotle's supposedly lost* Comedy *in a French monastery in the fourteenth century motivates a series of murders in Umberto Eco's* The Name of the Rose, *a novel that became a popular movie with Sean Connery.*

The selection here is from the translation by S. H. Butcher (London, 1895).

[Tragedy]

IV. Poetry in general seems to have sprung from two causes, each of the them lying deep in our nature. First, the instinct of imitation is implanted in man from childhood, one difference between him and other animals being that he is the most imitative of living creatures; and through imitation he learns his earliest lessons; and no less universal is the pleasure felt in things imitated. We have evidence of this in the facts of experience. Objects which in themselves we view with pain, we delight to contemplate when reproduced with minute fidelity: such as the forms of the most ignoble animals and of dead bodies. The cause of this again is, that to learn gives the liveliest pleasure, not only to philosophers but to men in general; whose capacity, however, of learning is more limited. Thus the reason why men enjoy seeing a likeness is, that in contemplating it they find themselves learning or inferring, and saying perhaps, 'Ah, that is he.' For if you happen not to have seen the original, the pleasure will be due not to the imitation as such, but to the execution, the colouring, or some such other cause. . . .

Poetry now diverged in two directions, according to the individual character of the writers. The graver spirits imitated noble actions, and the actions of good men. The more trivial sort imitated the actions of meaner persons, at first composing satires, as the former did hymns to the gods and the praises of famous men. A poem of the satirical kind cannot indeed be put down to any author earlier than Homer; though many such writers probably there were. But from Homer onward, instances can be cited,—his own Margites, for example, and other similar compositions. The appropriate metre was also here introduced; hence the measure is still called the iambic or lampooning measure, being that in which people lampooned one another. Thus the older poets were distinguished as writers of heroic or of lampooning verse.

As, in the serious style, Homer is pre-eminent among poets, for he alone combined dramatic form with excellence of imitation, so he too first laid down the main lines of Comedy, by dramatising the ludicrous instead of writing personal satire. His Margites bears the same relation to Comedy that the Iliad and Odyssey do to Tragedy. But when Tragedy and Comedy came to light, the two classes of poets still followed their natural bent: the lampooners became writers of Comedy, and the Epic poets were succeeded by Tragedians, since the drama was a larger and higher form of art.

Whether Tragedy has as yet perfected its proper types or not; and whether it is to be judged in itself, or in relation also to the audience,—this raises another question. Be that as it may, Tragedy—as also Comedy—was at first mere improvisation. The one originated with the leaders of the Dithyramb, the other with those of the phallic songs, which are still in use in many of our cities. Tragedy advanced by slow degrees; each new element that showed itself was in turn developed. Having passed through many changes, it found its natural form, and there it stopped.

Aeschylus first introduced a second actor; he diminished the importance of the Chorus, and assigned the leading part to the dialogue. Sophocles raised the number of actors to three, and added scene-painting. Moreover, it was not till late that the short plot was discarded for one of greater compass, and the grotesque diction of the earlier satyric form for the stately manner of Tragedy. The iambic measure then replaced the trochaic tetrameter, which was originally employed when the poetry was of the satyric order, and had greater affinities with dancing. Once dialogue had come in, Nature herself discovered the appropriate measure. For the iambic is, of all measures, the most colloquial: we see it in the fact that conversational speech runs into iambic lines more frequently than into any other kind of verse; rarely into hexameters, and only when we drop the colloquial intonation. The additions to the number of 'episodes' or acts, and the other improvements of which tradition tells, must be taken as already described; for to discuss them in detail would, doubtless, be a large undertaking.

V. Comedy is, as we have said, an imitation of characters of a lower type,—not, however, in the full sense of the word bad, the Ludicrous being merely a subdivision of the ugly. It consists in some defect or ugliness which is not painful or destructive. To take an obvious example, the comic mask is ugly and distorted, but does not imply pain.

The successive changes through which Tragedy passed, and the authors of these changes, are well known, whereas Comedy has had no history, because it was not at first treated seriously. It was late before the Archon granted a comic chorus to a poet; the performers were till then voluntary. Comedy had already taken definite shape when comic poets, distinctively so called, are heard of. Who introduced masks, or prologues, or increased the number of actors,—these and other similar details remain unknown. As for the plot, it came originally from Sicily; but of Athenian writers Crates was the first who, abandoning the 'iambic' or lampooning form, generalised his themes and plots.

Epic poetry agrees with Tragedy in so far as it is an imitation in verse of characters of a higher type. They differ, in that Epic poetry admits but one kind of metre, and is narrative in form. They differ, again, in their length: for Tragedy endeavours, as far as possible, to confine itself to a single revolution of the sun, or but slightly to exceed this limit; whereas the Epic action has no limits of time. This, then, is a second point of difference; though at first the same freedom was admitted in Tragedy as in Epic poetry.

Of their constituent parts some are common to both, some peculiar to Tragedy. Whoever, therefore, knows what is good or bad Tragedy, knows also about Epic poetry: for all the elements of an Epic poem are found in Tragedy, but the elements of a Tragedy are not all found in the Epic poem.

VI. Of the poetry which imitates in hexameter verse, and of Comedy, we will speak hereafter. Let us now discuss Tragedy, resuming its formal definition, as resulting from what has been already said.

Tragedy, then, is an imitation of an action that is serious, complete, and of a certain magnitude; in language embellished with each kind of artistic ornament, the several kinds being found in separate parts of the play; in the form of action, not of narrative; through pity and fear effecting the proper purgation of these emotions. By 'language embellished,' I mean language into which rhythm, 'harmony,' and song enter. By 'the several kinds in separate parts,' I mean, that some parts are rendered through the medium of verse alone, others again with the aid of song. . . .

Again, Tragedy is the imitation of an action; and an action implies personal agents, who necessarily possess certain distinctive qualities both of character and thought; for it is by these that we qualify actions themselves, and these—thought and character—are the two natural causes from which actions spring, and on actions again all success or failure depends. Hence, the Plot is the imitation of the action:—for by plot I here mean the arrangement of the incidents. By Character I mean that in virtue of which we ascribe certain qualities to the agents. Thought is required wherever a statement is proved, or, it may be, a general truth enunciated. Every Tragedy, therefore, must have six parts, which parts determine its quality—namely, Plot, Character, Diction, Thought, Spectacle, Song. Two of the parts constitute the medium of imitation, one of the manner, and three the objects of imitation. And these complete the list. . . .

But most important of all is the structure of the incidents. For Tragedy is an imitation, not of men, but of an action and of life, and life consists in action, and its end is a mode of action, not a quality. Now character determines men's qualities, but it is by their actions that they are happy or the reverse. Dramatic action, therefore, is not with a view to the representation of character: character comes in as subsidiary to the actions. Hence the incidents and the plot are the end of a tragedy; and the end is the chief thing of all. Again, without action there cannot be a tragedy; there may be without character. The tragedies of most of our modern poets fail in the rendering of character; and of poets in general this is often true. . . . Again, if you string together a set of speeches expressive of character, and well finished in point of diction and thought, you will not produce the essential tragic effect nearly so well as with a play which, however deficient in these respects, yet has a plot and artistically constructed incidents. Besides which, the most powerful elements of emotional interest in Tragedy—Peripeteia or Reversal of the Situation, and Recognition scenes—are parts of the plot. A further proof is, that novices in the art attain to finish of diction and precision of portraiture before they can construct the plot. It is the same with almost all the early poets. . . .

VII. These principles being established, let us now discuss the proper structure of the Plot, since this is the first and most important part of Tragedy.

Now, according to our definition, Tragedy is an imitation of an action that is complete, and whole, and of a certain magnitude; for there may be a whole that is wanting in magnitude. A whole is that which has a beginning, a middle, and an end. A beginning is that which does not itself follow anything by causal necessity, but after which something naturally is or comes to be. An end, on the contrary, is that which itself naturally follows some other thing, either by necessity, or as a rule, but has nothing following it. A middle is that which follows something as some other thing follows it. A well constructed plot, therefore, must neither begin nor end at haphazard, but conform to these principles. . . .

VIII. Unity of plot does not, as some persons think, consist in the unity of the hero. For infinitely various are the incidents in one man's life which cannot be reduced to unity; and so, too, there are many actions of one man out of which we cannot make one action. Hence the error, as it appears, of all poets who have composed a Heracleid, a Theseid, or other poems of the kind. They imagine that as Heracles was one man, the story of Heracles must also be a unity. But Homer, as in all else he is of surpassing merit, here too—whether from art or natural genius—seems to have happily discerned the truth. In composing the Odyssey he did not include all the adventures of Odysseus—such as his wound on Parnassus, or his feigned madness at the mustering of the host—incidents between which there was no necessary or probable connexion: but he made the Odyssey, and likewise the Iliad, to centre round an action that in our sense of the word is one. As therefore, in the other imitative arts, the imitation is one when the object imitated is one, so the plot, being an imitation of an action, must imitate one action and that a whole, the structural union of the parts being such that, if any one of them is displaced or removed, the whole will be disjointed and disturbed. For a thing whose presence or absence makes no visible difference, is not an organic part of the whole.

IX. It is, moreover, evident from what has been said, that it is not the function of the poet to relate what has happened, but what may happen,—what is possible according to the law of probability or necessity. The poet and the historian differ not by writing in verse or in prose. The work of Herodotus might be put into verse, and it would still be a species of history, with metre no less than without it. The true difference is that one relates what has happened, the other what may happen. Poetry, therefore, is a more philosophical and a higher thing than history: for poetry tends to express the universal, history the particular. By the universal I mean how a person of a certain type will on occasion speak or act, according to the law of probability or necessity; and it is this universality at which poetry aims in the names she attaches to the personages. The particular is—for example—what Alcibiades did or suffered. In Comedy this is already apparent: for here the poet first constructs the plot on the lines of probability, and then inserts characteristic names;—unlike the lampooners who write about particular individuals. But tragedians still keep to real names, the reason being that what is possible is credible: what has not happened we do not at once feel sure to be possible: but what has happened is manifestly possible: otherwise it would not have happened. Still there are some tragedies in which there are only one or two well known names, the rest being fictitious. In others, none are well known,—as in Agathon's Antheus, where incidents and names alike are fictitious, and yet they give none the less pleasure. We must not, therefore, at all costs keep to the received legends, which are the usual subjects of Tragedy. Indeed, it would be absurd to attempt it; for even subjects that are known are known only to a few, and yet give pleasure to all. It clearly follows that the poet or 'maker' should be the maker of plots rather than of verses; since he is a poet because he imitates, and what he imitates are actions. And even if he chances to take an historical subject, he is none the less a poet; for there is no reason why some events that have actually happened should not conform to the law of the probable and possible, and in virtue of that quality in them he is their poet or maker. . . .

But again, Tragedy is an imitation not only of a complete action, but of events terrible and pitiful. Such an effect is best produced when the events come on us by surprise; and the effect is heightened when, at the same time, they follow as cause and effect. The tragic wonder will then be greater than if they happened of themselves or by accident; for even coincidences are most striking when they have an air of design. We may instance the statue of Mitys at Argos, which fell upon his murderer while he was a spectator at a festival, and killed him. Such events seem not to be due to mere chance. Plots, therefore, constructed on these principles are necessarily the best.

X. Plots are either Simple or Complex, for the actions in real life, of which the plots are an imitation, obviously show a similar distinction. An action which is one and continuous in the sense above defined, I call Simple, when the change of fortune takes place without Reversal of the Situation and without Recognition.

A Complex action is one in which the change is accompanied by such Reversal, or by Recognition, or by both. These last should arise from the internal structure of the plot, so that what follows should be the necessary or probable result of the preceding action. It makes all the difference whether any given event is a case of *propter hoc* or *post hoc*.

XI. Reversal of the Situation is a change by which the action veers round to its opposite, subject always to our rule of probability or necessity. Thus in the Oedipus, the messenger comes to cheer Oedipus and free him from his alarms about his mother, but by revealing who he is, he produces the opposite effect. . . .

Recognition, as the name indicates, is a change from ignorance to knowledge, producing love or hate between the persons destined by the poet for good or bad fortune. The best form of recognition is coincident with a Reversal of the Situation, as in the Oedipus. There are indeed other forms. Even inanimate things of the most trivial kind may sometimes be objects of recognition. Again, we may recognise or discover whether a person has done a thing or not. But the recognition which is most intimately connected with the plot and action is, as we have said, the recognition of persons. This recognition, combined with Reversals, will produce either pity or fear; and actions producing these effects are those which, by our definition,

Tragedy represents. Moreover, it is upon such situations that the issues of good or bad fortune will depend. . . .

Two parts, then, of the Plot—Reversal of the Situation and Recognition—turn upon surprises. A third part is the Tragic Incident. The Tragic Incident is a destructive or painful action, such as death on the stage, bodily agony, wounds and the like. . . .

XIII. As the sequel to what has already been said, we must proceed to consider what the poet should aim at, and what he should avoid, in constructing his plots; and by what means the specific effect of Tragedy will be produced.

A perfect tragedy should, as we have seen, be arranged not on the simple but on the complex plan. It should, moreover, imitate actions which excite pity and fear, this being the distinctive mark of tragic imitation. It follows plainly, in the first place, that the change of fortune presented must not be the spectacle of a virtuous man brought from prosperity to adversity: for this moves neither pity nor fear; it merely shocks us. Nor, again, that of a bad man passing from adversity to prosperity: for nothing can be more alien to the spirit of Tragedy; it possesses no single tragic quality; it neither satisfies the moral sense nor calls forth pity or fear. Nor, again, should the downfall of the utter villain be exhibited. A plot of this kind would, doubtless, satisfy the moral sense, but it would inspire neither pity nor fear; for pity is aroused by unmerited misfortune, fear by the misfortune of a man like ourselves. Such an event, therefore, will be neither pitiful nor terrible. There remains, then, the character between these two extremes,—that of a man who is not eminently good and just, yet whose misfortune is brought about not by vice or depravity, but by some error or frailty. He must be one who is highly renowned and prosperous,—a personage like Oedipus, Thyestes, or other illustrious men of such families.

A well constructed plot should, therefore, be single in its issue, rather than double as some maintain. The change of fortune should be not from bad to good, but, reversely, from good to bad. It should come about as the result not of vice, but of some great error or frailty, in a character either such as we have described, or better rather than worse. . . .

Physics

Among Aristotle's many structures and concepts, the notion of causation has a pre-eminent place. Because Aristotle saw the world in terms of potentiality and "becoming"—of movement, therefore—he also had to account for the fact and the direction of the movement. Causes, then, are the motive forces of Aristotle's world, denoting the material from which something is made (material cause), the shape it takes (formal cause), who makes it (efficient cause), and why it is made (final cause). Aristotle's best exposition of his model of causation can be found in the Physics, *in the following passage.*

[The Four Causes]

II.3. Now that we have established these distinctions, we must proceed to consider causes, their character and number. Knowledge is the object of our inquiry, and men do not think they know a thing till they have grasped the "why" of it (which is to grasp its primary cause). So clearly we too must do this as regards both coming to be and passing away and every kind of

---

This translation is by R. P. Hardie (Oxford: Clarendon, 1930).

physical change, in order that, knowing their principles, we may try to refer to these principles each of our problems.

In one sense, then, (1) that out of which a thing comes to be and which persists, is called "cause," e.g. the bronze of the statue, the silver of the bowl, and the genera of which the bronze and the silver are species.

In another sense (2) the form or the archetype, i.e., the statement of the essence, and its genera, are called "causes" (e.g. of the octave the relation of 2:1, and generally number), and the parts in the definition.

Again (3) the primary source of the change or coming to rest; e.g. the man who gave advice is a cause, the father is cause of the child, and generally what makes of what is made and what causes change of what is changed.

Again (4) in the sense of end or "that for the sake of which" a thing is done, e.g. health is the cause of walking about. ("Why is he walking about?" we say. "To be healthy," and, having said that, we think we have assigned the cause.) The same is true also of all the intermediate steps which are brought about through the action of something else as means towards the end, e.g. reduction of flesh, urging, drugs, or surgical instruments are means towards health. All these things are "for the sake of" the end, though they differ from one another in that some are activities, others instruments.

This then perhaps exhausts the number of ways in which the term "cause" is used.

As the word has several senses, it follows that there are several causes of the same thing (not merely in virtue of a concomitant attribute), e.g. both the art of the sculptor and the bronze are causes of the statue. These are causes of the statue qua statue, not in virtue of anything else that it may be—only not in the same way, the one being the material cause, the other the cause whence the motion comes. Some things cause each other reciprocally, e.g. hard work causes fitness and vice versa, but again not in the same way, but the one as end, the other as the origin of change. Further the same thing is the cause of contrary results. For that which by its presence brings about one result is sometimes blamed for bringing about the contrary by its absence. Thus we ascribe the wreck of a ship to the absence of the pilot whose presence was the cause of its safety.

All the causes now mentioned fall into four familiar divisions. The letters are the causes of syllables, the material of artificial products, fire, &c., of bodies, the parts of the whole, and the premises of the conclusion, in the sense of "that from which." Of these pairs the one set are causes in the sense of substratum, e.g. the parts, the other set in the sense of essence—the whole and the combination and the form. But the seed and the doctor and the adviser, and generally the maker, are all sources whence the change or stationariness originates, while the others are causes in the sense of the end or the good of the rest; for "that for the sake of which" means what is best and the end of the things that lead up to it. (Whether we say the "good itself" or the "apparent good" makes no difference.) Such then is the number and nature of the kinds of cause.

Now the modes of causation are many, though when brought under heads they too can be reduced in number. For "cause" is used in many senses and even within the same kind one may be prior to another (e.g. the doctor and the expert are causes of health, the relation 2:1 and number of the octave), and always what is inclusive to what is particular. Another mode of causation is the incidental and its genera, e.g. in one way "Polyclitus," in another "sculptor" is the cause of a statue, because "being Polyclitus" and "sculptor" are incidentally conjoined. Also the classes in which the incidental attribute is included; thus "a man" could be said to be the cause of a statue or, generally, "a living creature." An incidental attribute too may be more or less remote, e.g. suppose that "a pale man" or "a musical man" were said to be the cause of the statue.

All causes, both proper and incidental, may be spoken of either as potential or as actual; e.g. the cause of a house being built is either "house-builder" or "house-builder building."

Similar distinctions can be made in the things of which the causes are cause, e.g. of "this statue" or of "statue" or of "image" generally, of "this bronze" or of "bronze" or of "material" generally. So too with the incidental attributes. Again we may use a complex expression for either and say, e.g. neither "Polyclitus" nor "sculptor" but "Polyclitus, sculptor."

All these various uses, however, come to six in number, under each of which again the usage is two-fold. Cause means either what is particular or a genus, or an incidental attribute or a genus of that, and these either as a complex or each by itself; and all six either as actual or as potential. The difference is this much, that causes which are actually at work and particular exist and cease to exist simultaneously with their effect, e.g. this healing person with this being-healed person and that house-building man with that being-built house; but this is not always true of potential causes—the house and the housebuilder do not pass away simultaneously.

In investigating the cause of each thing it is always necessary to seek what is most precise (as also in other things); thus man builds because he is a builder, and a builder builds in virtue of his art of building. This last cause then is prior: and so generally.

Further, generic effects should be assigned to generic causes, particular effects to particular causes, e.g. statue to sculptor, this statue to this sculptor; and powers are relative to possible effects, actually operating causes to things which are actually being effected.

This must suffice for our account of the number of causes and the modes of causation

Roman aqueduct. 19 BCE. Pont du Gard, Nîmes, France. Giraudon/Art Resource, NY.

The World of Rome

Besides being effective soldiers, administrators, and empire-builders, the Romans were brilliant engineers. They pioneered the use of the arch and invented the architectural forms based on it: the barrel vault (an arch extended in space), the groin vault (two barrel vaults crossing each other), and the dome and half-dome (an arch rotated on its axis). The discovery of pozzuolana, volcanic ash that made a slow-drying concrete, allowed the creation of structures that were essentially welded together. The genius of Roman construction has left visible signs of its prowess on the landscape. The straightest, fastest roads in Britain were the Roman roads. The largest dome in the world for centuries was the great temple of the Pantheon, built during the reign of the Emperor Hadrian. The Colosseum, apparently an open sports arena, is a great fantasy of arches, barrel vaults, and groin vaults. But the Romans invested even simple structures with great virtuosity and beauty. The Pont du Gard near Nîmes in southern France is a good example. Built as an aqueduct late in the first century BCE, this beautiful structure was part of a system that carried water from the springs at Uzès to Nîmes thirty miles south. The span of 900 feet has a height of 180 feet above the Gard River. Designed as both a bridge and an aqueduct, it delivered 100 gallons of water per person every day to the town for centuries, and its use as a bridge for carts and pedestrians continues to this day.

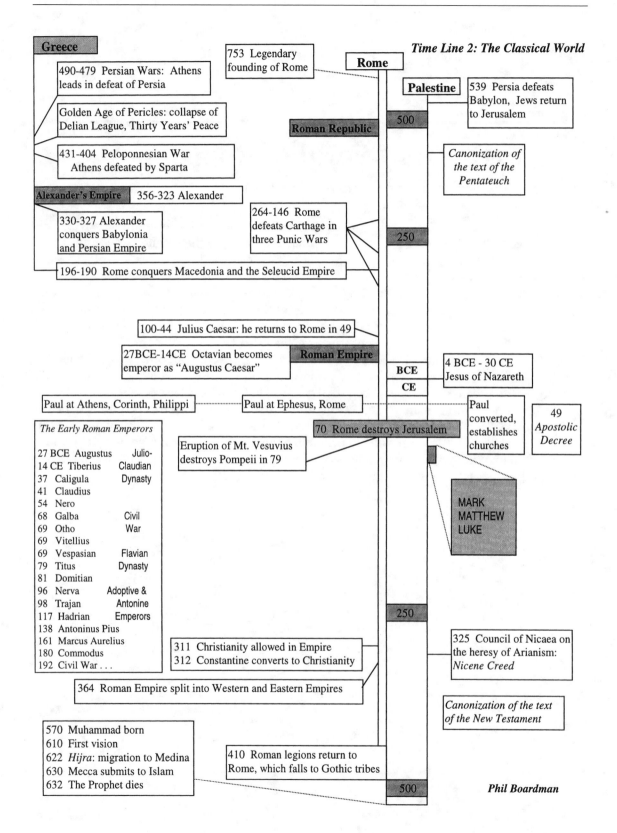

Time Line 2: The Classical World

Greece

490-479 Persian Wars: Athens leads in defeat of Persia

Golden Age of Pericles: collapse of Delian League, Thirty Years' Peace

431-404 Peloponnesian War Athens defeated by Sparta

Alexander's Empire   356-323 Alexander

330-327 Alexander conquers Babylonia and Persian Empire

196-190 Rome conquers Macedonia and the Seleucid Empire

753 Legendary founding of Rome

Rome

264-146 Rome defeats Carthage in three Punic Wars

100-44 Julius Caesar: he returns to Rome in 49

27BCE-14CE Octavian becomes emperor as "Augustus Caesar"

Roman Republic

Roman Empire

500

250

BCE

CE

250

500

Palestine

539 Persia defeats Babylon, Jews return to Jerusalem

Canonization of the text of the Pentateuch

4 BCE - 30 CE Jesus of Nazareth

Paul at Athens, Corinth, Philippi

Paul at Ephesus, Rome

Paul converted, establishes churches

49 *Apostolic Decree*

The Early Roman Emperors

27 BCE	Augustus	Julio-
14 CE	Tiberius	Claudian
37	Caligula	Dynasty
41	Claudius	
54	Nero	
68	Galba	Civil
69	Otho	War
69	Vitellius	
69	Vespasian	Flavian
79	Titus	Dynasty
81	Domitian	
96	Nerva	Adoptive &
98	Trajan	Antonine
117	Hadrian	Emperors
138	Antoninus Pius	
161	Marcus Aurelius	
180	Commodus	
192	Civil War . . .	

Eruption of Mt. Vesuvius destroys Pompeii in 79

70 Rome destroys Jerusalem

MARK MATTHEW LUKE

311 Christianity allowed in Empire
312 Constantine converts to Christianity

364 Roman Empire split into Western and Eastern Empires

325 Council of Nicaea on the heresy of Arianism: *Nicene Creed*

Canonization of the text of the New Testament

570 Muhammad born
610 First vision
622 *Hijra*: migration to Medina
630 Mecca submits to Islam
632 The Prophet dies

410 Roman legions return to Rome, which falls to Gothic tribes

Phil Boardman

CATULLUS (C.84–C.54 BCE)
Poems

Influenced by Greek lyric verse, Catullus wrote poems that were personal, informal, and emotional. Abandoning the pretentiousness of earlier Roman poetry, Catullus examined a wide range of subjects in language that is sometimes startlingly direct. Most successful were his poems addressed to his mistress, a married woman he calls Lesbia in the poems. The twenty-five poems to Lesbia are an encyclopedia of passionate love, showing in turns the emotions of infatuation, joy, passion, disappointment, despair, anger, and hatred—all that romantic love has come to mean in the modern West. His poems, written in the late republican Rome of Julius Caesar, Cicero, and Pompey, were influential with the next generation of poets under the new empire of Augustus. But while Latin poets like Virgil and Horace became part of the school curriculum and were on people's lips for centuries, Catullus suffered a very different fate. After the second century his poems disappeared from sight. A single manuscript surfaced around 1300, was copied twice, then was lost. One of those copies was copied twice and then it too was lost. Thus Catullus survives only in three manuscript copies dating from almost fourteen centuries after his death. It is fitting that this most modern of Roman poets should be known and admired now.

5

Vivamus, mea Lesbia, atque amemus
Lesbia, let's live and love
without one thought for gossip of
the boys grown old and stern.
Suns go down and can return,
but, once put out our own brief light,
we sleep through one eternal night.
Give me a thousand, a hundred kisses,
another thousand, a second hundred,
a thousand complete, a hundred repeat;
and when we've many thousand more,
we'll scramble them, forget the score
so Malice cannot know how high
the count, and cast its evil eye.

The translations, using standard numbering for the poems, are by Roy Arthur Swanson (New York: Liberal Arts Press, 1959).

8

Miser Catulle, desinas ineptire
Catullus, poor soul, stop playing the fool;
write off as loss what you see has been lost.
There used to be days full of sunshine for you,
when you followed the path laid out by your girl.
We loved her as no girl will ever be loved!
Those were the days when we had all the fun
which you dearly wanted and she didn't shun;
those were real days full of sunshine for you.
Now, though, she shuns it; so you, useless, don't
chase her and live a poor soul, as she runs:
instead, stick it out with a stubborn heart.
So long, girl; Catullus is sticking it out.
He won't look you up; he won't ask you out.
But you will be sorry when none asks you out.
What life—damn you, slut!—is left now for you?
Who'll come to you now or think you're a doll?
Whom now will you love or whose claim to be?
Whom will you kiss? Whose lips will you bite?
But you, then, Catullus, be stubborn; sit tight.

13

Cenabis bene, mi Fabulle, apud me
Fabullus, you will dine with me,
gods willing, in a day or three,
if you will bring the meal with you,
good and big, a bright girl too,
and wine and salt and lots of laughs.
If you bring this, my friend, why, look,
you will dine well: the pocketbook
of your Catullus is well filled
with cobwebs; but, in turn, you will
be unadulterably thrilled
by pleasure, taste—say what you will:
I'll have a perfume for you here,
which Love Gods proffered to my dear;
on smelling it, you will propose
that gods above make you all nose.

39

Egnatius, quod candidos habet dentes
Because Egnatius has white teeth, he smiles
without a stop. And should it come to trials
where lawyers move the court to tears, he smiles.
Suppose a mother mourns her only son,
he smiles. Whatever it is, whatever he's done,
wherever it is, he smiles. It's a disease,
not elegance, I think, nor does it please.

So, good Egnatius, I must give you warning,
were you a Roman, Sabine, Tiburtine,
or frugal Umbrian, or fat Etruscan,
or dark Lanuvian with big buck teeth,
or Transpadane—to bring my people in—
or one of any group which cleans its teeth
with water, constant smiles would still displease:
nothing's as far from tact as tactless grins.

But you're from Spain, and Spain's the spot
where teeth are scrubbed and red gums rubbed with what
is pissed the night before into a pot,
so that your tooth tells by its higher shine
how much you've drunk the dregs of bedroom wine.

58

Caeli, Lesbia nostra, Lesbia illa
Caelius, that Lesbia, my woman,
that—that Lesbia, whom once I, Catullus,
loved above himself and closest cronies,
now rubs up the grandsons of lordly Remus
on the corners and in the narrow alleys.

69

Noli admirari, quare tibi femina nulla
Don't wonder why no woman, Rufe, would want
to spread her tender thighs for you,
despite your gifts to her of high-class clothes
and charming bright translucent stones.
There's an ugly rumor that your underarms
are caves for a wild goat's stinking reek.
All are afraid of the goat; no wonder: no *bella*
puella would share her bed with a beast.
Dispose of this terrible plague to woman's nose,
or else don't wonder why she runs.

71

Si quoi iure bono sacer alarum obstitit hircus
If armpit odor ever rightly hurt
a guy, or gout cut down his speed,
that rival who cuts in on you has gained,
as he deserved, both maladies.
For, when he screws, he gives you your revenge:
the stink chokes her, the gout kills him.

72

Dicebas quondam solum te nosse Catullum
Catullus you once called your only love,
preferred to Jove, my Lesbia.
I loved you, not as men love mistresses,
but as a father loves his heirs.
I know you now: it makes my love more hot,
but you're more cheap, mere trash to me.
"How so?" you ask. Such dirt heaps up my love
but buries all my friendliness.

92

Lesbia mi dicit semper male nec tacet umquam
Lesbia loves to libel me, endlessly;
but she loves me I'm damned sure,
for I pay her back with dirty cracks, constantly,
and damned if I don't love her.

98

In te, si in quemquam, dici pote, putide Victi
Stinking Victius,
to you, if anyone, that can be said
which people say to loudmouthed louts:
that tongue of yours could wipe an ass or clean
a farmer's shoe, had you the chance.
Suppose you want to see us dead and gone:
to get your wish, just yawn, man, yawn.

101

Multas per gentes et multa per aequora vectus
I've sailed to many nations over many seas
and come now, brother, to this final rite,
these obsequies, to honor you in death and say
a word or two at unresponsive ash,
since fate, where I'm concerned, has been so rash
as uselessly to hasten you away.
So take this customary family mite—
our mourning duty, offerings like these:
they're moistened with your brother's many tears.
Goodbye for now: farewell for all the years.

VIRGIL (70–19 BCE)

Virgil's legacy to the west is enormous. Working from Homer's Iliad *and* Odyssey, *he transformed and preserved the epic conventions that inspired later works, like Spenser's* Faerie Queene, *Milton's* Paradise Lost, *James Joyce's* Ulysses, *even Ralph Ellison's* Invisible Man. *Useful for the study of poetry, of grammar, and of Latin, the* Aeneid *became the central text in European and American schools for nearly 1900 years, down to the end of the nineteenth century. Even the pattern of Virgil's career became the model for later poets. Virgil started by writing poems ("Eclogues") about shepherds based on the pastoral poems of the Greeks, and then wrote poems ("Georgics") about farming and farm life, before turning his hand to the great subject of his epic* The Aeneid. *Similarly, later poets felt that they should serve a poetic apprenticeship by writing pastoral poetry before they tackled the epic themes. Spenser, for instance, wrote the* Shepherd's Calendar *and Milton* Lycidas *before they composed their epics.*

Eclogues

The moral tone that tempers all of Virgil's poetry, including his great epic, the Aeneid, *was enough to bring Virgil the admiration of early Christians. But more compelling was a passage in the fourth of his pastoral poems, the* Eclogues, *in which he seemed to announce the coming of a baby boy who would usher in a reign of peace. Early Christians saw this as prophetic of the coming of Christ and recognized Virgil, who died only 15 years before Jesus was born, as a Christian prophet. Many Christians believed that had Virgil lived just a few years later, such a great and moral writer would have been among the most important of Christ's evangelists. So great was Virgil's reputation among literate Christians that early in the fifth century St. Augustine, in* On Christian Doctrine, *offered a defense of pagan writers like Virgil: "But we should not think that we ought not to learn literature because Mercury is said to be its inventor. . . . Rather, every good and true Christian should understand that wherever he may find truth, it is his Lord's." Similarly, when Dante wrote his great Christian epic, the* Divine Comedy, *in the early fourteenth century, he made Virgil, the greatest of the pre-Christian pagans, his guide through Hell.*

The translation of the *Fourth Eclogue* is by John Corrington Brown, published in London in 1872. It translates Virgil's Latin poem as English prose, and its language here has been somewhat modernized by the editor.

"The Fourth Eclogue"

Muses of Sicily, let us strike a somewhat louder chord. It is not for all that plantations have charms, or groundling tamarisks. If we are to sing of the woodland, let the woodland rise to a consul's dignity.

The last era of the song of Cuma has come at length; the grand file of the ages is being born anew; at length the virgin is returning, returning too the reign of Saturn; at length a new generation is descending from heaven on high. Smile your pure smile on the birth of the boy who shall at last bring the race of iron to an end, and bid the golden race spring up all the world over—you, Lucina—your own Apollo is at length on his throne. In your consulship it is—in yours, Pollio—that this glorious time shall come on, and the mighty months begin their march. Under your conduct, any remaining trace of our national guilt shall become void, and release the world from the thraldom of perpetual fear. He shall have the life of the gods conferred on him, and shall see gods and heroes mixing together, and shall himself be seen by them, and with his father's virtues shall govern a world at peace.

For you, sweet boy, the earth of her own unforced will shall pour forth a child's first presents—gadding ivy and foxglove everywhere, and Egyptian bean blending with the bright smiling acanthus. Of themselves, the goats shall carry home udders distended with milk; nor shall the herds fear huge lions in the way. Of itself, your grassy cradle shall pour out flowers to caress you. Death to the serpent, and to the treacherous plant of poisoned juice. Assyrian spices shall spring up by the wayside.

But soon as you shalt be of an age to read at length of the glories of heroes and your father's deeds, and to acquaint yourself with the nature of manly work, the yellow of the waving corn shall steal gradually over the plain, and from briers, that know nothing of culture, grapes shall hang in purple clusters, and the stubborn heart of oak shall exude dews of honey. Still, under all this show, some few traces shall remain of the sin and guile of old—such as may prompt men to defy the ocean goddess with their ships, to build towns with walls round them, to cleave furrows in the soil of earth. A second Tiphys shall there be in those days—a second Argo to convey the flower of chivalry; a second war of heroes, too, shall there be, and a second time shall Achilles be sent in his greatness to Troy.

Afterwards, when ripe years have at length made you a man, even the peaceful sailor shall leave the sea, nor shall the good ship of pine exchange merchandise—all lands shall produce all things; the ground shall not feel the harrow, nor the vineyard the pruning-hook; the sturdy ploughman, too, shall at length set his bulls free from the yoke; nor shall wool be taught to counterfeit varied hues, but of himself, as he feeds in the meadows, the ram shall transform his fleece, now into a lovely purple dye, now into saffron-yellow—of its own will, scarlet shall clothe the lambs as they graze. Ages like these, flow on!—so cried to their spindles the Fates, uttering in concert the fixed will of destiny.

Assume your august dignities—the time is at length at hand—you best-loved offspring of the gods, august scion of Jove! Look upon the world as it totters beneath the mass of its overhanging dome—earth and the expanse of sea and the deep of heaven—look how all are rejoicing in the age that is to be! O may my life's last days last long enough and breath be granted me enough to tell of your deeds! I will be overmatched in song by none—not by Orpheus of Thrace, nor by Linus, though that were backed by his mother, and this by his father—Orpheus by Calliope, Linus by Apollo in his beauty. Were Pan himself, with Arcady looking on, to enter the lists with me, Pan himself, with Arcady looking on, should own himself vanquished.

Begin, sweet child, with a smile, to take notice of your mother—that mother has had ten months of tedious sickness and loathing. Begin, sweet child—the babe on whom never parent smiled, never grew to deserve the table of a god or the bed of a goddess!

The Aeneid

Virgil's great masterpiece, the Aeneid, *is epic, public, and official; it celebrates the submission of the individual to the duties owed the gods and the state. In spite of Virgil's doubts about the tremendous power marshaled by the first emperor, Augustus, the poem also celebrates the triumph of Augustan peace, and Rome's potential to bring prosperity to the Western world.*

The Aeneid *tells the story of Aeneas, a Trojan who escaped from Troy when it fell to the Greek forces of Agamemnon. His destiny is to travel to Italy with his followers and found the colony from which later Romans will trace their ancestry. Like Odysseus among the Phaeacians, Aeneas lands in Carthage and during a respite he tells about his adventures, including an account of the fall of Troy (an event missing from Homer's two epics). Dido, the Queen of Carthage, falls in love with Aeneas, but reminded by the gods of his duty, Aeneas abandons her. Also like Odysseus, he journeys to the Underworld where he talks to the shade of Dido, who killed herself when he left her. He also confronts the shade of his father Anchises, who speaks prophetically about events that will lead to the founding of Rome. Later, in Italy, Aeneas fights to secure a safe abode for his followers but, like Moses, he does not live to see the city promised to his people.*

Aeneas's great virtue is piety, a devotion to the service of the gods and an awareness of his obligations to his family and his country. Aeneas is not a happy man; he suffers and comes to understand the suffering of others in the course of the epic. From Aeneas, Rome learns to temper its justice, dignity, and self-control with compassion. In the words offered to his son in the Underworld, Anchises spells out Rome's great destiny:

> Others, no doubt, will better mould the bronze
> To the semblance of soft breathing, draw, from marble,
> The living countenance; and others plead
> With greater eloquence, or learn to measure,
> Better than we, the pathways of the heaven,
> The risings of the stars: remember, Roman,
> To rule the people under law, to establish
> The way of peace, to battle down the haughty,
> To spare the meek. Our fine arts, these, forever.

from Book I [The Landing Near Carthage]

> Arms and the man I sing, the first who came,
> Compelled by fate, an exile out of Troy,
> To Italy and the Lavinian coast,
> Much buffeted on land and on the deep

The translation of *Aeneid* used here is by Rolfe Humphries, a poet who taught high school Latin for years before returning to his *alma mater*, Amherst, to teach. His *Aeneid* (New York: Scribner's, 1951) is a companion to a verse translation of Ovid's *Metamorphoses*.

By violence of the gods, through that long rage,
That lasting hate, of Juno's. And he suffered
Much, also, in war, till he should build his town
And bring his gods to Latium, whence, in time,
The Latin race, the Alban fathers, rose
And the great walls of everlasting Rome.
Help me, O Muse, recall the reasons: why,
Why did the queen of heaven drive a man
So known for goodness, for devotion, through
So many toils and perils? Was there slight,
Affront, or outrage? Is vindictiveness
An attribute of the celestial mind?

There was an ancient city, Carthage, once
Founded by Tyrians, facing Italy
And Tiber's mouth, far-off, a wealthy town,
War-loving, and aggressive; and Juno held
Even her precious Samos in less regard.
Here were her arms, her chariot, and here,
Should fate at all permit, the goddess burned
To found the empire of the world forever.
But, she had heard, a Trojan race would come,
Some day, to overthrow the Tyrian towers,
A race would come, imperious people, proud
In war, with wide dominion, bringing doom
For Libya. Fate willed it so. And Juno
Feared, and remembered: there was the old war
She fought at Troy for her dear Greeks; her mind
Still fed on hurt and anger; deep in her heart
Paris' decision rankled, and the wrong
Offered her slighted beauty; and the hatred
Of the whole race; and Ganymede's honors—
All that was fuel to fire; she tossed and harried
All over the seas, wherever she could, those Trojans
Who had survived the Greeks and fierce Achilles,
And so they wandered over many an ocean,
Through many a year, fate-hounded. Such a struggle
It was to found the race of Rome!

                              They were happy
Spreading the sail, rushing the foam with bronze,
And Sicily hardly out of sight, when Juno,
Still nourishing the everlasting wound,
Raged to herself: "I am beaten, I suppose;
It seems I cannot keep this Trojan king
From Italy. The fates, no doubt, forbid me.

Pallas, of course, could burn the Argive ships,
Could drown the sailors, all for one man's guilt,
The crazy acts of Ajax. Her own hand
Hurled from the cloud Jove's thunderbolt, and shattered
Their ships all over the sea; she raised up storm
And tempest; she spiked Ajax on the rocks,
Whirled him in wind, blasted his heart with fire.
And I, who walk my way as queen of the gods,
Sister of Jove, and wife of Jove, keep warring
With one tribe through the long, long years. Who cares
For Juno's godhead? Who brings sacrifice
Devoutly to her altars?"

                       Brooding, burning,
She sought Aeolia, the storm-clouds' dwelling,
A land that sweeps and swarms with the winds' fury,
Whose monarch, Aeolus, in his deep cave rules
Imperious, weighing down with bolt and prison
Those boisterous struggling roarers, who go raging
Around their bars, under the moan of the mountain.
High over them their sceptered lord sits watching,
Soothing, restraining, their passionate proud spirit,
Lest, uncontrolled, they seize, in their wild keeping,
The land, the sea, the arch of sky, in ruin
Sweeping through space. This Jupiter feared; he hid them
Deep in dark caverns, with a mass of mountain
Piled over above them, and a king to give them
Most certain regulation, with a knowledge
When to hold in, when to let go. Him Juno
Approached in supplication:—"Aeolus,
Given by Jove the power to still the waters,
Or raise them with a gale, a tribe I hate
Is on its way to Italy, and they carry
Troy with them, and their household gods, once beaten.
Shake anger into those winds of yours, turn over
Their ships, and drown them; drive them in all directions,
Litter the sea with bodies! For such service
The loveliest nymph I have, Deiopea,
Shall be your bride forever, and you wilt father
Fair children on her fairness." Aeolus
Made answer: "Yours, O Queen, the task of seeking
Whatever it is you will; and mine the duty
To follow with performance. All my empire,
My sceptre, Jove's indulgence, are beholden
To Juno's favor, by whose blessing I
Attend the feasts of the gods and rule this storm-land."

His spear-butt struck the hollow mountain-side,
And the winds, wherever they could, came sweeping forth,
Whirled over the land, swooped down upon the ocean.
East, South, Southwest, they heave the billows, howl,
Storm, roll the giant combers toward the shore.
Men cry; the rigging creaks and strains; the clouds
Darken, and men see nothing; a weight of darkness
Broods over the deep; the heavy thunder rumbles
From pole to pole; the lightning rips and dazzles;
There is no way out but death. Aeneas shudders
In the chill shock, and lifts both hands to heaven:—
"O happy men, thrice happy, four times happy,
Who had the luck to die, with their fathers watching,
Below the walls of Troy! Ah, Diomedes,
Bravest of Greeks, why could I not have fallen,
Bleeding my life away on plains of Ilium
In our encounter there, where mighty Hector
Went down before Achilles' spear, and huge
Sarpedon lay in dust, and Simois river
Rolled to the sea so many noble heroes,
All drowned in all their armor?" And the gale
Howls from the north, striking the sail, head on;
The waves are lifted to the stars; the oars
Are broken, and the prow slews round; the ship
Lies broadside on; a wall of water, a mountain,
Looms up, comes pouring down; some ride the crest,
Some, in the trough, can see the boil of the sand.
The South wind hurls three ships on the hidden rocks,
That sea-reef which Italians call the Altars;
The West takes three, sweeping them from the deep
On shoal and quicksand; over the stern of one,
Before Aeneas' eyes, a great sea falls,
Washing the helmsman overboard; the ship
Whirls thrice in the suck of the water and goes down
In the devouring gulf; and here and there
A few survivors swim, the Lycian men
Whose captain was Orontes; now their arms,
Their Trojan treasures, float with the broken timbers
On the swing and slide of the waves. The storm, triumphant,
Rides down more boats, and more; there goes Achates;
Abas, Aletes, Ilioneus,
Receive the hostile water; the walls are broken;
The enemy pours in.

    But meanwhile Neptune
Saw ocean in a welter of confusion,

The roar of storm, and deep and surface mingled.
Troublesome business, this; he rose, majestic,
From under the waves, and saw the Trojan vessels
Scattered all over the sea by the might of the waves
And the wreck of sky; he recognized the anger
And cunning of his sister, and he summoned
The winds by name:—"What arrogance is this,
What pride of birth, you winds, to meddle here
Without my sanction, raising all this trouble?
I'll—No, the waves come first: but listen to me,
You are going to pay for this! Get out of here!
Go tell your king the lordship of the ocean,
The trident, are not his, but mine. His realm
Reaches no further than the rocks and caverns
You brawlers dwell in; let him rule that palace,
Big as he pleases, shut you in, and stay there!"

This said, he calmed the swollen sea and cloud,
Brought back the sun; Cymothoe and Triton,
Heaving together, pulled the ships from the reef,
As Neptune used his trident for a lever,
Opened the quicksand, made the water smooth,
And the flying chariot skimmed the level surface.
Sometimes, in a great nation, there are riots
With the rabble out of hand, and firebrands fly
And cobblestones; whatever they lay their hands on
Is a weapon for their fury, but should they see
One man of noble presence, they fall silent,
Obedient dogs, with ears pricked up, and waiting,
Waiting his word, and he knows how to bring them
Back to good sense again. So ocean, roaring,
Subsided into stillness, as the sea-god
Looked forth upon the waters, and clear weather
Shone over him as he drove his flying horses.

Aeneas' weary children make for harbor,
Whichever lies most near, and the prows are turned
To Libya's coast-line. In a bay's deep curve
They find a haven, where the water lies
With never a ripple. A little island keeps
The sea-swell off, and the waves break on its sides
And slide back harmless. The great cliffs come down
Steep to deep water, and the background shimmers,
Darkens and shines, the tremulous aspen moving
And the dark fir pointing still. And there is a cave
Under the overhanging rocks, alive

With water running fresh, a home of the Nymphs,
With benches for them, cut from the living stone.
No anchor is needed here for weary ships,
No mooring-cable. Aeneas brings them in,
Seven weary vessels, and the men are glad
To be ashore again, to feel dry sand
Under the salt-stained limbs. Achates strikes
The spark from the flint, catches the fire on leaves,
Adds chips and kindling, blows and fans the flame,
And they bring out the soaked and salty corn,
The hand-mills, stone and mortar, and make ready,
As best they can, for bread.

                    Meanwhile Aeneas
Climbs to a look-out, for a view of the ocean,
Hoping for some good luck; the Phrygian galleys
Might meet his gaze, or Capys' boats, or a pennon
On a far-off mast-head flying. There is nothing,
Nothing to see out yonder, but near the water
Three stags are grazing, with a herd behind them,
A long line browsing through the peaceful valley.
He reaches for the bow and the swift arrows
Borne by Achates, and he shoots the leaders,
High-antlered, routs the common herd, and ceases
Only when seven are slain, a number equal
To the ships' tally, and then he seeks the harbor,
Divides the spoil, broaches the wine Acestes
Had stowed for them at Drepanum on their leaving,
A kingly present, and he calms their trouble,
Saying: "O comrades, we have been through evil
Together before this; we have been through worse,
Scylla, Charybdis, and the Cyclops' dwelling,
The sounding rocks. This, too, the god will end.
Call the nerve back; dismiss the fear, the sadness.
Some day, perhaps, remembering even this
Will be a pleasure. We are going on
Through whatsoever chance and change, until
We come to Latium, where the fates point out
A quiet dwelling-place, and Troy recovered.
Endure, and keep yourself for better days."
He kept to himself the sorrow in the heart,
Wearing, for them, a mask of hopefulness.
They were ready for the feasting. Part lay bare
The flesh from the torn hides, part cut the meat,
Impaling it, still quivering, on spits,
Setting the kettles, keeping the water boiling,

And strong with food again, sprawling stretched out
On comfortable grass, they take their fill
Of bread and wine and venison, till hunger
Is gone, and the board cleared. And then they talk
For a long time, of where their comrades are,
Are, or may be, hopeful and doubtful both.
Could they believe them living? or would a cry
Fall on deaf ears forever? All those captains,
Brave Gyas, brave Cloanthus, Amycus,
Lycus, Orontes,—in his secret heart
Aeneas mourns them.

             Meanwhile, from the heaven
Jupiter watched the lands below, and the seas
With the white points of sails, and far-off people,
Turning his gaze toward Libya. And Venus
Came to him then, a little sadly, tears
Brimming in those bright eyes of hers. "Great father,"
She said, "Great ruler of the world
Of men and gods, great wielder of the lightning,
What has my poor Aeneas done? what outrage
Could Trojans perpetrate, so that the world
Rejects them everywhere, and many a death
Inflicted on them over Italy?
There was a promise once, that as the years
Rolled onward, they would father Rome and rulers
Of Roman stock, to hold dominion over
All sea and land. That was a promise, father;
What changed it? Once that promise was my comfort;
Troy fell; I weighed one fate against another
And found some consolation. But disaster
Keeps on; the same ill-fortune follows after.
What end of it all, great king? One man, Antenor,
Escaped the Greeks, came through Illyrian waters
Safe to Liburnian regions, where Timavus
Roars underground, comes up nine times, and reaches
The floodland near the seas. One man, Antenor,
Founded a city, Padua, a dwelling
For Trojan men, a resting-place from labor,
And shares their quietude. But we, your children,
To whom heaven's height is granted, we are betrayed,
We have lost our ships, we are kept from Italy,
Kept far away. One enemy—I tell you
This is a shameful thing! Do we deserve it?
Is this our rise to power?"

He smiled, in answer,
The kind of smile that clears the air, and kissed her.
"Fear not, my daughter; fate remains unmoved
For the Roman generations. You will witness
Lavinium's rise, her walls fulfill the promise;
You will bring to heaven lofty-souled Aeneas.
There has been no change in me whatever. Listen!
To ease this care, I will prophesy a little,
I will open the book of fate. Your son Aeneas
Will wage a mighty war in Italy,
Beat down proud nations, give his people laws,
Found them a city, a matter of three years
From victory to settlement. His son,
The boy Ascanius, named Ilius once,
When Troy was standing, and now called Iulus,
Shall reign for thirty years, and great in power
Forsake Lavinium, transfer the kingdom
To Alba Longa, new-built capital.
Here, for three hundred years, the line of Hector
Shall govern, till a royal priestess bears
Twin sons to Mars, and Romulus, rejoicing
In the brown wolf-skin of his foster-mother,
Takes up the tribe, and builds the martial walls
And calls the people, after himself, the Romans.
To these I set no bounds in space or time;
They shall rule forever. Even bitter Juno
Whose fear now harries earth and sea and heaven
Will change to better counsels, and will cherish
The race that wears the toga, Roman masters
Of all the world. It is decreed. The time
Will come, as holy years wheel on, when Troy
Will subjugate Mycenae, vanquish Phthia,
Be lord of Argos. And from this great line
Will come a Trojan, Caesar, to establish
The limit of his empire at the ocean,
His glory at the stars, a man called Julius
Whose name recalls Iulus. Welcome waits
For him in heaven; all the spoils of Asia
Will weigh him down, and prayer be made before him.
Then wars will cease, and a rough age grow gentler,
White Faith and Vesta, Romulus and Remus,
Give law to nations. War's grim gates will close,
Tight-shut with bars of iron, and inside them
The wickedness of war sit bound and silent,
The red mouth straining and the hands held tight
In fastenings of bronze, a hundred hundred."

With that, he sent down Mercury from heaven
That Carthage might be kindly, and her land
And new-built towers receive them with a welcome,
And their queen, Dido, knowing the will of fate,
Swing wide her doors. On the oarage of his wings
He flies through the wide sweep of air to Libya,
Where, at the will of the god, the folk make ready
In kindliness of heart, and their queen's purpose
Is gracious and gentle.

from Book II [The Fall of Troy]

They all were silent, watching. From his couch
Aeneas spoke: "A terrible grief, O Queen,
You bid me live again, how Troy went down
Before the Greeks, her wealth, her pitiful kingdom,
Sorrowful things I saw myself, wherein
I had my share and more. Even Ulysses,
Even his toughest soldiery might grieve
At such a story. And the hour is late
Already; night is sliding down the sky
And setting stars urge slumber. But if you long
To learn our downfall, to hear the final chapter
Of Troy no matter how I shrink, remembering,
And turn away in grief, let me begin it.

Broken in war, set back by fate, the leaders
Of the Greek host, as years went by, contrived,
With Pallas' help, a horse as big as a mountain,
They wove its sides with planks of fir, pretending
This was an offering for their safe return,
At least, so rumor had it. But inside
They packed, in secret, into the hollow sides
The fittest warriors; the belly's cavern,
Huge as it was, was filled with men in armor.
There is an island, Tenedos, well-known,
Rich in the days of Priam; now it is only
A bay, and not too good an anchorage
For any ship to trust. They sailed there, hid
On the deserted shore. We thought they had gone,
Bound for Mycenae, and Troy was very happy,
Shaking off grief, throwing the gates wide open.
It was a pleasure, for a change, to go
See the Greek camp, station and shore abandoned;
Why, this was where Achilles camped, his minions,
The Dolopes, were here; and the fleet just yonder,

And that was the plain where we used to meet in battle.
Some of us stared in wonder at the horse,
Astounded by its vastness, Minerva's gift,
Death from the virgin goddess, had we known it.
Thymoetes, whether in treachery, or because
The fates of Troy so ordered, was the first one
To urge us bring it in to the heart of the city,
But Capys, and some others, knowing better,
Suspicious of Greek plotting, said to throw it
Into the sea, to burn it up with fire,
To cut it open, see what there was inside it.
The wavering crowd could not make up its mind.

And, at that point, Laocoön came running,
With a great throng at his heels, down from the hilltop
As fast as ever he could, and before he reached us,
Cried in alarm: 'Are you crazy, wretched people?
Do you think they have gone, the foe? Do you think that any
Gifts of the Greeks lack treachery? Ulysses,—
What was his reputation? Let me tell you,
Either the Greeks are hiding in this monster,
Or it's some trick of war, a spy, or engine,
To come down on the city. Tricky business
Is hiding in it. Do not trust it, Trojans,
Do not believe this horse. Whatever it may be,
I fear the Greeks, even when bringing presents.'
With that, he hurled the great spear at the side
With all the strength he had. It fastened, trembling,
And the struck womb rang hollow, a moaning sound.
He had driven us, almost, to let the light in
With the point of the steel, to probe, to tear, but something
Got in his way, the gods, or fate, or counsel,
Ill-omened, in our hearts; or Troy would be standing
And Priam's lofty citadel unshaken.

Meanwhile, some Trojan shepherds, pulling and hauling,
Had a young fellow, with his hands behind him,
Tied up, and they were dragging him to Priam.
He had let himself be taken so, on purpose,
To open Troy to the Greeks, a stranger, ready
For death or shifty cunning, a cool intriguer,
Let come what may. They crowd around to see him,
Take turns in making fun of him, that captive.
Listen, and learn Greek trickiness; learn all
Their crimes from one.
He stopped in the middle, frightened and defenseless,

Looked at the Trojan ranks,—'What land, what waters,
Can take me now?' he cried, 'There is nothing, nothing
Left for me any more, no place with the Greeks,
And here are the Trojans howling for my blood!'
Our mood was changed. We pitied him, poor fellow,
Sobbing his heart out. We bade him tell his story,
His lineage, his news: what can he count on,
The captive that he is? His fear had gone
As he began: 'O King, whatever happens,
I will tell the truth, tell all of it; to start with,
I own I am a Greek. Sinon is wretched,
Fortune has made him so, but she will never
Make him a liar. You may perhaps have heard
Rumors of Palamedes, son of Belus,
A man of glorious fame. But the Greeks killed him,—
He was against the war, and so they killed him,
An innocent man, by perjury and lying
False witness. Now that he is dead they mourn him.
My father, his poor relative, had sent me
To soldier in his company; I was then
Scarcely beyond my boyhood. Palamedes
Held, for some time, some influence and standing
In royal councils, and we shared his glory,
But, and all men know this, Ulysses' hatred,
His cunning malice, pulled him down; thereafter
I lived in darkness, dragging out a lifetime
In sorrow for my innocent lord, and anger,
And in my anger I was very foolish,
I talked; I vowed, if I got home to Argos,
I would have vengeance: so I roused Ulysses
To hate me in his turn, and that began it,
Downfall and evil, Ulysses always trying
To frighten me with hint and accusation,
With rumors planted where the crowd would listen;
Oh yes, Ulysses knew what he was doing,
He never stopped, until with Calchas working
Hand in glove with him—why am I telling this,
And what's the use? I am stalling. All the Greeks,
You think, are all alike; what more do you want?
Inflict the punishment. That would be something
Ulysses would rejoice in, and some others
Pay handsome money for!'
But we were all on fire to hear him further.
Pelasgian craft meant nothing to our folly.
Trembling and nervous, he resumed his lying:
'The Greeks were tired of the long war; they often

Wanted to sail from Troy for home. Oh, would
That they had only done it! But a storm
Would cut them off, or the wrong wind terrify them.
Especially, just after the horse was finished,
With the joined planks of maple, all the heaven
Roared loud with storm-clouds. In suspense and terror
We sent Eurypylus to ask Apollo
What could be done; the oracle was gloomy,
Foreboding: "Blood, O Greeks, and a slain virgin
appeased the winds when first you came here; blood
Must pay for your return, a life be given,
An Argive life." The word came to our ears
With terror in it, our blood ran cold in our veins,
For whom was fate preparing? who would be
The victim of Apollo? Then Ulysses
Dragged Calchas into our midst, with a great uproar,
Trying his best to make the prophet tell us
What the gods wanted. And there were many then
Who told me what was coming, or kept silent
Because they saw, and all too well, the scheme
Ulysses had in mind. For ten days Calchas
Said nothing at all, hid in his tent, refusing
To have a word of his pronounce the sentence,
And all the time Ulysses kept on shouting,
Till Calchas broke, and doomed me to the altar.
And all assented; what each man had feared
In his own case, he bore with great composure
When turned another way.
The terrible day was almost on me; fillets
Were ready for my temples, the salted meal
Prepared, the altars standing. But I fled,
I tore myself away from death, I admit it,
I hid all night in sedge and muddy water
At the edge of the lake, hoping, forever hoping,
They might set sail. And now I hope no longer
To see my home, my parents, or my children,
Poor things, whom they will kill because I fled them,
Whom they will murder for my sacrilege.
But oh, by the gods above, by any power
That values truth, by any uncorrupted
Remnant of faith in all the world, have pity,
Have pity on a soul that bears such sorrow,
More than I ever deserved.'
He had no need to ask us. Priam said,
Untie him, and we did so with a promise
To spare his life. Our king, with friendly words,

Addressed him, saying, 'Whoever you are, forget
The Greeks, from now on. You are ours; but tell me
Why they have built this monstrous horse? who made it,
Who thought of it? What is it, war-machine,
Religious offering?' And he, instructed
In every trick and artifice, made answer,
Lifting his hands, now free: 'Eternal fires,
Inviolable godhead, be my witness,
You altars, you accursed swords, you fillets
Which I as victim wore, I had the right
To break those solemn bonds, I had the right
To hate those men, to bring whatever they hide
Into the light and air; I am bound no longer
To any country, any laws, but, Trojans,
Keep to the promise, if I tell the truth,
If I pay back with interest.
All the Greek hope, since first the war began,
Rested in Pallas, always. But Ulysses,
The crime-contriver, and the son of Tydeus
Attacked Minerva's temple, stole her image
Out of the holy shrine, and slew the guards,
And laid their bloody hands upon the goddess,
And from that time the Danaan hopes were broken,
Faltered and failed. It was no doubtful anger
Pallas revealed; she gave them signs and portents.
From her image in the camp the upraised eyes
Shot fire, and sweat ran salty down the limbs,
Thrice from the ground she seemed to flash and leap
With vibrant spear and clashing shield. The priest,
Calchas, made prophecy: they must take to flight
Over the sea, and Troy could not be taken
Without new omens; they must go to Argos,
Bring back the goddess again, whom they have taken
In curved ships over the sea. And if they have gone,
They are bound for home, Mycenae, for new arms,
New gods, new soldiers; they will be here again
When least expected. Calchas' message warned them,
And so they built this image, to replace
The one they had stolen, a gigantic offering
For a tremendous sacrilege. It was Calchas,
Again, who bade them build a mass so mighty
It almost reached the stars, too big to enter
Through any gate, or be brought inside the walls.
For if your hands should damage it, destruction,
(May God avert it) would come upon the city,
But if your hands helped bring it home, then Asia

Would be invading Greece, and doom await
Our children's children.'

             We believed him, we
Whom neither Diomede nor great Achilles
Had taken, nor ten years, nor that armada,
A thousand ships of war. But Sinon did it
By perjury and guile.

            Then something else,
Much greater and more terrible, was forced
Upon us, troubling our unseeing spirits.
Laocoön, allotted priest of Neptune,
Was slaying a great bull beside the altars,
When suddenly, over the tranquil deep
From Tenedos,—I shudder even now,
Recalling it—there came a pair of serpents
With monstrous coils, breasting the sea, and aiming
Together for the shore. Their heads and shoulders
Rose over the waves, upright, with bloody crests,
The rest of them trailing along the water,
Looping in giant spirals; the foaming sea
Hissed under their motion. And they reached the land,
Their burning eyes suffused with blood and fire,
Their darting tongues licking the hissing mouths.
Pale at the sight, we fled. But they went on
Straight toward Laocoön, and first each serpent
Seized in its coils his two young sons, and fastened
The fangs in those poor bodies. And the priest
Struggled to help them, weapons in his hand.
They seized him, bound him with their mighty coils,
Twice round his waist, twice round his neck, they squeezed
With scaly pressure, and still towered above him.
Straining his hands to tear the knots apart,
His chaplets stained with blood and the black poison,
He uttered horrible cries, not even human,
More like the bellowing of a bull when, wounded,
It flees the altar, shaking from the shoulder
The ill-aimed axe. And on the pair went gliding
To the highest shrine, the citadel of Pallas,
And vanished underneath the feet of the goddess
And the circle of her shield.

                    The people trembled
Again; they said Laocoön deserved it,
Having, with spear, profaned the sacred image.
It must be brought to its place, they cried, the goddess
Must be appeased. We broke the walls, exposing
The city's battlements, and all were busy
Helping the work, with rollers underfoot
And ropes around the neck. It climbed our walls,
The deadly engine. Boys, unwedded girls
Sang alleluias round it, all rejoicing
To have a hand on the tow-rope. It came nearer,
Threatening, gliding, into the very city.
O motherland! O Ilium, home of gods,
O walls of Troy! Four times it stopped, four times
The sound of arms came from it, and we pressed on,
Unheedful, blind in madness, till we set it,
Ill-omened thing, on the citadel we worshipped.
And even when Cassandra gave us warning,
We never believed her; so a god had ordered.
That day, our last, poor wretches, we were happy,
Garlanding the temples of the gods
All through the town.

                    And the sky turned, and darkness
Came from the ocean, the great shade covering earth
And heaven, and the trickery of the Greeks.
Sprawling along the walls, the Trojans slumbered,
Sleep holding their weary limbs, and the Greek armada,
From Tenedos, under the friendly silence
Of a still moon, came surely on. The flagship
Blazed at the masthead with a sudden signal,
And Sinon, guarded by the fates, the hostile
Will of the gods, swung loose the bolts; the Greeks
Came out of the wooden womb. The air received them,
The happy captains, Sthenelus, Ulysses,
Thessandrus, Acamas, Achilles' son
Called Neoptolemus, Thoas, Machaon,
Epeos, who designed the thing,—they all
Came sliding down the rope, and Menelaus
Was with them in the storming of a city
Buried in sleep and wine. The watch was murdered,
The open doors welcome the rush of comrades,
They marshal the determined ranks for battle.
It was the time when the first sleep begins
For weary mortals, heaven's most welcome gift.
In sleep, before my eyes, I seemed to see

Hector, most sorrowful, black with bloody dust,
Torn, as he had been, by Achilles' car,
The thong-marks on his swollen feet. How changed
He was from that great Hector who came, once,
Triumphant in Achilles' spoil, from hurling
Fire at the Grecian ships. With ragged beard,
Hair matted with his blood, wearing the wounds
He earned around the walls of Troy, he stood there.
It seemed that I spoke first:—'O light of Troy,
Our surest hope, we have long been waiting for you,
What shores have kept you from us? Many deaths,
Much suffering, have visited our city,
And we are tired. Why do I see these wounds?
What shame has caused them?' Those were foolish questions;
He made no answer but a sigh or a groan,
And then: 'Alas, O goddess-born! Take flight,
Escape these flames! The enemy has the walls,
Troy topples from her lofty height; enough
Has been paid out to Priam and to country.
Could any hand have saved them, Hector's would have.
Troy trusts to you her household gods, commending
Her holy things to you; take them, companions
Of destiny; seek walls for them, and a city
To be established, a long sea-wandering over.
From the inner shrine he carried Vesta's chaplets
In his own hands, and her undying fire.

Livy (59 BCE–17 CE)
The History of Rome

Rome, always aware of its greatness, had no shortage of chroniclers, record keepers, letter writers, and historians. But only Livy was what we would call a professional historian, a person who sets as his life work the writing of a great history and does only that, without other occupation or preoccupation. In 142 books, Livy wrote the history of Rome down to his own time. His lack of connections to the military or to the Roman senate gave him a view of events that belonged to an outsider (as opposed, say, to Julius Caesar's insider's account of his conquest of Gaul). Livy saw the study of history as morally profitable, as he says in his preface, because "in history you have a record of the infinite variety of human experience plainly set out for all to see, and in that record you can find for yourself and your country both examples and warnings; fine things to take as models, base things, rotten through and through, to avoid." Of the 142 books that Livy completed, only books 1–10 and 21–45 survive.

[Romulus and Remus]

But (I must believe) it was already written in the book of fate that this great city of ours should arise, and the first steps be taken to the founding of the mightiest empire the world has known—next to God's. The Vestal Virgin was raped and gave birth to twin boys. Mars, she declared, was their father—perhaps she believed it, perhaps she was merely hoping by the pretence to palliate her guilt. Whatever the truth of the matter, neither gods nor men could save her or her babes from the savage hands of the king. The mother was bound and flung into prison; the boys, by the king's order, were condemned to be drowned in the river. Destiny, however, intervened; the Tiber had overflowed its banks; because of the flooded ground it was impossible to get to the actual river, and the men entrusted to do the deed thought that the flood-water, sluggish though it was, would serve their purpose. Accordingly they made shift to carry out the king's orders by leaving the infants on the edge of the first flood-water they came to, at the spot where now stands the Ruminal fig-tree—said to have once been known as the fig-tree of Romulus. In those days the country thereabouts was all wild and uncultivated, and the story goes that when the basket in which the infants had been exposed was left high and dry by the receding water, a she-wolf, coming down from the neighboring hills to quench her thirst, heard the children crying and made her way to where they were. She offered them her teats to suck and treated them with such gentleness that Faustulus, the king's herdsman, found her licking them with her tongue. Faustulus took them

---

The translation of Livy given here is by Aubrey de Selincourt (Penguin, 1960), an English school-master who retired to write his own history, *The World of Herodotus*.

to his hut and gave them to his wife Larentia to nurse. Some think that the origin of this fable was the fact that Larentia was a common whore and was called Wolf by the shepherds.

Such, then, was the birth and upbringing of the twins. By the time they were grown boys, they employed themselves actively on the farm and with the flocks and began to go hunting in the woods; their strength grew with their resolution, until not content only with the chase they took to attacking robbers and sharing their stolen goods with their friends the shepherds. Other young fellows joined them, and they and the shepherds would fleet the time together, now in serious talk, now in jollity.

Even in that remote age the Palatine hill (which got its name from the Arcadian settlement Pallanteum) is supposed to have been the scene of the gay festival of the Lupercalia. The Arcadian Evander, who many years before held that region, is said to have instituted there the old Arcadian practice of holding an annual festival in honor of Lycean Pan (afterwards called Inuus by the Romans), in which young men ran about naked and disported themselves in various pranks and fooleries. The day of the festival was common knowledge, and on one occasion when it was in full swing some brigands, incensed at the loss of their ill-gotten gains, laid a trap for Romulus and Remus. Romulus successfully defended himself, but Remus was caught and handed over to Amulius. The brigands laid a complaint against their prisoner, the main charge being that he and his brother were in the habit of raiding Numitor's land with an organized gang of ruffians and stealing the cattle. Thereupon Remus was handed over for punishment to Numitor.

Now Faustulus had suspected all along that the boys he was bringing up were of royal blood. He knew that two infants had been exposed by the king's orders, and the rescue of his own two fitted perfectly in point of time. Hitherto, however, he had been unwilling to declare what he knew, until either a suitable opportunity occurred or circumstances compelled him. Now the truth could no longer be concealed, so in his alarm he told Romulus the whole story; Numitor, too, when he had Remus in custody and was told that the brothers were twins, was set thinking about his grandsons; the young men's age and character, so different from the lowly born, confirmed his suspicions; and further inquiries led him to the same conclusion, until he was on the point of acknowledging Remus. The net was closing in, and Romulus acted. He was not strong enough for open hostilities, so he instructed a number of the herdsmen to meet at the king's house by different routes at a preordained time; this was done, and with the help of Remus, at the head of another body of men, the king was surprised and killed. Before the first blows were struck, Numitor gave it out that an enemy had broken into the town and attacked the palace; he then drew off all the men of military age to garrison the inner fortress, and, as soon as he saw Romulus and Remus, their purpose accomplished, coming to congratulate him, he summoned a meeting of the people and laid the facts before it: Amulius's crime against himself, the birth of his grandsons, and the circumstances attending it, how they were brought up and ultimately recognized, and, finally, the murder of the king for which he himself assumed responsibility. The two brothers marched through the crowd at the head of their men and saluted their grandfather as king, and by a shout of unanimous consent his royal title was confirmed.

Romulus and Remus, after the control of Alba had passed to Numitor in the way I have described, were suddenly seized by an urge to found a new settlement on the spot where they had been left to drown as infants and had been subsequently brought up. There was, in point of fact, already an excess of population at Alba, what with the Albans themselves, the Latins, and the addition of the herdsmen: enough, indeed, to justify the hope that Alba and Lavinium would one day be small places compared with the proposed new settlement. Unhappily the brothers' plans for the future were marred by the same source which had divided their grandfather and Amulius—jealousy and ambition. A disgraceful quarrel arose from a matter in itself trivial. As the brothers were twins and all question of seniority was thereby precluded, they determined to ask the tutelary gods of the countryside to declare by augury which of them should govern the new town once it was founded, and give his name to it. For this purpose Romulus took the Palatine hill and Remus the Aventine as their respective stations from which to observe the auspices. Remus, the story goes, was the first to receive a sign—six vultures; and no sooner was this made known to the people than double the number of birds appeared to Romulus. The followers of each promptly saluted their master as king, one side basing its claim upon priority, the other upon number. Angry words ensued, followed all too soon by blows, and in the course of the affray Remus was killed. There is another story, a commoner one, according to which Remus, by way of jeering at his brother, jumped over the half-built walls of the new settlement; whereupon Romulus killed him in a fit of rage, adding the threat, 'So perish whoever else shall overleap my battlements.'

This, then, was how Romulus obtained the sole power. The newly built city was called by its founder's name.

[The Abduction of the Sabine Women]

Rome was now strong enough to challenge any of her neighbors; but, great though she was, her greatness seemed likely to last only for a single generation. There were not enough women, and that, added to the fact that there was no intermarriage with neighboring communities, ruled out any hope of maintaining the level of population. Romulus accordingly, on the advice of his senators, sent representatives to the various peoples across his borders to negotiate alliances and the right of intermarriage for the newly established state. The envoys were instructed to point out that cities, like everything else, have to begin small; in course of time, helped by their own worth and the favor of heaven, some, at least, grow rich and famous, and of these Rome would assuredly be one: Gods had blessed her birth, and the valor of her people would not fail in the days to come. The Romans were men, as they were; why, then, be reluctant to intermarry with them?

Romulus's overtures were nowhere favorably received; it was clear that everyone despised the new community, and at the same time feared, both for themselves and for posterity, the growth of this new power in their midst. More often than not his envoys were dismissed with the question of whether Rome had thrown open her doors to female, as well as to male, runaways and vagabonds, as that would evidently be the most suitable way for Romans to get wives. The young Romans naturally resented this jibe, and a clash seemed inevitable. Romulus, seeing it must come, set the scene for it with elaborate care. Deliberately hiding his resentment, he prepared to celebrate the Consualia, a solemn festival in honor of Neptune, patron of the horse, and sent notice of his intention all over the neighboring countryside. The better to advertise it, his people lavished upon their preparations for the spectacle all the resources—such as they were in those days—at their command. On the appointed day crowds flocked to Rome, partly, no doubt, out of sheer curiosity to see the new town. The majority were from the neighboring settlements of Caenina, Crustumium, and Antemnae, but all the Sabines were there too, with their wives and children. Many houses offered hospitable entertainment to the visitors; they were invited to inspect the fortifications, layout, and numerous buildings of the town, and expressed their surprise at the rapidity of its growth. Then the great moment came; the show began, and nobody had eyes or thoughts for anything else. This was the Romans' opportunity: at a given signal all the able-bodied men burst through the crowd and seized the young women. Most of the girls were the prize of whoever got hold of them first, but a few conspicuously handsome ones had been previously marked down for leading senators, and these were brought to their houses by special gangs. There was one young woman of much greater beauty than the rest; and the story goes that she was seized by a party of men belonging to the household of someone called Thalassius, and in reply to the many questions about whose house they were taking her to, they, to prevent anyone else laying hands upon her, kept shouting, 'Thalassius, Thalassius!' This was the origin of the use of this word at weddings.

By this act of violence the fun of the festival broke up in panic. The girls' unfortunate parents made good their escape, not without bitter comments on the treachery of their hosts and heartfelt prayers to the God to whose festival they had come in all good faith in the solemnity of the occasion, only to be grossly deceived. The young women were no less indignant and as full of foreboding for the future.

Romulus, however, reassured them. Going from one to another he declared that their own parents were really to blame, in that they had been too proud to allow intermarriage with their neighbors; nevertheless, they need not fear; as married women they would share all the fortunes of Rome, all the privileges of the community, and they would be bound to their husbands by the dearest bond of all, their children. He urged them to forget their wrath and give their hearts to those to whom chance had given their bodies. Often, he said, a sense of injury yields in the end to affection, and their husbands would treat them all the more kindly in that they would try, each one of them, not only to fulfil their own part of the bargain but also to make up to their wives for the homes and parents they had lost. The men, too, played their part: they spoke honeyed words and vowed that it was passionate love which had prompted their offence. No plea can better touch a woman's heart.

[The Rape of Lucretia]

The young princes were drinking one day in the quarters of Sextus Tarquinius—Collatinus, son of Egerius, was also present—when someone chanced to mention the subject of wives. Each of them, of course, extravagantly praised his own; and the rivalry got hotter and hotter, until Collatinus suddenly cried: 'Stop! What need is there of words, when in a few hours we can prove beyond doubt the incomparable superiority of my Lucretia? We are all young and strong: why shouldn't we ride to Rome and see with our own eyes what kind of women our wives are? There is no better evidence, I assure you, than what a man finds when he enters his wife's room unexpectedly.'

They had all drunk a good deal, and the proposal appealed to them; so they mounted their horses and galloped off to Rome. They reached the city as dusk was falling; and there the wives of the royal princes were found enjoying themselves with a group of young friends at a dinner-party, in the greatest luxury. The riders then went on to Collatia, where they found Lucretia very differently employed: it was already late at night, but there, in the hall of her house, surrounded by her busy maid-servants, she was still hard at work by lamplight upon her spinning. Which wife had won the contest in womanly virtue was no longer in doubt.

With all courtesy Lucretia rose to bid her husband and the princes welcome, and Collatinus, pleased with his success, invited his friends to sup with him. It was at that fatal supper that Lucretia's beauty, and proven chastity, kindled in Sextus Tarquinias the flame of lust, and determined him to debauch her.

Nothing further occurred that night. The little jaunt was over, and the young men rode back to camp.

A few days later Sextus, without Collatinus's knowledge, returned with one companion to Collatia, where he was hospitably welcomed in Lucretia's house, and, after supper, escorted, like the honored visitor he was thought to be, to the guest-chamber. Here he waited till the house was asleep, and then, when all was quiet, he drew his sword and made his way to Lucretia's room determined to rape her. She was asleep. Laying his left hand on her breast, 'Lucretia,' he whispered, 'not a sound! I am Sextus Tarquinius. I am armed—if you utter a word, I will kill you.' Lucretia opened her eyes in terror; death was imminent, no help at hand. Sextus urged his love, begged her to submit, pleaded, threatened, used every weapon that might conquer a woman's heart. But all in vain; not even the fear of death could bend her will. 'If death will not move you,' Sextus cried, 'dishonor shall. I will kill you first, then cut the throat of a slave and lay his naked body by your side. Will they not believe that you have been caught in adultery with a servant—and paid the price?' Even the most resolute chastity could not have stood against this dreadful threat.

Lucretia yielded. Sextus enjoyed her, and rode away, proud of his success.

The unhappy girl wrote to her father in Rome and to her husband in Ardea, urging them both to come at once with a trusted friend and quickly, for a frightful thing had happened. Her father came with Valerius, Volesus's son, her husband with Brutus, with whom he was returning to Rome when he was met by the messenger. They found Lucretia sitting in her room, in deep distress. Tears rose to her eyes as they entered, and to her husband's question, 'Is it well with you?' she answered, 'No. What can be well with a woman who has lost her honor? In your bed, Collatinus, is the impress of another man. My body only has been violated. My heart is innocent, and death will be my witness. Give me your solemn promise that the adulterer shall be punished—he is Sextus Tarquinius. He it is who last night came as my enemy disguised as my guest, and took his pleasure of me. That pleasure will be my death—and his, too, if you are men.'

The promise was given. One after another they tried to comfort her. They told her she was helpless, and therefore innocent; that he alone was guilty. It was the mind, they said, that sinned, not the body: without intention there could never be guilt.

'What is due to him,' Lucretia said, 'is for you to decide. As for me I am innocent of fault, but I will take my punishment. Never shall Lucretia provide a precedent for unchaste women to escape what they deserve.' With these words she drew a knife from under her robe, drove it into her heart, and fell forward, dead.

Her father and husband were overwhelmed with grief. While they stood weeping helplessly, Brutus drew the bloody knife from Lucretia's body, and holding it before him cried: 'By this girl's blood—none more chaste till a tyrant wronged her—and by the gods, I swear that with sword and fire, and whatever else can lend strength to my arm, I will pursue Lucius Tarquinius the Proud, his wicked wife, and all his children, and never again will I let them or any other man be King in Rome.'

He put the knife into Collatinus's hands, then passed it to Lucretius, then to Valerius. All looked at him in astonishment: a miracle had happened—he was a changed man. Obedient to his command, they swore their oath. Grief was forgotten in the sudden surge of anger, and when Brutus called upon them to make war, from that instant, upon the tyrant's throne, they took him for their leader.

Lucretia's body was carried from the house into the public square. Crowds gathered, as crowds will, to gape and wonder—and the sight was unexpected enough, and horrible enough, to attract them. Anger at the criminal brutality of the king's son and sympathy with the father's grief stirred every heart; and when Brutus cried out that it was time for deeds not tears, and urged them, like true Romans, to take up arms against the tyrants who had dared to treat them as a vanquished enemy, not a man amongst them could resist the call.

. . . When news of the rebellion reached Ardea, the king immediately started for Rome, to restore order. Brutus got wind of his approach, and changed his route to avoid meeting him, finally reaching Ardea almost at the same moment as Tarquin arrived at Rome. Tarquin found the city gates shut against him and his exile decreed. Brutus the Liberator was enthusiastically welcomed by the troops, and Tarquin's sons were expelled from the camp. Two of them followed their father into exile at Caere in Etruria. Sextus Tarquinius went to Gabii—his own territory, as he doubtless hoped; but his previous record there of robbery and violence had made him many enemies, who now took their revenge and assassinated him.

OVID (43 BCE–C.17 CE)
Metamorphoses

Unlike Virgil, who was rescued from an early exile by Augustus and who during his career enjoyed the patronage of a wealthy friend of the emperor, Ovid was a brilliant poet who lost Augustus's favor and ended his life in bitter exile on the Black Sea. We are not sure what brought about the break in his relations with the emperor; he himself says the cause was "his poetry and his mistake," and his punishment was heightened by the removal of his books from libraries in Rome.

In spite of his bad end, Ovid became one of the most popular and influential poets during the centuries to follow, partly because of his brilliant and witty treatment of love in poems like the Art of Love, *a handbook of seduction. But his greatest poem is* Metamorphoses, *a compendium of Greek and Roman mythical stories, cleverly woven together around the central theme of change. Because the Greek (and Roman) myths show so many humans and gods changed into plants, birds, animals, trees, and stars, Ovid's theme allows him to retell a huge number of stories. In fact, his poem became a kind of encyclopedia of myth, the sourcebook for later writers and artists in the West who were seduced by Ovid's versions of the stories.*

But Ovid's style is very much unlike an encyclopedia: he draws from the stories all their emotion, sentiment, and irony. With great insight, Ovid searches the stories for deeper strains of passion, of terror, of fate. So successful is his enterprise that many of his stories, barely known in earlier versions, have become emblems for us of human psychology: the self-love of Narcissus, Pygmalion's possessive love for the image of the woman he crafted, Icarus's death in the sea after he fails to heed his father's warning about flying too close to the sun, Orpheus's winning his wife out of hell only to lose her again. And Arachne, in the story included here, who challenges to a weaving contest the very goddess who gave her her skill. Although she weaves a tapestry depicting the treachery of the gods toward humans, she fails to learn her own lesson and, in besting Minerva (Athena), invites the goddess's resentment and revenge.

[Creation and Flood]

My purpose is to tell of bodies which have been transformed into shapes of a different kind. You heavenly powers, since you were responsible for those changes, as for all else, look favourably on my attempts, and spin an unbroken thread of verse, from the earliest beginnings of the world, down to my own times.

Before there was any earth or sea, before the canopy of heaven stretched overhead, Nature presented the same aspect the world over, that to which men have given the name of Chaos.

Ovid's verse is translated here into English prose by Mary M. Innes (New York: Penguin, 1955).

This was a shapeless uncoordinated mass, nothing but a weight of lifeless matter, whose ill-assorted elements were indiscriminately heaped together in one place. There was no sun, in those days, to provide the world with light, no crescent moon ever filling out her horns: the earth was not poised in the enveloping air, balanced there by its own weight, nor did the sea stretch out its arms along the margins of the shores. Although the elements of land and air and sea were there, the earth had no firmness, the water no fluidity, there was no brightness in the sky. Nothing had any lasting shape, but everything got in the way of everything else; for, within that one body, cold warred with hot, moist with dry, soft with hard, and light with heavy.

This strife was finally resolved by a god, a natural force of a higher kind, who separated the earth from heaven, and the water from the earth, and set the clear air apart from the cloudy atmosphere. When he had freed these elements, sorting them out from the heap where they had lain, indistinguishable from one another, he bound them fast, each in its separate place, forming a harmonious union. The fiery aether, which has no weight, formed the vault of heaven, flashing upwards to take its place in the highest sphere. The air, next to it in lightness, occupied the neighbouring regions. Earth, heavier than these, attracted to itself the grosser elements, and sank down under its own weight, while the encircling sea took possession of the last place of all, and held the solid earth in its embrace. In this way the god, whichever of the gods it was, set the chaotic mass in order, and, after dividing it up, arranged it in its constituent parts.

When this was done, his first care was to shape the earth into a great ball, so that it might be the same in all directions. After that, he commanded the seas to spread out this way and that, to swell into waves under the influence of the rushing winds, and to pour themselves around earth's shores. Springs, too, he created, and great pools and lakes, and confined between sloping banks the rivers which flow down from the hills and continue, each in its own channel, until they are either swallowed up by the earth itself, or reach the sea and enter its expanse of wider waters, there to wash against shores instead of banks. Then the god further ordained that earth's plains should unroll, its valleys sink down, the woods be clothed with leaves, and rocky mountain peaks rise up.

As the sky is divided into two zones on the right hand, and two on the left, with a fifth in between, hotter than any of the rest, so the world which the sky encloses was marked off in the same way thanks to the providence of the god: he imposed the same number of zones on earth as there are in the heavens. The central zone is so hot as to be uninhabitable, while two others are covered in deep snow: but between these extremes he set two zones to which he gave a temperate climate, compounded of heat and cold.

Over all these regions hangs the air, as much heavier than the fiery aether as it is lighter than earth or water. To the air the god assigned mists and clouds, and thunder that was destined to cause human hearts to tremble: here too he placed the thunderbolts, and winds that strike out lightnings from the clouds. Nor did the builder of the world allow the winds, any more than the rest, to roam at will throughout the air—they can scarcely be prevented from tearing the world apart, even as it is, although each blows in a different direction: so violent is the strife between brothers. The East wind withdrew to the lands of the dawn, to the kingdoms of Arabia and Persia, and to the mountain ridges that lie close to the sun's morning rays. The West, and the shores which are warmed by the setting sun, are subject to Zephyr. Boreas, who makes men shudder with his chill breath, invaded Scythia and the North, while the lands opposite to those are continually drenched with rain and clouds, brought by the South wind.

Above all these, the god set the clear aether that has no weight, and is untainted by any earthly particles.

No sooner were all things separated in this way, and confined within definite limits, than the stars which had long been buried in darkness and obscurity began to blaze forth all through the sky. So that every region should have its appropriate inhabitants, stars and divine forms occupied the heavens, the waters afforded a home to gleaming fishes, earth harboured wild beasts, and the yielding air welcomed the birds.

There was as yet no animal which was more akin to the gods than these, none more capable of intelligence, none that could be master over all the rest. It was at this point that man was born: either the Creator, who was responsible for this better world, made him from divine seed, or else Prometheus, son of Iapetus, took the new-made earth which, only recently separated from the lofty aether, still retained some elements related to those of heaven and, mixing it with rainwater, fashioned it into the image of the all-governing gods. Whereas other animals hang their heads and look at the ground, he made man stand erect, bidding him look up to heaven, and lift his head to the stars. So the earth, which had been rough and formless, was moulded into the shape of man, a creature till then unknown.

In the beginning was the Golden Age, when men of their own accord, without threat of punishment, without laws, maintained good faith and did what was right. There were no penalties to be afraid of, no bronze tablets were erected, carrying threats of legal action, no crowd of wrong-doers, anxious for mercy, trembled before the face of their judge: indeed, there were no judges, men lived securely without them. Never yet had any pine tree, cut down from its home on the mountains, been launched on ocean's waves, to visit foreign lands: men knew only their own shores. Their cities were not yet surrounded by sheer moats, they had no straight brass trumpets, no coiling brass horns, no helmets and no swords. The peoples of the world, untroubled by any fears, enjoyed a leisurely and peaceful existence, and had no use for soldiers. The earth itself, without compulsion, untouched by the hoe, unfurrowed by any share, produced all things spontaneously, and men were content with foods that grew without cultivation. They gathered arbute berries and mountain strawberries, wild cherries and blackberries that cling to thorny bramble bushes: or acorns, fallen from Jupiter's spreading oak. It was a season of everlasting spring, when peaceful zephyrs, with their warm breath, caressed the flowers that sprang up without having been planted. In time the earth, though untilled, produced corn too, and fields that never lay fallow whitened with heavy ears of grain. Then there flowed rivers of milk and rivers of nectar, and golden honey dripped from the green holm-oak.

When Saturn was consigned to the darkness of Tartarus, and the world passed under the rule of Jove, the age of silver replaced that of gold, inferior to it, but superior to the age of tawny bronze. Jupiter shortened the springtime which had prevailed of old, and instituted a cycle of four seasons in the year, winter, summer, changeable autumn, and a brief spring. Then, for the first time, the air became parched and arid, and glowed with white heat, then hanging icicles formed under the chilling blasts of the wind. It was in those days that men first sought covered dwelling places: they made their homes in caves and thick shrubberies, or bound branches together with bark. The corn, the gift of Ceres, first began to be sown in long furrows, and straining bullocks groaned beneath the yoke.

After that came the third age, the age of bronze, when men were of a fiercer character, more ready to turn to cruel warfare, but still free from any taint of wickedness.

Last of all arose the age of hard iron: immediately, in this period which took its name from a baser ore, all manner of crime broke out; modesty, truth, and loyalty fled. Treachery and trickery took their place, deceit and violence and criminal greed. Now sailors spread their canvas to the winds, though they had as yet but little knowledge of these, and trees which had once clothed the high mountains were fashioned into ships, and tossed upon the ocean waves, far removed from their own element. The land, which had previously been common to all, like the sunlight and the breezes, was now divided up far and wide by boundaries, set by cautious surveyors. Nor was it only corn and their due nourishment that men demanded of the rich earth: they explored its very bowels, and dug out the wealth which it had hidden away, close to the Stygian shades; and this wealth was a further incitement to wickedness. By this time iron had been discovered, to the hurt of mankind, and gold, more hurtful still than iron. War made its appearance, using both those metals in its conflict, and shaking clashing weapons in bloodstained hands. Men lived on what they could plunder: friend was not safe from friend, nor father-in-law from son-in-law, and even between brothers affection was rare. Husbands waited eagerly for the death of their wives, and wives for that of their husbands. Ruthless stepmothers mixed brews of deadly aconite, and sons pried into their fathers' horoscopes, impatient for them to die. All proper affection lay vanquished and, last of the immortals, the maiden Justice left the blood-soaked earth.

The heights of heaven were no safer than the earth; for the giants, so runs the story, assailed the kingdom of the gods and, piling mountains together, built them up to the stars above. Then the almighty father hurled his thunderbolt, smashed through Olympus, and flung down Pelion from where it had been piled on top of Ossa. The terrible bodies of the giants lay crushed beneath their own massive structures, and the earth was drenched and soaked with torrents of blood from her sons. Then, they say, she breathed life into this warm blood and, so that her offspring might not be completely forgotten, changed it into the shape of men. But the men thus born, no less than the giants, were contemptuous of the gods, violent and cruel, with a lust to kill: it was obvious that they were the children of blood.

When the father of the gods, the son of Saturn, looked down from his high citadel, and saw what was going on, he groaned aloud. He recalled the horrid banquet of Lycaon which had not yet become common knowledge, so recent was the deed, and his heart swelled with dreadful wrath, worthy of Jupiter. He called together his council, and they did not delay when they heard his summons.

There is a track across the heavens, plain to see in the clear sky. It is called the Milky Way, and is famous for its brightness. It is by this road that the gods come to the palace of the mighty Thunderer, and to his royal home. On the right hand and on the left stand the houses of distinguished gods, filled with crowds that throng their open doors. The ordinary inhabitants of heaven live elsewhere, in different places. Here the powerful and noble divinities have made their homes. This is the spot which, were I allowed to speak boldly, I would not hesitate to call the Palatine district of high heaven.

So the gods took their seats in the marble council chamber, and their lord sat, throned high above them, leaning on his ivory sceptre. Three times, four times, he shook those awe-inspiring locks and with them moved the earth, the sea, the stars. Then he opened his lips, and spoke these indignant words: 'Never was I more anxious concerning the sovereignty of the universe, no, not even at that time when each of the snaky-footed giants was preparing to throw his hundred arms round the sky and take it captive. For then the attack was made by one small group of enemies and, although they were fierce ones, still the trouble originated from one source. Now the entire human race must be destroyed, throughout all the lands which Nereus surrounds with his roaring waters. I swear by the rivers of the underworld that flow through the Stygian grove beneath the earth: all other remedies have already been tried. This cancer is incurable, and must be cut out by the knife, in case the healthy part become infected. We have the demigods to care for, the spirits of the countryside, nymphs and fauns, satyrs and silvani, who roam the hills. Since we have not, as yet, considered them worthy of the honour of a place in heaven, let us at least ensure that they can live on the earth which we have given them. For can you believe, you gods, that they will go unmolested when Lycaon, a man notorious for his savagery, has laid plots against me, the lord and master of the thunderbolt, aye, and your king and master too?'

All the gods muttered uneasily, and eagerly demanded the punishment of the man who had dared to do such a deed. Their dismay was such as was felt by the human race, when a wicked band of fanatics tried to extinguish the Roman name by shedding Caesar's blood: all men were seized by panic fear of instant destruction, and the whole world shuddered. Just as the loyal devotion of your subjects pleases you, Augustus, so did that of the gods please Jupiter. He checked their murmurs with a word, and as he raised his hand, all fell silent. When the uproar had subsided, hushed by the authority of the king of heaven, Jupiter again broke the silence with these words: "As far as he is concerned, he has paid the penalty. Have no fear on that score. But I shall tell you what his crime was, and what his punishment."

"Scandalous rumours concerning the state of the times had reached my ears. Hoping to find them false, I descended from the heights of Olympus, and walked the earth, a god in human form. It would take long to tell what wickedness I found on every side. Even the scandalous rumours were less than the truth. I had crossed over the ridge of Maenalus, a place bristling with the lairs of wild beasts, over Cyllene, and through the pinewoods of chill Lycaeus. From there, when the last shades of twilight were heralding the night, I entered the inhospitable home of the Arcadian tyrant. I revealed myself as a god, and the people began to do me homage. Lycaon, however, first laughed at their pious prayers, and then exclaimed: 'I shall find out, by an infallible test, whether he be god or mortal: there will be no doubt about the truth.' His plan was to take me unawares, as I lay sound asleep at night, and kill me. This was the test of truth on which he was resolved. Not content with that, he took a hostage sent him by the Molossian people, slit the man's throat with his sharp blade, and cooked his limbs, still warm with life, boiling some and roasting others over the fire. Then he set this banquet on the table. No sooner had he done so, than I with my avenging flames brought the house crashing down upon its household gods, gods worthy of such a master. Lycaon fled, terrified, until he reached the safety of the silent countryside. There he uttered howling noises, and his attempts to speak were all in vain. His clothes changed into bristling hairs, his arms to legs, and he became a wolf. His own savage nature showed in his rabid jaws, and he now directed against the flocks his innate lust for killing. He had a mania, even yet, for shedding blood. But, though he was a wolf, he retained some traces of his original shape. The greyness of his hair was the same, his face showed the same violence, his eyes gleamed as before, and he presented the same picture of ferocity."

"One house has fallen, but far more than one have deserved to perish. To the ends of the earth, the dread Fury holds sway. You would think men had sworn allegiance to crime! They shall all be punished, forthwith, as they deserve. Such is my resolve."

Some of the gods shouted their approval of Jove's words, and sought to increase his indignation: others played the part of silent supporters. Yet all were grieved at the thought of the destruction of the human race, and wondered what the earth would be like, in future, when it had been cleared of mortal inhabitants. They inquired who would bring offerings of incense to their altars, whether Jove meant to abandon the world to the plundering of wild beasts. In answer to their questions, the kin of the gods assured them that they need not be anxious, for he himself would attend to everything. He promised them a new stock of men, unlike the former ones, a race of miraculous origin.

Now he was on the point of launching his thunderbolts against every part of the earth, when he felt a sudden dread lest he should set light to the pure upper air by so many fiery bolts, and send the whole vault of heaven up in flames. He remembered, too, one of fate's decrees, that a time would come when sea and earth and the dome of the sky would blaze up, and the massive structure of the universe collapse in ruins. So he laid aside the weapons forged by the hands of the Cyclopes, and resolved on a different punishment, namely to send rain pouring down from every quarter of the sky, and so destroy mankind beneath the waters.

He wasted no time, but imprisoned the North wind in Aeolus' cave, together with all the gusts which dispel the gathering clouds; and he let loose the South wind. On dripping wings the South wind flew, his terrible features shrouded in pitchy darkness. His beard was heavy with rain, water streamed from his hoary locks, mists wreathed his brow, his robes and feathers dripped with moisture. When he crushed the hanging clouds in his broad hand, there was a crash; thereafter sheets of rain poured down from heaven. Juno's messenger Iris, clad in rainbow hues, drew up water and supplied nourishment to the clouds. The corn was laid low, and the crops the farmer had prayed for now lay flattened and sadly mourned, the long year's toil was wasted and gone for nothing.

Nor was Jupiter's anger satisfied with the resources of his own realm of heaven: his brother Neptune, the god of the sea, lent him the assistance of his waves. He sent forth a summons to the rivers, and when they entered their king's home: "No time now for long exhortations!" he cried. "Exert your strength to the utmost: that is what we need. Fling wide your homes, withdraw all barriers, and give free course to your waters." These were his orders. The rivers returned to their homes and, opening up the mouths of their springs, went rushing to the sea in frenzied torrents.

Neptune himself struck the earth with his trident; it trembled, and by its movement threw open channels for the waters. Across the wide plains the rivers raced, overflowing their banks, sweeping away in one torrential flood crops and orchards, cattle and men, houses and temples, sacred images and all. Any building which did manage to survive this terrible disaster unshaken and remain standing, was in the end submerged when some wave yet higher than the rest covered its roof, and its gables lay drowned beneath the waters. Now sea and earth could no longer be distinguished: all was sea, and a sea that had no shores.

Some tried to escape by climbing to the hilltops, others, sitting in the curved boats, plied the oars where lately they had been ploughing; some sailed over cornlands, over the submerged roofs of their homes, while some found fish in the topmost branches of the elms. At times it happened that they dropped anchor in green meadows, sometimes the curved keels grazed vineyards that lay beneath them. Where lately sinewy goats cropped the grass, now ugly seals disported themselves. The Nereids wondered to see groves and towns and houses under the water; dolphins took possession of the woods, and dashed against high branches, shaking the oak trees as they knocked against them. Wolves swam among the flocks, and the waves supported tawny lions, and tigers too. The lightning stroke of his strong tusk was of no use, then, to the wild boar, nor his swift legs to the stag—both alike were swept away. Wandering birds searched long for some land where they might rest, till their wings grew weary and they fell into the sea. The ocean, all restrains removed, overwhelmed the hills, and waves were washing the mountain peaks, a sight never seen before. The greater part of the human race was swallowed up by the waters: those whom the sea spared died from lack of food, overcome by long-continued famine.

There is a land, Phocis, which separates the fields of Boeotia from those of Oeta. It was a fertile spot while it was land, but now had become part of the sea, a broad stretch of waters, suddenly formed. In that region a high mountain, called Parnassus, raises twin summits to the stars, and its ridges pierce the clouds. When the waters had covered all the rest of the earth, the little boat which carried Deucalion and his wife ran aground here. Of all the men who ever lived, Deucalion was the best and the most upright, no woman ever showed more reverence for the gods than Pyrrha, his wife. Their first action was to offer prayers to the Corycian nymphs, to the deities of the mountain, and to Themis, the goddess who foretold the future from its oracular shrine.

Now Jupiter saw the earth all covered with standing waters. He perceived that one alone survived of so many thousand men, one only of so many thousand women, and he knew that both were guiltless, both true worshippers of god. So, with the help of the North wind he drove away the storm clouds and, scattering the veils of mist, displayed heaven to earth and earth to heaven. The sea was no longer angry, for the ruler of ocean soothed the waves, laying aside his trident. Then he called to the sea-god Triton, who rose from the deep, his shoulders covered with clustering shellfish. Neptune bade him blow on his echoing conch shell, and recall waves and rivers by his signal. He lifted his hollow trumpet, a coiling instrument which broadens out in circling spirals from its base. When he blows upon it in mid-ocean, its notes fill the furthest shores of east and west. So now, too, the god put it to his lips, which were all damp from his dripping beard, and blew it, sending forth the signal for retreat as he had been bidden. The sound was heard by all the waters that covered earth and sea, and all the waves which heard it were checked in their course. The sea had shores once more, the swollen rivers were contained within their own channels, the floods sank down, and hills were seen to emerge. Earth rose up, its lands advancing as the waves retreated, and after a long interval the woods displayed their treetops uncovered, the mud left behind still clinging to their leaves.

The world was restored: but when Deucalion saw its emptiness, the desolate lands all deeply silent, tears started to his eyes, and he said to Pyrrha: "My cousin, my wife, the only woman left alive, related to me first by birth and blood, then joined to me in marriage—now, Pyrrha, our very dangers unite us. We two are the sole inhabitants of all the lands which east and west behold. The sea has taken the rest. Indeed, even yet, I feel no certainty that we shall survive; even now the clouds strike terror to my heart. What would your feelings be now, my poor wife, had fate snatched you to safety, without saving me? How could you have endured your fears, had you been left all alone? Who would have comforted you in your grief? For believe me, if the sea had taken you with the rest, I should follow you, my dear one, and the sea would have me too. If only I could create the nations anew, by my father's skill! If only I could mould the earth and give it breath: now the human race depends upon us two. It is god's will: we have been left as samples of mankind." So he spoke, and they wept together.

Then they decided to pray to the god in heaven, and to seek help from the holy oracle. Without delay, they went side by side to the waters of Cephisus which, though not yet clear, were already flowing in their accustomed channel. When they had sprinkled their heads and garments with water drawn from the river they turned their steps to the shrine of the holy goddess. The gables of the temple were discoloured with foul moss, and its altars stood unlit.

At the temple steps they both fell forward, prone upon the ground, and timidly kissed the chill rock, saying: "If the gods may be touched and softened by the prayers of the righteous, if divine anger may be thus turned aside, tell us, O Themis, how we may repair the destruction that has overtaken our race. Most gentle goddess, assist us in our distress."

The goddess pitied them, and uttered this oracle. "Depart from my temple, veil your heads, loosen the girdles of your garments and throw behind you the bones of your great mother." For long they stood in speechless wonder at this reply. Pyrrha was the first to break the silence, by declaring that she would not obey the commands of the goddess. With trembling lips she prayed to be excused: for she was afraid to injure her mother's ghost by disturbing her bones. But meanwhile they considered again the words of the oracle, so puzzling and obscure, and pondered them deeply: till after a time the son of Prometheus soothed the fears of Epimetheus' daughter with these comforting words: "Oracles are righteous, and never advise guilty action; so, unless my intuition deceives me, our great mother is the earth, and by her bones I think the oracle means the stones in the body of the earth. It is those we are instructed to throw behind our backs." The Titan's daughter was impressed by her husband's surmise; but she did not trust her hopes, for neither of them had any confidence in heaven's counsel. Still, there could be no harm in putting the matter to the test.

They went down the hillside, veiled their heads, loosened their tunics, and threw the stones behind them, as they had been bidden. Who would believe what followed, did not ancient tradition bear witness to it? The stones began to lose their hardness and rigidity, and after a little, grew soft. Then, once softened, they acquired a definite shape. When they had grown in size, and developed a tenderer nature, a certain likeness to a human form could be seen, though it was still not clear: they were like marble images, begun but not yet properly chiselled out, or like unfinished statues. The damp earthy parts, containing some moisture, were adapted to make the body: that which was solid and inflexible became bone. What was lately a vein in the rock kept the same name, and in a brief space of time, thanks to the divine will of the gods, the stones thrown from male hands took on the appearance of men, while from those the woman threw, women were recreated. So it comes about that we are a hardy race, well accustomed to toil, giving evidence of the origin from which we sprang.

Other animals of different kinds were produced by the earth, of its own accord, when the long-lingering moisture was warmed through by the rays of the sun. Then the mud and soggy marshes swelled under the heat, and fertile seeds, nourished in the life-giving earth as in a mother's womb, grew and in the fullness of time acquired a definite shape. This is what happens when the Nile, the river with seven mouths, recedes from the flooded fields and returns its streams to their original bed. The new mud becomes burning hot under the sun's rays, and the farmers, as they turn over the sods of earth, come upon many animals. Among these creatures they see some just begun, but already on the point of coming alive, others unfinished, lacking their full complement of limbs; and often in one and the same body one part is alive, while another is still only raw earth. Indeed, when heat and moisture have reached the proper balance, they bring forth life, and all things are born from these two elements. Although fire and water are always opposites, none the less moist heat is the source of everything, and this discordant harmony is suited to creation.

So when the earth, all muddied by the recent flood, grew warm again, under the kindly radiance of the sun in heaven, she brought forth countless forms of life. In some cases she reproduced shapes which had been previously known, others were new and strange.

[Arachne]

When Minerva had listened to such stories, she expressed her approval of the Muses' song, and of their righteous indignation. Then she said to herself: "It is not enough to praise other people: what I want is to be praised myself, and not to have others scorn my divine powers with impunity." As she spoke, her thoughts turned to the fortunes of Arachne, a young woman of Maeonia, whose skill in spinning, so the goddess had heard, was earning no less admiration than that of Minerva herself. Arachne was not of high rank, or noble family, but her talent had made her famous. Her father was a native of Colophon, called Idmon, who earned his living by dying absorbent wool with Phocaean purple. Her mother was dead, but she also had been of humble origin, no better than her husband. Their daughter, however, although she had been born in a cottage and still lived in the small village of Hypaepae, had gained a reputation throughout all Lydia by reason of her skill. Often the nymphs used to leave the vine-clad slopes of their beloved Tmolus to admire her work, and the river nymphs came from the waters of Pactolus. They enjoyed seeing the cloths, not only when they were completed, but even while they were still being woven. There was such grace in Arachne's skilful movements, whether she was winding the coarse yarn into balls in the first stages of her task, or working the stuff with her fingers, drawing out the fleecy cloud of wool, with constant handling, into one long soft thread, or whether she was twirling the slender spindle with deft thumb, or embroidering the finished material.

It was easy to see that she had been taught by Pallas: but the girl herself denied this. Offended at the suggestion that she had had any teacher, no matter how distinguished, "Let Pallas come and compete with me!" she cried. "If I am defeated, she can do what she likes with me!" Pallas made herself up as an old woman, put false streaks of grey in the hair at her temples, and took a stick to support her tottering steps. Then she began to speak to Arachne, saying: "Not all the things that old age brings in its train are to be shunned: with advancing years, we gain experience. Pay heed, then, to my advice; seek recognition as the best of all mortal spinners, but admit the supremacy of the goddess, and humbly ask her pardon for your hot-headed words. She will forgive you, if you ask her." Arachne left the piece of weaving which she had begun. She eyed the old woman sullenly, and could scarcely keep herself from striking her. Anger showed plainly on her face, as she answered Pallas, whom, of course, she did not recognize. "You have lived too long," she said, "that is what is wrong with you. You are worn out with old age, and your mind is feeble too. If you have any daughters or daughters-in-law, let them listen to what you have to say. I can look after myself. Don't imagine that your warnings have had any effect on me; I am still of the same opinion. Why does Pallas not come in person? Why does she avoid my challenge?" "She has come!" cried the goddess and, throwing off the disguise of an old woman, she revealed that she was indeed Pallas.

The nymphs and women of Mygdonia reverently humbled themselves before the goddess. They were all terrified, except Arachne, and even she leaped to her feet, and a sudden flush swept over her unwilling cheeks, and receded again, just as the sky crimsons when Aurora first stirs, but in a little while shines white with the light of sunrise. She persisted in going on with her plan and, in her eagerness for a victory which she foolishly thought she could win, rushed upon her fate. Jove's daughter uttered no more warnings; she accepted the challenge, and postponed the competition no further. Without wasting any time, she and Arachne took their stance in different parts of the room, and each stretched the slender threads on her loom. Then they bound their frames to the crossbeams, separated the threads of the warp with the heddle and, with flying fingers wove the crossthreads in between, by means of the sharp-tipped shuttles. As these threads were drawn through the warp, a blow from the comb with its notched teeth beat them into place. With their garments tucked up beneath their breasts, out of the way, the goddess and the girl worked with all speed, their hands moving skilfully over the looms. In their eagerness, they were not conscious of the labour involved. Into the cloth they wove threads dyed purple in Tyrian coppers, shades of colour differing so slightly that they could scarcely be distinguished: so, after a shower, when the sunlit rainbow paints heaven's vault with its long arc, though a thousand different colours shine there, the transition from one to another is so gradual that the eye of the beholder cannot perceive it. Where they met, the colours look the same, yet their outer bands are completely different. Pliant gold thread, too, was interwoven, as old stories were pictured on the looms.

Pallas' tapestry showed the rock of Mars, on the acropolis of Cecrops' city, and the ancient contest that took place there, to determine what name the land should have. Twelve gods, in all their glorious majesty, were seated on lofty thrones, with Jupiter in their midst. Each of the gods was recognized by his own particular features: the figure of Jove was one of royal dignity, while Neptune was standing up, striking the rugged rocks with his long trident. From the cleft, the sea gushed out, and by this token he claimed the city. To herself, Pallas gave a shield and a sharp-tipped spear. On her head she wore her helmet, and her breast was protected by the aegis. Then she showed the earth putting forth a hoary olive tree, complete with berries, where she had struck the ground with her spear. The gods were gazing in awe at this miracle, and the figure of Victory completed the picture.

Then, to give her rival illustrations of the reward she might expect for her insane audacity, the goddess added four scenes, depicting contests, one in each corner, all brilliantly coloured, though shown in miniature. One corner held Haemon and Thracian Rhodope, now icy mountains but once human beings, who dared to give themselves the names of the greatest of the gods. A second corner showed the unhappy fate of the queen of the Pygmies. Juno, after defeating her in a contest, had ordained that she become a crane, and declare war on her own people. The goddess portrayed Antigone too, who once dared to compete with the consort of almighty Jupiter: royal Juno changed her into a bird. Neither the city of Troy nor her father, Laomedon, could save her then. She grew wings and, as a shining white stork, still applauds herself with clattering beak. The remaining corner showed Cinyras after his bereavement, embracing the temple steps which had once been his daughters' limbs, and weeping as he lay on the stone. Then Pallas embroidered the edges with olives, the symbol of peace. This was the end of her task: she finished her weaving with her own tree.

Arachne wove a picture of Europa, deceived by Jupiter when he presented himself in the shape of a bull. You would have thought that the bull was a live one, and that the waves were real waves. Europa herself was seen, looking back at the shore she had left behind, crying to her companions, and timidly drawing up her feet, shrinking from the touch of the surging waters. The tapestry showed Asterie too, held fast by the struggling eagle, and Leda reclining under the swan's wings. Then the girl added further pictures of Jupiter in disguise, showing how he turned himself into a satyr to bestow twins on fair Antiope, and assumed the likeness of Amphitryon when he embraced the lady of Tiryns: how he tricked Danae by changing into a shower of gold, deceived Asopus' daughter as a flame, Mnemosyne as a shepherd, and Demeter's daughter, Proserpine, as a spotted snake.

She showed Neptune, too, changed into a fierce bull for his affair with Aeolus' daughter. Disguised as the river god Enipeus, he was making love to Aloeus' wife, who later bore him twin sons, and he was deceiving Bisaltis as a ram. The golden-haired mother of the corn crops, gentlest of goddesses, knew him in the shape of a horse, Melantho as a dolphin, and to the snaky-haired princess, who was the mother of the winged steed, he appeared as a bird. All these incidents were correctly depicted, people and places had their authentic features.

Phoebus was there, in peasant garb, and other scenes showed how he dressed himself, at one time in a hawk's plumage, at another in a lion's skin, and how he disguised himself as a shepherd to deceive Macareus' daughter, Isse. There was also a picture of Bacchus, tricking Erigone with the semblance of a bunch of grapes, and one of Saturn, in the shape of a horse, creating the centaur Chiron, half horse, half man. The outer edge of the cloth, bordered by a fine hem, was gay with flowers, intertwined with clustering ivy.

Neither Pallas nor even Jealousy personified could find any flaw in the work. The golden-haired goddess, wild with indignation at her rival's success, tore to pieces the tapestry which displayed the crimes committed by the gods. Then, with the shuttle of Cytorian boxwood which she held in her hand, three times, four times, she struck Idmon's daughter on the forehead. Arachne found her plight beyond endurance: with a fine show of spirit, she fastened a noose round her neck, to hang herself. But Pallas pitied her, as she hung there; lifting her up, the goddess said: "You may go on living, you wicked girl, but you must be suspended in the air like this, all the time. Do not hope for any respite in the future—this same condition is imposed on your race, to your remote descendants." Then, as she departed, she sprinkled Arachne with the juice of Hecate's herb. Immediately, at the touch of this baneful potion, the girl's hair dropped out, her nostrils and her ears went too, and her head shrank almost to nothing. Her whole body, likewise, became tiny. Her slender fingers were fastened to her sides, to serve as legs, and all the rest of her was belly; from that belly, she yet spins her thread, and as a spider is busy with her web as of old.

Interior View. Hagia Sophia, Istanbul, Turkey. Giraudon/Art Resource, NY.

The World Beyond Rome

The Church of *Hagia Sophia* ("Holy Wisdom") is a great work of architecture and also a perfect emblem for "the world beyond Rome." It is located on a promontory in Istanbul, the old city of Byzantium that the Emperor Constantine made the capital—Constantinople—of the Roman Empire early in the fourth century. Hagia Sophia was built under the direction of the Emperor Justinian; his architects, Anthermius of Tralles and Isidore of Miletus, saw to its completion in 537 after less than six years of construction. Its complex plan makes extravagant use of the triumphs of Roman engineering, the arch and the dome. It is, furthermore, a combination of the square Greek Cross common in eastern basilicas, with the longer Roman basilica common in the western church: the half-domes on opposite ends give the illusion of great length, while a triple aisle along the other two sides make for a square outline on the ground. The church also brilliantly uses the innovative pendentive, the curved triangle that joins the large supporting arches with the base of the dome. The pendentives and other open surfaces were covered with the mosaics (now lost or damaged) that glorified Byzantine churches. But Hagia Sophia shows signs of the other sea change in the post-Roman world. In 1453 the Ottoman (Turkish) emperor Mehmed II defeated Constantinople. When he entered the city, he is said to have marched straight to Hagia Sophia, the city's chief emblem of Byzantine Christianity, and converted it to an Islamic mosque. In the photograph at left the large medallions with Arabic calligraphy can be seen. On the walls the representational art of Byzantine Christianity has been replaced by the abstract arabesque of Islam.

Tacitus (c.55–c.117)

The great historian of the early Roman Empire, Tacitus, gives us a strong sense of the reach of the Roman Empire, both in territory and into peoples' lives. Tacitus was a senator who turned to the writing of history during the reigns of the "good emperors" in the second century, when it was again possible to write freely and critically of the empire. Writing about the great period of colonial expansion, Tacitus studied closely the enemies of Rome. Because he was intent on exposing the corruption of emperors like Nero, he was willing to look at the cultures and practices of the Jews or of the German tribes and praise their integrity where he found it, especially in contrast to Roman failures.

The groups that Tacitus described—the Jews, the Christians, the Germans—developed in important ways during the period of the empire and after. Other readings in this section show some of those developments. The Germans, who eventually would be the conquerors of the Romans, always threatened the outposts of the empire. Christianity rode with travelers, Roman soldiers, and other converts to all parts of the empire, becoming at the same time a convenient scapegoat for emperors like Nero. Yet when Rome collapsed, a skeleton of Roman Christianity was left standing. Judaism responded to Roman attempts to destroy its heart in Jerusalem by strengthening the preservation of its learning and tradition through rabbis at the periphery.

The Annals [The Burning of Rome]

38. There followed a dreadful disaster; whether fortuitously, or by the wicked contrivance of the prince, is not determined, for both are asserted by historians: but of all the calamities which ever befell this city from the rage of fire, this was the most terrible and severe. It broke out in that part of the Circus which is contiguous to mounts Palatine and Cœlius; where, by reason of shops in which were kept such goods as minister aliment to fire, the moment it commenced it acquired strength, and being accelerated by the wind, it spread at once through the whole extent of the Circus: for neither were the houses secured by enclosures, nor the temples environed with walls, nor was there any other obstacle to intercept its progress; but the flame, spreading every way impetuously, invaded first the lower regions of the city, then mounted to the higher; then again ravaging the lower, it baffled every effort to extinguish it, by the rapidity of its destructive course, and from the liability of the city to conflagration, in consequence of the narrow and intricate alleys, and the irregularity of the streets in ancient Rome. Add to this, the wailings of terrified women, the infirm condition of the aged, and the helplessness of childhood: such as strove to provide for themselves and those who laboured to assist others; these dragging the feeble, those waiting for them; some hurrying, others linger-

The versions used here are from *The Oxford Translation, Revised* (London: Bell, 1903), except for *Germania*, which is translated by Alfred John Church and William Jackson Brodribb, reprinted in Random House's Modern Library in 1942.

ing; altogether created a scene of universal confusion and embarrassment: and while they looked back upon the danger in their rear, they often found themselves beset before, and on their sides: or if they had escaped into the quarters adjoining, these too were already seized by the devouring flames; even the parts which they believed remote and exempt, were found to be in the same distress. At last, not knowing what to shun, or where to seek sanctuary, they crowded the streets, and lay along in the open fields. Some, from the loss of their whole substance, even the means of their daily sustenance, others, from affection for their relations, whom they had not been able to snatch from the flames, suffered themselves to perish in them, though they had opportunity to escape. Neither dared any man offer to check the fire: so repeated were the menaces of many who forbade to extinguish it; and because others openly threw firebrands, with loud declarations "that they had one who authorized them;" whether they did it that they might plunder with the less restraint, or in consequence of orders given.

39. Nero, who was at that juncture sojourning at Antium, did not return to the city till the fire approached that quarter of his house which connected the palace with the gardens of Mæcenas; nor could it, however, be prevented from devouring the house and palace, and everything around. But for the relief of the people, thus destitute, and driven from their dwellings, he opened the field of Mars and the monumental edifices erected by Agrippa, and even his own gardens. He likewise reared temporary houses for the reception of the forlorn multitude: and from Ostia and the neighbouring cities, were brought, up the river, household necessaries; and the price of grain was reduced to three sesterces the measure. All which proceedings, though of a popular character, were thrown away, because a rumour had become universally current, "that at the very time the city was in flames, Nero, going on the stage of his private theatre, sang 'The Destruction of Troy,' assimilating the present disaster to that catastrophe of ancient times."

40. At length, on the sixth day, the conflagration was stayed at the foot of Esquiliæ, by pulling down an immense quantity of buildings, so that an open space, and, as it were, void air, might check the raging element by breaking the continuity. But ere the consternation had subsided, the fire broke out afresh, with no little violence, but in regions more spacious, and therefore with less destruction of human life: but more extensive havoc was made of the temples, and the porticoes dedicated to amusement. This conflagration, too, was the subject of more censorious remark, as it arose in the Æmilian possessions of Tigellinus: and Nero seemed to aim at the glory of building a new city, and calling it by his own name: for, of the fourteen sections into which Rome is divided, four were still standing entire, three were levelled with the ground, and in the seven others there remained only here and there a few remnants of houses, shattered and half consumed.

41. It were no very easy task to recount the number of tenements and temples which were lost: but the following, most venerable for antiquity and sanctity, were consumed: that dedicated by Servius Tullius to the Moon; the temple and great altar consecrated by Evander the Arcadian to Hercules while present; the chapel vowed by Romulus to Jupiter Stator; the palace of Numa, with the temple of Vesta, and in it the tutelar gods of Rome. Moreover, the treasures accumulated by so many victories, the beautiful productions of Greek artists, ancient writings of authors celebrated for genius, and till then preserved entire, were consumed: and though great was the beauty of the city, in its renovated form, the older inhabitants remembered many decorations of the ancient which could not be replaced in the modern city. There were some who remarked that the commencement of the fire showed itself on

the fourteenth before the calends of July, the day on which the Senones set fire to the captured city. Others carried their investigation so far as to determine that an equal number of years, months, and days intervened between the two fires.

42. To proceed: Nero appropriated to his own purposes the ruins of his country, and founded upon them a palace; in which the old-fashioned, and, in those luxurious times, common ornaments of gold and precious stones, were not so much the objects of attraction as lands and lakes; in one part, woods like vast deserts; in another part, open spaces and expansive prospects. The projectors and superintendents of this plan were Severus and Celer, men of such ingenuity and daring enterprise as to attempt to conquer by art the obstacles of nature, and fool away the treasures of the prince: they had even undertaken to sink a navigable canal from the lake Avernus to the mouth of the Tiber, over an arid shore, or through opposing mountains: nor indeed does there occur anything of a humid nature for supplying water, except the Pomptine marshes; the rest is either craggy rock or a parched soil: and had it even been possible to break through these obstructions, the toil had been intolerable, and disproportioned to the object. Nero, however, who longed to achieve things that exceeded credibility, exerted all his might to perforate the mountains adjoining to Avernus: and to this day there remain traces of his abortive project.

43. But the rest of the old site not occupied by his palace was laid out, not as after the Gallic fire, without discrimination and regularity, but with the lines of streets measured out, broad spaces left for transit, the height of the buildings limited, open areas left, and porticoes added to protect the front of the clustered dwellings: these porticoes Nero engaged to rear at his own expense, and then to deliver to each proprietor the areas about them cleared. He moreover proposed rewards proportioned to every man's rank and private substance, and fixed a day within which, if their houses, single or clustered, were finished, they should receive them: he appointed the marshes of Ostia for a receptacle of the rubbish, and that the vessels which had conveyed the grain up the Tiber should return laden with rubbish; that the buildings themselves should be raised to a certain portion of their height without beams, and arched with stone from the quarries of Gabii or Alba, that stone being proof against fire: that over the water springs, which had been improperly intercepted by private individuals, overseers should be placed, to provide for their flowing in greater abundance, and in a greater number of places, for the supply of the public: that every housekeeper should have in his yard means for extinguishing fire; neither should there be party-walls, but every house should be enclosed by its own walls. These regulations, which were favourably received, in consideration of their utility, were also a source of beauty to the new city: yet some there were who believed that the ancient form was more conducive to health, as from the narrowness of the streets and the height of the buildings the rays of the sun were more excluded; whereas now, the spacious breadth of the streets, without any shade to protect it, was more intensely heated in warm weather.

44. Such were the provisions made by human counsels. The gods were next addressed with expiations; and recourse had to the Sibyl's books. By admonition from them to Vulcan, Ceres, and Proserpina, supplicatory sacrifices were made, and Juno propitiated by the matrons, first in the Capitol, then upon the nearest shore, where, by water drawn from the sea, the temple and image of the goddess were besprinkled; and the ceremony of placing the goddess in her sacred chair, and her vigil, were celebrated by ladies who had husbands. But not all the relief that could come from man, not all the bounties that the prince could bestow, nor all the atonements which could be presented to the gods, availed to relieve Nero of the infamy

of being believed to have ordered the conflagration. Hence, to suppress the rumour, he false-ly charged with the guilt, and punished with the most exquisite tortures, the persons com-monly called Christians, who were hated for their enormities. Christus, the founder of that name, was put to death as a criminal by Pontius Pilate, procurator of Judea, in the reign of Tiberius: but the pernicious superstition, repressed for a time, broke out again, not only through Judea, where the mischief originated, but through the city of Rome also, whither all things horrible and disgraceful flow, from all quarters, as to a common receptacle, and where they are encouraged. Accordingly, first those were seized who confessed they were Christians: next, on their information, a vast multitude were convicted, not so much on the charge of burning the city, as of hating the human race. And in their deaths they were also made the subjects of sport, for they were covered with the hides of wild beasts, and worried to death by dogs, or nailed to crosses, or set fire to, and when day declined, burnt to serve for nocturnal lights. Nero offered his own gardens for that spectacle, and exhibited a Circensian game, indiscriminately mingling with the common people in the habit of a charioteer, or else stand-ing in his chariot. Whence a feeling of compassion arose towards the sufferers, though guilty and deserving to be made examples of by capital punishment, because they seemed not to be cut off for the public good, but victims to the ferocity of one man.

The History [The Jews]

1. In the beginning of the same year, Titus, who was appointed by his father to complete the subjugation of Judaea, and who, when both were no higher than subjects, had gained a repu-tation for military talents, now exercised a more extended influence, and shone with aug-mented lustre; the provinces and armies emulating each other in their zeal and attachment to him. Titus, on his part, that he might be thought deserving of still higher distinctions, appeared in all the splendour of external embellishments, and showed himself a prompt and resolute soldier, challenging respect by courtesy and affability; mixing with the common sol-diers when engaged in the works and on their march, without impairing the dignity of the general. He succeeded to the command of three legions in Judaea, the fifth, the tenth, and the fifteenth; who had long served under Vespasian. To these he added the twelfth, from Syria, and the third and twenty-second, withdrawn from Alexandria. He was attended, besides, by twenty cohorts of the allies, and eight squadrons of horse, with the two kings Agrippa and Sohemus, and auxiliaries from Antiochus. He had also a band of Arabs, formidable in them-selves, and harbouring towards the Jews the bitter animosity usually subsisting between neighbouring nations. Many persons had come from Rome and Italy, each impelled by the hopes he had of preoccupying the favour of a prince who had not yet chosen his friends. With this force Titus, advancing into the enemy's country in order of battle, by his scouts diligent-ly exploring the motions of the enemy, and prepared for action, formed a camp a short dis-tance from Jerusalem.

2. Being now about to relate the catastrophe of that celebrated city, it seems fitting that I should unfold the particulars of its origin. The Jews, we are told, escaping from the island of Crete, at the time when Saturn was driven from his throne by the violence of Jupiter, settled in the extreme parts of Libya. Their name is adduced as a proof. Ida, it is alleged, is a well-known mountain in Crete: the neighbouring Idaeans, by an addition to the name to adapt it to the language of barbarians, are ordinarily called Judaeans. Some say that the population, overflowing throughout Egypt, in the reign of Isis, was relieved by emigration into the neigh-

bouring countries, under the conduct of Hierosolymus and Juda. Many state that they are the progeny of the Aethiopians, who were impelled by fear and detestation to change their abode in the reign of king Cepheus. There are those who report that they are a heterogeneous band from Assyria, a people who, being destitute of a country, made themselves masters of a portion of Egypt, and subsequently settled in cities of their own in the Hebrew territories, and the parts bordering on Syria. Others, ascribing to the Jews an illustrious origin, say that the Solymi, a nation celebrated in the poetry of Homer, called the city which they built Hierosolyma from their own name.

3. Very many authors agree in recording that a pestilential disease, which disfigured the body in a loathsome manner, spreading over Egypt, Bocchoris, at that time king, repairing to the oracle of Jupiter Hammon, in quest of a remedy, was directed to purify his kingdom, and exterminate that race of men as being detested by the gods: that a mass of people thus searched out and collected together were in a wild and barren desert abandoned to their misery, when, all the rest being bathed in tears and torpid with despair, Moses, one of the exiles, admonished them not to look for any aid from gods or men, being deserted of both, but to trust themselves to him as a heaven-commissioned guide, by whose aid already they had warded off the miseries that beset them. They assented, and commenced a venturous journey, not knowing whither they went. But nothing distressed them so much as want of water; and now they lay stretched through all the plains, ready to expire, when a herd of wild asses, returning from pasture, went up a rock shaded with a grove. Moses followed them, and forming his conjecture by the herbage that grew upon the ground, opened copious springs of water. This was a relief; and pursuing their journey for six days without intermission, on the seventh, having expelled the natives, they took possession of a country where they built their city, and dedicated their temple.

4. In order to bind the people to him for the time to come, Moses prescribed to them a new form of worship, and opposed to those of all the world beside. Whatever is held sacred by the Romans, with the Jews is profane: and what in other nations is unlawful and impure, with them is permitted. The figure of the animal through whose guidance they slaked their thirst, and were enabled to terminate their wanderings, is consecrated in the sanctuary in their temple; while in contempt of Jupiter Hammon, they sacrifice a ram. The ox, worshipped in Egypt for the god Apis, is slain as a victim by the Jews. They abstain from the flesh of swine, from the recollection of the loathsome affliction which they had formerly suffered from leprosy, to which that animal is subject. The famine, with which they were for a long time distressed, is still commemorated by frequent fastings; and the Jewish bread, made without leaven, is a standing evidence of their seizure of corn. They say that they instituted a rest on the seventh day because that day brought them rest from their toils; but afterwards, charmed with the pleasures of idleness, the seventh year also was devoted to sloth. Others allege that this is an honour rendered to Saturn, either because their religious institutes were handed down by the Idaeans, who, we are informed, were expelled from their country with Saturn, and were the founders of the nation; or else because, of the seven stars by which men are governed, the star of Saturn moves in the highest orbit, and exercises the greatest influence; and most of the heavenly bodies complete their effects and course by the number seven.

5. These rites and ceremonies, howsoever introduced, have the support of antiquity. Their other institutions, which have been extensively adopted, are tainted with execrable knavery; for the scum and refuse of other nations, renouncing the religion of their country, were in the habit of bringing gifts and offerings to Jerusalem,—hence the wealth and grandeur of the

state; and also because faith is inviolably observed, and compassion is cheerfully shown towards each other, while the bitterest animosity is harboured against all others. They eat and lodge with one another only; and though a people of unbridled lust, they admit no intercourse with women from other nations. Among themselves no restraints are imposed. That they may be known by a distinctive mark, they have established the practice of circumcision. All who embrace their faith submit to the same operation. The first thing instilled into their proselytes is to despise the gods, to abjure their country, to set at nought parents, children, brothers. They show concern, however, for the increase of their population, for it is forbidden to put any of their brethren to death; and the souls of such as die in battle, or by the hand of the executioner, are thought to be immortal. Hence their desire of procreation, and contempt of death. The bodies of the deceased they choose rather to bury than burn, following in this the Egyptian custom; with whom they also agree in their attention to the dead, and their persuasion as to the regions below, but are opposed to them in their notions about celestial things. The Egyptians worship various animals and images, the work of men's hands; the Jews acknowledge one God only, and conceive of him by the mind alone, condemning, as impious, all who, with perishable materials, wrought into the human shape, form representations of the Deity. That Being, they say, is above all, and everlasting, neither susceptible of likeness nor subject to decay. In consequence they allow no resemblance of him in their city, much less in their temples. In this way they do not flatter their kings, nor show their respect for the Caesars. But because their priests performed in concert with the pipe and timbrels, were crowned with ivy, and a golden vine was found in the temple, some have supposed that Bacchus, the conqueror of the East, was the object of their adoration; but the Jewish institutions have no conformity whatever to the rites of Bacchus. For Bacchus has ordained festive and jocund rites, while the usages of the Jews are dull and repulsive. . . .

9. Pompey was the first Roman that subdued the Jews, and by right of conquest entered their temple. Thenceforward it became generally known that the habitation was empty, and the sanctuary unoccupied, no representation of the Deity being found within it. The walls of the city were levelled to the ground; the Temple remained. In the civil wars that afterwards shook the empire, when the eastern provinces fell to the lot of Mark Antony, Pacorus, the Parthian king, made himself master of Judaea; but was, in a short time after, put to death by Ventidius, and his forces retired beyond the Euphrates. Caius Sosius once more reduced the Jews to obedience. Herod was placed on the throne by Mark Antony, and Augustus enlarged his privileges. On the death of Herod, a man of the name of Simon, without waiting for the authority of the emperor, seized the sovereignty. He, however, was punished for his ambition by Quinctilius Varus, the governor of Syria; and the nation, reduced to submission, was divided in three portions between the sons of Herod. During the reign of Tiberius things remained in a state of tranquillity. Afterwards, being ordered by Caligula to place his statue in the Temple, the Jews, rather than submit, had recourse to arms. This commotion the death of Caligula extinguished. Claudius, the Jewish kings being either dead, or the dominion reduced to narrow limits, committed the province of Judaea to Roman knights, or his freedmen. One of these, Antonius Felix, exercised the prerogatives of a king with the spirit of a slave, rioting in cruelty and licentiousness. He married Drusilla, the granddaughter of Antony and Cleopatra, that he might be grandson-in-law of Mark Antony, who was the grandfather of Claudius.

10. The patience, however, of the Jews held out to the time of Cassius Florus, the procurator. Under him a war broke out. Cestius Gallus, the governor of Syria, endeavoured to crush the revolt. He fought some obstinate battles, most of them unsuccessfully. After his death,

which happened either by destiny or from disappointment and vexation, Vespasian, who was sent by Nero, succeeded to the command. By his character, the good fortune that attended his arms, and with the advantage of excellent officers, in two summer campaigns he overran the whole country, and made himself master of all the cities except Jerusalem. The following year, which was devoted to civil war, passed in tranquillity so far as concerned the Jews. The peace of Italy restored, the care of foreign affairs returned. It inflamed his resentment that the Jews were the only nation that had not submitted. At the same time it was deemed politic for Titus to remain at the head of the armies, with a view to any events or casualties that might arise under the new reign. Accordingly the prince, as already mentioned, encamped under the walls of Jerusalem, and displayed his legions in the face of the enemy.

11. The Jews formed in order of battle under the very walls, determined, if successful, to push forward; and, if obliged to give ground, secure of a retreat. The cavalry, with the light-armed cohorts, sent against them, fought with doubtful success. Soon the enemy gave way, and on the following days engaged in frequent skirmishes before the gates, till at length, after a series of losses, they were forced to retire within the walls. The Romans resolved now to carry the place by storm. To linger before it till famine compelled a surrender, appeared indeed unworthy of them, and the soldiers demanded the post of danger, some from courage, many from hardihood and the hope of gaining rewards. Rome, her splendours and her pleasures, kept flitting before the eyes of Titus himself; and if Jerusalem did not fall at once, he looked upon it as obstructing his enjoyments. But Jerusalem, standing upon an eminence, naturally difficult of approach, was rendered still more impregnable by redoubts and bulwarks by which even places on a level plain would have been competently fortified. Two hills that rose to a prodigious height were enclosed by walls constructed so as in some places to project in angles, in others to curve inwards. In consequence the flanks of the besiegers were exposed to the enemy's weapons. The extremities of the rock were abrupt and craggy; and the towers were built, upon the mountain, sixty feet high; in the low ground, a hundred and twenty feet. These works presented a spectacle altogether astonishing. To the distant eye they seemed to be an equal elevation. Within the city there were other fortifications enclosing the palace of the kings, and the tower of Antonia, with its conspicuous pinnacles, so called by Herod, in honour of Mark Antony.

12. The Temple itself was in the nature of a citadel, enclosed in walls of its own, and more elaborate and massy than the rest. The very porticoes that surrounded it were a capital defence. A perennial spring supplied the place with water. Subterraneous caverns were scooped out in the mountains, and there were basins and tanks as reservoirs of rain-water. It was foreseen by the founders of the city, that the manners and institutions of the nation, so repugnant to the rest of mankind, would be productive of frequent wars; hence every kind of provision against a siege, howsoever protracted; and exposed as they had been to the successful assault of Pompey, their fears and experience had taught them many expedients. On the other hand, having purchased the privilege of raising fortifications through the venality of the Claudian times, they constructed such walls in a period of peace as showed they had an eye to war; while their numbers were augmented by a conflux of people from every quarter, and from the overthrow of other cities; for all the most indomitable spirits took refuge with them and by consequence they lived in a state of greater dissension. They had three armies, and as many generals. The outward walls, which were of the widest extent, were defended by Simon: John, otherwise called Bargioras, guarded the middle precinct; and Eleazar the Temple. The two former were strong in the number of men; the latter in situation.

But battles, plots, and burnings occurred among themselves, and a large quantity of grain was consumed by fire. After a short time, John, sending a band of assassins under colour of performing a sacrifice, to cut off Eleazar and his party, gained possession of the Temple. From that time the citizens separated into two factions; and in this state they continued till, the Romans approaching, an enemy without produced unanimity within.

13. Prodigies had occurred which that race, enslaved to superstition, but opposed to religion, held it unlawful, either by vows or victims, to expiate. Embattled armies were seen rushing to the encounter, with burnished arms, and the whole Temple appeared to blaze with fire that flashed from the clouds. Suddenly the portals of the sanctuary were flung wide open, and a voice, in more than mortal accents, was heard to announce that the gods were going forth; at the same time, a prodigious bustle, as of persons taking their departure: occurrences which few interpreted as indicative of impending woe: the majority were deeply impressed with a persuasion that it was contained in the ancient writings of the priests, that it would come to pass at that very time, that the East would renew its strength, and they that should go forth from Judaea should be rulers of the world. Mysterious words, which foreshowed Vespasian and Titus: but the people, according to the usual course of human fondness, interpreting this consummation of destiny as referring to themselves, were not induced to abandon their error even by affliction. We learn that the number of the besieged of every age, male and female, was six hundred thousand; all that were capable bore arms, and more than could be expected out of that number had the fortitude to do so. The devotion of the women was equal to that of the men; and if they must needs move their seat, and quit the habitation of their fathers, they dreaded to live more than to die. Such was the city, such the nation, against which Titus Caesar determined to act by means of mounds and mantelets, since the nature of the locality was adverse to assault and sudden attacks. The legions had each their several duties assigned them, and there was a cessation of fighting until all the engines and appliances for reducing cities, invented by ancient or modern genius, were prepared. . . .

Germania [The Germans]

4. For my own part, I agree with those who think that the tribes of Germany are free from all taint of inter-marriages with foreign nations, and that they appear as a distinct, unmixed race, like none but themselves. Hence, too, the same physical peculiarities throughout so vast a population. All have fierce blue eyes, red hair, huge frames, fit only for a sudden exertion. They are less able to bear laborious work. Heat and thirst they cannot in the least endure; to cold and hunger their climate and their soil inure them.

7. They choose their kings by birth, their generals for merit. These kings have not unlimited or arbitrary power, and the generals do more by example than by authority. If they are energetic, if they are conspicuous, if they fight in the front, they lead because they are admired. But to reprimand, to imprison, even to flog, is permitted to the priests alone, and that not as a punishment, or at the general's bidding, but, as it were, by the mandate of the god whom they believe to inspire the warrior. They also carry with them into battle certain figures and images taken from their sacred groves. And what most stimulates their courage is, that their squadrons or battalions, instead of being formed by chance or by a fortuitous gathering, are composed of families and clans. Close by them, too, are those dearest to them, so that they hear the shrieks of women, the cries of infants. They are to every man the most sacred witnesses of his bravery—they are his most generous applauders. The soldier brings

his wounds to mother and wife, who shrink not from counting or even demanding them and who administer both food and encouragement to the combatants.

8. Tradition says that armies already wavering and giving way have been rallied by women who, with earnest entreaties and bosoms laid bare, have vividly represented the horrors of captivity, which the Germans fear with such extreme dread on behalf of their women, that the strongest tie by which a state can be bound is the being required to give, among the number of hostages, maidens of noble birth. They even believe that the sex has a certain sanctity and prescience, and they do not despise their counsels, or make light of their answers. In Vespasian's days we saw Veleda, long regarded by many as a divinity. In former times, too, they venerated Aurinia, and many other women, but not with servile flatteries, or with sham deification.

11. About minor matters the chiefs deliberate, about the more important the whole tribe. Yet even when the final decision rests with the people, the affair is always thoroughly discussed by the chiefs. They assemble, except in the case of a sudden emergency, on certain fixed days, either at new or at full moon; for this they consider the most auspicious season for the transaction of business. Instead of reckoning by days as we do, they reckon by nights, and in this manner fix both their ordinary and their legal appointments. Night they regard as bringing on day. Their freedom has this disadvantage, that they do not meet simultaneously or as they are bidden, but two or three days are wasted in the delays of assembling. When the multitude think proper, they sit down armed. Silence is proclaimed by the priests, who have on these occasions the right of keeping order. Then the king or the chief, according to age, birth, distinction in war, or eloquence, is heard, more because he has influence to persuade than because he has power to command. If his sentiments displease them, they reject them with murmurs; if they are satisfied, they brandish their spears. The most complimentary form of assent is to express approbation with their weapons.

12. In their councils an accusation may be preferred or a capital crime prosecuted. Penalties are distinguished according to the offence. Traitors and deserters are hanged on trees; the coward, the unwarlike, the man stained with abominable vices, is plunged into the mire of the morass, with a hurdle put over him. This distinction in punishment means that crime, they think, ought, in being punished, to be exposed, while infamy ought to be buried out of sight. Lighter offences, too, have penalties proportioned to them; he who is convicted, is fined in a certain number of horses or of cattle. Half of the fine is paid to the king or to the state, half to the person whose wrongs are avenged and to his relatives. In these same councils they also elect the chief magistrates, who administer law in the cantons and the towns. Each of these has a hundred associates chosen from the people, who support him with their advice and influence.

13. They transact no public or private business without being armed. It is not, however, usual for anyone to wear arms till the state has recognised his power to use them. Then in the presence of the council one of the chiefs, or the young man's father, or some kinsman, equips him with a shield and a spear. These arms are what the "toga" is with us, the first honour with which youth is invested. Up to this time he is regarded as a member of a household, afterwards as a member of the commonwealth. Very noble birth or great services rendered by the father secure for lads the rank of a chief; such lads attach themselves to men of mature strength and of long approved valour. It is no shame to be seen among a chief's followers. Even in his escort there are gradations of rank, dependent on the choice of the man to whom

they are attached. These followers vie keenly with each other as to who shall rank first with his chief, the chiefs as to who shall have the most numerous and the bravest followers. It is an honour as well as a source of strength to be thus always surrounded by a large body of picked youths; it is an ornament in peace and a defence in war. And not only in his own tribe but also in the neighbouring states it is the renown and glory of a chief to be distinguished for the number and valour of his followers, for such a man is courted by embassies, is honoured with presents, and the very prestige of his name often settles a war.

14. When they go into battle, it is a disgrace for the chief to be surpassed in valour, a disgrace for his followers not to equal the valour of the chief. And it is an infamy and a reproach for life to have survived the chief, and returned from the field. To defend, to protect him, to ascribe one's own brave deeds to his renown, is the height of loyalty. The chief fights for victory; his vassals fight for their chief. If their native state sinks into the sloth of prolonged peace and repose, many of its noble youths voluntarily seek those tribes which are waging some war, both because inaction is odious to their race, and because they win renown more readily in the midst of peril, and cannot maintain a numerous following except by violence and war. Indeed, men look to the liberality of their chief for their war-horse and their bloodstained and victorious lance. Feasts and entertainments, which, though inelegant, are plentifully furnished, are their only pay. The means of this bounty come from war and rapine. Nor are they as easily persuaded to plough the earth and to wait for the year's produce as to challenge an enemy and earn the honour of wounds. Nay, they actually think it tame and stupid to acquire by the sweat of toil what they might win by their blood.

15. Whenever they are not fighting, they pass much of their time in the chase, and still more in idleness, giving themselves up to sleep and to feasting, the bravest and the most warlike doing nothing, and surrendering the management of the household, of the home, and of the land, to the women, the old men, and all the weakest members of the family. They themselves lie buried in sloth, a strange combination in their nature that the same men should be so fond of idleness, so averse to peace. It is the custom of the states to bestow by voluntary and individual contribution on the chiefs a present of cattle or of grain, which, while accepted as a compliment, supplies their wants. They are particularly delighted by gifts from neighboring tribes, which are sent not only by individuals but also by the state, such as choice steeds, heavy armour, trappings, and neckchains. We have now taught them to accept money also.

18. Their marriage code, however, is strict, and indeed no part of their manners is more praiseworthy. Almost alone among barbarians they are content with one wife, except a very few among them, and these not from sensuality, but because their noble birth procures for them many offers of alliance. The wife does not bring a dower to the husband, but the husband to the wife. The parents and relatives are present, and pass judgment on the marriage-gifts, gifts not meant to suit a woman's taste, nor such as a bride would deck herself with, but oxen, a caparisoned steed, a shield, a lance, and a sword. With these presents the wife is espoused, and she herself in her turn brings her husband a gift of arms. This they count their strongest bond of union, these their sacred mysteries, these their gods of marriage. Lest the woman should think herself to stand apart from aspirations after noble deeds and from the perils of war, she is reminded by the ceremony which inaugurates marriage that she is her husband's partner in toil and danger, destined to suffer and to dare with him alike both in peace and in war. The yoked oxen, the harnessed steed, the gift of arms, proclaim this fact. She

must live and die with the feeling that she is receiving what she must hand down to her children neither tarnished nor depreciated, what future daughters-in-law may receive, and may be so passed on to her grand-children.

19. Thus with their virtue protected they live uncorrupted by the allurements of public shows or the stimulant of feastings. Clandestine correspondence is equally unknown to men and women. Very rare for so numerous a population is adultery, the punishment for which is prompt, and in the husband's power. Having cut off the hair of the adulteress and stripped her naked, he expels her from the house in the presence of her kinsfolk, and then flogs her through the whole village. The loss of chastity meets with no indulgence; neither beauty, youth, nor wealth will procure the culprit a husband. No one in Germany laughs at vice, nor do they call it the fashion to corrupt and to be corrupted. Still better is the condition of those states in which only maidens are given in marriage, and where the hopes and expectations of a bride are then finally terminated. They receive one husband, as having one body and one life, that they may have no thoughts beyond, no further-reaching desires, that they may love not so much the husband as the married state. To limit the number of their children or to destroy any of their subsequent offspring is accounted infamous, and good habits are here more effectual than good laws elsewhere.

20. In every household the children, naked and filthy, grow up with those stout frames and limbs which we so much admire. Every mother suckles her own offspring, and never entrusts it to servants and nurses. The master is not distinguished from the slave by being brought up with greater delicacy. Both live amid the same flocks and lie on the same ground till the freeborn are distinguished by age and recognised by merit. The young men marry late, and their vigour is thus unimpaired. Nor are the maidens hurried into marriage: the same age and a similar stature is required; well-matched and vigorous they wed, and the offspring reproduce the strength of the parents. Sister's sons are held in as much esteem by their uncles as by their fathers; indeed, some regard the relation as even more sacred and binding, and prefer it in receiving hostages, thinking thus to secure a stronger hold on the affections and a wider bond for the family. But every man's own children are his heirs and successors, and there are no wills. Should there be no issue, the next in succession to the property are his brothers and his uncles on either side. The more relatives he has, the more numerous his connections, the more honoured is his old age; nor are there any advantages in childlessness.

21. It is a duty among them to adopt the feuds as well as the friendships of a father or a kinsman. These feuds are not implacable; even homicide is expiated by the payment of a certain number of cattle and of sheep, and the satisfaction is accepted by the entire family, greatly to the advantage of the state, since feuds are dangerous in proportion to a people's freedom.

No nation indulges more profusely in entertainments and hospitality. To exclude any human being from their roof is thought impious; every German, according to his means, receives his guest with a well-furnished table. When his supplies are exhausted, he who was but now the host becomes the guide and companion to further hospitality, and without invitation they go to the next house. It matters not; they are entertained with like cordiality. No one distinguishes between an acquaintance and a stranger, as regards the rights of hospitality. It is usual to give the departing guest whatever he may ask for, and a present in return is asked with as little hesitation.

27. In their funerals there is no pomp; they simply observe the custom of burning the bodies of illustrious men with certain kinds of wood. They do not heap garments or spices on the funeral pile. The arms of the dead man and in some cases his horse are consigned to the fire.

A turf mound forms the tomb. Monuments with their lofty elaborate splendour they reject as oppressive to the dead. Tears and lamentations they soon dismiss; grief and sorrow but slowly. It is thought becoming for women to bewail, for men to remember, the dead.

Such on the whole is the account which I have received of the origin and manners of the entire German people.

MARCUS AURELIUS (121–180)
Meditations

Marcus Annius Verus was born during the reign of the Emperor Hadrian to noble parents, who died when he was young. Marcus was raised by his grandfather, who provided him with excellent tutors devoted to the stoic philosophy. When Marcus was seventeen, Hadrian died and was succeeded by Aurelius Antoninus. Antoninus was married to Faustina, who was Marcus's aunt. The childless emperor adopted Marcus, placed him in the succession as Marcus Aurelius Antoninus, and married him to his daughter Faustina. For the next 23 years, Marcus studied in preparation to become emperor. When Antoninus died in 161, Marcus took as co-emperor the other adopted son of Antoninus, Lucius Verus, who only reigned until his death in 169. The long-lasting Roman Peace finally yielded to turmoil during the reign of Marcus Aurelius. An epidemic of plague, followed by floods and famine, ravaged the empire, and barbarians began to push at the eastern borders. Marcus had to travel to Asia to put down a rebellion by the leader of his troops; his wife died during this campaign. Otherwise he spent most of his time with his legions along the Danube, attempting to quell invasions by marauding tribes. Until his death of disease in 180, he was camped on the borderlands of empire, occupying his mind by recording in a journal or commonplace book his musings about how to live the perfect life. His Meditations *are simply a collection of reflections that give voice to the stoic philosophy in which he had been trained and which presumably gave him the strength to face years of military campaigns.*

I

1. Courtesy and serenity of temper I first learnt to know from my grandfather Verus.

2. Manliness without ostentation I learnt from what I have heard and remember of my father.

3. My mother set me an example of piety and generosity, avoidance of all uncharitableness—not in actions only, but in thought as well—and a simplicity of life quite unlike the usual habits of the rich.

4. To my great-grandfather I owed the advice to dispense with the education of the schools and have good masters at home instead—and to realize that no expense should be grudged for this purpose.

5. It was my tutor who dissuaded me from patronizing Green or Blue at the races, or Light or Heavy in the ring; and encouraged me not to be afraid of work, to be sparing in my wants, attend to my own needs, mind my own business, and never listen to gossip.

6. Thanks to Diognetus I learnt not to be absorbed in trivial pursuits; to be sceptical of wizards and wonder-workers with their tales of spells, exorcisms, and the like; to eschew

---

These selections are translated by Maxwell Staniforth (Baltimore: Penguin, 1964).

cockfighting and other such distractions; not to resent outspokenness; to familiarize myself with philosophy, beginning with Bacchius and going on to Tandasis and Marcian; to write compositions in my early years; and to be ardent for the plank-and-skin pallet and other rigours of the Greek discipline.

7.   From Rusticus I derived the notion that my character needed training and care, and that I must not allow myself to be led astray into a sophist's enthusiasm for concocting speculative treatises, edifying homilies, or imaginary sketches of The Ascetic or The Altruist. He also taught me to avoid rhetoric, poetry, and verbal conceits, affectations of dress at home, and other such lapses of taste, and to imitate the easy epistolary style of his own letter written at Sinuessa to my mother. If anyone, after falling out with me in a moment of temper, showed signs of wanting to make peace again, I was to be ready at once to meet them half-way. Also I was to be accurate in my reading, and not content with a mere general idea of the meaning; and not to let myself be too quickly convinced by a glib tongue. Through him, too, I came to know Epictetus's *Dissertations*, of which he gave me a copy from his library.

8.   Apollonius impressed on me the need to make decisions for myself instead of depending on the hazards of chance, and never for a moment to leave reason out of sight. He also schooled me to meet spasms of acute pain, the loss of my son, and the tedium of a chronic ailment with the same unaltered composure. He himself was a living proof that the fieriest energy is not incompatible with the ability to relax. His expositions were always a model of clarity; yet he was evidently one who rated practical experience and an aptitude for teaching philosophy as the least of his accomplishments. It was he, moreover, who taught me how to accept the pretended favours of friends without either lowering my own self-respect or giving the impression of an unfeeling indifference.

9.   My debts to Sextus include kindliness, how to rule a household with paternal authority, the real meaning of the Natural Life, an unselfconscious dignity, an intuitive concern for the interests of one's friends, and a good-natured patience with amateurs and visionaries. The aptness of his courtesy to each individual lent a charm to his society more potent than any flattery, yet at the same time it exacted the complete respect of all present. His manner, too, of determining and systematizing the essential rules of life was as comprehensive as it was methodical. Never displaying a sign of anger nor any kind of emotion, he was at once entirely imperturbable and yet full of kindly affection. His approval was always quietly and undemonstratively expressed, and he never paraded his encyclopaedic learning.

10. It was the critic Alexander who put me on my guard against unnecessary faultfinding. People should not be sharply corrected for bad grammar, provincialisms, or mispronunciation; it is better to suggest the proper expression by tactfully introducing it oneself in, say, one's reply to a question or one's acquiescence in their sentiments, or into a friendly discussion of the topic itself (not of the diction), or by some other suitable form of reminder. . . .

III

6.   If mortal life can offer you anything better than justice and truth, self-control and courage—that is, peace of mind in the evident conformity of your actions to the laws of reason, and peace of mind under the visitations of a destiny you cannot control—if, I say, you can discern any higher ideal, why, turn to it with your whole soul, and rejoice in the prize you have found. But if nothing seems to you better than the deity which dwells within you, directing each impulse, weighing each impression, abjuring (in the Socratic phrase) the temptations

of the flesh, and avowing allegiance to the gods and compassion for mankind; if you find all else to be mean and worthless in comparison, then leave yourself no room for any rival pursuits. For if you once falter and turn aside, you will no longer be able to give unswerving loyalty to this ideal you have chosen for your own. No ambitions of a different nature can contest the title to goodness which belongs to reason and civic duty; not the world's applause, nor power, nor wealth, nor the enjoyment of pleasure. For a while there may seem to be no incongruity in these things, but very quickly they get the upper hand and sweep a man off his balance. Do you then, I would say, simply and spontaneously make your choice of the highest, and cleave to that. `But what is best for myself is the highest,' you say? If it is best for you as a reasonable being, hold fast to it; but if as an animal merely, then say so outright, and maintain your view with becoming humility—only be very sure that you have probed the matter aright. . . .

10.   Letting go all else, cling to the following few truths. Remember that man lives only in the present, in this fleeting instant: all the rest of his life is either past and gone, or not yet revealed. This mortal life is a little thing, lived in a little corner of the earth; and little, too, is the longest fame to come—dependent as it is on a succession of fast-perishing little men who have no knowledge even of their own selves, much less of one long dead and gone.

11.   To these maxims add yet another. When an object presents itself to your perception, make a mental definition or at least an outline of it, so as to discern its essential character, to pierce beyond its separate attributes to a distinct view of the naked whole, and to identify for yourself both the object itself and the elements of which it is composed, and into which it will again be resolved. Nothing so enlarges the mind as this ability to examine methodically and accurately every one of life's experiences, with an eye to determining its classification, the ends it serves, its worth to the universe, and its worth to men as the members of that supreme City in which all other cities are as households. . . .

IV

3.   Men seek for seclusion in the wilderness, by the seashore, or in the mountains—a dream you have cherished only too fondly yourself. But such fancies are wholly unworthy of a philosopher, since at any moment you choose you can retire within yourself. Nowhere can man find a quieter or more untroubled retreat than in his own soul; above all, he who possesses resources in himself, which he need only contemplate to secure immediate ease of mind—the ease that is but another word for a well-ordered spirit. Avail yourself often, then, of this retirement, and so continually renew yourself. Make your rules of life brief, yet so as to embrace the fundamentals; recurrence to them will then suffice to remove all vexation, and send you back without fretting to the duties to which you must return.

After all, what is it that frets you? The vices of humanity? Remember the doctrine that all rational beings are created for one another; that toleration is a part of justice; and that men are not intentional evildoers. Think of the myriad enmities, suspicions, animosities, and conflicts that are now vanished with the dust and ashes of the men who knew them; and fret no more.

Or is it your allotted portion in the universe that chafes you? Recall once again the dilemma, 'if not a wise Providence, then a mere jumble of atoms', and consider the profusion of evidence that this world is as it were a city. Do the ills of the body afflict you? Reflect that the mind has but to detach itself and apprehend its own powers, to be no longer involved with the movements of the breath, whether they be smooth or rough. In short, recollect all you have learnt and accepted regarding pain and pleasure.

Or does the bubble reputation distract your Keep before your eyes the swift onset of oblivion, and the abysses of eternity before us and behind; mark how hollow are the echoes of applause, how fickle and undiscerning the judgements of professed admirers, and how puny the arena of human fame. For the entire earth is but a point, and the place of our own habitation but a minute corner in it; and how many are therein who will praise you, and what sort of men are they?

Remember then to withdraw into the little field of self. Above all, never struggle or strain; but be master of yourself, and view life as a man, as a human being, as a citizen, and as a mortal. Among the truths you will do well to contemplate most frequently are these two: first, that things can never touch the soul, but stand inert outside it, so that disquiet can arise only from fancies within; and secondly, that all visible objects change in a moment, and will be no more. Think of the countless changes in which you yourself have had a part. The whole universe is change, and life itself is but what you deem it.

4.   If the power of thought is universal among mankind, so likewise is the possession of reason, making us rational creatures. It follows, therefore, that this reason speaks no less universally to us all with its 'thou shalt' or 'thou shalt not'. So then there is a world-law; which in turn means that we are all fellow-citizens and share a common citizenship, and that the world is a single city. Is there any other common citizenship that can be claimed by all humanity? And it is from this world-polity that mind, reason, and law themselves derive. If not, whence else? As the earthy portion of me has its origin from earth, the watery from a different element, my breath from one source and my hot and fiery parts from another of their own elsewhere (for nothing comes from nothing, or can return to nothing), so too there must be an origin for the mind.

5.   Death, like birth, is one of Nature's secrets; the same elements that have been combined are then dispersed. Nothing about it need give cause for shame. For beings endowed with mind it is no anomaly, nor in any way inconsistent with the plan of their creation. . . .

48. Remind yourself constantly of all the physicians, now dead, who used to knit their brows over their ailing patients; of all the astrologers who so solemnly predicted their clients' doom; the philosophers who expatiated so endlessly on death or immortality; the great commanders who slew their thousands; the despots who wielded powers of life and death with such terrible arrogance, as if themselves were gods who could never die; the whole cities which have perished completely, Helice, Pompeii, Herculaneum, and others without number. After that, recall one by one each of your own acquaintances; how one buried another, only to be laid low himself and buried in turn by a third, and all in so brief a space of time. Observe, in short, how transient and trivial is all mortal life; yesterday a drop of semen, tomorrow a handful of spice or ashes. Spend, therefore, these fleeting moments on earth as Nature would have you spend them, and then go to your rest with a good grace, as an olive falls in its season, with a blessing for the earth that bore it and a thanksgiving to the tree that gave it life.

49. Be like the headland against which the waves break and break: it stands firm, until presently the watery tumult around it subsides once more to rest. 'How unlucky I am, that this should have happened to me!' By no means; say rather, 'How lucky I am, that it has left me with no bitterness; unshaken by the present, and undismayed by the future.' The thing could have happened to anyone, but not everyone would have emerged unembittered. So why put the one down to misfortune, rather than the other to good fortune? Can a man call anything at

all a misfortune, if it is not a contravention of his nature; and can it be a contravention of his nature if it is not against that nature's will? Well, then: you have learnt to know that will. Does this thing which has happened hinder you from being just, magnanimous, temperate, judicious, discreet, truthful, self-respecting, independent, and all else by which a man's nature comes to its fulfillment? So here is a rule to remember in future, when anything tempts you to feel bitter: not, 'This is a misfortune,' but 'To bear this worthily is good fortune.' . . .

VI

13. When meat and other dainties are before you, you reflect: This is dead fish, or fowl, or pig; or: This Falernian is some of the juice from a bunch of grapes; my purple robe is sheep's wool stained with a little gore from a shellfish; copulation is friction of the members and an ejaculatory discharge. Reflections of this kind go to the bottom of things, penetrating into them and exposing their real nature. The same process should be applied to the whole of life. When a thing's credentials look most plausible, lay it bare, observe its triviality, and strip it of the cloak of verbiage that dignifies it. Pretentiousness is the arch deceiver, and never more delusive than when you imagine your work is most meritorious. Note what Crates has to say about Xenocrates himself. . . .

15. One thing hastens into being, another hastens out of it. Even while a thing is in the act of coming into existence, some part of it has already ceased to be. Flux and change are for ever renewing the fabric of the universe, just as the ceaseless sweep of time is for ever renewing the face of eternity. In such a running river, where there is no firm foothold, what is there for a man to value among all the many things that are racing past him? It would be like setting the affections on some sparrow flitting by, which in the selfsame moment is lost to sight. A man's life is no more than an inhalation from the air and an exhalation from the blood; and there is no true difference between drawing in a single breath, only to emit it again, as we do every instant, and receiving the power to breathe at all, as you did but yesterday at your birth, only to yield it back one day to the source from which you drew it. . . .

21. If anyone can show me, and prove to me, that I am wrong in thought or deed, I will gladly change. I seek the truth, which never yet hurt anybody. It is only persistence in self-delusion and ignorance which does harm. . . .

24. In death, Alexander of Macedon's end differed no whit from his stable-boy's. Either both were received into the same generative principle of the universe, or both alike were dispersed into atoms. . . .

42. All of us are working together for the same end; some of us knowingly and purposefully, others unconsciously (as Heraclitus, I think, has remarked that `even in their sleep men are at work' and contributing their share to the cosmic process). To one man falls this share of the task, to another that; indeed, no small part is performed by that very malcontent who does all he can to hinder and undo the course of events. The universe has need even of such as he. It remains for you, then, to consider with whom you will range yourself; for in any case he who directs all things will find some good use to make of you, and give you your place among his helpmates and fellow-labourers. Only, have a care that yours is not that sorry function which, according to Chrysippus, is performed by the clown's part on the stage. . . .

44. If the gods took counsel together about myself, and what should befall me, then their counsel was good. For it were hard to conceive of divinity counselling unwisely. After all, what incentive would they have to work my hurt? Where would be the gain, either to them-

selves, or to the universe which is their chief care? Even if they took no special thought for myself, at least they took thought for the universe; and I ought to welcome and feel kindly disposed towards anything that happens as a result. If, of course, they took no thought for anything at all—an impious thing to believe—why then, let us make an end of sacrifice and prayer and vow, and all other actions whereby we acknowledge the presence of living gods in our midst. Yet even so, and even if it is true that they care nothing for our mortal concerns, I am still able to take care of myself and to look to my own interests; and the interest of every creature lies in conformity with its own constitution and nature. My own nature is a rational and civic one; I have a city, and I have a country; as Marcus I have Rome, and as a human being I have the universe; and consequently, what is beneficial to these communities is the sole good for me. . . .

VIII

50. Is your cucumber bitter? Throw it away. Are there briars in your path? Turn aside. That is enough. Do not go on to say, 'Why were things of this sort ever brought into the world?' The student of nature will only laugh at you; just as a carpenter or a shoemaker would laugh, if you found fault with the shavings and scraps from their work which you saw in the shop. Yet they, at least, have somewhere to throw their litter; whereas Nature has no such out-place. That is the miracle of her workmanship: that in spite of this self-limitation, she nevertheless transmutes into herself everything that seems worn-out or old or useless, and re-fashions it into new creations, so as never to need either fresh supplies from without, or a place to discard her refuse. Her own space, her own materials and her own skill are sufficient for her. . . .

IX

30. Look down from above on the numberless herds of mankind, with their mysterious ceremonies, their divers voyagings in storm and calm, and all the chequered pattern of their comings and gatherings and goings. Go on to consider the life of bygone generations; and then the life of all those who are yet to come; and even at the present day, the life of the hordes of far-off savages. In short, reflect what multitudes there are who are ignorant of your very name; how many more will have speedily forgotten it; how many, perhaps praising you now, who will soon enough be abusing you; and that therefore remembrance, glory, and all else together are things of no worth. . . .

Pirke Avot

Hebrew tradition held that on Sinai Moses was given both the tablets of written law, the Torah, and oral law, the so-called "Oral Torah." The oral law was memorized and handed down orally for centuries, accumulating interpretations alongside the central texts of the Torah in a process of elaboration and commentary known as midrash. *The rabbis, who inherited the traditions of the Pharisees, as well as their commitment to extend the reach and joy of the law into all aspects of daily life, after the destruction of Jerusalem in 70 CE began to write down these complex constructions of law and legal interpretation. The central text in this tradition is the Mishnah, the written version of the oral law. The Mishnah is organized according to general categories of subject matter, and attaches to the authoritative interpretations of the law the names of individual influential early rabbis. As time went on, the Mishnah itself became the subject of additional commentary and interpretation, and the written accumulation of this body of law, interpretation, story, folklore, and debate, came to be called the Talmud.*

The tradition of the rabbis grew out of influential debates over interpretation of the law between Hillel and Shammai and their followers. Hillel (70 BCE–10 CE) was a liberal teacher in Jerusalem who emphasized personal piety and a concern for others in his teachings. His central teachings, grounded in a love both of peace and of study, anticipated and influenced the teachings of another early Jewish teacher, Jesus. Shammai (50 BCE–30 CE) represented a stricter, more conservative, attitude toward the law. Because he was a leader of the Sanhedrin, his views probably dominated during the years leading up to the destruction of Jerusalem; afterward those of Hillel achieved greater currency. For almost five centuries, beginning with Gamaliel the Elder (20 CE–50 CE), the first rabbi to be honored with the title "rabban" (teacher or master), the leaders of the Sanhedrin were descendants of Hillel.

Another student of Hillel, Johanan ben Zakkai (d. 80 CE), is reputed to have preserved the laws and rituals of Judaism at the time of the destruction of Jerusalem in 70 CE; according to tradition, he escaped from Jerusalem in a coffin carried by his students. These and other rabbis, such as Rabbi Akiba and Judah the Prince, were responsible for preserving—and inspiring—the traditions, the commentaries, the commentaries on commentaries, that give rabbinic literature its peculiar flavor. As a reward, their names run throughout the teachings, sayings, and stories preserved in the Talmud, especially in the Pirke Avot, *the "sayings of the fathers."*

The source of these selections is *Torah from our Sages: Pirke Avot,* translated by Jacob Neusner (Dallas: Rossel Books, 1984).

Chapter 1

1. Moses received Torah at Sinai and handed it on to Joshua, Joshua to elders, and elders to prophets. And prophets handed it on to the men of the great assembly.

   They said three things:
   Be prudent in judgment.
   Raise up many disciples.
   Make a fence for the Torah.

2. Simeon the Righteous was one of the last survivors of the great assembly. He would say:
   On three things does the world stand:
   On the Torah,
   and on the Temple service,
   and on deeds of lovingkindness.

3. Antigonus of Sokho received [the Torah] from Simeon the Righteous. He would say:
   Do not be like servants who serve the master on condition of receiving a reward,
   but [be] like servants who serve the master not on condition of receiving a reward.
   And let the fear of Heaven be upon you.

4. Yose ben Yoezer of Zeredah and Yose ben Yohanan of Jerusalem received [the Torah] from them. Yose ben Yoezer says:
   Let your house be a gathering place for sages.
   And wallow in the dust of their feet,
   And drink in their words with gusto.

5. Yose ben Yohanan of Jerusalem says:
   Let your house be open wide.
   And seat the poor at your table ["make the poor members of your household"].
   And don't talk too much with women.
   (He referred to a man's wife, all the more so is the rule to be applied to the wife of one's fellow. In this regard did sages say:
   So long as a man talks too much with a woman,
   he brings trouble on himself,
   wastes time better spent on studying Torah,
   and ends up an heir of Gehenna.)

6. Joshua ben Perahyah and Nittai the Arbelite received [the Torah] from them. Joshua ben Perahyah says:
   Set up a master for yourself.
   And get yourself a companion-disciple.
   And give everybody the benefit of the doubt.

7. Nittai the Arbelite says:
   Keep away from a bad neighbor.
   And don't get involved with a bad person.
   And don't give up hope of retribution.

8. Judah ben Tabbai and Simeon ben Shetah received [the Torah]
   from them. Judah ben Tabbai says:
   Don't make yourself like one of those who advocate before
   judges [while you yourself are judging a case].
   And when the litigants stand before you, regard them as guilty.
   But when they leave you, regard them as acquitted (when they
   have accepted your judgment).

9. Simeon ben Shetah says:
   Examine the witnesses with great care.
   And watch what you say,
   lest they learn from what you say how to lie.

10. Shemaiah and Avtalyon received [the Torah] from them.
    Shemaiah says:
    Love work.
    Hate authority.
    Don't get friendly with the government.

11. Avtalyon says:
    Sages, watch what you say,
    lest you become liable to the punishment of exile, and go into
    exile to a place of bad water, and disciples who follow you
    drink bad water and die, and the name of Heaven be thereby
    profaned.

12. Hillel and Shammai received [the Torah] from them. Hillel says:
    Be disciples of Aaron,
    loving peace and pursuing grace,
    loving people and drawing them near to the Torah.

13. He would say [in Aramaic]:
    A name made great is a name destroyed,
    And one who does not add, subtracts.
    And who does not learn is liable to death.
    And the one who uses the crown, passes away.

14. He would say:
    If I am not for myself, who is for me?
    And when I am for myself, what am I?
    And if not now, when?

15. Shammai says:
    Make your learning of Torah a fixed obligation.
    Say little and do much.
    Greet everybody cheerfully.

16. Rabban Gamaliel says:
    Set up a master for yourself.
    Avoid doubt.
    Don't tithe by too much guesswork.

17. Simeon his son says:
    All my life I grew up among the sages, and I found nothing better for a
    person [the body] than silence.
    And not the learning is the thing, but the doing.
    And whoever talks too much causes sin.

18. Rabban Simeon ben Gamaliel says: On three things does the world
    stand:
    on justice,
    on truth,
    and on peace.
    As it is said, *Execute the judgment of truth and peace in your gates.*

Chapter 2

4. He [Rabban Gamaliel] would say: Make His wishes into your own
   wishes, so that He will make your wishes into His wishes. Put aside
   your wishes on account of His wishes, so that He will put aside the
   wishes of other people in favor of your wishes.

   Hillel says:

   Do not walk out on the community.
   And do not have confidence in yourself until the day you die.
   And do not judge your companion until you are in his place.
   And do not say anything which cannot be heard, for in the end
   it will be heard.
   And do not say: When I have time, I shall study, for you may
   never have time.

5. He would say:
   A coarse person will never fear sin,
   nor will an *am ha-Aretz* ever be pious,
   nor will a shy person learn,
   nor will an ignorant person teach,
   nor will anyone too occupied in business get wise.
   In a place where there are no individuals, try to be an
   individual.

6. Also, he saw a skull floating on the water and said to it [in
   Aramaic]:
   Because you drowned others, they drowned you,
   and in the end those who drowned you will be drowned.

7. He would say:
    Lots of meats, lots of worms;
    lots of property, lots of worries;
    lots of women, lots of witchcraft;
    lots of slave girls, lots of lust;
    lots of slave boys, lots of robbery.

    Lots of Torah, lots of life;
    lots of discipleship, lots of wisdom;
    lots of counsel, lots of understanding;
    lots of righteousness, lots of peace.

    [If] one has gotten a good name, he has gotten it for himself.
    [If] he has gotten teachings of Torah, he has gotten himself life
    eternal.

Chapter 3

14. He [Rabbi Akiba] would say:
    Precious is the human being, who was created in the image [of
    God].
    It was an act of still greater love that it was made known to him
    that he was created in the image [of God], as it is said, *For in the
    image of God He made man.*
    Precious are the Israelites, who are called children to the
    Omnipresent.
    It was an act of still greater love that it was made known to
    them that they were called the children of the Omnipresent, as
    it is said, *You are the children of the Lord your God.*
    Precious are Israelites, to whom was given that precious thing.
    It was an act of still greater love that it was made known to
    them that to them was given that precious thing with which the
    world was made, as it is said, *For I give you a good doctrine. Do
    not forsake My Torah.*

15. Everything is foreseen; and free choice is given.
    In goodness the world is judged.
    And all is in accord with the abundance of deed[s].

16. He would say: All is handed over as a pledge, and a net is cast over all
    the living.
    The store is open,
    the storekeeper gives credit;
    the account book is open,
    and the hand is writing.
    Whoever wants to borrow may come and borrow.
    The charity collectors go around every day and collect from man
    whether he knows it or not.

And they have grounds for what they do.
And the judgment is a true judgment.
And everything is ready for the meal.

Chapter 4

16. Rabbi Jacob says: This world is like an antechamber before the world to come.
    Get ready in the antechamber, so that you can go into the great hall.

17. He would say:
    Better is a single moment spent in penitence and good deeds in this world than the whole of the world to come.
    And better is a single moment of inner peace in the world to come than the whole lifetime spent in this world.

Chapter 5

7. There are seven traits to an unformed clod, and seven to a sage.
   A sage does not speak before someone greater than he in wisdom;
   and he does not interrupt his companion;
   and he is not at a loss for an answer;
   he asks a relevant question and answers properly;
   and he addresses each matter in its proper sequence—first, then second;
   and concerning something he has not heard, he says: I have not heard the answer;
   and he concedes the truth [when another person demonstrates it].
   And the opposite of these traits apply to a clod.

11. There are four sorts of personality:
    easily angered, easily calmed—he loses what he gains;
    hard to anger, hard to calm—what he loses he gains;
    hard to anger and easy to calm—a truly pious man;
    easy to anger and hard to calm—a truly wicked man.

12. There are four types of disciples:
    quick to grasp, quick to forget—he loses what he gains;
    slow to grasp, slow to forget—what he loses he gains;
    quick to grasp, slow to forget—a sage;
    slow to grasp, quick to forget—a bad lot indeed.

13. There are four traits among people who give charity:
    he who wants to give but does not want others to give—he begrudges what belongs to others;
    he who wants others to give but does not want to give—he begrudges what belongs to himself;

he who will give and he wants others to give—is truly pious;
he who will not give and he does not want others to give—he is
truly wicked.

14. There are four sorts among those who go to the study house:
he who goes but does not carry out [what he learns]—he has at
least the reward for the going;
he who practices but does not go [to study]—he has at least the
reward for the doing;
he who both goes and practices—he is truly pious;
he who neither goes nor practices—he is truly wicked.

Chapter 6

8. Rabbi Simeon ben Manasia in the name of Rabbi Simeon
ben Yohai says:
Beauty,
strength,
wealth,
honor,
wisdom,
old age and gray hair,
and children,
adorn the righteous and adorn the world, as it is written, *Gray hair is
a crown of glory. It is attained through righteousness.*
It is written, *The glory of young men is their strength. The majesty of
older men is gray hair.*
It is written, *The crown of sages is their riches.*
It is written, *Grandchildren are the crown of older men. The glory of children is their parents.*
It is written, *The moon is embarrassed. The sun is ashamed, because the
Lord of Hosts reigns on Mount Zion and in Jerusalem. The Presence will
be revealed to His elders.*

Rabbi Simeon ben Manasia says: These seven qualities that the sages
attribute to the righteous, were found in Rabbi and his sons.

9. Said Rabbi Yose ben Kisma: One time when I was walking
along the road, I met a man who greeted me. I returned his
greeting.

He said to me: My teacher, where do you come from?

I answered him: I am from a great city of sages and scribes.

He said to me: My teacher, if you agree to live with us in our
place, I will give you a million golden *dinars*, precious stones,
and pearls.

I answered him: Even if you give me all the gold, silver, precious stones and pearls in the world, I would only live in a place [filled with study] of Torah. So it is written in the book of Psalms by David, King of Israel, *I prefer the Torah You proclaimed to thousands of gold and silver pieces.*

Moreover, when a person dies nothing accompanies him, not silver, gold, precious stones, nor pearls—rather [his knowledge of] Torah and [his] good deeds [alone], as it is written, *Torah will lead you where you walk, guard you while you sleep, and speak to you when you are awake.* [The words] [Torah] *will lead you where you walk* [refer] to this life; [the words] *guard you while you sleep* [refer] to the grave; [the words] *speak to you when you are awake* [refer] to the world to come.

As it is written, *Gold and silver belong to Me, says the Lord of Hosts.*

Christian Documents

Christianity grew out of the first flowerings of rabbinic culture, but, as the book of Acts in the New Testament makes clear, it quickly defined itself over against Judaism. This is somewhat ironic, for Jesus's teachings fell within the tenor of the teachings of Hillel and other liberal rabbis. And Paul, in the book of Acts, claimed to be a student of the rabbi Gamaliel. But the intellectual move away from, first, Judaic law, and then Judaic practice, along with the definitive movement toward the western reaches of the Roman Empire, meant that Christianity was kept from dissolving back into Judaism, like so many other sects started by roving messiahs.

Correspondence between Pliny the Younger and Trajan

After his father died, Pliny (61 or 62–c.113) was adopted by his famous uncle Pliny the Elder, a Roman lawyer specializing in property law. During his lifetime in public administration he collected and published his private letters in ten volumes. These letters, following a fashion among wealthy Romans, were litterae curiosius scriptae *("letters written with special care"), and Pliny came to be admired as a master of this rhetorical art. The letters, which focus on details of life and politics at the turn of the second century, are a treasure trove for historians. Volume 10, devoted entirely to letters to the Emperor Trajan, contains the letter reproduced here; it includes an important account of early Christianity.*

It is my custom, my Lord, to refer to you all things concerning which I am in doubt. For who can better guide my indecision or enlighten my ignorance?

I have never taken part in the trials of Christians: hence I do not know for what crime nor to what extent it is customary to punish or investigate. I have been in no little doubt as to whether any discrimination is made for age, or whether the treatment of the weakest does not differ from that of the stronger; whether pardon is granted in case of repentance, or whether he who has ever been a Christian gains nothing by having ceased to be one; whether the *name* itself without the proof of crimes, or the crimes, inseparably connected with the *name*, are punished. Meanwhile, I have followed this procedure in the case of those who have been brought before me as Christians. I asked them whether they were Christians a second and a third time and with threats of punishment; I questioned those who confessed; I ordered those who were obstinate to be executed. For I did not doubt that, whatever it was that they confessed, their stubbornness and inflexible obstinacy ought certainly to be punished. There were others of similar madness, who because they were Roman citizens, I have noted for sending to the City. Soon, the crime spreading, as is usual when attention is called to it, more cases arose. An

The translation is by Dana Munro and Edith Bramhall (Philadelphia: University of Pennsylvania Press, 1898).

anonymous accusation containing many names was presented. Those who denied that they were or had been Christians, ought, I thought, to be dismissed since they repeated after me a prayer to the gods and made supplication with incense and wine to your image, which I had ordered to be brought for the purpose together with the statues of the gods, and since besides they cursed Christ, not one of which things they say, those who are really Christians can be compelled to do. Others, accused by the informer, said that they were Christians and afterwards denied it; in fact they had been but had ceased to be, some many years ago, some even twenty years before. All both worshipped your image and the statues of the gods, and cursed Christ. They continued to maintain that this was the amount of their fault or error, that on a fixed day they were accustomed to come together before daylight and to sing by turns a hymn to Christ as a god, and that they bound themselves by oath, not for some crime but that they would not commit robbery, theft, or adultery, that they would not betray a trust nor deny a deposit when called upon. After this it was their custom to disperse and to come together again to partake of food, of an ordinary and harmless kind, however; even this they had ceased to do after the publication of my edict in which according to your command I had forbidden associations. Hence I believed it the more necessary to examine two female slaves, who were called deaconesses, in order to find out what was true, and to do it by torture. I found nothing but a vicious, extravagant superstition. Consequently I have postponed the examination and make haste to consult you. For it seemed to me that the subject would justify consultation, especially on account of the number of those in peril. For many of all ages, of every rank, and even of both sexes are and will be called into danger. The infection of this superstition has not only spread to the cities but even to the villages and country districts. It seems possible to stay it and bring about a reform. It is plain enough that the temples, which had been almost deserted, have begun to be frequented again, that the sacred rites, which had been neglected for a long time, have begun to be restored, and that fodder for victims, for which till now there was scarcely a purchaser, is sold. From which one may readily judge what a number of men can be reclaimed if repentance is permitted.

Trajan's Reply:
You have followed the correct procedure, my Secundus, in conducting the cases of those who were accused before you as Christians, for no general rule can be laid down as a set form. They ought not to be sought out; if they are brought before you and convicted they ought to be punished; provided that he who denies that he is a Christian, and proves this by making supplication to our gods, however much he may have been under suspicion in the past, shall secure pardon on repentance. In the case of no crime should attention be paid to anonymous charges, for they afford a bad precedent and are not worthy of our age.

Apocryphal Gospels

The collection of Christian scriptures, the New Testament, like the writings in the Hebrew Bible, give the appearance of completeness. The two gospel examples offered here serve as a reminder of the process of selection that went into the making of the canonical scriptures. Recent discoveries of whole libraries of ancient texts, like the Dead Sea Scrolls and the Nag Hammadi Library, have added to our store of gospels, letters, and apocalypses that were not considered authoritative enough to make it into the finished collection of the New Testament. The New Testament as we know it took on its present shape in the third and fourth centuries and included only those texts that seemed to bear the ancient weight of authority. The "books" that didn't make it in sometimes survived in a separate existence, often contributing to Christian legends and doctrines that sound biblical but are nowhere to be found in the Bible. For instance, the reader will look in vain in the Bible for an account of the "Harrowing of Hell," when Jesus descended into hell and released the souls of all the beloved Old Testament figures that Christians admired; that story is told in the Gospel of Nicodemus, which was not accepted into the New Testament canon.

[The Gospel of Thomas]

Perhaps the best known event in biblical archeology in this century was the discovery of the Dead Sea Scrolls in caves at Qumran near the Dead Sea in 1947. The scrolls, dating from the time of Jesus, include documents from a group, perhaps of Essenes, who had withdrawn into the wilderness in reaction against perceived abuses by the powers within Judaism. The scrolls included texts and fragments of books of the Hebrew Bible in Hebrew—the oldest such texts to survive. Less well known was a discovery of ancient religious texts near the Egyptian town of Nag Hammadi in 1945. Among the texts is the complete Gospel of Thomas in the common Egyptian language Coptic, probably translated from Greek. Although the existence of Thomas in early Christian times had been known, scholars believed that no actual text had survived. Thomas is remarkable because, unlike the four gospels collected in the New Testament, it is a sayings gospel, without stories, biography, or narrative order. It is therefore much more like the sayings of Greek philosophers or like Jewish wisdom literature (Proverbs in the Bible, or the Pirke Avot *in this volume) than like the gospel accounts that became central in Christian literature. Thomas is important to many scholars because they had already judged that the writers of Matthew and Luke, while they were writing their gospels, had before them both Mark and some other collection of sayings of Jesus. Scholars have reconstructed this other source, calling it "Q" (German* Quelle, *"source") and including in it sayings found in the same order in both Matthew and Luke, but not in Mark. The main argument against some such text as Q was that the known gospels were narratives, not collections of sayings. The existence of the Gospel of Thomas therefore allowed the possibility of a source like Q. Thomas also suggested, in its portrait of Jesus, that some in the earliest Christian communities viewed Jesus as a teacher of wisdom rather than as a healer or miracle worker. Scholars date Thomas to the same period as the synoptic gospels (70–100 CE), and believe it originated in Greek in the region in Syria most associated with traditions of the disciple Thomas. Students who have seen the recent film* Stigmata (1999) *will remember that the plot hinges on the suppression of a secret text that has Jesus saying, "The Kingdom of God is inside you and all around you, not in buildings of wood and stone. Split a piece of wood and I am there; lift a stone and you will find me." These sayings are to be found in Thomas 3 and 77, and the opening lines of Thomas are also quoted in the film. A postscript to the film mentions the discovery of the Nag Hammadi Library and announces, probably erroneously, that the Catholic Church judges the Gospel of Thomas to be heretical. Most conservatives who want to downplay the importance of Thomas will argue that it is a much later text, like some of the other noncanonical gospels.*

Prologue

These are the secret sayings that the living Jesus spoke and Didymos Judas Thomas recorded.

    1   And he said, "Whoever discovers the interpretation of these sayings will not taste death."

    2   Jesus said, "Those who seek should not stop seeking until they find. ²When they find, they will be disturbed. ³When they are disturbed, they will marvel, and will rule over all."

    3   Jesus said, If your leaders say to you, 'Look, the (Father's) imperial rule is in the sky,' then the birds of the sky will precede you. ²If they say to you, 'It is in the sea,' then the fish

will precede you. ³Rather, the (Father's) imperial rule is inside you and outside you. ⁴When you know yourselves, then you will be known, and you will understand that you are children of the living Father. ⁵But if you do not know yourselves, then you live in poverty, and you are the poverty."

12   The disciples said to Jesus, "We know that you are going to leave us. Who will be our leader?"

²Jesus said to them, "No matter where you are, you are to go to James the Just, for whose sake heaven and earth came into being."

13   Jesus said to his disciples, "Compare me to something and tell me what I am like."

²Simon Peter said to him, "You are like a just angel."

³Matthew said to him, "You are like a wise philosopher."

⁴Thomas said to him, "Teacher, my mouth is utterly unable to say what you are like."

⁵Jesus said, "I am not your teacher. Because you have drunk, you have become intoxicated from the bubbling spring that I have tended."

⁶And he took him, and withdrew, and spoke three sayings to him.

⁷When Thomas came back to his friends, they asked him, "What did Jesus say to you?"

⁸Thomas said to them, "If I tell you one of the sayings he spoke to me, you will pick up rocks and stone me, and fire will come from the rocks and devour you."

15   Jesus said, "When you see one who was not born of woman, fall on your faces and worship. That one is your Father."

16   Jesus said, "Perhaps people think that I have come to cast peace upon the world. ²They do not know that I have come to cast conflicts upon the earth: fire, sword, war. ³For there will be five in a house: there'll be three against two and two against three, father against son and son against father, ⁴and they will stand alone."

17   Jesus said, "I will give you what no eye has seen, what no ear has heard, what no hand has touched, what has not arisen in the human heart."

18   The disciples said to Jesus, "Tell us, how will our end come?" ²Jesus said, "Have you found the beginning, then, that you are looking for the end? You see, the end will be where the beginning is. ³Congratulations to the one who stands at the beginning: that one will know the end and will not taste death."

24   His disciples said, "Show us the place where you are, for we must seek it."

²He said to them, "Anyone here with two ears had better listen!

³There is light within a person of light, and it shines on the whole world. If it does not shine, it is dark."

25   Jesus said, "Love your friends like your own soul, ²protect them like the pupil of your eye."

28   Jesus said, "I took my stand in the midst of the world, and in flesh I appeared to them. ²I found them all drunk, and I did not find any of them thirsty. ³My soul ached for the children of humanity, because they are blind in their hearts and do not see, for they came into the world empty, and they also seek to depart from the world empty. ⁴But meanwhile they are drunk. When they shake off their wine, then they will change their ways."

31   Jesus said, "No prophet is welcome on his home turf; ²doctors don't cure those who know them."

34   Jesus said, "If a blind person leads a blind person, both of them will fall into a hole."

35 Jesus said, "One can't enter a strong man's house and take it by force without tying his hands. ²Then one can loot his house."

36   Jesus said, "Don't fret, from morning to evening and from evening to morning, about what you're going to wear."

37   His disciples said, "When will you appear to us, and when will we see you?"

2Jesus said, "When you strip without being ashamed, and you take your clothes and put them under your feet like little children and trample them, 3then [you] will see the son of the living one and you will not be afraid."

38   Jesus said, "Often you have desired to hear these sayings that I am speaking to you, and you have no one else from whom to hear them. 2There will be days when you will seek me and you will not find me."

44   Jesus said, "Whoever blasphemes against the Father will be forgiven, 2and whoever blasphemes against the son will be forgiven, 3but whoever blasphemes against the holy spirit will not be forgiven, either on earth or in heaven."

62   Jesus said, "I disclose my mysteries to those [who are worthy] of [my] mysteries. 2Do not let your left hand know what your right hand is doing."

63   Jesus said,

There was a rich man who had a great deal of money. 2He said, "I shall invest my money so that I may sow, reap, plant, and fill my storehouses with produce, that I may lack nothing." 3These were the things he was thinking in his heart, but that very night he died. 4Anyone here with two ears had better listen!

74   He said, "Lord, there are many around the drinking trough, but there is nothing in the well."

75   Jesus said, "There are many standing at the door, but those who are alone will enter the bridal suite."

76   Jesus said,

The Father's imperial rule is like a merchant who had a supply of merchandise and then found a pearl. 2That merchant was prudent; he sold the merchandise and bought the single pearl for himself.

3"So also with you, seek his treasure that is unfailing, that is enduring, where no moth comes to eat and no worm destroys."

77   Jesus said, "I am the light that is over all things. I am all: from me all came forth, and to me all attained. 2Split a piece of wood; I am there. 3Lift up the stone, and you will find me there."

89   Jesus said, "Why do you wash the outside of the cup? 2Don't you understand that the one who made the inside is also the one who made the outside?"

90   Jesus said, "Come to me, for my yoke is comfortable and my lordship is gentle, 2and you will find rest for yourselves."

113 His disciples said to him, "When will the (Father's) imperial rule come?"

2"It will not come by watching for it. 'It will not be said, 'Look, here!' or 'Look, there!' 'Rather, the Father's imperial rule is spread out upon the earth, and people don't see it."

114 Simon Peter said to them, "Make Mary leave us, for females don't deserve life."

2Jesus said, "Look, I will guide her to make her male, so that she too may become a living spirit resembling you males. 3For every female who makes herself male will enter the domain of Heaven."

[The Secret Gospel of Mark]

The existence of the Secret Gospel of Mark *was only revealed in the discovery of a copy of an ancient letter in a Judean monastery in 1958. The letter was written by Clement of Alexandria (c.150–c.211), an Athenian leading the Christian school in Alexandria. Clement was an opponent of gnostic dualists who believed in salvation through esoteric knowledge that revealed to Christians their spiritual origins, identities, and destinies. The letter, written to a certain Theodore, attacks the authenticity of a version of Mark used by a gnostic sect, and then says that there are only two authentic versions of the gospel, one for the general public and the second, "a more spiritual gospel for the use of those being perfected." According to Clement, when Mark died he left this second version in the care of the Church at Alexandria, "where it even now is very carefully guarded, being read only to those being initiated into the great mysteries." Clement then cites the two short passages that are in the* Secret Gospel *but not in the public version. Whether the initiation hinted at in the* Secret Gospel *is sexual in nature is unclear, and it is, naturally, the subject of heated debate.*

The existence of a separate insider's text simply carries a step further one of the themes found in the gospel of Mark as it appears in the New Testament. In Mark, knowledge and understanding are reserved for a special group of insiders and Jesus tells his disciples that they are initiated into a wisdom that most will be unable to understand. Jesus even suggests that the parables are designed to be difficult so that not everyone can understand them. Over and over, in fact, the gospel shows that even the disciples can barely make sense of what Jesus is trying to get them to see. The two passages in the Secret Gospel *also parallel the story of the raising of Lazarus and the references to the "Beloved Disciple" in the gospel of John.*

Fragment 1: To be located between Mark 10:34 and 10:35. Clement to Theodore, Folio 1, verso, line 23–Folio 2, recto, line 11.

1. And they come into Bethany, and this woman was there whose brother had died. She knelt down in front of Jesus and says to him, "Son of David, have mercy on me." But the disciples rebuked her. And Jesus got angry and went with her into the garden where the tomb was. Just then a loud voice was heard from inside the tomb. Then Jesus went up and rolled the stone away from the entrance to the tomb. He went right in where the young man was, stuck out his hand, grabbed him by the hand, and raised him up. The young man looked at Jesus, loved him, and began to beg him to be with him. Then they left the tomb and went into the young man's house. (Incidentally, he was rich.) Six days later Jesus gave him an order; and when evening had come, the young man went to him, dressed only in a linen cloth. He spent that night with him, because Jesus taught him the mystery of God's domain. From there [Jesus] got up and returned to the other side of the Jordan.

Fragment 2: To be located between 10:46a ("Then they came to Jericho") and 10:46b ("As he was leaving Jericho . . ."). Clement to Theodore, Folio 2, recto, lines 14–16

2. The sister of the young man whom Jesus loved was there, along with his mother and Salome, but Jesus refused to see them.

The three gospel texts here are translated by members of the Jesus Seminar and included in *The Complete Gospels: Annotated Scholars Version*, first published by the Polebridge Press in San Francisco, 1992.

[The Infancy Gospel of Thomas]

The many rejected biblical texts arose partly because there was often disagreement about what the core beliefs of Christianity were to be, even, as we see in the Infancy Gospel of Thomas, *about what the essential nature of Jesus was meant to be. This strange text shows us Jesus as a child, barely in control of the tremendous power he wields and behaving toward his fellow humans with insolence. The trouble his parents face is similar to that shown in the single infancy story that made it into the canonical gospels, when Jesus debates with rabbis and then talks back to his mother in the gospel of Luke. This text was apparently very popular among early Christians, for it survives in many versions in thirteen different languages. As a written text, it may date from the second century (probably in Syria), but it contains popular folk stories that would have been handed down orally from the time that Jesus's followers began to be curious about his youthful years.*

Boyhood deeds of our Lord Jesus Christ.

1. *I, Thomas* the Israelite, am reporting to you, all my non-Jewish brothers and sisters, to make known the extraordinary childhood deeds of our Lord Jesus Christ—what he did after his birth in my region. This is how it all started:

2. *When this boy, Jesus,* was five years old, he was playing at the ford of a rushing stream. He was collecting the flowing water into ponds and made the water instantly pure. He did this with a single command. He then made soft clay and shaped it into twelve sparrows. He did this on the sabbath day, and many other boys were playing with him.

But when a Jew saw what Jesus was doing while playing on the sabbath day, he immediately went off and told Joseph, Jesus' father: "See here, your boy is at the ford and has taken mud and fashioned twelve birds with it, and so has violated the sabbath."

So Joseph went there, and as soon as he spotted him he shouted, "Why are you doing what's not permitted on the sabbath?"

But Jesus simply clapped his hands and shouted to the sparrows: "Be off, fly away, and remember me, you who are now alive!" And the sparrows took off and flew away noisily.

The Jews watched with amazement, then left the scene to report to their leaders what they had seen Jesus doing.

3. *The son of Annas the scholar,* standing there with Jesus, took a willow branch and drained the water Jesus had collected. Jesus, however, saw what had happened and became angry, saying to him, "Damn you, you irreverent fool! What harm did the ponds of water do to you? From this moment you, too, will dry up like a tree, and you'll never produce leaves or root or bear fruit."

In an instant the boy had completely withered away. Then Jesus departed and left for the house of Joseph. The parents of the boy who had withered away picked him up and were carrying him out, sad because he was so young. And they came to Joseph and accused him: "It's your fault—your boy did all this."

4. *Later he was going* through the village again when a boy ran by and bumped him on the shoulder. Jesus got angry and said to him, "You won't continue your journey." And all of a sudden he fell down and died.

Some people saw what had happened and said, "Where has this boy come from? Everything he says happens instantly!"

The parents of the dead boy came to Joseph and blamed him, saying, "Because you have such a boy, you can't live with us in the village, or else teach him to bless and not curse. He's killing our children!"

5. So Joseph summoned his child and admonished him in private, saying, "Why are you doing all this? These people are suffering and so they hate and harass us." Jesus said, "I know that the words I spoke are not my words. Still, I'll keep quiet for your sake. But those people must take their punishment." There and then his accusers became blind.

Those who saw this became very fearful and at a loss. All they could say was, "Every word he says, whether good or bad, has became a deed—a miracle, even!" When Joseph saw that Jesus had done such a thing, he got angry and grabbed his ear and pulled very hard. The boy became infuriated with him and replied, "It's one thing for you to seek and not find; it's quite another for you to act this unwisely. Don't you know that I don't really belong to you? Don't make me upset."

Two Christian Creeds

Paul's letters in the New Testament show a constant struggle to keep far-flung groups of converts from very different backgrounds focused on a single set of accepted beliefs and practices. Christianity's response to the strain of opposed orthodoxies and differences in interpretation was very different from that of Judaism. The Talmud essentially collects and places in direct juxtaposition the accumulated and often contradictory teachings of the sages. It does not often choose winners or pick sides. Instead, wisdom was found to lie in the accumulation, in the conflict itself, and in the magnificence of its expressions.

The teachings of Jesus, similar to those of other rabbis, were open to many interpretations and uses. But as Christianity spread, faced with alternations of official support and persecution, many sought decisive resolution of doctrinal disputes. Where beliefs clashed, it seemed wise to determine a winner. Councils were held to debate doctrinal issues, and the losing views were declared heresies. The arguments over some beliefs lasted centuries and sometimes resulted in open warfare. One such controversy can be perceived in the two creeds in common liturgical use in the Christian church over the centuries. The Apostle's Creed is a well-known and concise statement of Christian belief, elaborating the central mystery of the Trinity—Father, Son, and Holy Spirit—and mentioning the church, baptism, resurrection, and the afterlife as important articles of Christian faith. This creed probably developed out of a question-and-answer baptism ritual in the early church, reached its present form in the seventh century, and became the church's official creed about 1200. Through its name, it pretends to greater antiquity and authority than it really had, however, for many of the doctrines it enshrines would have been unknown to the original followers of Jesus.

The Nicene Creed, while structurally similar to the Apostle's Creed, is actually intended to stamp out a particularly stubborn heresy. Arius, the bishop in Alexandria, Egypt, after the year 300, proposed that if God was absolutely one (as Plato believed), Christ had to be a created being, subject to the kind of growth and change some readers see in the gospels. Because this seemed to deny full Godhead to Christ and therefore to undercut the doctrine of the Trinity, Arius's teachings aroused a controversy so great that the Emperor Constantine convened a Council at Nicaea in 325 to discuss the issue. The Council declared the Arian doctrine a heresy and issued a declaration that clarified the church's official position. The liturgical version of that declaration, the Nicene Creed, with its decisive phrases, "of one substance with the Father" and "begotten not made," is thus a banner of victory in a war over a theological argument.

Apostles' Creed

I believe in God the Father Almighty, Maker of Heaven and Earth:

And in Jesus Christ his only Son our Lord; Who was conceived by the Holy Ghost, Born of the Virgin Mary, Suffered under Pontius Pilate, Was crucified, dead, and buried: He descended into hell; The third day he rose again from the dead; He ascended into Heaven, And sitteth on the right hand of God, the Father Almighty; From thence he shall come to judge the quick and the dead.

I believe in the Holy Ghost; The Holy Catholic Church, the Communion of Saints; The Forgiveness of sins; The Resurrection of the body, And the Life everlasting. Amen.

Nicene Creed

I believe in one God, the Father Almighty, Maker of heaven and earth, And of all things visible and invisible.

And in one Lord Jesus Christ, the only begotten Son of God, Begotten of his Father before all worlds, God of God, Light of Light, Very God of very God, Begotten, not made, Being of one substance with the Father, By whom all things were made: Who for us men, and for our salvation, came down from heaven, And was incarnate by the Holy Ghost of the Virgin Mary, And was made man; And was crucified also for us under Pontius Pilate. He suffered and was buried; And the third day he rose again according to the Scriptures, And ascended into heaven, And sitteth at the right hand of the Father. And he shall come again with glory to judge both the quick and the dead: Whose kingdom shall have no end.

And I believe in the Holy Ghost, the Lord and Giver of Life, Who procedeth from the Father and the Son, Who with the Father and the Son together is worshipped and glorified, Who spake by the Prophets. And I believe one Holy Catholic and Apostolic Church. I acknowledge one Baptism for the remission of sins. And I look for the Resurrection of the dead, And the Life of the World to come. Amen.

St. Augustine (354–430)
The Confessions

There was no more vociferous debater in arguments about heresy than Augustine, the bishop of Hippo in North Africa. Although he is best known for his autobiographical account of his belated conversion, the Confessions, *his greatest achievement lay in his providing a coherent philosophical and theological ground for developing Christian doctrines. All of this important work occurred after the events he describes in the* Confessions. *His account of his early life displays his shifting adherence to a number of leading philosophies, including Manichaeism and Platonism. Augustine's early commitment to philosophy actually gave him the foundation for his expositions of Christian doctrine, and the deeply infused Platonism in Christianity is largely his creation. Educated early Christians, like Augustine, had a great love of the Roman classics. They were aware, furthermore, that the style of Cicero and the moral teachings of Virgil seemed in some ways to surpass those of the Bible. St. Jerome recounted a harrowing experience in which he was wracked by a visionary voice which asked him to identify himself. When he announced he was a Christian, the voice countered, "You are a Ciceronian, not a Christian!"*

While some Christians were willing simply to banish the classics, Augustine worked for a humanist accommodation, allowing that where Virgil seemed to speak truth, that truth came from God. On the other hand, Augustine argued in On Christian Doctrine, *the Bible contained everything a Christian needed to know to recognize what to avoid and what to embrace: "Scripture teaches nothing but charity, nor condemns anything except cupidity." These great opposites,* caritas *and* cupiditas, *are dimensions of the human will. Charity is "the motion of the soul toward the enjoyment of God for His own sake, and the enjoyment of one's self and of one's neighbor for the sake of God"; cupidity is "a motion of the soul toward the enjoyment of one's self, one's neighbor, or any corporal thing for the sake of something other than God."*

Augustine's Confessions *is the first autobiography, but the book is more than memoir: it is a celebration of God's power over human intransigence, and it is deeply colored by the perspective of the writer, a bishop looking back on events that reached a climax twelve years before, in 386. By the time of his conversion, Augustine could recognize God as the* One *he had met in Platonism, but was unable to abandon a life of cupidity in order to believe whole-heartedly in the faith of his pious mother. In the climactic scene, a model for thousands of conversions through the ages, Augustine is kicked over the edge by reading a random scripture passage in which God seems to speak directly to him.*

[Conversion to Christianity]

VIII. 11. Thus I was soul-sick and tormented, accusing myself much more severely than usual, rolling and turning in my chain, awaiting the time that chain would be wholly broken in which I now was only barely held, but held nevertheless. And you, O Lord, pressed upon me—in my soul—with a severe mercy, redoubling the lashes of fear and shame, so that I should not again give way, and rather than bursting that last weak bit of chain, should find it instead stronger and more binding than ever. For I said to myself, "Let it be done now; let it be done now." And as I spoke, I all but accomplished it: I almost did it, but not quite. Yet I didn't sink back to my former state, but kept my stand near by, and caught my breath. And I tried again, and fell somewhat less short of it, and somewhat less, and all but touched and laid hold of it—and yet I didn't come close enough to touch or lay hold of it. Still I hesitated to die to death and to live to life: and the bad things I was used to carried more weight with me than the good things which were new to me. As the very moment in which I was to become a new person drew nearer, the more horror it struck into me. Still, it didn't strike me back or turn me away; it held me in suspense.

Mere toys of toys, and vanities of vanities—my ancient mistresses, as it were—still held me; they plucked at my garment of flesh and whispered softly: "Do you cast us off?" and "From this moment shall we no longer be with you forever?" and "From now on will this or that no longer be lawful for you?" And what was it which they meant in what I just wrote—"this" or "that?" What were they suggesting, O my God? Let your mercy keep it away from the soul of your servant! What defilements did they suggest! What shame! And now I only partly heard them; they no longer openly showed themselves to contradict me, but muttered as it were behind my back, pulling at me as I was leaving to get me to look back on them. Yet they did hold me back, for I hesitated to burst free and shake them off, and to leap in the direction I was called. Violent habits warned me, "Do you think you can live without them?"

But now it spoke very faintly. For in the direction toward which I had turned my face, even though I still trembled to go there, I could see the chaste dignity of Continence: she was

---

This account of Augustine's conversion has been translated for this collection by the editor.

serene and self-possessed, friendly but not wanton, beckoning honestly for me to come without fear or doubt. She stretched forth her holy hands to receive and embrace me, full of multitudes of good examples. There were so many boys and girls here, a multitude of youth and every age, grave widows and aged virgins; and Continence herself in all of them, not barren, but a fruitful mother of children—of joys—by you her husband, O Lord. And she smiled on me with a pleasant persuasiveness, as if she were saying, "Can't you do what these men and women are doing? Can they even do it by themselves, without the help of the Lord their God? The Lord their God gave me to them. Why do you try to stand by yourself, and therefore not at all? Let him support you as well. Don't be afraid. He won't pull away and let you fall. Cast yourself fearlessly upon him, for he will receive you; he will heal you." And I blushed in shame, for I still heard the voices of those vanities, and I hung back, hesitating. And then she seemed to say, "Stop your ears against those unclean members of yours, so that they may be mortified. They tell you of delights, but those delights can't compare with delight in the law of the Lord your God." This controversy took place in my heart, self warring against self. . . .

VIII. 12. . . . There rose within me a mighty storm, bringing with it a shower of tears. . . . I somehow cast myself down under a fig-tree, giving full vent to my tears; and the floods of my eyes gushed out an acceptable sacrifice to you. And then I spoke to you words to this effect: "And you, O Lord, how long? How long, Lord? Will you be angry for ever? Remember not our former iniquities"—for I felt that my sins were still holding me back. I raised my voice in sorrow: "How long, how long, this 'tomorrow, and tomorrow?' Why not now? Why not end my uncleanness this very hour?"

So I was speaking and weeping in the bitter contrition of my heart. Suddenly I heard from a neighboring house a chanting voice, like that of a boy or a girl (I couldn't tell which), repeating, "Take up and read. Take up and read." My face changed at once, and I began to think most intently whether children ever sang such words in their games, but I couldn't remember ever hearing words like that before. So I stopped the flow of my tears and rose to go, certain that this sign could only be a command from God to open the book, and read the first passage I should find. For indeed I had heard that Antony, coming in during the reading of the Gospel, had received the admonition, as if what was being read was spoken directly to him: "Go, sell all that you have, and give to the poor, and you shall have treasure in heaven, and come and follow me." And by such an oracle he had been immediately converted to you.

So I returned eagerly to the place where Alypius was sitting, for I had left there the volume of the Apostle. I seized the book, opened it, and read in silence that passage on which my eyes first fell: "Not in rioting and drunkenness, not in chambering and wantonness, not in strife and envying; but put on the Lord Jesus Christ, and make not provision for the flesh, in concupiscence." I had no wish to read further; there was no need to. For at the end of this sentence, instantly a light of serenity infused my heart, and all the shadows of my former doubt vanished.

Then putting my finger or some other marker between the pages to mark my place, I shut the book, and with a calm countenance made known to Alypius what had happened. . . .

Next we go in to my mother. We tell her, and she rejoices. We describe for her how it all took place, and in triumph she leaps for joy. She blessed you, "Who are able to do above that which we ask or think"; for she perceived that you had given her more with regard to me than she used to ask for in her pitiful and sorrowful groanings. For you converted me to you in such a way that I no longer sought a wife nor any other worldly hope. I was now standing in that rule of faith where you had shown me to her in a vision so many years before. And so you changed her mourning into joy, a joy more plentiful than she had imagined, and in a purer and more precious way than she had earlier sought when she desired grandchildren of my body.

The Mass

In the tradition of Christian liturgy, the mass is the musical setting, either polyphonic or in plainchant, of the service of the Eucharist (Communion). In the Roman Catholic church, a well-established ordering of texts in Latin was in place from about the 4th century to 1966, when vernacular languages were required in place of Latin. The mass is made up of two parts: the Ordinary, *those texts that remain the same for every mass; and the* Proper, *the liturgical and scriptural texts that change daily throughout the seasons of the church calendar. The parts of the Ordinary, sung by the choir and occasionally by the celebrant, are the Kyrie, Gloria, Credo, Sanctus (sometimes divided into Sanctus and Benedictus), and Agnus Dei. The Proper texts, sung by the choir with the participation of soloists, are the Introit, Gradual, Alleluia or Tract, Sequence, Offertory, and Communion. The standard order of service followed this pattern:*

| Chants | | Prayers and |
Proper	Ordinary	lessons
I. INTRODUCTORY RITES		
Introit		
	Kyrie	
	Gloria	
		Collect (opening prayer)
II. LITURGY OF THE WORD		
		Epistle
Gradual		
Alleluia/tract		
Sequence (rare)		
		Gospel
		Homily (sermon)
	Credo	
		(general intercessions)
III. LITURGY OF THE EUCHARIST		
Offertory		
		Preface
	Sanctus	
		Te igitur, etc. to the conclusion of the Eucharistic Prayer, which began with Preface, Sanctus
		Pater noster (Lord's Prayer)
	Agnus Dei	
Communion		Post-Communion prayer
	Ite missa est (dismissal)	

The standardized texts of the Ordinary proved to be one of the greatest impulses to creativity in Western music, for from the ninth century on, through the addition of tropes (additional texts), through settings in plainchant, then through polyphonic settings, musicians and composers offered praise to God in specially composed masses. Most of the composers of the late Middle Ages whose names come down to us were best known for their settings of the mass texts. The great classical composers, like Haydn, Mozart, and Beethoven, wrote mass settings for chorus, soloists, and orchestra, in a tradition that continues with modern and contemporary composers.

Kyrie (Greek)

Kyrie eleison. (three times)   Lord have mercy.
Christe eleison. (three times)   Christ have mercy.
Kyrie eleison. (three times)   Lord have mercy.

Gloria

Gloria in excelsis Deo.   Glory to God on high.
Et in terra pax hominibus   And on earth peace to men
bonae voluntatis.   of good will.
Laudamus te.   We praise you.
Benedicimus te.   We bless you.
Adoramus te.   We adore you.
Glorificamus te.   We glorify you.
Gratias agimus te   We give thanks to you
propter magnam gloriam tuam.   for your great glory.
Domine Deus, Rex caelestis,   O Lord God, heavenly King,
Deus Pater omnipotens.   God the Father almighty.
Domine fili unigenite,   O Lord the only-begotten son,
Jesu Christe.   Jesus Christ.
Domine Deus,   O Lord God,
Agnus Dei,   Lamb of God,
Filius Patris,   Son of the Father,
Qui tollis peccata mundi,   who takes away the sins of the world,
miserere nobis,   have mercy upon us,
suscipe deprecationem nostram,   receive our prayer,
Qui sedes ad dexteram Patris,   you who sit at the right hand of the Father,
miserere nobis.   have mercy on us.
Suscipe deprecationem nostram,   Receive our prayer,
Qui sedes ad dexteram Patris,   you who sit at the right hand of the Father,
miserere nobis.   have mercy on us.
Quoniam tu solus sanctus.   For you alone are holy.
Tu solus Dominus.   You alone are the Lord.
Tu solus altissimus,   You alone are the most high,
Jesu Christe.   Jesus Christ.
Cum Sancto Spiritu,   With the Holy Spirit,
in gloria Dei Patris. Amen.   in the glory of God the Father. Amen.

Credo

The text of the Credo is the Nicene Creed, the English translation of which is given earlier in this section.

Sanctus (with Benedictus)

Sanctus, Dominus Deus Sabaoth.
Pleni sunt caeli et terra gloria tua.

Holy, holy, holy, Lord God of Hosts.
Heaven and earth are full of your glory.

Osanna, Osanna in excelsis.

Hosanna in the highest.

Benedictus qui venit
in nomine Domini.

Blessed is he who comes
in the name of the Lord.

Osanna, Osanna in excelsis.

Hosanna in the highest.

Agnus Dei

Agnus Dei,
qui tollis peccata mundi,
miserere nobis.
Agnus Dei,
qui tollis peccata mundi,
miserere nobis.
Agnus Dei,
qui tollis peccata mundi,
dona nobis pacem.

Lamb of God,
who takes away the sins of the world,
have mercy on us,

grant us peace.

The "Quem quaeritis" Trope

A trope is an addition to the existing liturgy, either by adding new words to existing melodic lines, or by inserting new words and music into an existing liturgical section. Because the Alleluia of the mass ended with florid musical passages on the last syllable of "Alleluia," tropes called Sequences *were commonly added between the Alleluia and the Gospel, using the existing chanted melodies and new texts appropriate to the season. These sequences became popular creative additions to the liturgy that in their turn influenced secular dances and songs. Among the best known sequences is the "Dies irae" (see below) added to the Mass for the Dead. Among the most influential of tropes may have been one added to the Introit for the Easter morning service during the tenth century: the voices were alternated so that a small scene could be enacted in which the angel at the now empty tomb of Jesus asks the three Marys as they approach: "Quem quaeritis in sepulchro?" ("Whom do you seek in the tomb?"). As liturgical scenes like this became popular, they came to be acted on the church steps and eventually grew into full scale dramatic cycles portraying biblical stories. Because knowledge of Greek and Roman drama had effectively disappeared during the early Middle Ages, many scholars believe that the enactment of these liturgical scenes was the first step in a reinvention of drama in Western Europe. The simplest of these tropes, which spread widely and elaborately in the middle of the tenth century, dates from about 950 from the monastery in St. Gall (St. Gall Stiftsbibliothek MS 484) .*

Quem quaeritis in sepulchro, Christicolae?	Whom do you seek in the tomb, O followers of Christ?
Jesum Nazarenum crucifixum, o caelicolae.	Jesus of Nazareth, the crucified, O heaven-dwellers
Non est hic, surrexit sicut praedixerat; ite, nuntiate quia surrexit de sepulchro.	He is not here, he has risen as he foretold; go, announce that he has risen from the tomb.
Resurrexi.	I have risen . . . (the first word of the Introit of the Easter Mass to which the trope has been added as an Introduction)

The *Requiem* Mass

One of the best known of the specialized masses is the Mass for the Dead, *called the* Requiem *from the opening words of its Introit, "Requiem aeternam dona eis Domine" ("Give them eternal rest, O Lord"). Its musical setting contains the Kyrie, the Sanctus, and the Agnus Dei from the Ordinary, the Introit and Gradual from the Proper, a tract and the special sequence "Dies irae" ("Day of wrath"). The "Dies irae," because of its dramatic evocation of the terrors of the Last Judgment, became a special focus of attention in musical settings of the Requiem. Many great composers have written settings of the Requiem Mass for orchestra, soloists, and chorus, including Mozart, Dvorák, Verdi, Fauré, and Durufle. Brahms'* German Requiem *uses German scriptural passages instead of the usual Latin texts. The* War Requiem *of Benjamin Britten intersperses the traditional Latin text with anti-war poems of the British poet Wilfred Owen.*

"Dies irae"

Dies irae, dies illa, Solvet saeclum in favilla Teste David cum Sibylla.	Day of wrath, that day when the world will be reduced to ashes, as David prophesied with the Sibyl.
Quantus tremor est futurus, Quando judex est venturus, Cuncta stricte discussurus.	What trembling will there be when the judge ventures forth to thresh all out strictly.
Tuba, mirum spargens sonum Per sepulchra regionum, Coget omnes ante thronum.	The trumpet, scattering a wondrous sound through the tombs of all lands, shall drive all before the throne.
Mors stupebit et natura Cum resurget creatura Judicanti responsura.	Death and nature will be astounded when every creature arises to answer the judge.

This version of "Quem quaeritis" is translated by the editor for this collection.

Liber scriptus proferetur
In quo totum continetur
Unde mundus judicetur.

Judex ergo cum sedebit,
Quidquid latet apparebit:
Nil inultum remanebit.

Quid sum miser tunc dicturus,
Quem patronum rogaturus,
Cum vix justus sit securus?

Rex tremendae majestatis,
Qui salvandos salvas gratis,
Salva me, fons pietatis.

. . . .

Lacrimosa dies illa
Qua resurget ex favilla
Judicandus homo reus.

Huic ergo parce, Deus,
Pie Jesu Domine:
Dona eis requiem. Amen.

A written book will be brought forth
in which all is contained
by which the world will be judged.

Therefore when the judge shall sit,
whatever was hidden will be revealed,
And nothing will remain unpunished.

What shall I say in misery?
Whom shall I seek as patron,
when even the just are not secure?

King of tremendous majesty,
who freely saves the saved,
save me, fount of mercy.

. . . .

Full of tears will be that day
when from the ashes will arise
the guilty man to be judged.

Then spare this one, O God,
merciful Lord Jesus.
Grant them rest. Amen.

The editor has provided the English translation for this collection.

BENEDICT OF NURSIA (480–542)
The Rule of St. Benedict

Benedict, from a good family and educated in good Roman schools, had a temperament well-suited to the monastic movement which was spreading during his lifetime. His response to the growing corruption and decay in Rome was to retreat to a cave outside the city to live a life of contemplation. He lived alone there, wearing borrowed monastic garb, for three years. His reputation for sanctity led to his being named abbot of a nearby monastery and soon the number of his followers led him to found a large order at Monte Cassino, between Rome and Naples.

While he admired the life of the solitary hermit, Benedict realized that most Christians dedicated to a life of absolute devotion would thrive better in a community, and he developed his Rule *as a guide for that working and praying community. The* Rule *takes notice of all aspects of monastic life, from the times of religious observances, to the duties of every level of worker and monk. More impressive is Benedict's care for spiritual growth and for human concerns, and his careful provision of sufficient food, clothing, and sleep to balance the routines of work, prayer, and study. Young men entering orders would take vows that acknowledged the permanence of the arrangement. One typical vow recorded in the early church ran like this:*

> I, brother Gerald, in the presence of abbot Gerald and the other brothers, promise steadfastness in this monastery according to the rule of St. Benedict and the precepts of Sts. Peter and Paul; and I hereby surrender all my possessions to this monastery, built in the honor of St. Peter and governed by the abbot Gerald.

A more detailed vow announced the kind of life that lay ahead:

> I hereby renounce my parents, my brothers and relatives, my friends, my possessions and my property, and the vain and empty glory and pleasure of this world. I also renounce my own will, for the will of God. I accept all the hardships of the monastic life, and take the vows of purity, chastity, and poverty, in the hope of heaven; and I promise to remain a monk in this monastery all the days of my life.

The Rule *remained the chief guide to the monastic life for monks of many orders for more than fifteen centuries. The order founded by Benedict is known as the Benedictine order. In 1964, because of the civilizing work of Benedictine monks in Europe during the Middle Ages, Pope Paul VI proclaimed Benedict the patron saint of Europe. Benedict's famous abbey at Monte Cassino, the parent house of European monasticism, was not so peaceful a place as Benedict's* Rule *would dictate. It was taken by Lombards in 589, by Saracens in 884, and by Normans in 1030. During the Black Death an earthquake damaged the buildings, which were rebuilt in the sixteenth and seventeenth centuries. In 1944, falsely*

The selections here are translated by Cardinal Gasquet (London: Chatto and Windus, 1925).

believing the monastery to be a German stronghold, the Allies bombed the building to rubble, then rebuilt it to its original plans after the war.

What the Abbot Should Be

An abbot to be fit to rule a monastery should ever remember what he is called, and in his acts illustrate his high calling. For in a monastery he is considered to take the place of Christ, since he is called by His name as the apostle saith, *Ye have received the spirit of the adoption of sons, whereby we cry, Abba, Father.* Therefore the abbot should neither teach, ordain, nor require anything against the command of our Lord (God forbid!), but in the minds of his disciples let his orders and teaching be mingled with the leaven of divine justice.

The abbot should ever be mindful that at the dread judgment of God there will be inquiry both as to his teaching and as to the obedience of his disciples. Let the abbot know that any lack of goodness, which the master of the family shall find in his flock, will be accounted the shepherd's fault. On the other hand, he shall be acquitted in so far as he shall have shown all the watchfulness of a shepherd over a restless and disobedient flock: and if as their pastor he shall have employed every care to cure their corrupt manners, he shall be declared guiltless in the Lord's judgment, and he may say with the prophet, *I have not hidden Thy justice in my heart; I have told Thy truth and Thy salvation; but they contemned and despised me.* And then in the end shall death be inflicted as a meet punishment upon the sheep which have not responded to his care. When, therefore, any one shall receive the name of abbot, he ought to rule his disciples with a twofold teaching: that is, he should first show them in deeds rather than words all that is good and holy. To such as are understanding, indeed, he may expound the Lord's behests by words; but to the hard-hearted and to the simple-minded he must manifest the divine precepts in his life. Thus, what he has taught his disciples to be contrary to God's law, let him show in his own deeds that such things are not be done, lest preaching to others *he himself become a castaway,* and God say unto him thus sinning, *why dost thou declare My justices, and take My testament in thy mouth? Thou hast hated discipline, and cast My speeches behind thee.* And *Thou, who didst see the mote in thy brother's eye, hast thou not seen the beam that is in thine own?*

Let him make no distinction of persons in the monastery. Let not one be loved more than another, save such as be found to excel in obedience or good works. Let not the free-born be put before the serf-born in religion, unless there be other reasonable cause for it. If upon due consideration the abbot shall see such cause he may place him where he pleases; otherwise let all keep their own places, because *whether bond or free we are all one in Christ,* and bear an equal burden of service under one Lord: *for with God there is no accepting of persons.* For one thing only are we preferred by Him, if we are found better than others in good works and more humble. Let the abbot therefore have equal love for all, and let all, according to their deserts, be under the same discipline.

The abbot in his teaching should always observe that apostolic rule which saith, Reprove, entreat, rebuke. That is to say, as occasions require he ought to mingle encouragement with reproofs. Let him manifest the sternness of a master and the loving affection of a father. He must reprove the undisciplined and restless severely, but he should exhort such as are obedient, quiet and patient, for their better profit. We charge him, however, to reprove and punish the stubborn and negligent. Let him not shut his eyes to the sins of offenders; but, directly they begin to show themselves and to grow, he must use every means to root them up utterly. . . .

To the more virtuous and apprehensive, indeed, he may for the first or second time use words of warning; but in dealing with the stubborn, the hard-headed, the proud and the disobedient, even at the very beginning of their sin, let him chastise them with stripes and with bodily punishments; knowing that it is written, *The fool is not corrected with words.* And again, *strike thy son with a rod and thou shalt deliver his soul from death.*

The abbot ought ever to bear in mind what he is and what he is called; he ought to know that to whom more is entrusted, from him more is exacted. Let him recognize how difficult and how hard a task he has undertaken, to rule souls and to make himself a servant to the humours of many. One, forsooth, must be led by gentle words, another by sharp reprehension, another by persuasion; and thus shall he so shape and adapt himself to the character and intelligence of each, that he not only suffer no loss in the flock entrusted to his care, but may even rejoice in its good growth. Above all things let him not slight nor make little of the souls committed to his care, heeding more fleeting, worldly and frivolous things; but let him remember always that he has undertaken the government of souls, of which he shall also have to give an account. And that he may not complain of the want of temporal means, let him remember that it is written, *Seek first the kingdom of God, and His justice, and all things shall be given to you.* And again, *Nothing is wanting to such as fear Him.*

He should know that whoever undertakes the government of souls must prepare himself to account for them. And however great the number of the brethren under him may be, let him understand for certain that at the Day of Judgment he will have to give to our Lord an account of all their souls as well as of his own. In this way, by fearing the inquiry concerning his flock which the Shepherd will hold, he is solicitous on account of others' souls as well as of his own, and thus whilst reclaiming other men by his corrections, he frees himself also from all vice.

On Taking Counsel of the Brethren

Whenever any weighty matters have to be transacted in the monastery let the abbot call together all the community and himself propose the matter for discussion. After hearing the advice of the brethren let him consider it in his own mind, and then do what he shall judge most expedient. We ordain that all must be called to council, because the Lord often reveals to younger members what is best. And let the brethren give their advice with all humble subjection, and presume not stiffly to defend their own opinion. Let them rather leave the matter to the abbot's discretion, so that all submit to what he shall deem best. As it becometh disciples to obey their master, so doth it behoove the master to dispose of all things with forethought and justice. . . .

The Instruments of Good Works

First of all, to love the Lord God with all our heart, with all our soul, with all our strength.

> Then, to love our neighbor as ourselves.
> Then, not to kill.
> Not to commit adultery.
> Not to steal.
> Not to be covetous.
> Not to bear false witness.

To respect all men.
Not to do to another what one would not have done to
oneself.
To deny oneself in order to follow Christ.
To chastise the body.
Not to be fond of pleasures.
To love fasting.
To give refreshment to the poor.
To clothe the naked.
To visit the sick.
To bury the dead.
To come to the help of those in trouble.
To comfort those in sadness. . . .
Not to wish to be called holy before one is so; but to be holy
        first so as to be called such with truth.
Daily in one's acts to keep God's commandments.
To love chastity.
To hate no man.
Not to be jealous or envious.
Not to love wrangling.
To show no arrogant spirit.
To reverence the old.
To love the young.
To pray for one's enemies for the love of Christ.
To make peace with an adversary before the sun sets.
And, never to despair of God's mercy.

Behold these are the tools of our spiritual craft; when we shall have made use of them constantly day and night, and shall have proved them at the day of judgment, that reward shall be given us by our Lord, which He has promised, *Which eye hath not seen, nor ear heard, nor hath it entered into the heart of man to conceive what God hath prepared for those that love Him.* Steadfastly abiding in the community, the workshop where all these instruments are made use of is the cloister of the monastery.

How Young Children Are to Be Corrected

Every age and state of intelligence ought to be governed in the way suitable to it. Thus the faults of those who are children or youths, or who cannot understand the seriousness of the penalty of excommunication, shall be punished by rigorous fasting or corrected by sharp stripes.

Ought Monks to Have Anything of Their Own

Above all others, let this vice be extirpated in the monastery. No one, without leave of the abbot, shall presume to give, or receive, or keep as his own, anything whatever: neither book, nor tablets, nor pen: nothing at all. For monks are men who can claim no dominion even over their own bodies or wills. All that is necessary, however, they may hope from the Father of the monastery; but they shall keep nothing which the abbot has not given or allowed. All things are to be common to all, as it is written, *Neither did any one say or think that aught was his own.* Hence if any one shall be found given to this most wicked vice let him be admonished once or twice, and if he do not amend let him be subjected to correction.

Whether All Ought to Receive Necessary Things Uniformly

It is written, *Distribution was made to every one, according as he had need.* By this we do not mean that there is to be a personal preference (which God forbid), but a consideration for infirmities. In this wise let him who needs less thank God and be not distressed, and let him who requires more be humiliated because of his infirmity, and not puffed up by the mercy that is shown him: so all the members shall be in peace. Above all things let not the pest of murmuring, for whatever cause, by any word or sign, be manifested. If any one shall be found faulty in this let him be subjected to the most severe punishment.

Of the Weekly Servers in the Kitchen

The brethren are so to serve each other that no one be excused from work of the kitchen unless on the score of health, or because he is occupied in some matter of great utility, for thence great reward is obtained and charity is exercised. Let the weaker brethren, however, have help that they may not do their work in sadness; and let all generally be helped according to the circumstances of the community or the position of the place (i.e. kitchen). If the community be large the cellarer may be eased from the service of the kitchen, and any others who (as we have said) are engaged in matters of greater utility. Let the rest serve one another in charity. On Saturday, he who ends his weekly service must clean up everything. He must wash the towels with which the brethren wipe their hands and feet; and he who finishes his service, and he who enters on it, are to wash the feet of all. He shall give back to the cellarer all the vessels used in his ministry, cleaned and unbroken, and the cellarer shall hand them to the one entering on his office, that he may know what he gives and what he receives. . . .

The Weekly Reader

There ought always to be reading whilst the brethren eat at table. Yet no one shall presume to read there from any book taken up at haphazard; but whoever is appointed to read for the whole week is to enter on his office on the Sunday. Let the brother when beginning his service after Mass and Communion ask all to pray for him, that God may preserve him from the spirit of pride. And let the following verse be thrice repeated by all in the oratory, he, the reader, first beginning: *O Lord, Thou wilt open my lips, and my mouth shall declare Thy praise,* then, having received a blessing, let the reader enter upon his office. The greatest silence shall be kept, so that no whispering, nor noise, save the voice of the reader alone, be heard there.

Whatever is required for eating and drinking the brethren shall minister to each other so that no one need ask for anything. Yet should anything be wanted it ought to be demanded by sign rather than by word. Let no one ask any question there about what is being read or about anything else, lest occasion be given to the evil one; unless, perhaps, the prior shall wish to say something briefly for the purpose of edification. The brother who is reader for the week may take a mess of pottage before beginning to read, on account of Holy Communion, and lest perchance it may be too long for him to fast. He shall eat afterwards with the weekly servers and kitchen helpers. The brethren, however, are not all to read or sing in course, but only such as may edify the hearers.

Of the Amount of Food

We believe that it is enough to satisfy just requirement if in the daily meals, at both the sixth and ninth hours, there be at all seasons of the year two cooked dishes, so that he who cannot eat of the one may make his meal of the other. Therefore two dishes of cooked food must suffice for all the brethren, and if there be any fruit or young vegetables these may be added to the meal as a third dish. Let a pound weight of bread suffice for each day, whether there be one meal or two, that is, for both dinner and supper. If there is to be supper a third of the pound is to be kept back by the cellarer and given to the brethren at that meal.

If however, the community has been occupied in any great labor it shall be at the will, and in the power of the abbot, if he think fit, to increase the allowance, so long as every care be taken to guard against excess, and that no monk be incapacitated by surfeiting. For nothing is more contrary to the Christian spirit than gluttony, as our Lord declares, *Take heed to yourselves lest perhaps your hearts be overcharged with surfeiting.* And the same quantity shall not be given to young children, but a lesser amount than those older; frugality being maintained in everything. All, save the very weak and sick, are to abstain wholly from eating the flesh of quadrupeds [animals with four feet].

Of the Measure of Drinks

Every one hath his proper gift from God, one thus, another thus. For this reason the amount of other people's food cannot be determined without some misgiving. Still, having regard to the weak state of the sick, we think that a pint of wine a day is sufficient for any one. But let those whom God gives the gift of abstinence know that they shall receive their proper reward. If either local circumstances, the amount of labour, or the heat of the summer require more, it can be allowed at the will of the prior, care being taken in all things that gluttony and drunkenness creep not in.

Although we read that "wine is not the drink of monks at all," yet, since in our days they cannot be persuaded of this, let us at least agree not to drink to satiety, but sparingly, *Because wine maketh even the wise to fall away.*

The Koran

The Koran is the holy book of Islam, one of the three great monotheistic religions of the West. The Koran is actually a collection of the prophetic utterances of Muhammad, as they were given to him in visions by messengers of God. Recognized as the same God worshipped in their own ways by Jews and by Christians, the God of Islam is starkly alone, all-powerful, and deeply concerned with humans. Islam means submission, and the proper stance of the Muslim is undisputing obedience. Acknowledging the importance of the stories and traditions of both Jews and Christians, Islam gives special place to Abraham, who submitted to God in his willingness to sacrifice his son Isaac at God's command, and who was the father of Ishmael.

The founder of Islam, Muhammad, was born into the Quraysh, the tribe who controlled the city of Mecca and its sacred shrine, the Kaaba. The Kaaba was a structure which held a sacred black stone traditionally believed to have been carried by Adam as he left Eden. Before Muhammad's time, the Kaaba was a holy place to many Arabian tribes, each recognizing it as a shrine. Thus, as keepers of the shrine, the Quraysh managed a lucrative pilgrimage trade in Mecca.

His father died just before Muhammad was born in 570 CE, and his mother died when he was young. Raised first by his grandfather and then by an uncle, Muhammad early sought a living in trade, and didn't learn to read or write. When he was about 25, he began running the caravans of the wealthy widow, Kadijah, who asked him to marry her, though she was 15 years older than he.

In 610, during the month of Ramadan, when Muhammad had retreated to a cave outside of Mecca for meditation and reflection, a powerful voice ordered him to read or to recite "in the name of your Lord, who created humankind from a clot of blood!" When Muhammad returned home, Kadijah recognized that he had had a revelation and she became the first convert to Islam, which sees Muhammad as the last in a line of prophets that includes Adam, Noah, Abraham, Moses, and Jesus.

Attempts to convert other Meccans were not entirely successful: submission to God was one thing, but when Muhammad began to claim that the Kaaba was the shrine of Allah alone, he became a threat to the economy of the city. Finally in 622, having gathered very few followers in twelve years, he was forced, under cover of night, to flee the city and journey to the city later called Medina. This journey, about 300 miles, is called the hijra (or "hegira"), and marks the beginning date of the Islamic calendar. After the hijra, Muhammad moved actively to strengthen Islam by becoming an administrator and political leader as well as a prophet. He expelled Jewish and pagan groups in Medina who failed to respond to his announcements of God's commands, and increasingly his visions dealt in the legal and ethical details of running a community.

Throughout his years in Medina, Muhammad continued his conflict with his former tribe in Mecca, who were routed in several skirmishes and saw their trade dwindle. Finally in 629, Muhammad

---

This translation of the Koran is a recent one by Thomas Cleary (San Francisco: HarperCollins, 1993).

led a force against the city, which surrendered without bloodshed, leaving Muhammad in control of both city and sacred shrine. After the prophet's death three years later, Mecca became the center of Islam, with a pilgrimage to Mecca (hajj) required of Muslims who are able to undertake the journey.

The revelations to Muhammad were collected by his friends and followers into a book called the Koran (Qu'ran). It is strikingly different from both the Hebrew Bible and the Christian New Testament. The chapters (or surahs) are arranged simply in order of length, longest first; because the earlier revelations tended to be shorter and simpler, they fall near the end of the book. The traditional titles of the Surahs do not announce a theme for the whole chapter; instead, they are simply a striking word or phrase that occurs early in the chapter. There is almost no narrative or story-telling in the Koran; instead the collection has the quality of almost random pronouncements, with much repetition. Throughout there are demands of submission to God's absolute will, colored by continual reminders of God's great mercy and kindness. The language of the Koran, a written dialect of Arabic, is considered sacred and perfect, the language of God himself.

The Muslim religion is based centrally on the Koran, with peripheral importance attached to customs, sayings, and traditions associated with Muhammad. But Muhammad insisted that he not be viewed as divine or extraordinary: he was simply the messenger who carried the Koran to the people. The emphasis, then, is upon acting in accordance with God's will, beginning with five practices so important they have come to be called the Pillars of Islam. First, the Muslim must make a profession of faith. To say "There is no God but God, and Muhammad is his prophet" with sincerity is all that is required to become a Muslim. This simple statement, in striking contrast with the Christian creeds earlier in this section, captures the key doctrines of Islam, that God is one and that his last messenger was Muhammad.

The second pillar is prayer. Five times a day, at set times, the Muslim must bow down toward Mecca and pray in Arabic. This prayer can be done with others at a mosque, but the worship of God is primarily a private act and the relationship with God does not depend on intercessors or intermediaries.

The third pillar is giving, both charitable giving to the poor and needy, and the giving of a levied amount to support the religious and political policies of the government in certain Islamic countries. The fourth pillar is fasting, required every year during the month of Ramadan, the time of Muhammad's first vision. Food and drink are prohibited during daylight hours. Because Muslims follow a lunar calendar, Ramadan moves from season to season, which means that in some years the fasting occurs during long days in hot summer weather and in other years in cooler winter.

The fifth pillar is pilgrimage. Every Muslim who is able and can afford it is supposed to make the pilgrimage (hajj) to Mecca once during his or her lifetime. Because the pilgrimage most properly happens at a given time each year, tens of thousands of pilgrims from all over the world converge on Mecca at the same time, living in huge tent cities.

The hajj is a personal experience that makes manifest the notion that Islam creates a new brotherhood of faith that transcends the rivalries of tribes, nations, and races. In actual practice, of course, Islam itself split within a few generations of the death of Muhammad into a number of sects based on differences in belief. The chief split came about over the question of whether the leaders (caliphs) of Islam had to be direct descendants of Muhammad through his daughter Fatima. That division, alive today, separates the conservative shiites (based in Iran) from the sunnis, based in Saudi Arabia. With perhaps 700 million believers worldwide, Islam is still rapidly gaining converts, and is reported to be the fastest growing religion in the United States.

1. The Opening

In the name of God, the compassionate, the merciful

> All praise belongs to God,
> Lord of all worlds,
>
> The Compassionate, The Merciful,
>
> Ruler of Judgment Day.
>
> It is You that we worship,
> and to You we appeal for help.
>
> Show us the straight way,
>
> the way of those You have graced,
> not of those on whom is Your wrath,
> nor of those who wander astray.

2. The Cow

In the name of God, the compassionate, the merciful

> (2–7)
>
> This book, without doubt,
> has guidance in it for the conscientious;
>
> those who believe in the unseen,
> and steadily practice prayer,
> and give of what We have provided them,
>
> and those who believe
> what has been sent down to you
> and what was sent down before you,
> and are certain of the Hereafter.
>
> They follow guidance from their Lord,
> and they are the happy ones.
>
> As for the ungrateful who refuse,
> it is the same to them
> whether you warn them or not;
> they do not believe.
>
> God has sealed their hearts
> and their hearing,
> and covered their eyes;
> for them there is a great torment.

(8–14)

And among humankind
are those who say
they believe in God and the Last Day
but they do not believe.

They try to deceive God
and those who believe,
but they do not deceive anyone
except themselves,
although they do not know it.

There is a sickness in their hearts,
and God has made them sicker;
and theirs is a painful torment,
because they were in fact lying.

And when they are told not to make trouble on earth,
they say they are only doing good.

Is it not that they are in fact
the troublemakers,
without even knowing it?

And when it is said to them,
"Believe as the people believe,"
they say, "Shall we believe
as imbeciles believe?"
No, it is they,
they who are the imbeciles,
though they do not know.

And when they encounter
those who believe,
they say, "We believe."
But when they are alone
with their obsessions,
they say,
"We are in fact with you;
we were only joking."

(42–46)

And do not obscure truth by falsehood,
or knowingly conceal the truth;

and be constant in prayer,
and give charity,
and worship with the worshipful.

Do you command people to be just
when you forget yourselves
even though you read the Book?
Now won't you understand?

And seek help
with patience and prayer;
though it is indeed hard
except for the humble,

those who consider
that they will meet their Lord,
and that they will return to God.

(48)

And be wary of a day
when no soul can compensate
for another soul at all,
and no intercession is accepted from it,
and no ransom is taken from it,
and they will not be helped.

(62)

Be they Muslims, Jews,
Christians, or Sabians,
those who believe in God and the Last Day
and who do good
have their reward with their Lord.
They have nothing to fear,
and they will not sorrow.

(83)

Worship nothing but God;
be good to your parents and relatives,
and to the orphan and the poor.
Speak nicely to people,
be constant in prayer,
and give charity.

(84–85)

And when We took your promise
that you would not shed the blood of your own,
and would not drive your own from their homes,
you then confirmed it,
as you yourselves bear witness.

But then you yourselves
killed your own people,
and drove a group from among you
out of their homes,
assisting efforts against them
with iniquity and enmity.

(87)

We gave Moses the Book,
and caused messengers to follow after him.
And We gave clear proofs
to Jesus son of Mary,
and We strengthened him
with the holy spirit.
Are you not haughty and arrogant
whenever a messenger comes to you
with what your selves do not desire?
Some you have branded liars,
others you have killed.

(136)

Say,
"We believe in God,
and what was revealed to us,
and what was revealed to Abraham and Ishmael,
and Isaac and Joseph and the Tribes,
and what was given to Moses and Jesus,
and what was given to the prophets
from their Lord.
And we do not make any distinction
between individuals among them,
for we submit to God."

(163–164)

And your God is one God:
there is no God but The One,
the Compassionate,
the Merciful.

Behold, in the creation
of the heavens and the earth,
and the alternation of night and day,
and the ships that sail on the sea
to profit the people,
and the water God rains from the skies,
thereby enlivening the earth
after it has died,

and spreading animals of all kinds
thereupon,
and in the shifting of the winds
and the clouds
enslaved between the heavens and the earth:
therein are signs
for a discerning people.

(255)

God!
There is no God but The One,
the Living, the Self-subsistent:
drowsiness does not overtake God,
nor sleep.
To God belongs
what is in the heavens and the earth:
who could there be
who can intercede with God
except by leave of God?
God knows what is in front of them,
and what is behind them;
but they do not comprehend
anything of God's knowledge
except as God wills.
The throne of God
extends over the heavens and the earth,
and the preservation of them both
is not oppressive to God,
for God is most exalted, most sublime.

(256)

There is to be no compulsion in religion.
True direction is in fact distinct from error:
so whoever disbelieves in idols
and believes in God
has taken hold
of the most reliable handle,
which does not break.
For God is all-hearing and all-knowing.

(262–264)

Those who spend their wealth
in the way of God
and then do not follow what they spend
with reminders of their generosity
or with abusive treatment,
they have their reward

with their Lord.
And there is nothing for them to fear,
and they will not sorrow.

Kind and forgiving words
are better than charity
followed by abuse.
And God,
having no needs,
is most supremely clement.

Believers,
do not nullify your charities
by reminders of your generosity,
or by abusive behavior,
as do those who spend their wealth
to be seen by the people,
without believing in God
and the last day.
And what that is like
is a hard stone with dust on it
on which a heavy rain falls
and leaves it barren:
they cannot do a thing
with what they have earned.
And God does not guide
the people who refuse.

3. The Family of Imraan

In the name of God, the compassionate, the merciful

(2–7)

God:
there is nothing worth worship but God
the Living, the Self-subsistent.

God sent to you the Book with the truth
confirming the truth of what preceded it.
And God sent the Torah and the Gospel before,
as guidance to humankind;
and God sent the Criterion.

Surely for those who reject
the signs of God
there is a torment most severe;
and God is a mighty avenger.

Nothing is concealed from God,
on earth or in heaven.

God it is who forms you
in the wombs,
as God wills:
there is nothing worth worship but God,
the Almighty, the All-wise.

God it is who sent
the Book to you:
in it are verses definitive,
these the matrix of the Book;
while others are metaphorical.
And those in whose hearts is distortion
follow the metaphorical in it seeking discord,
seeking esoteric interpretation.
But no one knows
its original meaning
but God.
And those deeply rooted in knowledge say,
"We believe in it;
all is from God."
But none will be admonished
except for those of heart.

(18–22)

God attests
that there is in fact
nothing worth worship but God,
and so do the angels
and those with knowledge,
standing on justice.
There is nothing worth worship but God,
epitome of power and wisdom.

Indeed, religion with God
is surrender:
and those to whom the Book was given
did not differ
until after knowledge came to them,
out of conceit and envy among them.
And as for those who reject
the signs of God,
God indeed is quick to take account.

And if they dispute with you,
then say,

"I have surrendered my being to God,
and so have those who follow me."
And say to those
to whom the Book has been given,
and to the unlettered folk,
"Do you surrender to God?"
And if they have surrendered,
they are rightly guided.
But if they turn away,
your only responsibility
is to deliver a message;
and God sees the servants of God.

As for those who reject the signs of God
and kill the prophets,
alienated from truth,
and kill those who call for justice from the people,
inform them of an excruciating pain.

They are those whose works are futile
in this world and the hereafter;
and they have no helpers or protectors.

(29)

Say,
"Whether you conceal
what is in your hearts
or reveal it,
God knows.
And God knows
what is in the heavens
and what is in the earth;
and God has power over all things.

4. Women

In the name of God, the compassionate, the merciful

(1–10)

O humanity,
be reverent toward your Lord
who created you from one soul
and created its mate from it,
and from these two
disseminated many men and women.
Be reverent toward God
by whom you ask of each other,

and be reverent toward relationships;
for God is watching over you.

And give orphans their property
without exchanging bad for good
or consuming their wealth
commingled with your own,
for that is a grave misdeed.

And if you fear
you may not be able
to do justice by the orphans,
then marry women who please you,
two, three, or four;
but if you fear
you may not be able
to treat them equitably,
then marry one,
or a ward in your custody:
that would be more fitting,
so you do not go awry.

And give the women
their dowries as gifts;
but if they favor you
with anything from it
of their own accord,
then enjoy it
as wholesome and salutary.

And do not give to incompetents
your property that God has granted you for subsistence,
but provide for them from it, and clothe them,
and speak fair words to them.

And test orphans
until they reach the age of marriage;
and if you perceive in them
integrity and reason,
then turn their property over to them.

And do not consume it in extravagance,
or in a hurry before their majority.
And let one who is rich
take nothing from it,
and let one who is poor
partake of it fairly.
And then when you turn over
their property to them,

have evidence or witness made of it,
though God is sufficient
in taking account.

There is a portion for men
from what is left by their parents and closest kin,
and there is a portion for women
from what is left by their parents and closest kin:
whether there is little or much,
there is a determined portion.

And when relatives, orphans, or paupers
are present at the division,
then give them something of it,
and speak fair words to them.

And be as apprehensive as those
who leave behind them helpless children fear for them;
and be wary of God,
and speak to them fittingly.

For surely those who consume
the property of orphans unjustly
only ingest a fire;
and they will be burning
in a furious blaze.

(26–28)

God wants to clarify for you
and guide you in the ways
of those who were before you,
and to turn toward you;
for God is most knowing, most wise.

God wants to turn toward you,
but the wish of those who follow their lusts
is that you turn away,
turn utterly from God.

God wants to lighten your burden,
for humanity was created weak.

7. The Heights

(156–157)

God said,
"I strike with My punishment
whomever I will.
But My mercy extends to all things;

so I will make it the destiny of those
who are conscientious and charitable,
and those who believe in Our signs:"

"those who follow the Messenger,
the Unlettered Prophet,
of whom they find notice
in their own writings,
in the Torah and the Gospel:
he directs them to what is fair,
and restrains them from iniquity;
and he makes good things lawful to them,
and prohibits what is bad.
And he relieves them of their burden,
and the yokes that were upon them.
So those who have faith in him,
and who honor and assist him,
and who follow the light
sent down with him—
those are the happy, successful ones."

36. Yaa Siin

(48–70)

And they say,
"When is this promise to be fulfilled,
if you are telling the truth?"

They have nothing to look forward to
but a single blast:
it will seize them
even as they are disputing,

so they won't be able
to make their last will,
and they won't return to their families.

And the trumpet will be sounded,
and from the graves to their Lord
they will hasten.

They will say,
"Woe to us!
Who has roused us
from our beds?"
This is what God
The Compassionate has promised,
for the Prophets spoke the truth.

It will be just one single blast,
whereupon all of them
will be brought together before Us.

And on that day
no soul will be wronged in anything,
and you will not be rewarded
except for what you did.

The people of the Garden
will be happy at work that day;

they and their mates
will be in the shade
reclining on couches,

every amenity there for them,
and they have whatever they call for.

Peace:
a word from a merciful Lord.

And stand aside this day,
you who are sinners;

did I not command you,
children of Adam,
not to serve Obsession,
an obvious enemy to you,

and to serve Me,
this being a straight Path?

It has in fact led
a great many of you astray;
did you not understand?

This is hell,
which you were promised:

burn in it today,
for having been ungrateful.

On that day We will seal their mouths,
and their hands will speak to Us,
and their feet will bear witness
to what they have earned.

And if We wished,
We could have put out their eyes;
and they would have rushed for the path,
but how could they see?

And if We wished,
We could have transformed them
in their places,
so they could neither
progress nor go back.

And whomever We grant long life,
We reverse in nature:
so will they not understand?

And We did not teach him poetry,
as it is not proper for him.
This is but a Reminder
and a clear Recital,

to warn those who are alive,
and prove the Word against
the ungrateful who disbelieve.

96. Recite!

In the name of God, the compassionate, the merciful

(1–19)

Recite,
in the name of your Lord,
who created:

who created humankind
from a clot of blood.

Recite,
for your Lord is most generous,

who taught by the pen,

taught humankind
what it did not know.

Oh, no!
Humankind does indeed go too far

in regarding itself as self-sufficient:

in fact the return is to your Lord.

Do you see the one who forbids

the servant from prayer?

Do you see if he is on guidance,

or directs others to be conscientious?

Do you see if he repudiates truth and turns away?

Does he not know God sees?

Oh, no!
If he does not desist,
We will drag him by the forelock,

a lying, sinning forelock.

Let him call upon his associates then:

We will call the keepers of hell.

Oh, no!
Do not obey him:
bow down and draw closer to God.

Arthurian Source Documents

The small collection of excerpts collected here provide an example of the kinds of materials historians have to work with when they make decisions about sometimes compelling questions. In this case, the question is one that occurs to almost every reader acquainted with the Arthurian legends: Did King Arthur really exist? The documentary evidence below is surprisingly slim, and it is cast in such a way as to defeat a decisive answer to that question. The documents point to a real certainty, that if Arthur existed, he lived in that time after 410 when the Roman legions had pulled out of Britain and left the native Britons (a Celtic people) to fend for themselves. To ward off invading Pictish tribes in the north, the Britons hired Germanic settlers as mercenaries to fight for them. Within a few years, as the Germans themselves tell us in the Anglo-Saxon Chronicle, *the payments stopped and the German tribes themselves became the enemy, settling in the fertile land to the south and inviting over more of their people, the Angles, Saxons, and Jutes. Two chronicles written by the monks Gildas and Nennius tell this story from the side of the British. Nennius identifies as crucial a battle that occurred at Mount Badon and names Arthur as the winning war-leader. But Nennius is writing in 800, nearly 300 years after the key battle.*

As it happens, there is an earlier, almost contemporary, mention of the Battle of Mount Badon. The Welsh monk Gildas, in an attack upon his countrymen for their spinelessness in the face of the treacherous Germans, also calls the Battle of Mount Badon decisive. He says that it occurred in the very year of his birth, within living memory of friends or relatives. But Gildas doesn't mention Arthur!

These chronicles are in Latin. It is interesting to note that the Welsh themselves mention Arthur in works that are decidedly more imaginative. But only one poem might bear on the historical question because it has such an early date. The Welsh poem, the Gododdin, *is an account of a battle in which only the poet, Aneirin, is reputed to have escaped alive. In a portion of the poem that dates from around the year 600, the poet says, in praise of a warrior named Gwawddur, that he was brave and generous, "but he was no Arthur."*

What are we to make of this evidence? A strict historian might have to agree with the view put forward by J. N. L. Myres in The English Settlements *(Oxford History of England, 1986):*

"What is certainly more significant is that Gildas, in writing the only contemporary narrative of these momentous events, has no mention whatever of Arthur. His silence is decisive in determining the historical insignificance of this enigmatic figure. It is inconceivable that Gildas, with his intense interest in the outcome of a struggle that he believed had been decisively settled in the year of his own birth, should not have mentioned Arthur's part in it had that part been of any political consequence. The fact is that there is no contemporary or near-contemporary evidence for Arthur playing any decisive part

---

The Anglo-Saxon Chronicle, originally written in Old English, is taken from the translation of G. N. Garmonsway (London: J. M. Dent, 1953). The other documents, all originally in Latin, have been translated for this anthology by the editor.

in these events at all. No figure on the borderline of history and mythology has wasted more of the historian's time. There are just enough casual references in later Welsh legend, one or two of which may go back to the seventh century, to suggest that a man with this late Roman name Artorius may have won repute at some ill-defined point of time and place during the struggle. But if we add anything to the bare statement that Arthur may have lived and fought the Saxons, we pass at once from history to romance."

But that is certainly not the view of history itself, for it has embraced this enigmatic figure, made him a medieval king and showered him with stories of love, adventure, treachery, incest, violence, and spiritual longing. More than 7,000 works based on the Arthurian legends exist in English alone, including novels, plays, poems, movies, comic books, and computer games. And from these slim beginnings!

The Anglo-Saxon Chronicles: *Laud Chronicle,* Early 12th Century

443. In this year the Britons sent overseas to Rome and asked them for troops against the Picts, but they had none there because they were at war with Attila, king of the Huns; and then they sent to the Angles and made the same request to the princes of the Angles.

449. . . . In this year Marcian and Valentinian obtained the kingdom and reigned seven years. In their days Vortigern invited the Angles hither, and they then came hither to Britain3 in three ships at a place *Hoepwinesfleot* [Ebbsfleet, K]. King Vortigern gave them land to the south-east of this land on condition that they fought against the Picts. They then fought against the Picts and had victory wherever they came. Then they sent to Angel; ordered (them) to send more aid and to be told of the worthlessness of the Britons and of the excellence of the land. They then at once sent hither a larger force to help the others. These men came from three nations of Germany: from the Old Saxons, from the Angles, from the Jutes. From the Jutes came the people of Kent and the people of the Isle of Wight, that is the race which now dwells in the Isle of Wight, and the race among the West Saxons which is still called the race of the Jutes. From the Old Saxons came the East Saxons and South Saxons and West Saxons. From Angel, which has stood waste ever since between the Jutes and the Saxons, came the East Angles, Middle Angles, Mercians and all the Northumbrians. Their leaders were two brothers, Hengest and Horsa; they were sons of Wihtgils. Wihtgils was the son of Witta, the son of Weeta, the son of Woden; from this Woden sprang all our4 royal family and that of the peoples dwelling south of the Humber.

455. In this year Hengest and Horsa fought against king Vortigern at a place which is called *Ægelesthrep [Aylesford, K]*, and his brother Horsa was slain. And after that Hengest succeeded to the kingdom and Æsc, his son.

456. In this year Hengest and Æsc fought against the Britons at a place which is called *Crecganford [Crayford, K]*, and there slew four companies; and the Britons then forsook Kent and fled to London in great terror.

Gildas: *De Excidio et Conquestu Britanniae* (c.550)

Then some time passed, and the cruel invaders returned to their homes. . . . The survivors collected their strength under their leader, Ambrosius Aurelianus, a moderate man, who by chance alone of the Roman people had survived the catastrophe in which his parents, who had undoubtedly once worn the royal purple toga, had been killed, and whose present-day descendants have greatly degenerated from their former virtue. He and his men challenged their previous conquerors to battle, and by God's favor, victory was theirs. . . . From that time, now our countrymen and now the enemy have triumphed . . . up to the year of the siege of Mount Badon, when the last but certainly not the least slaughter of these scoundrels took place, which, I know, makes forty-four years and one month, and which was also the year of my birth.

Nennius: *Historia Brittonum* (c.800)

At that time the Saxons thrived in multitudes and increased in Britain. With Hengist dead, his son Octha crossed over from the left side of Britain to the realm of the Kentish people, and from him are descended the kings of the Kentish people. Then Arthur fought against them in those days along with the kings of the Britons, and he was himself the leader in their battles. His first battle was at the mouth of the river which is called Glein. The second, third, fourth, and fifth were upon another river, which is called Dubglas and is in the region of Linnuis. The sixth battle was upon the river which is called Bassas. The seventh battle was in the Wood of Celidon, that is Cat Coit Celidon. The eighth was at Castle Guinnion, in which Arthur carried an image of St. Mary, the Perpetual Virgin, on his shoulders, and the pagans were put to flight on that day, and there was a great slaughter of them by the virtue of Our Lord Jesus Christ and by the virtue of Saint Mary the Virgin his mother. The ninth battle was fought in the City of the Legion. The tenth was fought on the banks of the river which is called Tribruit. The eleventh battle occurred on the mountain which is called Agned. The twelfth battle was on Mount Badon, in which nine hundred and sixty men fell from a single attack of Arthur, and nobody overthrew them but he alone, and in all of the battles he emerged as victor. But although the others were overcome in the battle, they sent for help from Germany, and their forces were ceaselessly reinforced. The Saxons brought over leaders from Germany to rule the Britons. . . .

There is another wonder in the region which is called Ercing. It is a tomb near a fountain that is called Licat Anir, and the name of the man who is buried there was called Anir. He was the son of Arthur the soldier, who himself killed and buried him in that place. Men come to measure the mound, which is sometimes six, sometimes nine, sometimes twelve, or sometimes fifteen feet in length. However you measure it again and again, you will never get the same figure—and I have tested this myself.

Annales Cambriae (c.960)

An. 72 [c.518]. The battle of Badon, in which Arthur carried the cross of our Lord Jesus Christ for three days and three nights on his shoulders, and the Britons were victorious.

An. 93 [c.539]. The battle of Camlann, in which Arthur and Medraut fell, and there was death in Britain and in Ireland.

William of Malmesbury: *De Rebus Gestis Regum Anglorum* (c.1125)

But with Vortimer [son of Vortigern] dead, the vigor of the Britons faded, and their diminishing hopes flowed away, and indeed would have vanished entirely if Ambrosius, the lone survivor of the Romans who after Vortigern was monarch of the realm, had not checked the proud barbarians with the exemplary assistance of the warlike Arthur. This is that Arthur who is raved about even today in the trifles of the Bretons—a man who is surely worthy of being described in true histories rather than dreamed about in fallacious myths—for he truly sustained his tottering homeland for a long time and aroused the broken spirits of his fellow citizens to battle. Finally at the siege of Mount Badon, relying on the image of the mother of the Lord, which he had sewn on his armor, rising up alone, he routed nine hundred of the enemy in an incredible slaughter. . . .

But the tomb of Arthur is nowhere to be seen, so ancient dirges fable that he is still to come.

The Medieval World

Literature in the Middle Ages circulated primarily in manuscript, and had to be copied by hand, at great expense of time and money. As a result, many works have been lost, and many others exist only in single copies that have somehow managed to survive (*Beowulf* and *Sir Gawain and the Green Knight*, for instance). Other works that exist in numerous versions (like Chaucer's *Canterbury Tales*) vary widely because of the carelessness of scribes or because of changes deliberately introduced in copying. Furthermore, because paper did not come into wide use until late in the Middle Ages, manuscripts, made of animal skins, were very expensive, reserved for wealthy patrons, collectors, and church libraries. The growth of administrative bureaucracies stimulated a demand for literate scribes who specialized in legal and government documents. But the best-known of the scribes were the monks, many of whom worked in monasteries that specialized in producing prayer books, liturgies, religious texts, and sometimes secular texts. The most expensive and elaborate of these were illuminated with paintings and marginal decorations, even sometimes highlighted with gold leaf. The manuscript illumination at left is from *De operatione Dei* by Hildegard of Bingen. Prepared in the thirteenth century, after Hildegard's death, the manuscript illustrates visions that Hildegard described in words. In this vision the entire cosmos is a fiery wheel within the body of God, held there by an additional figure Hildegard calls "Love appearing in a human form, the Love of our heavenly Father." Man, the center of this cosmos, is surrounded by figures of stars, planets, and animals. In the lower corner is Hildegard, writing down the vision as she perceives it, "with the innermost eyes and ears of a person."

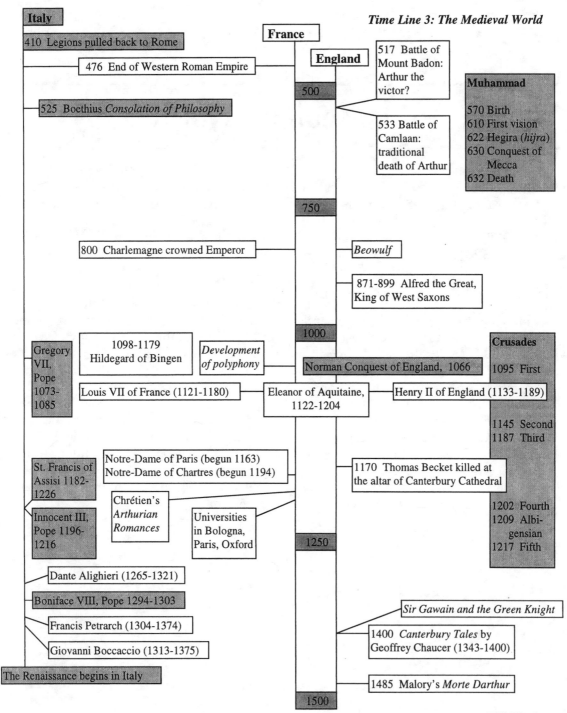

Time Line 3: The Medieval World

Italy

410 Legions pulled back to Rome

476 End of Western Roman Empire

525 Boethius *Consolation of Philosophy*

France

England

500

517 Battle of Mount Badon: Arthur the victor?

533 Battle of Camlaan: traditional death of Arthur

Muhammad

570 Birth
610 First vision
622 Hegira (*hijra*)
630 Conquest of Mecca
632 Death

750

800 Charlemagne crowned Emperor

Beowulf

871-899 Alfred the Great, King of West Saxons

1000

Gregory VII, Pope 1073-1085

1098-1179 Hildegard of Bingen

Development of polyphony

Norman Conquest of England, 1066

Crusades

1095 First

Louis VII of France (1121-1180)

Eleanor of Aquitaine, 1122-1204

Henry II of England (1133-1189)

1145 Second
1187 Third

St. Francis of Assisi 1182-1226

Notre-Dame of Paris (begun 1163)
Notre-Dame of Chartres (begun 1194)

1170 Thomas Becket killed at the altar of Canterbury Cathedral

Innocent III, Pope 1196-1216

Chrétien's *Arthurian Romances*

Universities in Bologna, Paris, Oxford

1202 Fourth
1209 Albigensian
1217 Fifth

1250

Dante Alighieri (1265-1321)

Boniface VIII, Pope 1294-1303

Sir Gawain and the Green Knight

Francis Petrarch (1304-1374)

1400 *Canterbury Tales* by Geoffrey Chaucer (1343-1400)

Giovanni Boccaccio (1313-1375)

The Renaissance begins in Italy

1485 Malory's *Morte Darthur*

1500

Phil Boardman

Feudal Documents

Feudalism was a system of rights and duties that drew its power from land ownership and was common in Western Europe from the ninth to the fourteenth centuries. Land was held "in fief" (as a source of income) in return for specified services, like military service. The hierarchies built into medieval society—kings, nobles, knights, peasants, common serfs—ensured that people were entangled in a web of loyalties and obligations. The king might grant land to a noble in return for military service or the provision of troops in time of war. A vassal *was anyone who held land (a fief) in return for service to an overlord. In a feudal contract, the lord was obligated to provide the fief to the vassal, to protect him, and to offer justice in his court. In return, the lord had the right to demand the services attached to the fief, and these services might be military, but they might also be judicial, administrative, or religious. The two homages below are actual feudal contracts. The second one, through its escape clauses, shows the loyalties demanded of a vassal might often be in conflict. In fact the chivalric literature that grew out of the tempering of late feudalism with doctrines of love and social grace often has as its main theme the problem of conflicting loyalties, such as Lancelot's duties both to Guinevere and to King Arthur in the Arthurian legends.*

[Homage, Somme rurale]

The man should put his hands together as a sign of humility, and place them between the two hands of his lord as a token that he vows everything to him and promises faith to him; and the lord should receive him and promise to keep faith with him. Then the man should say: "Sir, I enter your homage and faith and become your man by mouth and hands [i.e., by taking the oath and placing his hands between those of the lord], and I swear and promise to keep faith and loyalty to you against all others, and to guard your rights with all my strength."

[Homage of John of Toul]

I, John of Toul, make known that I am the liege man of the lady Beatrice, countess of Troyes, and of her son, Theobald, count of Champagne, against every creature, living or dead, saving my allegiance to lord Enjorand of Coucy, lord John of Arcis, and the count of Grandpré. If it should happen that the count of Grandpré should be at war with the countess and count of Champagne on his own quarrel, I will aid the count of Grandpré in my own person, and will

---

These documents are taken from the *Source Book for Mediæval History,* edited by Oliver J. Thatcher and Edgar H. McNeal (New York: Scribner's, 1905).

send to the count and the countess of Champagne the knights whose service I owe to them for the fief which I hold of them.

But if the count of Grandpré shall make war on the countess and the count of Champagne on behalf of his friends and not in his own quarrel, I will aid in my own person the countess and count of Champagne, and will send one knight to the count of Grandpré for the service which I owe him for the fief which I hold of him, but I will not go myself into the territory of the count of Grandpré to make war on him.

[Formula for the Ordeal by Hot Iron]

The ordeal is popularly seen as an example of the strange idiosyncrasies of medieval notions of justice. Ordeals were tests which allowed (or forced) God to step in and decide whether a defendant was guilty or not. Most ordeals were tortures in which God had to protect his righteous servants as a matter of judicial practice, saving them from being burned or drowned or killed in combat if they were innocent. Because of this, the formula for the ordeal has strong echoes of religious liturgies.

(1) First the priest says the prescribed mass; then he has the fire lighted, and blesses the water and sprinkles it over the fire, over the spectators, and over the place where the ordeal is to be held; then he says this prayer:

(2) O Lord, our God, the omnipotent Father, the unfailing Light, hear us, for thou art the maker of all lights. Bless, O God, the fire which we have sanctified and blessed in thy name, thou who hast illumined the whole world, that we may receive from it the light of thy glory. As thou didst illumine Moses with the fire, so illumine our hearts and minds that we may win eternal life.

(3) Then he shall say the litany. . . .

(4) The prayers. . . .

(5) Then the priest approaches the fire and blesses the pieces of iron, saying: O God, the just judge, who art the author of peace and judgest with equity, we humbly beseech thee so to bless this iron, which is to be used for the trial of this case, that if this man is innocent of the charge he may take the iron in his hand, or walk upon it, without receiving harm or injury; and if he is guilty this may be made manifest upon him by thy righteous power; that iniquity may not prevail over justice, nor falsehood over truth.

(6) O Lord, the holy Father, we beseech thee by the invocation of thy most holy name, by the advent of thy Son, our Lord Jesus Christ, and by the gift of the Holy Spirit, the Comforter, to bless these pieces of iron to the manifestation of thy righteous judgment, that they may be so sanctified and dedicated that thy truth may be made known to thy faithful subjects in this trial. In the name of our Lord Jesus Christ, etc.

(7) Omnipotent God, we humbly beseech thee that in the trial which we are about to make, iniquity may not prevail over justice, nor falsehood over truth. And if anyone shall attempt to circumvent this trial by witchcraft or dealing with herbs, may it be prevented by thy power.

(8) May the blessing of God the Father, Son, and Holy Spirit descend upon these pieces of iron, that the judgment of God may be manifest in them.

(9) Then this psalm shall be said on behalf of the accused: Hear my prayer, O Lord, and give ear unto my cry. . . .

(10) Prayer: Hear, we beseech thee, O Lord, the prayer of thy suppliants, and pardon those that confess their sins, and give us pardon and peace.

(11) Then those who are to be tried shall be adjured as follows: I adjure you (name), by omnipotent God who made heaven and earth, the sea, and all that in them is, by Jesus Christ his Son, who was born and suffered for us, by the Holy Spirit, by the holy Mary, the Mother of God, and by all the holy angels, apostles, martyrs, confessors, and virgins, that you do not yield to the persuasions of the devil and presume to take the iron in your hand, if you are guilty of the crime of which you are accused, or if you know the guilty person. If you are guilty and are rash enough to take the test, may you be put to confusion and condemned, by the virtue of our Lord Jesus Christ, and by the sign of his holy cross. But if you are innocent of the crime, in the name of our Lord Jesus Christ and by the sign of his holy cross, may you have faith to take this iron in your hand; and may God, the just Judge, keep you from harm, even as he saved the three children from the fiery furnace and freed Susanna from the false accusation; may you go through the ordeal safe and secure, and may the power of our Lord be made manifest in you this day.

(12) Then he who is about to be tried shall say: In this ordeal which I am about to undergo, I put my trust rather in the power of God the omnipotent Father to show his justice and truth in this trial, than in the power of the devil or of witchcraft to circumvent the justice and the truth of God.

(13) Then the man who is accused takes the sacrament and carries the iron to the designated place. After that the deacon shall bind up his hand and place the seal upon it. And until the hand is unwrapped [*i.e.*, at the end of three days] the man should put salt and holy water in all his food and drink.

NJAL'S SAGA

Iceland was discovered by the Scandinavians in the middle of the ninth century. Settlement began in the 870s, and continued for about sixty years. According to Icelandic sources, most of the settlers came from western Norway, fleeing the tyranny of Harold Fair-Hair, who conquered all the small kingdoms of Norway and united them under his rule. The actual situation was probably more complex than that. Settlement began when Harold was only a boy, and many immigrants came from the Hebrides and northern Scotland, where Norse settlers had established colonies a generation earlier. Many of these Hebrideans were of mixed Norse and Celtic descent; some were Christians, although in the absence of a Church establishment, their descendants adopted the polytheistic beliefs of their neighbors.

The leaders of the settlement were local chieftains—aristocrats of middling rank—from Norway and Scotland. Such men resisted the increasing centralization of power in Europe, and devised a system in Iceland with no central government whatsoever. The only national official was the Lawspeaker, whose role was simply to recite one-third of the law at the Althing (Assembly) each year. Decisions were reached through consensus. Although only the chieftains could vote at the Althing (originally thirty-six, their numbers were later increased to forty-eight), they had to consider the wishes of their supporters, since as free men they could transfer their allegiance to another chieftain whenever they wished. The peaceful adoption of Christianity at the Althing in 1000 was perhaps the greatest achievement of this form of government, and illustrates quite strikingly the supreme value that the Icelanders placed upon the law.

[The Conversion of Iceland]

100. There was a change of rulers in Norway. Jarl Hakon died, and Olaf Tryggvason became king. Hakon had been killed by a thrall named Kark who cut his throat at Rimul in Gaulardale. It was also learned that there was a change of faith in Norway, that they had cast off the old faith, and the king had also Christianized the western lands: the Shetland, Orkeney and Faroe islands.

Many said in Njal's hearing that it was a great abomination to abandon the old faith. Njal replied to them: "It seems to me that the new faith will be much better, and they who receive it will be fortunate. If the men who preach that faith come out to Iceland, then I shall do everything I can to further it." He often said this, and frequently went away from other men and meditated aloud by himself.

That same autumn a ship landed in the Eastfjords at Berufjord, at a place called Gautavik. The captain was named Thangbrand, the son of count Willibald of Saxony. Thangbrand was

The introduction and the translation were provided for this collection by Dennis Cronan.

sent to Iceland by king Olaf Tryggvason to preach the faith. With him was an Icelander named Gudleif, the son of Ari, the son of Mar, the son of Atli, the son of Ulf the Squinter, the son of Hogni the White, the son of Otrygg, the son of Oblaud, the son of Hjorleif the Amorous, king of Hordaland. Gudleif was a renowned fighter, very brave and hardy.

Two brothers named Thorleif and Ketil dwelt at Beruness. They were the sons of Holmstein, the son of Ozur from Broad-dale. They called a meeting and forbade men to trade with the new arrivals. Hall of Sida, who dwelt at Thvattriver in Alptafjord, heard about that, and rode to the ship with thirty men. He went at once to meet Thangbrand and said to him, "Isn't the trading going well?"

Thangbrand replied that it wasn't.

"Now I want to tell you the purpose of my errand," said Hall; "I want to invite you and your crew to my home; I am willing to take the risk in marketing your goods."

Thangbrand thanked him and went to Thvattriver.

One morning that autumn Thangbrand went out early and had a tent pitched. Then he sang mass in the tent with great ceremony, for it was an important feast-day.

Hall asked, "In whose honor are you celebrating this day?"

"The angel Michael's," he replied.

"What powers belong to this angel? asked Hall.

"Many," replied Thangbrand, "he shall weigh everything you do, both good and evil, and he is so merciful that he will weigh the good more."

Hall said, "I would like to have him for my friend."

"You can do that," said Thangbrand. " Give yourself to him today in the name of God."

"I want to stipulate," said Hall, "that you promise, on his behalf, that he will be my guardian angel."

"I promise that," said Thangbrand.

Hall and all his household were baptized.

101. Next spring Thangbrand travelled about preaching the faith, and Hall went with him. When they came west across Lonsheath to Stafafell, a man who dwelt there named Thorkel spoke against the faith and challenged Thangbrand to a duel. Thangbrand defended himself with a crucifix instead of a shield, but nonetheless he won the duel and slew Thorkel.

From there they travelled to Hornafjord and were guests at Borgarhofn, to the west of Heinabergsand. Hildir the Old dwelt there, the father of Glum, who later went to the burning with Flosi. Hildir and all his household received the faith.

From there they went to the cluster of farms at Fell and lodged at Kalfafell, the home of Kol Thorstein, Hall's kinsman. He and all his household received the faith. From there they went to Breidriver, where Ozur Hroaldsson dwelt, another kinsman of Hall's. He accepted preliminary baptism. From there they went to Svinafell. Flosi accepted preliminary baptism, and promised to accompany them to the Althing. From there they travelled west to the cluster of farms at Skog and were guests at Kirkby, the home of Surt the son of Asbjorn, the son of Thorstein, the son of Ketil the Foolish. Surt, like his father, grandfather and great-father before him, was already a Christian. From Skog they moved on to Hofdabrekka. By then the news of their journey had spread everywhere.

There was a man named Sorcerer-Hedin, who dwelt in Kerlingardale. The heathens there hired him to kill Thangbrand and his companions. He went up on Arnarrstakksheath and held a great sacrifice. When Thangbrand was riding westward, the earth burst apart beneath his horse. He leaped from his horse and reached safety on the edge of the chasm, but the earth swallowed the horse with all its harness, and it was never seen again. Then Thangbrand praised God.

Gudleif searched for Sorcerer-Hedin and found him on the heath and pursued him down to Kerlingardale River. When he came within range he cast a spear through him.

102. From there they travelled to Dyrholm, where they held a meeting and preached the faith. Ingjald the son of Thorkel Haeyjar-Tyrdil was baptized there.

From there they went to Fljotshlid and preached the faith. Vetrlidi the skald and his son Ari spoke against the faith the most strongly, so they killed Vetrlidi. This verse was composed about Vetrlidi's slaying:

> The tester of shields came south
> to wield the tools of war
> against the smithy of prayers
> in the warrior's breast.
> The valiant prover of battle-faith
> made the hammer of death
> scream on the skull-anvil
> under Veterlidi's hood.

From there Thangbrad went to Bergthorsknoll, and Njal and all his household received the faith. However Mord and his father Valgerd opposed it very strongly. From there they went west across the river into Haukadale, where they baptized Hall Thorarinsson who was only three years old at the time.

From there they travelled to Grimsness, where Thorvald the Infirm raised a band of men against them and sent word to Ulf Uggason that he should attack Thangbrand and kill him. Thorvald sent this verse to him:

> I send this message
> to Ulf Uggason,
> the wolf with metalled skin
> —there is no enmity between us:
> Thrust the craven betrayer
> who curses our gods
> over the echoing cliff,
> and I will push the other.

Ulf Uggason spoke another verse in reply:

> I will not rise to the bait,
> though it leap toward my teeth,
> from the slapping waves
> of Odin's mead-verse.
> I am far too wise
> to swallow the leaping fly
> in these troubled times.
> I guard myself against harm.

"I do not intend," he said, "to run a fool's errand for him. Let him take care that his tongue doesn't strangle him."

The messenger returned to Thorvald and told him Ulf's reply. Thorvald had many men with him and declared that he was going to ambush the Christians on Blaskoga heath. When Thangbrand and Gudleif were riding from Haukadale they met a man who rode towards them; he asked for Gudleif, and when he found him said: "For the sake of your brother Thorgils at Reykjahills I bring you warning that your enemies have set many ambushes for you, and that Thorvald the Infirm and his men are at Hest Brook in Grimsness."

"All the same," said Gudleif, "we shall ride to meet them."

After that they turned down to Hest Brook. Thorvald had just then crossed over the brook.

"Here's Thorvald now," said Gudleif to Thangbrand, "let's rush him."

Thangbrand hurled his spear through Thorvald, Gudleif hacked his arm off at the shoulder, and Thorvald died.

After that they rode to the Althing. Thorvald's kinsmen wanted to attack them, but Njal and the men from the Eastfjords stood by Thangbrand. Hjalti Skeggjason recited this ditty:

> I'm not afraid to mock the gods:
> I think Freyja's a bitch
> and Odin's another.

Hjalti and Gizur the White went abroad that summer. Thangbrand's ship, the Bison, broke apart off Bulandsness, in the east. Thangbrand travelled through all the western districts.

Steinunn the mother of Skald-Ref came to meet him; she talked to him for a long time, trying to convert him to paganism. Thangbrand was silent while she talked, and spoke for a long time afterwards, turning everything she said aside.

"Have you heard," she said, " that Thor challenged Christ to a duel, and he did not dare to fight against Thor?"

"I have heard," said Thangbrand, "that Thor would be nothing but mould and ashes, if God did not permit him to live."

"Do you know," she said, "who has wrecked your ship?"

"What do you have to say about that?" he asked.

"I will tell you," she said:

> Thor, the hammerer of giants,
> smashed the Bison to chips and bits;
> the gods drove the bobbing
> bell-ringer's sea-steed ashore.
> Christ did not keep the treader
> of the wake from bursting.
> I do not think your god
> protected the sea-buffalo.

Then she spoke another verse:

> Thor drove the sea-beast far
> .from its harbor; he shook
> its frame, beat it
> and hurled it aground.
> Never again will the Bison
> glide over the sea,

> since the rage of Thor's storm
> smashed it to bits.

After that they parted, and Thangbrand went west to Bardastrand.

103. Gest Oddleifsson lived at Hagi on Bardastrand. He was a very wise man, who could foresee men's destinies. He prepared a feast for Thangbrand and his companions. They went to Hagi, sixty men in all. It is reported that there were two hundred heathens there before them. A berserk named Otrygg, whom they all feared, was expected to come there. Otrygg reportedly feared neither fire nor sword. The heathens were terrified of him.

Thangbrand asked if men were willing to receive the faith, but all the heathens spoke out against it.

"I will give you the opportunity," said Thangbrand, "to test which faith is better. We shall make three fires; you heathens shall hallow one, I another, and the third shall be unhallowed. If the berserk is afraid of the one I hallow, and wades through your fire, then you shall receive the faith."

"This is well spoken," said Gest, "and I'll agree to it on behalf of myself and my household."

And when Gest had said this, many more agreed, and there was loud approval.

Then it was reported that the berserk was coming to the farm, and the fires were kindled so that they blazed. Men took their weapons and leaped up on the benches to await him. The berserk rushed with his weapons through the door; he came into the sitting room and immediately waded through the fire which the heathens had hallowed. When he came to the fire which Thangbrand had hallowed, he did not dare wade through it and said that he was burning all over. He swung his sword to strike at the benches, but when he raised it up it stuck in a crossbeam. Thangbrand struck his hand with a crucifix, and a great wonder happened: the sword fell from the berserk's hand. Then Thangbrand thrust a sword into his breast, and Gudleif cut off his arm. Thereupon many more attacked him and they slew the berserk.

After that Thangbrand asked if they were willing to receive the faith. Gest replied that he promised only what he intended to fulfill. Then Thangbrand baptized Gest and all his household, along with many others.

Thangbrand conferred with Gest, asking whether he should travel farther into the west fjords. Gest advised against this, and said that the men there were harsh and difficult to deal with, "And if it is your intention that this faith shall be accepted, then it will be accepted at the Althing, and all the chieftains from every district will be there."

"I have already spoken for it at the Thing," said Thangbrand, "and that is where I met my greatest difficulty." "Yet it is you who has done the most work," said Gest, "though it will fall to others to make the faith into law. As the saying goes, no one fells a tree with the first blow."

Afterwards Gest gave Thangbrand good gifts, and he travelled south again, going first to the Southern Quarter and then to the East fjords. He stayed at Bergthorsknoll, and Njal gave him good gifts. Then he rode east to Alptafjord to stay with Hall. He had his ship repaired; the heathens called it the Iron-Basket. He sailed abroad in this ship with Gudleif.

During that summer Hjalti Skeggjason was outlawed at the Thing for blasphemy against the gods.

104. Thangbrand told king Olaf about the offences of the Icelanders against him, that they were so steeped in sorcery that the earth split asunder beneath his horse and swallowed it.

King Olaf became so enraged that he had all the Icelanders in Norway seized and thrown into dungeons, and he intended to execute them. Then Gizur the White and Hjalti came to him and offered to submit themselves as sureties for these men, and to go out to Iceland to preach the faith; the king took this offer well, and all the Icelanders were set free.

Then Gizur and Hjalti prepared their ship for Iceland, and were away early. They landed at Eyra in the eleventh week of summer. They got horses for themselves at once, as well as men to unload the ship. They rode in a band of thirty men to the Thing, and sent word to the Christians to hold themselves ready. Hjalti remained behind at Reydarmull, because he had heard that he was outlawed for blasphemy. But when they came to Vellandkatla, below Gjabakki, Hjalti came riding after them, and said that he did not want to show the heathens that he was afraid of them. Many Christian men came to meet them, and they rode with a great troop to the Thing. The heathens had also massed their forces, and it seemed as though the entire assembly would become a battle. But that did not happen.

105.   There was a man named Thorgeir, who dwelt at Ljosawater. He was the son of Tjorvi, the son of Thorkel tha Long. His mother was called Thorunn and was the daughter of Thorstein, the son of Sigmund, the son of Gnupa-Bard. Thorgeir's wife was called Gudrid; she was the daughter of Thorkell the black from Hleidrargard; his brother was Orm Trunkback, the father of Hlenni the Old from Saurby. Thorkell and Orm were the sons of Thorir Snippet, the son of Ketil Seal, the son of Ornulf, the son of Bjornolf, the son of Grim Shaggy Cheek, the son of Ketil Trout, the son of Hallbjorn Half-Troll from Hrafnista.

The Christians tented their booths at the Althing. Gizur and Hjalti were in Mosfell Booth. The next day both sides went to the law rock, Christians and heathens, and naming witnesses, each declared the community of laws dissolved. There was such an uproar at the law rock that no one could hear what anyone else said. Then everyone left the law rock, and they all thought the situation looked very bad. The Christians took Hall of Sida as their lawspeaker. Hall went to meet Thorgeir the chieftain from Ljosawater and gave him three marks of silver, so that he would proclaim the law. This was a risky move, because Thorgeir was a heathen.

Thorgeir lay all day with a cloak spread over his head, and no one spoke to him. On the next day men went to the law rock. Thorgeir asked them to hear him and said: "It seems to me that our affairs are dead-locked if everyone does not have the same law. If the law is split apart, then peace will be split apart, and that can not be endured. Now I will ask both the heathens and the Christians, whether they will abide by the laws which I proclaim."

They all consented to this. He demanded oaths and binding pledges from them. They agreed to that, and he received their pledges.

"That is the foundation of our law," he said, "that all men in this land shall be Christians and believe in one God, the Father, the Son and the Holy Spirit, and abandon idolatry. No one shall expose children or eat horse-flesh. Anyone who does these things openly shall be outlawed for three years. But if they are done secretly, there shall be no penalty." (However, these heathen practices were all abolished a few years later, and could not be done secretly any more than openly.) He then spoke about the observance of the Lord's day and fast days, Christmas and Easter, and all the most important holy days. The heathens thought that they had been betrayed, but nonetheless the faith became law and everyone became Christian here in this land. With that, everyone returned home from the Thing.

PETER ABELARD (1079–1142)
The History of My Misfortunes

The story of Abelard and Heloise is among the best-known of medieval love stories, and it has moved people since the time the lovers were still living. Abelard was a brilliant and contentious student who went from teacher to teacher and town to town, finally establishing himself in Paris as a popular teacher.

Abelard's immersion in philosophy and his commitment to logic and the study of language led him to conclusions that often ran counter to the teachings of the church. For much of his life, even ignoring the sensational affair with Heloise, he was the center of controversy, facing charges of heresy, and escaping from attempts on his life. Abelard was never one to back down, and during his career he published tract after tract that offended clerics in authority.

The flames of notoriety were fanned by Abelard and Heloise themselves. The story of Abelard's castration would have spread among his many rivals and his students in any event. But Abelard wrote an account of his life which made clear the contempt he felt for other thinkers and described the passion of his love. Near the ends of their lives, Abelard and Heloise jointly published their correspondence, usually called the Letters of Abelard and Heloise. *After spending all the later years of their lives in various nunneries and monasteries, they can today be found buried together in the cemetery of Père-Lachaise in Paris.*

[The University of Paris and Heloise]

While these things were happening, it became needful for me again to repair to my old home, by reason of my dear mother, Lucia, for after the conversion of my father, Berengarius, to the monastic life, she so ordered her affairs as to do likewise. When all this had been completed, I returned to France, above all in order that I might study theology, since now my oft-mentioned teacher, William, was active in the episcopate of Châlons. In this field of learning Anselm of Laon, who was his teacher therein, had for long years enjoyed the greatest renown.

I sought out, therefore, this same venerable man, whose fame, in truth, was more the result of long-established custom than of the potency of his own talent or intellect. If any one came to him impelled by doubt on any subject, he went away more doubtful still. He was wonderful, indeed, in the eyes of these who only listened to him, but those who asked him questions perforce held him as nought. He had a miraculous flow of words, but they were

---

This translation by Henry Adams Bellows was first published by the Free Press in 1922.

contemptible in meaning and quite void of reason. When he kindled a fire, he filled his house with smoke and illumined it not at all. He was a tree which seemed noble to those who gazed upon its leaves from afar, but to those who came nearer and examined it more closely was revealed its barrenness. . . .

It was not long before I made this discovery, and stretched myself lazily in the shade of that same tree. I went to his lectures less and less often, a thing which some among his eminent followers took sorely to heart, because they interpreted it as a mark of contempt for so illustrious a teacher. Thenceforth they secretly sought to influence him against me, and by their vile insinuations made me hated of him. . . .

In truth at [my] first lecture . . . only a few were present, for it seemed quite absurd to all of them that I, hitherto so inexperienced in discussing the Scriptures, should attempt the thing so hastily. However, this lecture gave such satisfaction to all those who heard it that they spread its praises abroad with notable enthusiasm, and thus compelled me to continue my interpretation of the sacred text. When word of this was bruited about, those who had stayed away from the first lecture came eagerly, some to the second and more to the third, and all of them were eager to write down the glosses which I had begun on the first day, so as to have them from the very beginning.

Now this venerable man of whom I have spoken was acutely smitten with envy, and straightway incited, as I have already mentioned, by the insinuations of sundry persons, began to persecute me for my lecturing on the Scriptures no less bitterly than my former master, William, had done for my work in philosophy. At that time there were in this old man's school two who were considered far to excel all the others: Alberic of Rheims and Lotulphe the Lombard. The better opinion these two held of themselves, the more they were incensed against me. Chiefly at their suggestion, as it afterwards transpired, yonder venerable coward had the impudence to forbid me to carry on any further in his school the work of preparing glosses which I had thus begun. The pretext he alleged was that if by chance in the course of this work I should write anything containing blunders—as was likely enough in view of my lack of training—the thing might be imputed to him. When this came to the ears of his scholars, they were filled with indignation at so undisguised a manifestation of spite, the like of which had never been directed against any one before. The more obvious this rancour became, the more it redounded to my honour, and his persecution did nought save to make me more famous.

And so, after a few days, I returned to Paris, and there for several years I peacefully directed the school which formerly had been destined for me, nay, even offered to me, but from which I had been driven out. At the very outset of my work there, I set about completing the glosses on Ezekiel which I had begun at Laon. These proved so satisfactory to all who read them that they came to believe me no less adept in lecturing on theology than I had proved myself to be in the field of philosophy. Thus my school was notably increased in size by reason of my lectures on subjects of both these kinds, and the amount of financial profit as well as glory which it brought me cannot be concealed from you, for the matter was widely talked of. But prosperity always puffs up the foolish, and worldly comfort enervates the soul, rendering it an easy prey to carnal temptations. Thus I, who by this time had come to regard myself as the only philosopher remaining in the whole world, and had ceased to fear any further disturbance of my peace, began to loosen the rein on my desires, although hitherto I had always lived in the utmost continence. And the greater progress I made in my lecturing on philosophy or theology, the more I departed alike from the practice of the philosophers and the spirit of the divines in the uncleanness of my life. For it is well known, methinks, that philosophers, and still more those who have devoted their lives to arousing the love of sacred study, have been strong above all else in the beauty of chastity.

Thus did it come to pass that while I was utterly absorbed in pride and sensuality, divine grace, the cure for both diseases, was forced upon me, even though I, forsooth, would fain have shunned it. First was I punished for my sensuality, and then for my pride. For my sensuality I lost those things whereby I practiced it; for my pride, engendered in me by my knowledge of letters—and it is even as the Apostle said: "Knowledge puffeth itself up" (i Cor. viii, i)—I knew the humiliation of seeing burned the very book in which I most gloried. And now it is my desire that you should know the stories of these two happenings, understanding them more truly from learning the very facts than from hearing what is spoken of them, and in the order in which they came about. Because I had ever held in abhorrence the foulness of prostitutes, because I had diligently kept myself from all excesses and from association with the women of noble birth who attended the school, because I knew so little of the common talk of ordinary people, perverse and subtly flattering chance gave birth to an occasion for casting me lightly down from the heights of my own exaltation. Nay, in such case not even divine goodness could redeem one who, having been so proud, was brought to such shame, were it not for the blessed gift of grace.

Now there dwelt in that same city of Paris a certain young girl named Heloise, the niece of a canon who was called Fulbert. Her uncle's love for her was equalled only by his desire that she should have the best education which he could possibly procure for her. Of no mean beauty, she stood out above all by reason of her abundant knowledge of letters. Now this virtue is rare among women, and for that very reason it doubly graced the maiden, and made her the most worthy of renown in the entire kingdom. It was this young girl whom I, after carefully considering all those qualities which are wont to attract lovers, determined to unite with myself in the bonds of love, and indeed the thing seemed to me very easy to be done. So distinguished was my name, and I possessed such advantages of youth and comeliness, that no matter what woman I might favour with my love, I dreaded rejection of none. Then, too, I believed that I could win the maiden's consent all the more easily by reason of her knowledge of letters and her zeal therefor; so, even if we were parted, we might yet be together in thought with the aid of written messages. Perchance, too, we might be able to write more boldly than we could speak, and thus at all times could we live in joyous intimacy.

Thus, utterly aflame with my passion for this maiden, I sought to discover means whereby I might have daily and familiar speech with her, thereby the more easily to win her consent. For this purpose I persuaded the girl's uncle, with the aid of some of his friends, to take me into his household—for he dwelt hard by my school—in return for the payment of a small sum. My pretext for this was that the care of my own household was a serious handicap to my studies, and likewise burdened me with an expense far greater than I could afford. Now, he was a man keen in avarice, and likewise he was most desirous for his niece that her study of letters should ever go forward, so, for these two reasons, I easily won his consent to the fulfillment of my wish, for he was fairly agape for my money, and at the same time believed that his niece would vastly benefit by my teaching. More even than this, by his own earnest entreaties he fell in with my desires beyond anything I had dared to hope, opening the way for my love; for he entrusted her wholly to my guidance, begging me to give her instruction whensoever I might be free from the duties of my school, no matter whether by day or by night, and to punish her sternly if ever I should find her negligent of her tasks. In all this the man's simplicity was nothing short of astounding to me; I should not have been more smitten with wonder if he had entrusted a tender lamb to the care of a ravenous wolf. When he had thus given her into my charge, not alone to be taught but even to be disciplined, what had he done save to give free scope to my desires, and to offer me every opportunity, even if I had not sought it, to bend her to my will with threats and blows if I failed to do so with caresses? There were, however, two things which particularly served to allay any foul suspicion: his own love for his niece, and my former reputation for continence.

Why should I say more? We were united first in the dwelling that sheltered our love, and then in the hearts that burned with it. Under the pretext of study we spent our hours in the happiness of love, and learning held out to us the secret opportunities that our passion craved. Our speech was more of love than of the books which lay open before us; our kisses far outnumbered our reasoned words. Our hands sought less the book than each other's bosoms; love drew our eyes together far more than the lesson drew them to the pages of our text. In order that there might be no suspicion, there were, indeed, sometimes blows, but love gave them, not anger; they were the marks, not of wrath, but of a tenderness surpassing the most fragrant balm in sweetness. What followed? No degree in love's progress was left untried by our passion, and if love itself could imagine any wonder as yet unknown, we discovered it. And our inexperience of such delights made us all the more ardent in our pursuit of them, so that our thirst for one another was still unquenched.

In measure as this passionate rapture absorbed me more and more, I devoted ever less time to philosophy and to the work of the school. Indeed it became loathsome to me to go to the school or to linger there; the labour, moreover, was very burdensome, since my nights were vigils of love and my days of study. My lecturing became utterly careless and lukewarm; I did nothing because of inspiration, but everything merely as a matter of habit. I had become nothing more than a reciter of my former discoveries, and though I still wrote poems, they dealt with love, not with the secrets of philosophy. Of these songs you yourself well know how some have become widely known and have been sung in many lands, chiefly, methinks, by those who delighted in the things of this world. As for the sorrow, the groans, the lamentations of my students when they perceived the preoccupation, nay, rather the chaos, of my mind, it is hard even to imagine them.

A thing so manifest could deceive only a few, no one, methinks, save him whose shame it chiefly bespoke, the girl's uncle, Fulbert. The truth was often enough hinted to him, and by many persons, but he could not believe it, partly, as I have said, by reason of his boundless love for his niece, and partly because of the well-known continence of my previous life. Indeed we do not easily suspect shame in those whom we most cherish, nor can there be the blot of foul suspicion on devoted love. Of this St. Jerome in his epistle to Sabinianus (Epist. 48) says: "We are wont to be the last to know the evils of our own households, and to be ignorant of the sins of our children and our wives, though our neighbours sing them aloud." But no matter how slow a matter may be in disclosing itself, it is sure to come forth at last, nor is it easy to hide from one what is known to all. So, after the lapse of several months, did it happen with us. Oh, how great was the uncle's grief when he learned the truth, and how bitter was the sorrow of the lovers when we were forced to part! With what shame was I overwhelmed, with what contrition smitten because of the blow which had fallen on her I loved, and what a tempest of misery burst over her by reason of my disgrace! Each grieved most, not for himself, but for the other. Each sought to allay, not his own sufferings, but those of the one he loved. The very sundering of our bodies served but to link our souls closer together; the plentitude of the love which was denied to us inflamed us more than ever. Once the first wildness of shame had passed, it left us more shameless than before, and as shame died within us the cause of it seemed to us ever more desirable. And so it chanced with us as, in the stories that the poets tell, it once happened with Mars and Venus when they were caught together.

It was not long after this that Heloise found that she was pregnant, and of this she wrote to me in the utmost exultation, at the same time asking me to consider what had best be done. Accordingly, on a night when her uncle was absent, we carried out the plan we had determined on, and I stole her secretly away from her uncle's house, sending her without delay to my own country. She remained there with my sister until she gave birth to a son, whom she named Astrolabe. Meanwhile her uncle, after his return, was almost mad with grief; only one who had then seen him could rightly guess the burning agony of his sorrow and the bitterness of his shame. What steps to take against me, or what snares to set for me, he did not know. If he should kill me or do me some bodily hurt, he feared greatly lest his dear-loved niece should be made to suffer for it among my kinsfolk. He had no power to seize me and imprison me somewhere against my will, though I make no doubt he would have done so quickly enough had he been able or dared, for I had taken measures to guard against any such attempt.

At length, however, in pity for his boundless grief, and bitterly blaming myself for the suffering which my love had brought upon him through the baseness of the deception I had practiced, I went to him to entreat his forgiveness, promising to make any amends that he himself might decree. I pointed out that what had happened could not seem incredible to any one who had ever felt the power of love, or who remembered how, from the very beginning of the human race, women had cast down even the noblest men to utter ruin. And in order to make amends even beyond his extremest hope, I offered to marry her whom I had seduced, provided only the thing could be kept secret, so that I might suffer no loss of reputation thereby. To this he gladly assented, pledging his own faith and that of his kindred, and sealing with kisses the pact which I had sought of him—and all this that he might the more easily betray me.

Forthwith I repaired to my own country, and brought back thence my mistress, that I might make her my wife. She, however, most violently disapproved of this, and for two chief reasons: the danger thereof, and the disgrace which it would bring upon me. She swore that her uncle would never be appeased by such satisfaction as this, as, indeed, afterwards proved only too true. She asked how she could ever glory in me if she should make me thus inglorious, and should shame herself along with me. What penalties, she said, would the world rightly demand of her if she should rob it of so shining a light! What curses would follow such a loss to the Church, what tears among the philosophers would result from such a marriage! How unfitting, how lamentable it would be for me, whom nature had made for the whole world, to devote myself to one woman solely, and to subject myself to such humiliation! She vehemently rejected this marriage, which she felt would be in every way ignominious and burdensome to me. . . .

Her final argument was that it would be dangerous for me to take her back to Paris, and that it would be far sweeter for her to be called my mistress than to be known as my wife; nay, too, that this would be more honourable for me as well. In such case, she said, love alone would hold me to her, and the strength of the marriage chain would not constrain us. Even if we should by chance be parted from time to time, the joy of our meetings would be all the sweeter by reason of its rarity. But when she found that she could not convince me or dissuade me from my folly by these and like arguments, and because she could not bear to offend me, with grievous sighs and tears she made an end of her resistance, saying: "Then there is no more left but this, that in our doom the sorrow yet to come shall be no less than the love we two have already known." Nor in this, as now the whole world knows, did she lack the spirit of prophecy.

So, after our little son was born, we left him in my sister's care, and secretly returned to Paris. A few days later, in the early morning, having kept our nocturnal vigil of prayer unknown to all in a certain church, we were united there in the benediction of wedlock, her uncle and a few friends of his and mine being present. We departed forthwith stealthily and by separate ways, nor thereafter did we see each other save rarely and in private, thus striving our utmost to conceal what we had done. But her uncle and those of his household, seeking solace for their disgrace, began to divulge the story of our marriage, and thereby to violate the pledge they had given me on this point. Heloise, on the contrary, denounced her own kin and swore that they were speaking the most absolute lies. Her uncle, aroused to fury thereby, visited her repeatedly with punishments. No sooner had I learned this than I sent her to a convent of nuns at Argenteuil, not far from Paris, where she herself had been brought up and educated as a young girl. I had them make ready for her all the garments of a nun, suitable for the life of a convent, excepting only the veil, and these I bade her put on.

When her uncle and his kinsmen heard of this, they were convinced that now I had completely played them false and had rid myself forever of Heloise by forcing her to become a nun. Violently incensed, they laid a plot against me, and one night, while I, all unsuspecting, was asleep in a secret room in my lodgings, they broke in with the help of one of my servants, whom they had bribed. There they had vengeance on me with a most cruel and most shameful punishment, such as astounded the whole world, for they cut off those parts of my body with which I had done that which was the cause of their sorrow. This done, straightway they fled, but two of them were captured, and suffered the loss of their eyes and their genital organs. One of these two was the aforesaid servant, who, even while he was still in my service, had been led by his avarice to betray me.

When morning came the whole city was assembled before my dwelling. It is difficult, nay, impossible, for words of mine to describe the amazement which bewildered them, the lamentations they uttered, the uproar with which they harassed me, or the grief with which they increased my own suffering. Chiefly the clerics, and above all my scholars, tortured me with their intolerable lamentations and outcries, so that I suffered more intensely from their compassion than from the pain of my wound. In truth I felt the disgrace more than the hurt to my body, and was more afflicted with shame than with pain. My incessant thought was of the renown in which I had so much delighted, now brought low, nay, utterly blotted out, so swiftly by an evil chance. I saw, too, how justly God had punished me in that very part of my body whereby I had sinned. I perceived that there was indeed justice in my betrayal by him whom I had myself already betrayed; and then I thought how eagerly my rivals would seize upon this manifestation of justice, how this disgrace would bring bitter and enduring grief to my kindred and my friends, and how the tale of this amazing outrage would spread to the very ends of the earth. What path lay open to me thereafter? How could I ever again hold up my head among men, when every finger should be pointed at me in scorn, every tongue speak my blistering shame, and when I should be a monstrous spectacle to all eyes? I was overwhelmed by the remembrance that, according to the dread letter of the law, God holds eunuchs in such abomination that men thus maimed are forbidden to enter a church, even as the unclean and filthy; nay, even beasts in such plight were not acceptable as sacrifices. Thus in Leviticus (xxii, 24) is it said: "Ye shall not offer unto the Lord that which hath its stones bruised, or crushed, or broken, or cut." And in Deuteronomy (xxiii, i), "He that is wounded in the stones, or hath his privy member cut off, shall not enter into the congregation of the Lord."

I must confess that in my misery it was the overwhelming sense of my disgrace rather than any ardour for conversion to the religious life that drove me to seek the seclusion of the monastic cloister. Heloise had already, at my bidding, taken the veil and entered a convent. Thus it was that we both put on the sacred garb, I in the abbey of St. Denis, and she in the convent of Argenteuil, of which I have already spoken.

HELOISE (C.1100–C.1163)
Personal Letters

Heloise's name will forever be bound up with Abelard's (see the previous selection). We know nothing about her background and parentage except what we can learn from Abelard's description of her in his History of My Calamities *and from her own correspondence. By reputation she was lively, intelligent, and independent, qualities that shine through her letters. She was fortunate that her guardian, Fulbert, sought for her an education that would have been unusual for a young woman in her day. And she was fortunate that he chose as tutor the greatest teacher of the day, Abelard, although their passionate affair and disastrous marriage became a real-life counterpart to the tragic story of Tristan and Iseult that was popular at the same time. The published correspondence started when, after a period in the abbey without word from Abelard, Heloise received a copy of his "letter to a friend," that is, his account of his misfortunes. Hurt at her own isolation, and chafing with the knowledge that her religious vocation was a sham, she wrote to him of her grievance. The correspondence continued, focusing first on the deep wounds left by their notorious affair, their hasty and deceptive marriage, and his castration. In her third letter, Heloise described the difficulty of breaking away from fantasies which afflicted her: "Everything we did and also the times and places are stamped on my heart along with your image, so that I live through it all again with you." In his response Abelard confessed that his love was actually "unbridled lust" and that "as yours was the weaker nature I often forced you to consent with threats and blows." Arguing that their punishment had been just, he then urged her to turn truly to Christ through a devotion to the vows of her order. Heloise replied to Abelard as a transformed person, a sign of her strength and resolution: from that point on, their correspondence dealt importantly with theological questions, the rigors of monastic life, and the practicalities of monastic administration, in what have come to be called "the letters of direction." Already an Abbess, Heloise proved an able administrator and spiritual guide: during her lifetime her abbey founded six daughter houses. Heloise remained ever devoted to an ideal, an "ethic of intention," that she expressed in her first letter (below): "It is not the deed but the intention of the doer which makes the crime, and justice should weigh not what was done but the spirit in which it is done."*

Letter 1. Heloise to Abelard

Not long ago, my beloved, by chance someone brought me the letter of consolation you had sent to a friend. I saw at once from the superscription that it was yours, and was all the more eager to read it since the writer is so dear to my heart. I hoped for renewal of strength, at least

---

Heloise's letter is translated by Betty Radice and collected in *The Letters of Abelard and Heloise* (Baltimore: Penguin, 1974).

from the writer's words which would picture for me the reality I have lost. But nearly every line of this letter was filled, I remember, with gall and wormwood, as it told the pitiful story of our entry into religion and the cross of unending suffering which you, my only love, continue to bear.

In that letter you did indeed carry out the promise you made your friend at the beginning, that he would think his own troubles insignificant or nothing, in comparison with your own. . . .

No one, I think, could read or hear it dry-eyed; my own sorrows are renewed by the detail in which you have told it, and redoubled because you say your perils are still increasing. All of us here are driven to despair of your life, and every day we await in fear and trembling the final word of your death. And so in the name of Christ, who is still giving you some protection for his service, we beseech you to write as often as you think fit to us who are his handmaids and yours, with news of the perils in which you are still storm-tossed. We are all that are left you, so at least you should let us share your sorrow or your joy.

It is always some consolation in sorrow to feel that it is shared, and any burden laid on several is carried more lightly or removed. And if this storm has quietened down for a while; you must be all the more prompt to send us a letter which will be the more gladly received. But whatever you write about will bring us no small relief in the mere proof that you have us in mind. Letters from absent friends are welcome indeed, . . .

Thank God that here at least is a way of restoring your presence to us which no malice can prevent, nor any obstacle hinder; then do not, I beseech you, allow any negligence to hold you back.

You wrote your friend a long letter of consolation, prompted no doubt by his misfortunes, but really telling of your own. The detailed account you gave of these may have been intended for his comfort, but it also greatly increased our own feeling of desolation; in your desire to heal his wounds you have dealt us fresh wounds of grief as well as re-opening the old. I beg you, then, as you set about tending the wounds which others have dealt, heal the wounds you have yourself inflicted. You have done your duty to a friend and comrade, discharged your debt to friendship and comradeship, but it is a greater debt which binds you in obligation to us who can properly be called not friends so much as dearest friends, not comrades but daughters, or any other conceivable name more tender and holy. How great the debt by which you have bound yourself to us needs neither proof nor witness, were it in any doubt; if the whole world kept silent, the facts themselves would cry out. For you after God are the sole founder of this place, the sole builder of this oratory, the sole creator of this community. You have built nothing here upon another man's foundation. Everything here is your own creation. This was a wilderness open to wild beasts and brigands, a place which had known no home nor habitation of men. In the very lairs of wild beasts and lurking-places of robbers, where the name of God was never heard, you built a sanctuary to God and dedicated a shrine in the name of the Holy Spirit. To build it you drew nothing from the riches of kings and princes, though their wealth was great and could have been yours for the asking: whatever was done, the credit was to be yours alone. Clerks and scholars came flocking here, eager for your teaching, and ministered to all your needs; and even those who had lived on the benefices of the Church and knew only how to receive offerings, not to make them, whose hands were held out to take but not to give, became pressing in their lavish offers of assistance.

And so it is yours, truly your own, this new plantation for God's purpose, but it is sown with plants which are still very tender and need watering if they are to thrive. Through its feminine nature this plantation would be weak and frail even if it were not new; and so it needs a more careful and regular cultivation, according to the words of the Apostle: 'I planted the seed and Apollos watered it; but God made it grow.' . . . You devote your care to another's vineyard; think what you owe to your own. You teach and admonish rebels to no purpose, and in vain you throw the pearls of your divine eloquence to the pigs. While you spend so much on the stubborn, consider what you owe to the obedient; you are so generous to your enemies but should reflect on how you are indebted to your daughters. Apart from everything else, consider the close tie by which you have bound yourself to me, and repay the debt you owe a whole community of women dedicated to God by discharging it the more dutifully to her who is yours alone.

Your superior wisdom knows better than our humble learning of the many serious treatises which the holy Fathers compiled for the instruction or exhortation or even the consolation of holy women, and of the care with which these were composed. And so in the precarious early days of our conversion long ago I was not a little surprised and troubled by your forgetfulness, when neither reverence for God nor our mutual love nor the example of the holy Fathers made you think of trying to comfort me, wavering and exhausted as I was by prolonged grief, either by word when I was with you or by letter when we had parted. Yet you must know that you are bound to me by an obligation which is all the greater for the further close tie of the marriage sacrament uniting us, and are the deeper in my debt because of the love I have always borne you, as everyone knows, a love which is beyond all bounds.

You know, beloved, as the whole world knows, how much I have lost in you, how at one wretched stroke of fortune that supreme act of flagrant treachery robbed me of my very self in robbing me of you; and how my sorrow for my loss is nothing compared with what I feel for the manner in which I lost you. Surely the greater the cause for grief the greater the need for the help of consolation, and this no one can bring but you; you are the sole cause of my sorrow, and you alone can grant me the grace of consolation. You alone have the power to make me sad, to bring me happiness or comfort; you alone have so great a debt to repay me, particularly now when I have carried out all your orders so implicitly that when I was powerless to oppose you in anything, I found strength at your command to destroy myself. I did more, strange to say—my love rose to such heights of madness that it robbed itself of what it most desired beyond hope of recovery, when immediately at your bidding I changed my clothing along with my mind, in order to prove you the sole possessor of my body and my will alike. God knows I never sought anything in you except yourself; I wanted simply you, nothing of yours. I looked for no marriage-bond, no marriage portion, and it was not my own pleasures and wishes I sought to gratify, as you well know, but yours. The name of wife may seem more sacred or more binding, but sweeter for me will always be the word mistress, or, if you will permit me, that of concubine or whore. I believed that the more I humbled myself on your account, the more gratitude I should win from you, and also the less damage I should do to the brightness of your reputation.

You yourself on your own account did not altogether forget this in the letter of consolation I have spoken of which you wrote to a friend; there you thought fit to set out some of the reasons I gave in trying to dissuade you from binding us together in an ill-starred marriage. But you kept silent about most of my arguments for preferring love to wedlock and freedom to chains. God is my witness that if Augustus, Emperor of the whole world, thought fit to honour me with marriage and conferred all the earth on me to possess for ever, it would be dearer and more honourable to me to be called not his Empress but your whore.

For a man's worth does not rest on his wealth or power; these depend on fortune, but worth on his merits. And a woman should realize that if she marries a rich man more readily than a poor one, and desires her husband more for his possessions than for himself, she is offering herself for sale. Certainly any woman who comes to marry through desires of this kind deserves wages, not gratitude, for clearly her mind is on the man's property, not himself, and she would be ready to prostitute herself to a richer man, if she could. . . .

It is a holy error and a blessed delusion between man and wife, when perfect love can keep the ties of marriage unbroken not so much through bodily continence as chastity of spirit. But what error permitted other women, plain truth permitted me, and what they thought of their husbands, the world in general believed, or rather, knew to be true of yourself; so that my love for you was the more genuine for being further removed from error. What king or philosopher could match your fame? What district, town or village did not long to see you? When you appeared in public, who did not hurry to catch a glimpse of you, or crane his neck and strain his eyes to follow your departure? Every wife, every young girl desired you in absence and was on fire in your presence; queens and great ladies envied me my joys and my bed.

You had besides, I admit, two special gifts whereby to win at once the heart of any woman—your gifts for composing verse and song, in which we know other philosophers have rarely been successful. This was for you no more than a diversion, a recreation from the labours of your philosophic work, but you left many love-songs and verses which won wide popularity for the charm of their words and tunes and kept your name continually on every-one's lips., The beauty of the airs ensured that even the unlettered did not forget you; more than anything this made women sigh for love of you. And as most of these songs told of our love, they soon made me widely known and roused the envy of many women against me. For your manhood was adorned by every grace of mind and body, and among the women who envied me then, could there be one now who does not feel compelled by my misfortune to sympathize with my loss of such joys? Who is there who was once my enemy, whether man or woman, who is not moved now by the compassion which is my due? Wholly guilty though I am, I am also, as you know, wholly innocent. It is not the deed but the intention of the doer which makes the crime, and justice should weigh not what was done but the spirit in which it is done. What my intention towards you has always been, you alone who have known it can judge. I submit all to your scrutiny, yield to your testimony in all things.

Tell me one thing, if you can. Why, after our entry into religion, which was your decision alone, have I been so neglected and forgotten by you that I have neither a word from you when you are here to give me strength nor the consolation of a letter in absence? I Tell me, I say, if you can—or I will tell you what I think and indeed the world suspects. It was desire, not affection which bound you to me, the flame of lust rather than love. So when the end came to what you desired, any show of feeling you used to make went with it. This is not merely my own opinion, beloved, it is everyone's. There is nothing personal or private about it; it is the general view which is widely held. I only wish that it were mine alone, and that the love you professed could find someone to defend it and so comfort me in my grief for a while. I wish I could think of some explanation which would excuse you and somehow cover up the way you hold me cheap.

I beg you then to listen to what I ask—you will see that it is a small favour which you can easily grant. While I am denied your presence, give me at least through your words—of which you have enough and to spare—some sweet semblance of yourself. It is no use my hoping for generosity in deeds if you are grudging in words. Up to now I had thought I deserved much of you, seeing that I carried out everything for your sake and continue up to the present moment in complete obedience to you. It was not any sense of vocation which brought me as a young girl to accept the austerities of the cloister, but your bidding alone, and if I deserve no gratitude from you, you may judge for yourself how my labours are in vain. I can expect no reward for this from God, for it is certain that I have done nothing as yet for love of him. When you hurried towards God I followed you, indeed, I went first to take the veil-perhaps you were thinking how Lot's wife turned back, when you made me put on the religious habit and take my vows before you gave yourself to God. Your lack of trust in me over this one thing, I confess, overwhelmed me with grief and shame. I would have had no hesitation, God knows, in following you or going ahead at your bidding to the flames of Hell. My heart was not in me but with you, and now, even more, if it is not with you it is nowhere; truly, without you it cannot exist. See that it fares well with you, I beg, as it will if it finds you kind, if you give grace in return for grace, small for great, words for deeds. If only your love had less confidence in me, my dear, so that you would be more concerned on my behalf! But as it is, the more I have made you feel secure in me, the more I have to bear with your neglect.

Remember, I implore you, what I have done, and think how much you owe me. While I enjoyed with you the pleasures of the flesh, many were uncertain whether I was prompted by love or lust; but now the end is proof of the beginning. I have finally denied myself every pleasure in obedience to your will, kept nothing for myself except to prove that now, even more, I am yours. Consider then your injustice, if when I deserve more you give me less, or rather, nothing at all, especially when it is a small thing I ask of you and one you could so easily grant. And so, in the name of God to whom you have dedicated yourself, I beg you to restore your presence to me in the way you can-by writing me some word of comfort, so that in this at least I may find increased strength and readiness to serve God. When in the past you sought me out for sinful pleasures your letters came to me thick and fast, and your many songs put your Heloise on everyone's lips, so that every street and house echoed with my name. Is it not far better now to summon me to God than it was then to satisfy our lust? I beg you, think what you owe me, give ear to my pleas, and I will finish a long letter with a brief ending: farewell, my only love.

Hildegard of Bingen (1098–1179)

Hildegard recently celebrated her 900th birthday, and a great party it continues to be. New CD's of her music are issued monthly, some dressed up electronically, some marketed as New Age. Web sites tell about her life, offer translations of her poetry, and allow fans to download images of her music in the original notation. There are also testimonials from people whose lives she has changed. Every year San Francisco plays host to a weekend-long celebration of her work, through readings, music performances, and displays of images. Part of her popularity comes from feminist interest in a truly remarkable woman living in an age of great men. Another part results from a new interest in things medieval, associated with albums of Gregorian Chant showing up on the pop charts. Another part simply arises from familiarity, now that people have more opportunity to view, read, and listen to the artistic works of a woman who was, after all, a phenomenon in her own time.

Hildegard entered a Benedictine monastery when she was only 8 and became abbess in that monastery before she was forty. A few years later she began writing down the visions that first troubled her and later brought her fame and attention. In 1151 she published Scivias ("Know the Ways"), a collection of prophecies, music, and illuminations prepared under her supervision. The following year she fought a long battle to move her nuns to a female monastery at Rupertsberg, near Bingen. For the next 28 years her reputation and her political power grew, as kings, popes, and nobles sought her advice.

More than 100 letters to and from Hildegard survive, dealing with all aspects of public and private life. Three books record her visions and prophecies. Her manuscript paintings (many produced under her supervision), music and song texts, The Play of the Virtues (a liturgical play with music)—all of these attest to Hildegard's creative ability and her talent for accomplishing great things. She is a striking example of a person who successfully united the active life with the contemplative life.

Scivias
"Protestificatio"

In the year 1141 of the incarnation of Jesus Christ, the Word of God, when I was forty-two years and seven months old, a burning light coming from heaven poured into my mind. Like a flame which does not burn but rather enkindles, it inflamed my heart and my breast, just as the sun warms something with its rays. And I was able to understand books suddenly, the psaltery clearly, the evangelists and the volumes of the Old and New Testament, but I did not have the interpretation of the words of their texts nor the division of their syllables nor the knowledge of their grammar. Previously though, I had felt within myself the gift of secret mysteries and wondrous visions from the time I was a little girl, certainly from the time I was

---

The "Protestificatio," Hildegard's introduction to *Scivias,* is translated by Bruce Hozeski (Santa Fe: Bear, 1986).

five years old right up to the present time. I revealed my gift to no one except to a select few and some religious who were living in my area, and I concealed my gift continuously in quiet silence until God wished it to be manifest by God's own grace. I truly saw those visions; I did not perceive them in dreams, nor while sleeping, nor in a frenzy, nor with the human eyes or with the external ears of a person, nor in remote places; but I received those visions according to the will of God while I was awake and alert with a clear mind, with the innermost eyes and ears of a person, and in open places. There may be a reason why I received those visions in this manner, but it is difficult for a human person to understand why. But after I had passed through the turning point of young womanhood, when I had arrived at the beginning of the age of perfect fortitude, I again heard a heavenly voice speaking to me:

> *I, the living light and the obscured illumination, appointed the person whom I wished, and I drove out the person whom I wished, wondrously according to what pleased me, with great wonders across the boundary of ancient people, who have seen many secrets in me; indeed I struck people down on earth, so that they might not lift themselves up in any exaltation of their own minds. The world also had no joy in it nor playfulness nor practice in those things which belong to the world, because I restrained it from stubborn daring, having fear and quaking in its own labors. People indeed suffered pain in their hearts and in the veins of their flesh, having bound together soul and senses, and sustaining the many passions of the body so that diverse peace of mind was not concealed in them, but they judged themselves blameworthy in all their motives. For I surrounded the fissures of their hearts, lest their minds might raise themselves up through pride or through glory; but that they might have in all these things fear and sorrow rather than delight and wantonness. Whence they searched through my love in their own souls, where they came upon the one who hastened the way of salvation. And the one came upon those people and loved them, acknowledging that they had been faithful and similar to the one in some part of that labor which they had done for me. And holding themselves together with that one, they strained in all these things with heavenly zeal, so that my hidden miracles might be revealed. And the same people did not place themselves above that one, but when they came to that one with an ascent of humility and with the intention of good will, the one bent over them with warm protection. You therefore, o person, who receive these things not in the turmoil of deceit, but in the purity of simplicity, who receive these things straight for the manifestation of the things concealed, write what you see and hear.*

Although I saw and heard these things, I nevertheless refused to write them because of doubt and evil opinion and because of the diversity of other people's words, not so much out of stubbornness, but out of humility, until I became sick, pressed down by the scourge of God. I was sick for a long time with many different illnesses. Eventually, with the testimony of a certain noble man and a young woman of good wishes, I started to write what I had searched out and come upon secretly. As soon as I did that, I became healthy with a received strength, and knowing—as I said—the profoundness of the narration of books, I was able to bring my work to completion with difficulty, taking ten years. . . .

Letters
[to Bernard of Clairvaux, 1147]

Most praiseworthy Father Bernard, through God's power you stand wonderfully in highest honor. You are formidable against the indecent foolishness of this world. Full of lofty zeal and in ardent love for God's Son, you capture men with the banner of the holy cross so that they will wage war in the Christian army against the wrath of the pagans. I beseech you, father, by the living God, hear me in what I ask you.

I am very concerned about this vision which opens before me in spirit as a mystery. I have never seen it with the outer eyes of the flesh. I am wretched and more than wretched in my existence as a woman. And yet, already as a child, I saw great things of wonder which my tongue could never have given expression to, if God's spirit hadn't taught me to believe.

Gentle father, you are so secure, answer me in your goodness, me, your unworthy servant girl, who from childhood has never, not even for one single hour, lived in security. In your fatherly love and wisdom search in your soul, since you are taught by the Holy Spirit, and from your heart give some comfort to your servant girl.

I know in Latin text the meaning of the interpretation of the psalms, the gospels, and the other books which are shown to me through this vision. It stirs my heart and soul like a burning flame and teaches me the depth of interpretation. And yet this vision doesn't teach me writings in the German language; these I don't know. I can simply read them but have no ability to analyze them. Please answer me: what do you make of all of this? I am a person who received no schooling about external matters. It is only within, in my soul, that I have been trained. And that is why I speak in such doubt. But I take consolation from all that I have heard of your wisdom and fatherly love. I have not talked about this to anyone else, because, as I hear it said, there is so much divisiveness among people. There is just one person with whom I have shared this, a monk [Volmar] whom I have tested and whom I have found reliable in his cloistered way of life. I have revealed all of my secrets to him and he has consoled me with the assurance that they are sublime and awe-inspiring.

I beg you, father, for God's sake, that you comfort me. Then I will be secure. More than two years ago, I saw you in my vision as a person who can look at the sun and not be afraid, a very bold man. And I cried because I blushed at my faintheartedness.

Gentle father, mildest of men, I rest in your soul so that through your word you can show me, if you wish, whether I should say these things openly or guard them in silence. For this vision causes me a lot of concern about the extent to which I should talk about what I have seen and heard. For a time, when I was silent about these things, I was confined to my bed with serious illnesses, so intense that I was unable to sit up. This is why I complain to you in such sadness: I will be so easily crushed by the falling wooden beams in the winepress of my nature, that heavy wood growing from the root which sprang up in Adam through Satan's influence and cast him out into a world where there was no fatherland.

But now I lift myself up and hasten to you. I say to you: you will not be crushed. On the contrary, you constantly straighten the wooden beam and hold it upright; in your soul you are a conqueror. But it's not only yourself that you hold upright; you raise the world up towards its salvation. You are the eagle who gazes at the sun.

I ask you by the radiant clarity of the Divine and by the marvelous Word and by sweet tear-gifted repentance, the Spirit of truth, and by the holy sound which echoes through the whole creation: by him, the Word, from whom the world has come to be. By the majesty of the Divine, who in sweet greening power sent the Word into the womb of the Virgin, from whom he took flesh, as the honey is built up around the honeycomb.

The letters here are from *Hildegard of Bingen's Book of Divine Works,* translated by Matthew Fox (Santa Fe: Bear, 1987).

And may this sound, the power of the Divine, strike your heart and elevate your soul, so that you do not grow stiffly indifferent through the words of this woman [Hildegard], since you yourself seek out everything with God or with human beings or with any mystery until you press so far forward through the opening of your soul that you discern all of these things in God. Farewell, live well in your soul and be a strong warrior for God. Amen.

[to Pope Anastasius IV, 1153]

O shining bulwark, peak of guiding power in the lovely city prepared as Christ's bride, hear him, whose life is without beginning and never dissipates into fatigue.

O man, the eye of your discernment weakens; you are becoming weary, too tired to restrain the arrogant boastfulness of people to whom you have trusted your heart. Why do you not call these shipwrecked people back? They can be rescued from serious danger only through your help. And why do you not cut out the roots of the evil which chokes out the good, useful, fine-tasting, sweet-smelling plants? You are neglecting justice, the King's daughter, the heavenly bride, the woman who was entrusted to you. And you are even tolerant that this princess be hurled to the ground. Her crown and jewelled raiments are torn to pieces through the moral crudeness of men who bark like dogs and make stupid sounds like chickens which sometimes begin to cackle in the middle of the night. They are hypocrites. With their words they make a show of illusory peace; but within, in their hearts, they grind their teeth, like a dog who wags its tail at a recognized friend but bites with his sharp teeth an experienced warrior who fights for the King's house. Why do you tolerate the evil ways of people who in the darkness of foolishness draw everything harmful to themselves? They are like hens who make noise during the night and terrify themselves. People who act like this aren't rooted in goodness.

Listen then, O man, to him who loves exceedingly sharp discrimination. For he has put in place a strong instrument of uprightness, one that should do battle with evil. But that is precisely what you aren't doing when you don't dig out by the root that evil which suffocates the good. And you tolerate even more than that, allowing the evil to raise itself up proudly. And why? Because of your fear of the evil men who lay snares in nocturnal ambush and love the gold of death more than the beautiful King's daughter, justice.

But all the works made by God radiate the brightest light. Listen, O man. Before the world came to be, God spoke in divine inwardness the Word: "O my Son!" And the world came to be because it picked up the sound that went forth from God. The various kinds of creatures still lay hidden in darkness. As it is written, when God said: "Let it be!" the various types of creatures came forth. So it was through the Word of the Father and for the sake of the Word that all creatures were fashioned through God's will.

God sees and knows everything beforehand. But evil, on the other hand, through itself can neither by its rising or falling do anything or create anything or cause anything—for it is nothing. Evil should be valued only as the deceptive product of wishes and rebellious fantasies. For human beings do evil when they deal deceptively and rebelliously.

God sent the divine Son into the world so that through him the Devil, who had produced evil in its entirety and seduced humanity, might be conquered and thereby the human race, given over to corruption through that evil, might be saved. Therefore God abhors the perverted works of indecency, murder, theft, rebellion, tyranny, and hypocrisy of the godless. For

God has crushed all of these under foot through the divine Son, who has totally scattered the plunder of the hellish tyrants.

Therefore, O man, you who sit on the papal throne, you despise God when you don't hurl from yourself the evil but, even worse, embrace it and kiss it by silently tolerating corrupt men. The whole Earth is in confusion on account of the ever recurring false teaching whereby human beings love what God has brought to nothing. And you, O Rome, are like one in the throes of death. You will be so shaken that the strength of your feet, the feet on which you now stand, will disappear. For you don't love the King's daughter, justice, with glowing love but as in a delirium of sleep so that you push her away from you. And that is why she also will flee from you, unless you call her back. Nevertheless, the high mountains will still offer the strength of their help to you; they will raise you up and support you with the strong branches of their high trees, so that you don't completely collapse in your dignity, namely in the dignity of your marriage to Christ. So there still remain for you a few blades of your beauty, until the snow of manifold sarcasm comes and blows out much foolishness. Protect yourself that you don't fall, since you open the doors to the ways of the pagans.

Therefore, hear him who lives and who cannot be pushed out of the way. Already the world is full of aberration; later it will be in sadness, and then in such a horrible state that it will not matter to people if they are killed. But from the heart comes healing, when the red sky of morning becomes visible, like the light of the first sunrise. Words cannot express the new longings and enthusiasm that follow.

But he who is great without limit has in our time touched a small tent so that it might behold wonders, fashion unknown letters, and let an unknown language be heard. And it was said to this little tent: "What you express in the language announced to you from above will not be in the ordinary human forces of expression, for that was not given to you. But let him who has the file eagerly smooth this speech so that it receives the right sound for human ears."

And you, O man, who have been placed as the visible shepherd, rise up and hasten quickly to justice, so that you will not be criticized by the great Doctor for not having cleansed your flock from dirt and for not having anointed them with oil. But if the will knows nothing about these things that have passed and the man does not cling to these cravings, he will not incur heavy judgment. But the guilt of this ignorance will be washed away through acts of penance.

And so, O man, stand upon the right way and God will rescue you. God will lead you back to the fold of blessing and election and you will live forever.

[to the Monks of Zwiefalten]

The clear-shining brightness speaks: *The strong light of the Godhead knows and recognizes all things even to their last details. Who rests on this insight and who grasps it, if not that person who sees with sapphire-blue eyes that God who is over all is so changeless in divine justice that God lets no injustice stand, for injustice can find no rest in God!*

God the Father had such delight in himself that he called forth the whole creation through the divine Word. And then the divine creation pleased God, too, and every creature that God lovingly touched, God took in divine arms. O what great delight you have in your work!

God the Father is changeless in justice and spares the unjust only because they pray to the divine Son for forgiveness. For God looks at the divine Word made flesh and is reminded that it is through the Word that all creatures were made. God's saints, too, in a similar way touch God through their pleas with their clear voices, like shining clouds on a gentle mist over the water.

Listen, therefore, you who break out in your evil deeds! You were called "Mountain of the Lord" because you should imitate the Son of God through your cloistered behavior. So why do you transgress the motherly inner realm of love and modesty, like those who on Horeb disciplined their bodies according to the Law but then went astray on another path? Or like sentinels at the gate, who call up the guard with loud voice and thereby insidiously clear a way into the city. Your spirits are like storm-pregnant clouds—first they give themselves over to slothful anger, but then they turn about and give themselves in high spirits to bestial filth. And thus you neglect the sacrifice you are called to make and say: "We don't have the will to oppose our own natures, for we cannot gird the loins of our bodies since we're born from Adam." For even though your life in the cloister puts you in the palace of the Divine, you don't want to tame the fire in your loins. You were rescued from the stall of the ass and placed by the highest Lord in the exalted service of honor in the festivals of the holy Church. Why then are you not ashamed to run back again like dummies to the stall of the ass? Alas, in this you are like Balaam who, rabid with wounds and burning scars, took his repose in the land of the shadow of death. (cf. Numbers 31:8 & 16; II Peter 2:16; Revelation 2:14) Don't, therefore, abandon the holy mountain in scandalous adultery. Woe to the disgrace of the prostitute who is cast forth abroad! For those who fail against the holy institution go to ruin.

So take hold of the discipline [of the Lord] so that you don't wander from the ways of justice, as though you had no law and as though the sun didn't shine over the blessed censer, so that the Lord isn't angered and that you don't go to ruin far from the right way. For ruin is what lies under your feet because of your transgressions. O awesome offering deserving of every honor, to which neither the unbelief of idols nor the burden of mortal wounds clings.

Alas, what pain over this misery! For God will throw you down with all your grumbling just like the Ninevites, unless you hasten quickly to the olive tree of salvation in Christ. A sweet fragrance streams forth from this tree and it allows the blossoms of the just fulfillment of the law to sprout. Why are you so twisted in your lies that you don't realize your blindness? For you are blind, because you have not kept earnestly in mind the guilt in which you were born through Adam's fall. But you have embraced that guilt with laughter and jokes, as though it didn't exist for you. Avoid this so that your salvation may quickly come. Use your eyes and walk on the paths of justice.

[to Elisabeth of Schönau]

. . . I am but a poor creature and fragile vessel; yet what I speak to you comes not from me but from the clear light. Human beings are vessels God had made and filled with the Spirit so that the divine work might come to perfection in them. For God does not do things the way we humans do. It was through the divine Word of command alone that everything came into existence perfect. The grasses, the woods, the trees came forth. The sun too and the moon and the stars went to their appointed places to perform their service. The waters sent out fish and birds. Cattle too and wild beasts arose. All of these creatures—each according to the assignment given it by God—came into being to serve human beings with all of creation.

It was only humans themselves who did not know their Creator. For although God bestowed great knowledge on humans, they raised themselves up in their hearts and turned away from God. It had been God's intention that all of the divine works should be brought to completion in humankind. And yet the old trickster deceived those first human beings and in a flattering whisper infected them with the virus of disobedience, so that they strove for more than they were supposed to. Alas, all the elements got entangled in the confusion of light and darkness, just as humankind did through its transgression of God's command.

But God endowed certain persons with insight so that humankind should not completely fall into derision. Abel was good; Cain a murderer. And many saw God in a mysterious light, while others committed very serious sins until that time came in which the Word of God shone forth, as it is written: "You are the fairest of the sons of men." (Psalm 45:2) Then the sun of justice arose and it made humans shine with good works in faith and deed, just as it is when the redness of morning first appears in the sky and then the other hours of the day follow till the night breaks in.

How the world changes, O daughter Elisabeth: The world no longer has the driving force from which the green of virtues blossoms, neither in the early morning nor in the first, the third, nor especially in the sixth hour of the day. It is truly necessary in our time that God choose certain people so that the divine instruments are not idle.

Listen, then, my troubled daughter: The whispering of the ambitious serpent sometimes seeks to wear down precisely those people our God instructed through divine inspiration. For when the old snake spots a gem of special worth, he hisses, raising himself up, and says: "What is that?" And then he torments with many afflictions the heart that longs to fly above the clouds (as the old serpent himself once did), as though human beings were gods.

And now I want you to listen further to me. Those who long to bring God's words to completion must always remember that, because they are human, they are vessels of clay and so should continually focus on what they are and what they will be. They should leave heavenly things to the One who is heavenly, for they are themselves exiles who do not recognize what is heavenly. They only announce the mysteries like a trumpet which indeed allows the sound but is not itself the source that produces the note. For someone else is blowing into the trumpet and causing the note to be produced.

They should put on the armor of faith, being mild, gentle, poor, and despised. This was the condition of that Lamb whose trumpet notes sound in them from the childlike intuition of their behavior. But God always disciplines those who blow God's trumpets and God sees to it that the earthen vessel does not break but pleases the Divine.

O daughter, may God make you a mirror of life! But even I who suffer from a heart of little courage and am again and again disturbed and crippled by fear, even I sometimes sound with a weak note from the trumpet of the living light. And may God help me to persevere in divine service!

[to Wibert of Gembloux, 1175]

. . . The words which I speak are not my own nor those of any human being, but what I say comes from the vision which I received from above.

O true servant of God, if it had pleased God to raise not only my soul but my body as well to a prophetic vision, still that could not cause the fear to diminish from my spirit and my heart. For I know that I am a human being, even though I have been cloistered from my childhood. There have been many who were wise and whose lives were so filled with wonders that they proclaimed a great number of mysteries. And yet, from a vain pursuit of glory, they ascribed these things to themselves, and thus came to their downfall. But those, on the other hand, who in their spiritual advancement derived their wisdom from God and regarded themselves as nothing—they became pillars of heaven. This is what happened in the case of

St. Paul who, although he excelled the other apostles in preaching, regarded himself as nothing. The same is true of the evangelist John who was filled with tender humility, and because of this was able to obtain so much from the divine spring.

How would it be understood if a poor creature like myself were not to recognize this gift? God works where God wills, for the honor of the divine name and not for the honor of earthbound mortals. But I am continuously filled with fear and trembling. For I do not recognize in myself security through any kind of personal ability. And yet I raise my hands aloft to God, that I might be held by God, just like a feather which has no weight from its own strength and lets itself be carried by the wind.

I cannot fully understand the things I see, not as long as I remain in bondage to the body and the invisible soul. For in both cases we human beings suffer from want.

I also saw in my vision that the first book of my visions should be called Scivias, because it would proclaim the way of the living light and not derive from any other teaching.

From my childhood days, when my limbs, nerves, and veins were not yet strong, the gift of this vision brought joy to my soul; and this has remained true up to this very time when I am a woman of more than 70 years. And as God wants, my soul climbs in this vision high above, even to the height of the firmament. But I do not see these things with my external eyes nor do I hear them with my external ears. I do not perceive them through the thoughts of my heart or through the mediation of my five senses. I see them much more in my soul alone, with my physical eyes open, in such a way that I never experience the unconsciousness of ecstasy, but I see all of this awake, whether by day or night.

The light which I see is not bound by space. It is much, much more light-filled than a cloud that carries the sun in itself. There is nothing in it to recognize of height, length, or breadth. It was described to me as the "shadow of the living light." And just as the sun, the moon, and the stars are reflected in water, so writings, talks, powers, and certain actions of people are illuminated for me in this light.

I was often severely hindered by sickness and involved with heavy sufferings that threatened to bring me to death's door. And yet God has always made me alive again, even to this day.

I keep for a long time in memory all the things I see and learn in the vision, because as soon as I see or hear it, it enters my memory. I simultaneously see, hear, and understand. In an instant I learn what I know through the vision. But whatever I do not see in the vision, I have no knowledge of, for I am without formal education and was only instructed to read simple letters. And I write what I see and hear in the vision and I don't add any other words. I communicate the plain Latin words just as I hear them in the vision. For I do not become educated in my vision so that I can write like the philosophers. The words in the vision do not sound like words from a human mouth, but they are like flaming lightning and like a cloud moving in the pure ether. I am not able to perceive the shape of this light, just as I cannot look with unprotected eyes at the disk of the sun.

It is in this light that I sometimes see, though not often, another light that I call "the living light." When and how I see this, I cannot say. But as long as I see this "living light" all sadness and anxiety are taken away from me. The result is that I feel like a simple young girl and not like an old lady.

[During these experiences] I do not know myself, either in body or soul. And I consider myself as nothing. I reach out to the living God and turn everything over to the Divine that God, who has neither beginning nor end, can preserve me from evil in every situation. And that is why I ask you to pray for me too, since you have requested this reply from me. And ask all of those to pray for me, too, who, like you, desire to hear these words in good faith. Pray that I may persevere in God's service.

But I want to say something to you, too, O son of God, for you seek God in faith and are filled with desire for the Divine. God wants to save you. Pay attention to the eagle who with his two wings flies towards the clouds. If he lost his wings, he would fall down to the Earth and not be able to raise himself up again, no matter how eagerly he sought to lift himself up in flight. Human beings also fly with two wings; the right wing is the knowledge of good and the left wing is the knowledge of evil. The knowledge of evil serves the good, insofar as the good is sharpened and highlighted through the knowledge of evil; and so through this knowledge human beings become wise in all things.

O true son of God, may God raise the wings of your knowledge so that you can fly the right paths. Thus when sin hankers after you and touches you—for you are born such that you cannot exist without sin—you will be able not to satisfy it through action. Then you will have a good flight. The heavenly choir sings the praises of God for people who conduct themselves in this way and they praise such people. For though they are created out of ashes, they love God so much that, for God's sake, they are able completely to despise themselves. So persevere in this battle, strong warrior, so that you may enter into the heavenly harmony where God will say to you: you belong to the children of Israel. For in the zeal of your desire for heaven, you have kept your eyes on the mountain peak, past all the craggy clefts. And may all of those names you included in your letter to me be so guided by the Holy Spirit that they will be inscribed in the book of life.

Songs

When Hildegard was a girl the Rhineland was electrified at the discovery in 1106 of a mass grave containing many bones outside of Cologne. This discovery seemed to support an old legend about Ursula, a fifth-century British princess who, not wanting to marry a pagan prince, received her father's permission to postpone the wedding until she and her handmaids could complete a pilgrimage to Rome. (She actually intended to remain a virgin dedicated to God.) In earlier versions of the legend Ursula was accompanied by five, eight, even eleven virgin companions. By the tenth century, Ursula was said to travel with 11,000 virgins for three years, until, while returning from Rome to Britain, she was stopped in Cologne and urged to marry the chief of a tribe of Huns. When she refused, she and all of her followers were martyred. Hildegard's younger contemporary, the visionary Elisabeth of Schönau, claimed to have received visions about the bones and in 1157 wrote a book about the revelations, adding details to the accepted story. (Elisabeth herself had visited Hildegard once and written to her three times, troubled about her visions. Hildegard's letter of reassurance is reproduced above.) In light of these events, the Feast of St. Ursula became very popular in the Rhineland and Hildegard wrote the music for several services in her honor. Here songs are chosen from the services of Matins, of Lauds, and of Vespers.

The songs are translated for this collection by the editor

"Spiritui Sancto" (Matins)

All honor be to the holy spirit,
who in the mind of the virgin Ursula
gathered a virginal flock, like doves;
because of this, like Abraham, she left her fatherland.

And, indeed, because of the lamb's embrace, she freed herself
from betrothal to a man.

For this most chaste and golden army
with maidenly, flowing hair
crossed the sea:
O who had ever heard of such a thing?

And, indeed, because of the lamb's embrace,
she freed herself from betrothal to a man.

Glory to the father and to the son
and to the holy spirit.

And, indeed, because of the lamb's embrace,
she freed herself from betrothal to a man.

"O Ecclesia" (Lauds)

O Ecclesia, your eyes are like sapphire,
your ears like Mount Bethel,
your nose like a mountain of myrrh and incense,
and your mouth like the sound of many waters.

In a vision of true faith
Ursula loved the son of God,
gave up both man and this world,
and looked into the sun
and called to a most handsome youth, saying:

With great desire I have desired to come to you,
to sit with you at the heavenly wedding,
running to you through strange ways
just as the clouds float through air
that is pure as sapphire.

And after Ursula had spoken in this way
a report ran among all the people,
and they said: this is the innocence and ignorance
of a girl who doesn't understand what she is saying.

And they mocked her in a great symphony,
until a fiery burden fell upon her.
Then they all recognized
that contempt for the world is like Mount Bethel.

And they all noticed also
the sweetest odor of myrrh and incense,
because contempt for the world
rises above everything else.

Then the devil inspired his allies
to put these most noble women to death.
And all the elements heard this deed cry out,
and before the throne of God they said:

Woe! The ruby blood of an innocent lamb
has been poured out for her betrothal.
Let all the heavens listen
and in a great symphony praise the lamb of God,
because the throat of the ancient serpent
has choked on these pearls
formed from the word of God.

"Cum vox sanguinis" (Vespers)

When the voice of blood
of Ursula and her innocent company
resounds before the throne of God,
an ancient prophecy comes
from the root of Mamre
in a true revelation of the Trinity
and it says:

This blood touches us,
now let us all rejoice.

And after that comes the congregation of the lamb,
for the sake of the ram caught among the thorns,
 and it says:

Praise be in Jerusalem,
because of the redness of this blood.

Then comes the sacrifice of the calf
as ancient law laid out,
a sacrifice of praise in colorful garments,
which veiled God's face from Moses,
showing only his back.

Here are the priests who show God through their words
and are not able to see him perfectly,
and they say:

O most noble throng,
this virgin who on earth is called Ursula
in heaven is named Columba [Dove],
because she gathered around her an innocent throng.

O Ecclesia, you are to be praised for this multitude:
like the un-burning bush which Moses saw
and which God had planted in the first root
of the man whom he had formed of clay,
this great throng signifies that they would live
without sexual union with men.

They cried out with the clearest voice,
in purest gold, topaz,
and sapphire wrapped in gold.
Now let all the heavens rejoice,
and all peoples be adorned with these. Amen.

Marie de France (fl. late 12th century)
Lais

Marie is the earliest known French woman poet. We know virtually nothing about her. She presumably was called "of France" because she was not there, but in England, attached to the French speaking court of Henry II. Her audience, then, would have been a group of Anglo-Norman nobles and ladies. Although she wrote a collection of fables in the style of Aesop and a work called "St. Patrick's Purgatory," she is best known for her wonderful collection of twelve Breton lais. These lais are narrative poems in the form of short romances about love, sometimes unhappy or treacherous love, with elements of magic and the supernatural. Her lais are remarkable for their psychological realism, and she seems strikingly honest, too, in divulging her desire to make a name for herself as a writer but having to search for the right form and subject matter.

Prologue

Those to whom God has given the gift of comely speech, should not hide their light beneath a bushel, but should willingly show it abroad. If a great truth is proclaimed in the ears of men, it brings forth fruit a hundred-fold; but when the sweetness of the telling is praised of many, flowers mingle with the fruit upon the branch.

According to the witness of Priscian, it was the custom of ancient writers to express obscurely some portions of their books, so that those who came after might study with greater diligence to find the thought within their words. The philosophers knew this well, and were the more unwearied in labour, the more subtle in distinctions, so that the truth might make them free. They were persuaded that he who would keep himself unspotted from the world should search for knowledge, that he might understand. To set evil from me, and to put away my grief, I purposed to commence a book. I considered within myself what fair story in the Latin or Romance I could turn into the common tongue. But I found that all the stories had been written, and scarcely it seemed the worth my doing, what so many had already done. Then I called to mind those Lays I had so often heard. I doubted nothing—for well I know—that our fathers fashioned them, that men should bear in remembrance the deeds of those who have gone before. Many a one, on many a day, the minstrel has chanted to my ear. I would not that they should perish, forgotten, by the roadside. In my turn, therefore, I have made them a song, rhymed as well as I am able, and often has their shaping kept me sleepless in my bed.

Marie's Old French poetry is here translated into English prose by Eugene Mason, *French Mediaeval Romances* (London: Dent, 1911).

In your honour, most noble and courteous King, to whom joy is a handmaid, and in whose heart all gracious things are rooted, I have brought together these Lays, and told my tales in seemly rhyme. Ere they speak for me, let me speak with my own mouth, and say,

"Sire, I offer you these verses. If you are pleased to receive them, the fairer happiness will be mine, and the more lightly I shall go all the days of my life. Do not deem that I think more highly of myself than I ought to think, since I presume to proffer this, my gift." Hearken now to the commencement of the matter.

The Were-Wolf

Amongst the tales I tell you once again, I would not forget the Lay of the Were-Wolf. Such beasts as he are known in every land. Bisclavaret he is named in Brittany; whilst the Norman calls him Garwal.

It is a certain thing, and within the knowledge of all, that many a christened man has suffered this change, and ran wild in the woods, as a Were-Wolf. The Were-Wolf is a fearsome beast. He lurks within the thick forest, mad and horrible to see. All the evil that he may, he does. He goeth to and fro, about the solitary place, seeking man, in order to devour him. Hearken, now, to the adventure of the Were-Wolf, that I have to tell.

In Brittany there dwelt a baron who was marvelously esteemed of all his fellows. He was a stout knight, and a comely, and a man of office and repute. Right private was he to the mind of his lord, and dear to the counsel of his neighbours. This baron was wedded to a very worthy dame, right fair to see, and sweet of semblance. All his love was set on her, and all her love was given again to him. One only grief had this lady. For three whole days in every week her lord was absent from her side. She knew not where he went, nor on what errand. Neither did any of his house know the business which called him forth.

On a day when this lord was come again to his house, altogether joyous and content, the lady took him to task, right sweetly, in this fashion,

"Husband," said she, "and fair, sweet friend, I have a certain thing to pray of you. Right willingly would I receive this gift, but I fear to anger you in the asking. It is better for me to have an empty hand, than to gain hard words."

When the lord heard this matter, he took the lady in his arms, very tenderly, and kissed her.

"Wife," he answered, "ask what you will. What would you have, for it is yours already?"

"By my faith," said the lady, "soon shall I be whole. Husband, right long and wearisome are the days you spend away from your home. I rise from my bed in the morning, sick at heart, I know not why. So fearful am I, lest you do aught to your loss, that I may not find any comfort. Very quickly shall I die for reason of my dread. Tell me now, where you go, and on what business! How may the knowledge of one who loves so closely, bring you to harm?"

"Wife," made answer the lord, "nothing but evil can come if I tell you this secret. For the mercy of God do not require it of me. If you but knew, you would withdraw yourself from my love, and I should be lost indeed."

When the lady heard this, she was persuaded that her baron sought to put her by with jesting words. Therefore she prayed and required him the more urgently, with tender looks and speech, till he was overborne, and told her all the story, hiding naught.

"Wife, I become Bisclavaret. I enter in the forest, and live on prey and roots, within the thickest of the wood."

After she had learned his secret, she prayed and entreated the more as to whether he ran in his raiment, or went spoiled of vesture.

"Wife," said he, "I go naked as a beast."

"Tell me, for hope of grace, what you do with your clothing?"

"Fair wife, that will I never. If I should lose my raiment, or even be marked as I quit my vesture, then a Were-Wolf I must go for all the days of my life. Never again should I become man, save in that hour my clothing were given back to me. For this reason never will I show my lair."

"Husband," replied the lady to him, "I love you better than all the world. The less cause have you for doubting my faith, or hiding any tittle from me. What savour is here of friendship? How have I made forfeit of your love; for what sin do you mistrust my honour? Open now your heart, and tell what is good to be known."

So at the end, outwearied and overborne by her importunity, he could no longer refrain, but told her all.

"Wife," said he, "within this wood, a little from the path, there is a hidden way, and at the end thereof an ancient chapel, where oftentimes I have bewailed my lot. Near by is a great hollow stone, concealed by a bush, and there is the secret place where I hide my raiment, till I would return to my own home."

On hearing this marvel the lady became sanguine of visage, because of her exceeding fear. She dared no longer to lie at his side, and turned over in her mind, this way and that, how best she could get her from him. Now there was a certain knight of those parts, who, for a great while, had sought and required this lady for her love. This knight had spent long years in her service, but little enough had he got thereby, not even fair words or a promise. To him the dame wrote a letter, and meeting, made her purpose plain.

"Fair friend," said she, "be happy. That which you have coveted so long a time, I will grant without delay. Never again will I deny your suit. My heart, and all I have to give, are yours, so take me now as love and dame."

Right sweetly the knight thanked her for her grace, and pledged her faith and fealty. When she had confirmed him by an oath, then she told him all this business of her lord—why he went, and what he became, and of his ravening within the wood. So she showed him of the chapel, and of the hollow stone, and of how to spoil the Were-Wolf of his vesture. Thus, by the kiss of his wife, was Bisclavaret betrayed. Often enough had he ravished his prey in desolate places, but from this journey he never returned. His kinsfolk and acquaintance came together to ask of his tidings, when this absence was noised abroad. Many a man, on many a day, searched the woodland, but none might find him, nor learn where Bisclavaret was gone.

The lady was wedded to the knight who had cherished her for so long a space. More than a year had passed since Bisclavaret disappeared. Then it chanced that the King would hunt in that self-same wood where the Were-Wolf lurked. When the hounds were unleashed they ran this way and that, and swiftly came upon his scent. At the view the huntsman winded on his horn, and the whole pack were at his heels. They followed him from morn to eve, till he was torn and bleeding, and was all adread lest they should pull him down. Now the King was very close to the quarry, and when Bisclavaret looked upon his master, he ran to him for pity and for grace. He took the stirrup within his paws, and fawned upon the prince's foot. The King was very fearful at this sight, but presently he called his courtiers to his aid.

"Lords," cried he, "hasten hither, and see this marvellous thing. Here is a beast who has the sense of man. He abases himself before his foe, and cries for mercy, although he cannot speak. Beat off the hounds, and let no man do him harm. We will hunt no more to-day, but return to our own place, with the wonderful quarry we have taken."

The King turned him about, and rode to his hall, Bisclavaret following at his side. Very near to his master the Were-Wolf went, like any dog, and had no care to seek again the wood. When the King brought him safely to his own castle, he rejoiced greatly, for the beast was fair and strong, no mightier had any man seen. Much pride had the King in his marvelous beast. He held him so dear, that he bade all those who wished for his love, to cross the Wolf in naught, neither to strike him with a rod, but ever to see that he was richly fed and kennelled warm. This commandment the Court observed willingly. So all the day the wolf sported with the lords, and at night he lay within the chamber of the King. There was not a man who did not make much of the beast, so frank was he and debonair. None had reason to do him wrong, for ever was he about his master, and for his part did evil to none. Every day were these two companions together, and all perceived that the King loved him as his friend.

Hearken now to that which chanced.

The King held a high Court, and bade his great vassals and barons, and all the lords of his venery to the feast. Never was there a goodlier feast, nor one set forth with sweeter show and pomp. Amongst those who were bidden, came that same knight who had the wife of Bisclavaret for dame. He came to the castle, richly gowned, with a fair company, but little he deemed whom he would find so near. Bisclavaret marked his foe the moment he stood within the hall. He ran towards him, and seized him with his fangs, in the King's very presence, and to the view of all. Doubtless he would have done him mischief, had not the King called and chidden him, and threatened him with a rod. Once, and twice, again, the Wolf set upon the knight in the very light of day. All men marvelled at his malice, for sweet and serviceable was the beast, and to that hour had shown hatred of none. With one consent the household deemed that this deed was done with full reason, and that the Wolf had suffered at the knight's hand some bitter wrong. Right wary of his foe was the knight until the feast had ended, and all the barons had taken farewell of their lord, and departed, each to his own house. With these, amongst the very first, went that lord whom Bisclavaret so fiercely had assailed. Small was the wonder that he was glad to go.

No long while after this adventure it came to pass that the courteous King would hunt in that forest where Bisclavaret was found. With the prince came his wolf, and a fair company. Now at nightfall the King abode within a certain lodge of that country, and this was known of that dame who before was the wife of Bisclavaret. In the morning the lady clothed her in her most dainty apparel, and hastened to the lodge, since she desired to speak with the King, and to offer him a rich present. When the lady entered in the chamber, neither man nor leash might restrain the fury of the Wolf. He became as a mad dog in his hatred and malice. Breaking from his bonds he sprang at the lady's face, and bit the nose from her visage. From every side men ran to the succour of the dame. They beat off the wolf from his prey, and for a little would have cut him in pieces with their swords. But a certain wise counsellor said to the King,

"Sire, hearken now to me. This beast is always with you, and there is not one of us all who has not known him for long. He goes in and out amongst us, nor has molested any man, neither done wrong or felony to any, save only to this dame, one only time as we have seen. He has done evil to this lady, and to that knight, who is now the husband of the dame. Sire, she was once the wife of that lord who was so close and private to your heart, but who went, and none might find where he had gone. Now, therefore, put the dame in a sure place, and question her straitly, so that she may tell—if perchance she knows thereof—for what reason this Beast holds her in such mortal hate. For many a strange deed has chanced, as well we know, in this marvellous land of Brittany."

The King listened to these words, and deemed the counsel good. He laid hands upon the knight, and put the dame in surety in another place. He caused them to be questioned right straitly, so that their torment was very grievous. At the end, partly because of her distress, and partly by reason of her exceeding fear, the lady's lips were loosed, and she told her tale. She showed them of the betrayal of her lord, and how his raiment was stolen from the hollow stone. Since then she knew not where he went, nor what had befallen him, for he had never come again to his own land. Only, in her heart, well she deemed and was persuaded, that Bisclavaret was he.

Straightway the King demanded the vesture of his baron, whether this were to the wish of the lady, or whether it were against her wish. When the raiment was brought him, he caused it to be spread before Bisclavaret, but the Wolf made as though he had not seen. Then that cunning and crafty counsellor took the King apart, that he might give him a fresh rede.

"Sire," said he, "you do not wisely, nor well, to set this raiment before Bisclavaret, in the sight of all. In shame and much tribulation must he lay aside the beast, and again become man. Carry your wolf within your most secret chamber, and put his vestment therein. Then close the door upon him, and leave him alone for a space. So we shall see presently whether the ravening beast may indeed return to human shape."

The King carried the Wolf to his chamber, and shut the doors upon him fast. He delayed for a brief while, and taking two lords of his fellowship with him, came again to the room. Entering therein, all three, softly together, they found the knight asleep in the King's bed, like a little child. The King ran swiftly to the bed and taking his friend in his arms, embraced and kissed him fondly, above a hundred times. When the man's speech returned once more, he told him of his adventure. Then the King restored to his friend the fief that was stolen from him, and gave such rich gifts, moreover, as I cannot tell. As for the wife who had betrayed Bisclavaret, he bade her avoid his country, and chased her from the realm. So she went forth, she and her second lord together, to seek a more abiding city, and were no more seen.

The adventure that you have heard is no vain fable. Verily and indeed it chanced as I have said. The Lay of the Were-Wolf, truly, was written that it should ever be borne in mind.

ANDREAS CAPELLANUS (FL. LATE 12TH CENTURY)
The Art of Courtly Love

Andrew the Chaplain's De arte honeste amandi *is usually translated as* The Art of Courtly Love, *even though the term "courtly love" was an invention of the nineteenth century. It characterizes a kind of romantic love which idealizes passion and worship of the beloved, or, as some might say, makes a virtue out of sexual frustration. Andreas's work was part of the revolution in style that occurred in the twelfth century—a move away from literary works that were martial, heroic, and male-centered and toward works that were more intimate and at least pretended to notice the place and attitudes of women.*

Important in this development were the court circles that grew up around Eleanor of Aquitaine, the wife of King Louis VII of France (and later of King Henry II of England), and their two daughters, Alix and especially Marie, the Countess of Champagne. Eleanor was the granddaughter of the first troubadour, William IX of Aquitaine, the first known secular love poet of the later Middle Ages. She took under her patronage troubadours who sang about courtly love and poets who revived the Celtic stories about Merlin and King Arthur. Andreas describes her court as a true love court, *in the legal sense: in one case about adulterous love, Andreas tells us, Eleanor handed down the decision that love can only exist outside of marriage and not within marriage. Andreas wrote his treatise about 1182 at the court of Champagne for Marie, Eleanor's daughter; Marie also commissioned the first romance about the adulterous affair of Lancelot and Guinevere,* The Knight of the Cart, *by Chrétien de Troyes.*

The Art of Courtly Love is a handbook of love addressed to a young cleric. The first two-thirds offers a series of sample dialogues in which male speakers of varying social ranks try to win to their sides (and their beds) women of varying social ranks. That section of the work ends with Andreas's summary of the rules that characterize and guide this kind of secular, passionate love. Then Andreas does a sudden and complete about-face, rejecting the folly of all such love, and suggesting that only the love of God is truly important. Much of this last part of the work is devoted to a detailed, virulent, and entirely conventional, medieval attack upon women for bringing about men's downfall and for their vanity, drunkenness, wantonness, and greed. Whatever the ultimate meaning of this enigmatic work, the rules below and their reflections in countless poems, novels, operas, and films, came to shape what later ages recognized as romantic love.

[The Rules of Love]

1. Marriage is not a good excuse for not loving.
2. The person who is not jealous cannot love.

The "Rules of Love" have been translated for this collection by the editor.

3. No one can be bound by two loves.
4. Love is known to be always increasing or decreasing.
5. What a lover takes from an unwilling partner is bitter.
6. A male usually does not love until he reaches puberty.
7. When a lover dies, the survivor is required to remain without a partner for two years.
8. No one should be deprived of love except for the strongest reason.
9. No one can love unless he is compelled by Love's persuasion.
10. Love is always an exile from the home of avarice.
11. One should not love a woman whom one would be ashamed to seek to marry.
12. A true lover does not desire the embraces of any but his beloved.
13. Love rarely survives being made public.
14. A love easily achieved will be regarded with contempt; love achieved with difficulty will be valued.
15. Every lover turns pale when he is near his beloved.
16. When a lover suddenly sees his beloved, his heart pounds.
17. A new love drives out an old one.
18. Good character alone makes a man worthy of love.
19. If love diminishes, it quickly fades and rarely regains strength.
20. One in love is always fearful.
21. True jealousy always causes the feeling of love to grow.
22. When one begins to suspect his beloved, jealousy and the feeling of love both grow.
23. One who is vexed by the thought of love sleeps and eats very little.
24. Every act of a lover ends in thoughts of his beloved.
25. A true lover regards as good only what he thinks will please his beloved.
26. Love can deny nothing to love.
27. A lover can never have enough of the solaces of his beloved.
28. The slightest presumption causes a lover to harbor sinister suspicions about his beloved.
29. One who is vexed by excessive passion is usually not in love.
30. A true lover is constantly and without intermission preoccupied by thoughts of his beloved.
31. Nothing prevents one woman from being loved by two men, or one man by two women.

STATUTES OF GREGORY IX FOR THE
UNIVERSITY OF PARIS IN 1231

Gregory IX, pope from 1227 to 1241, was an expert in canon law and theology and a staunch defender of papal prerogatives and powers. A stern and often angry man, he engaged in political struggles with secular nobles who seemed to act on their own authority in violation of his. As with other popes in the twelfth and thirteenth centuries, he supported the crusades and worried about heresy in southern France and northern Italy. In 1231, the year of these university statutes, he established the papal Inquisition as a way to root out heresy. Under later popes, the Inquisition became a tool against alchemy, witchcraft, and sorcery.

Gregory's interest in the University of Paris arose early. As a young man, Ugo di Segni, he studied theology there and discovered his skills in diplomacy. The late twelfth and early thirteenth centuries were a time of ferment in the church. St. Dominic and St. Francis, both friends of Ugo, founded their orders of mendicant friars then. And the University of Paris was founded about the time Gregory was born, shortly before 1170. Before that time—in the time of Abelard, for instance—the schools were attached to the Cathedral of Notre-Dame. The chancellor at Notre-Dame had the power to license a master of arts degree, which meant that students in schools at Notre-Dame could themselves become teachers, that is, be recognized as a master instead of an apprentice ("bachelor"). In the early thirteenth century, Paris had three superior faculties, each headed by a dean—theology, canon law, and medicine—and one inferior (this is a title, not a judgment!) faculty, headed by a rector—the arts. In addition, the students and faculties were organized into four "nations," each headed by a proctor—French, Picard, Norman, and English.

The first university was that at Bologna, specializing in law. The University of Paris, famous for theology, was the first university in northern Europe, and it was the model for a similar university in England, at Oxford. Armed with a charter granted by pope, king, or emperor, and a caveat against teaching heresy or atheism, teachers and students essentially formed corporations and ruled themselves, with the students paying the teachers. Teachers had to be popular, therefore, or students would wander off to other universities. Sometimes the students even started their own, as in the case of Cambridge, which was started by some students unhappy with their experience at Oxford.

Removed from the world in the "ivory towers" of their colleges, students became accustomed to living by rules that were different from those in the surrounding towns. Reports of drunkenness and fighting were common, and occasionally brawls occurred between students and townspeople. On the Feast of St. Scholastica (the sister of St. Benedict) in Oxford in 1355, for example, a fight broke out in an Oxford tavern which quickly erupted into the streets and escalated into a pitched battle between "town and

---

This translation is by D. C. Munro in *University of Pennsylvania Translations and Reprints* (Philadelphia, 1897).

gown." In the end, 63 students were killed and many more left the university in fear. As self-govern-ing entities, universities established principles of conduct, like these for the University of Paris.

Gregory, the bishop, servant of the servants of God, to his beloved sons, all the masters and students of Paris—greeting and apostolic benediction.

Paris, the mother of sciences, like another Cariath Sepher, a city of letters, stands forth illustrious, great indeed, but concerning herself she causes greater things to be desired, full of favor for the teachers and students. There, as in a special factory of wisdom, she has silver as the beginnings of her veins, and of gold is the spot in which according to law they flow together; from which the prudent mystics of eloquence fabricate golden necklaces inlaid with silver, and making collars ornamented with precious stones of inestimable value, adorn and decorate the spouse of Christ. There the iron is raised from the earth, because when the earthly fragility is solidified by strength, the breastplate of faith, the sword of the spirit, and the other weapons of the Christian soldier, powerful against the brazen powers, are formed from it. And the stone melted by heat, is turned into brass, because the hearts of stone, enkindled by the fervor of the Holy Ghost, at times glow, burn and become sonorous, and by preaching herald the praises of Christ.

Accordingly, it is undoubtedly very displeasing to God and men that any one in the afore-said city should strive in any way to disturb so illustrious grace, or should not oppose himself openly and with all his strength to any who do so. Wherefore, since we have diligently investigated the questions referred to us concerning a dissension which, through the instigation of the devil, has arisen there and greatly disturbed the university, we have decided, by the advice of our brethren, that these should be set at rest rather by precautionary measures, than by a judicial sentence.

Therefore, concerning the condition of the students and schools, we have decided that the following should be observed: each chancellor, appointed hereafter at Paris, at the time of his installation, in the presence of the bishop, or at the command of the latter in the chapter at Paris—two masters of the students having been summoned for this purpose and present in behalf of the university—shall swear that, in good faith, according to his conscience, he will not receive as professors of theology and canon law any but suitable men, at a suitable place and time, according to the condition of the city and the honor and glory of those branches of learning; and he will reject all who are unworthy without respect to persons or nations. Before licensing anyone, during three months, dating from the time when the license is requested, the chancellor shall make diligent inquiries of all the masters of theology present in the city, and of all other honest and learned men through whom the truth can be ascertained, concerning the life, knowledge, capacity, purpose, prospects and other qualities needful in such persons; and after the inquiries, in good faith and according to his conscience, he shall grant or deny the license to the candidate, as shall seem fitting and expedient. The masters of theology and canon law, when they begin to lecture, shall take a public oath that they will give true testimony on the above points. The chancellor shall also swear, that, he will in no way reveal the advice of the masters, to their injury; the liberty and privileges being maintained in their full vigor for the canons at Paris, as they were in the beginning. Moreover, the chancellor shall promise to examine in good faith the masters in medicine and arts and in the other branches, to admit only the worthy and to reject the unworthy.

In other matters, because confusion easily creeps in where there is no order, we grant to you the right of making constitutions and ordinances regulating the manner and time of lectures and disputations, the costume to be worn, the burial of the dead; and also concerning the bachelors, who are to lecture and at what hours, and on what they are to lecture; and concerning the prices of the lodgings or the interdiction of the same; and concerning a fit punishment for those who violate your constitutions or ordinances, by exclusion from your society. And if, perchance, the assessment of the lodgings is taken from you, or anything else is lacking, or an injury or outrageous damage, such as death or the mutilation of a limb, is inflicted on one of you; unless through a suitable admonition satisfaction is rendered within fifteen days, you may suspend your lectures until you have received full satisfaction. And if it happens that any one of you is unlawfully imprisoned, unless the injury ceases on a remonstrance from you, you may, if you judge it expedient, suspend your lectures immediately.

We command, moreover, that the bishop of Paris shall so chastise the excesses of the guilty, that the honor of the students shall be preserved and evil deeds shall not remain unpunished. But in no way shall the innocent be seized on account of the guilty; nay rather, if a probable suspicion arises against anyone, he shall be detained honorably and on giving suitable bail he shall be freed, without any exactions from the jailors. But if, perchance, such a crime has been committed that imprisonment is necessary, the bishop shall detain the criminal in his prison. The chancellor is forbidden to keep him in his prison. We also forbid holding a student for a debt contracted by another, since this is interdicted by canonical and legitimate sanctions. Neither the bishop, nor his official, nor the chancellor shall exact a pecuniary penalty for removing an excommunication or any other censure of any kind. Nor shall the chancellor demand from the masters who are licensed an oath, or obedience, or any pledge; nor shall he receive any emolument or promise for granting a license, but be content with the above-mentioned oath.

Also, the vacation in summer is not to exceed one month, and the bachelors, if they wish, can continue their lectures in vacation time. Moreover, we prohibit more expressly the students from carrying weapons in the city, and the university from protecting those who disturb the peace and study. And those who call themselves students but do not frequent the schools, or acknowledge any master, are in no way to enjoy the liberties of the students.

Moreover, we order that the masters in arts shall always read one lecture on Priscian, and one book after the other in the regular courses. Those books on natural philosophy which for a certain reason were prohibited in a provincial council, are not to be used at Paris until they have been examined and purged of all suspicion of error. The masters and students in theology shall strive to exercise themselves laudably in the branch which they profess; they shall not show themselves philosophers, but they shall strive to become God's learned. And they shall not speak in the language of the people, confounding the sacred language with the profane. In the schools they shall dispute only on such questions as can be determined by theological books and the writings of the holy fathers.

Also, about the property of the scholars who die intestate or do not commit the arrangement of their affairs to others, we have determined to arrange thus: namely, that the bishop and one of the masters, whom the university shall appoint for this purpose, shall receive all the property of the defunct, and placing it in a suitable and safe spot, shall fix a certain date, before which his death can be announced in his native country, and those who ought to succeed to his property can come to Paris or send a suitable messenger. And if they come or send, the goods shall be restored to them, with the security which shall have been given. If no one appears, then the bishop and masters shall expend the property for the soul of the departed, as seems expedient; unless, perchance, the heirs shall have been prevented from coming by some good reason. In that case, the distribution shall be deferred to a fitting time.

Truly, because the masters and students, who harassed by damages and injuries, have taken a mutual oath to depart from Paris and have broken up the school, have seemed to be waging a contest not so much for their own benefit as for the common good; we consulting the needs and advantage of the whole church, wish and command that after the privileges have been granted to the masters and students by our most dearly beloved son in Christ, the illustrious King of the French, and amends have been paid by the malefactors, they shall study at Paris and shall not be marked by any infamy or irregularity on account of their staying away or return.

It is not lawful for any man whatever to infringe this deed of our provision, constitution, concession, prohibition and inhibition or to act contrary to it, from rash presumption. If anyone, however, should dare to attempt this, let him know that he incurs the wrath of almighty God and of the blessed Peter and Paul, his apostles.

Given at the Lateran, on the Ides of April [April 13], in the fifth year of our pontificate.

THOMAS AQUINAS (C. 1225–1274)
Summa Theologica

Thomas Aquinas came from a wealthy land-owning family who wanted their son to become an abbot of a monastery. They placed him as a young boy in the famous abbey at Monte Cassino near their home. When the emperor closed the abbey and expelled the monks, Thomas decided against the monastic life in favor of the newest order of mendicant friars, the Dominicans, founded 30 years before. Monks made vows of personal poverty, but lived in the luxury of religious communities that had accumulated great wealth over the years. The fraternal orders, beginning with St. Francis, who founded the Franciscans in 1209, were devoted to poverty, both individually and as a brotherhood. They sustained themselves by becoming expert street preachers and teachers. To Aquinas, the dedication to learning that characterized the order founded by St. Dominic, must have felt like a new freedom. When he was sent by his order to the Dominican house at the University of Paris, he was put in contact with revolutionary old ideas. (To keep this from happening, his family had him abducted on his way to Paris, and held him prisoner for a year before releasing him in 1245.)

The ideas that were shaking up Paris were Aristotle's, available in Latin translations for the first time by way of Muslim Spain (Aristotle's works had been preserved among Arabic scholars). Christian theology, cast in Platonic terms for more than a thousand years, suddenly faced the challenge of Aristotle's scientific rationalism. In the course of earning a bachelor's degree, a "license to teach," and a master's degree (1256), Thomas studied theology and the new science. After a sojourn in Italy, he returned to Paris to find the view growing among intellectuals that scientific investigation based on reason might lead to truths that contradicted those asserted by faith. He began to lecture and write, taking the position that reason could operate within the faith, so that theology itself could be organized on a rational basis. Beginning with a few simple truths revealed by God, the entire edifice of Christian belief could be constructed by means of the question and answer method then popular in the university. In terms of Aristotle's causes, the final cause, which set all in motion, was God, the summum bonum *"highest good," or happiness.*

In 1272, Thomas was sent to Naples to found a Dominican school in the University of Naples. At that time his ideas, which were laid out in two large treatises, were being attacked as part of the general religious reaction against radical scientific rationalism. After his death, however, his logical constructions were seen as ways of preserving doctrinal clarity, and even in the last century renewal movements within Roman Catholicism were grounded in his teachings. He became a saint in 1323. His philosophy, in which revelations of God's truth become the basis of an orderly examination of the human and natural worlds, came to be called scholasticism *or* Thomism.

This excerpt is translated by the Fathers of the English Dominican Province (Benziger Brothers, 1947).

On the Existence of God

Question 2: The Existence of God (in Three Articles)

Third Article

Whether God Exists?

We proceed thus to the Third Article:—

Objection 1. It seems that God does not exist; because if one of two contraries be infinite, the other would be altogether destroyed. But the word "God" means that He is infinite goodness. If, therefore, God existed, there would be no evil discoverable; but there is evil in the world. Therefore God does not exist.

Obj. 2. Further, it is superfluous to suppose that what can be accounted for by a few principles has been produced by many. But it seems that everything we see in the world can be accounted for by other principles, supposing God did not exist. For all natural things can be reduced to one principle, which is nature; and all voluntary things can be reduced to one principle, which is human reason, or will. Therefore there is no need to suppose God's existence.

On the contrary, It is said in the person of God: *I am Who am* (Exod. iii. 14).

I answer that, The existence of God can be proved in five ways.

The first and more manifest way is the argument from motion. It is certain, and evident to our senses, that in the world some things are in motion. Now whatever is in motion is put in motion by another, for nothing can be in motion except it is in potentiality to that towards which it is in motion; whereas a thing moves inasmuch as it is in act. For motion is nothing else than the reduction of something from potentiality to actuality. But nothing can be reduced from potentiality to actuality, except by something in a state of actuality. Thus that which is actually hot, as fire, makes wood, which is potentially hot, to be actually hot, and thereby moves and changes it. Now it is not possible that the same thing should be at once in actuality and potentiality in the same respect, but only in different respects. For what is actually hot cannot simultaneously be potentially hot; but it is simultaneously potentially cold. It is therefore impossible that in the same respect and in the same way a thing should be both mover and moved, i.e., that it should move itself. Therefore, whatever is in motion must be put in motion by another. If that by which it is put in motion be itself put in motion, then this also must needs be put in motion by another, and that by another again. But this cannot go on to infinity, because then there would be no first mover, and, consequently, no other mover; seeing that subsequent movers move only inasmuch as they are put in motion by the first mover; as the staff moves only because it is put in motion by the hand. Therefore it is necessary to arrive at a first mover, put in motion by no other; and this everyone understands to be God.

The second way is from the nature of the efficient cause. In the world of sense we find there is an order of efficient causes. There is no case known (neither is it, indeed, possible) in which a thing is found to be the efficient cause of itself; for so it would be prior to itself, which is impossible. Now in efficient causes it is not possible to go on to infinity, because in all efficient causes following in order, the first is the cause of the intermediate cause, and the intermediate is the cause of the ultimate cause, whether the intermediate cause be several, or one only. Now to take away the cause is to take away the effect. Therefore if there be no first cause among efficient causes, there will be no ultimate, nor any intermediate cause. But if in efficient causes it is possible to go on to infinity, there will be no first efficient cause, neither will there be an ultimate effect, nor any intermediate efficient causes; all of which is plainly false. Therefore it is necessary to admit a first efficient cause, to which everyone gives the name of God.

The third way is taken from possibility and necessity, and runs thus. We find in nature things that are possible to be and not to be, since they are found to be generated, and to corrupt, and consequently, they are possible to be and not to be. But it is impossible for these always to exist, for that which is possible not to be at some time is not. Therefore, if everything is possible not to be, then at one time there could have been nothing in existence. Now if this were true, even now there would be nothing in existence, because that which does not exist only begins to exist by something already existing. Therefore, if at one time nothing was in existence, it would have been impossible for anything to have begun to exist; and thus even now nothing would be in existence—which is absurd. Therefore, not all beings are merely possible, but there must exist something the existence of which is necessary. But every necessary thing either has its necessity caused by another, or not. Now it is impossible to go on to infinity in necessary things which have their necessity caused by another, as has been already proved in regard to efficient causes. Therefore we cannot but postulate the existence of some being having of itself its own necessity, and not receiving it from another, but rather causing in others their necessity. This all men speak of as God.

The fourth way is taken from the gradation to be found in things. Among beings there are some more and some less good, true, noble, and the like. But "more" and "less" are predicated of different things, according as they resemble in their different ways something which is the maximum, as a thing is said to be hotter according as it more nearly resembles that which is hottest; so that there is something which is truest, something best, something noblest, and, consequently, something which is uttermost being; for those things that are greatest in truth are greatest in being, as it is written in *Metaph.* ii. Now the maximum in any genus is the cause of all in that genus; as fire, which is the maximum of heat, is the cause of all hot things. Therefore there must also be something which is to all beings the cause of their being, goodness, and every other perfection; and this we call God.

The fifth way is taken from the governance of the world. We see that things which lack intelligence, such as natural bodies, act for an end, and this is evident from their acting always, or nearly always, in the same way, so as to obtain the best result. Hence it is plain that not fortuitously, but designedly, do they achieve their end. Now whatever lacks intelligence cannot move towards an end, unless it be directed by some being endowed with knowledge and intelligence; as the arrow is shot to its mark by the archer. Therefore some intelligent being exists by whom all natural things are directed to their end; and this being we call God.

Reply Obj. 1. As Augustine says (*Enchir.* xi): *Since God is the highest good, He would not allow any evil to exist in His works, unless His omnipotence and goodness were such as to bring good even out of evil.* This is part of the infinite goodness of God, that He should allow evil to exist, and out of it produce good.

Reply Obj. 2. Since nature works for a determinate end under the direction of a higher agent, whatever is done by nature must needs be traced back to God, as to its first cause. So also whatever is done voluntarily must also be traced back to some higher cause other than human reason or will, since these can change and fail; for all things that are changeable and capable of defect must be traced back to an immovable and self-necessary first principle, as was shown in the body of the *Article.*

POPE BONIFACE VIII (1235–1303)
Unam Sanctam

Benedetto Gaetani was born in 1235 to an Italian noble family. Late in his life, in 1294, he was invested as Pope Boniface VIII and immediately became embroiled in controversies with the European kings. In 1295 Edward I of England and Philip IV of France, in order to pay for ongoing wars, sought money from clergy in their countries. Boniface responded by issuing a bull forbidding the taxation of the clergy by secular authorities. The kings responded by declaring the clergy outlaws and stopping the transfer of any money to Rome. Boniface backed down for a time, but the issue returned in broader terms when Philip accused a bishop of treason. Both Philip and Boniface claimed the case for trial in their own courts. In the papal bull Unam Sanctam *(1302) Boniface set forth sweeping claims of papal supremacy. Asserting the unity of the church and the necessity of belonging to the church to achieve salvation, Boniface then requires absolute submission to the pope in order to belong to the church and achieve salvation. In response to Boniface's claim that spiritual authority is greater than secular authority, Philip plotted to abduct Boniface and bring him to France. In 1303, Boniface was attacked in his residence. Although the abduction was not successful, the injuries caused his death a month later.*

We are compelled, our faith urging us, to believe and to hold—and we do firmly believe and simply confess—that there is one holy catholic and apostolic church, outside of which there is neither salvation nor remission of sins; her Spouse proclaiming it in the canticles: "My dove, my undefiled is but one, she is the choice one of her that bare her"; which represents one mystic body, of which body the head is Christ; but of Christ, God. In this church there is one Lord, one faith and one baptism. There was one ark of Noah, indeed, at the time of the flood, symbolizing one church; and this being finished in one cubit had, namely, one Noah as helmsman and commander. And, with the exception of this ark, all things existing upon the earth were, as we read, destroyed. This church, moreover, we venerate as the only one, the Lord saying through His prophet: "Deliver my soul from the sword, my darling from the power of the dog." He prayed at the same time for His soul—that is, for Himself the Head—and for His body—which body, namely, he called the one and only church on account of the unity of the faith promised, of the sacraments, and of the love of the church. She is that seamless garment of the Lord which was not cut but which fell by lot. Therefore of this one and only church there is one body and one head—not two heads as if it were a monster:—Christ, namely, and the vicar of Christ, St. Peter, and the successor of Peter. For the Lord Himself said to Peter, Feed my sheep. My sheep, He said, using a general term, and not designating these or those particular

---

The translation by E. F. Henderson (London: 1896) is reprinted from Norton *Downs' Basic Documents in Medieval History* (Princeton: Van Nostrand, 1959).

sheep; from which it is plain that He committed to Him all His sheep. If, then, the Greeks or others say that they were not committed to the care of Peter and his successors, they necessarily confess that they are not of the sheep of Christ; for the Lord says, in John, that there is one fold, one shepherd and one only. We are told by the word of the gospel that in this His fold there are two swords,—a spiritual, namely, and a temporal. For when the apostles said "Behold here are two swords"—when, namely, the apostles were speaking in the church—the Lord did not reply that this was too much, but enough. Surely he who denies that the temporal sword is in the power of Peter wrongly interprets the word of the Lord when He says: "Put up thy sword in its scabbard." Both swords, the spiritual and the material, therefore, are in the power of the church; the one, indeed, to be wielded for the church, the other by the church; the one by the hand of the priest, the other by the hand of kings and knights, but at the will and sufferance of the priest. One sword, moreover, ought to be under the other, and the temporal authority to be subjected to the spiritual. For when the apostle says "there is no power but of God, and the powers that are of God are ordained," they would not be ordained unless sword were under sword and the lesser one, as it were, were led by the other to great deeds. For according to St. Dionysius the law of divinity is to lead the lowest through the intermediate to the highest things. Not therefore, according to the law of the universe, are all things reduced to order equally and immediately; but the lowest through the intermediate, the intermediate through the higher. But that the spiritual exceeds any earthly power in dignity and nobility we ought the more openly to confess the more spiritual things excel temporal ones. This also is made plain to our eyes from the giving of tithes, and the benediction and the sanctification; from the acceptation of this same power, from the control over those same things. For, the truth bearing witness, the spiritual power has to establish the earthly power, and to judge it if it be not good. Thus concerning the church and the ecclesiastical power is verified the prophecy of Jeremiah: "See, I have this day set thee over the nations and over the kingdoms," and the other things which follow. Therefore if the earthly power err it shall 'be judged by the spiritual power; but if the lesser spiritual power err, by the greater. But if the greatest, it can be judged by God alone, not by man, the apostle bearing witness. A spiritual man judges all things, but he himself is judged by no one. This authority, moreover, even though it is given to man and exercised through man, is not human but rather divine, being given by divine lips to Peter and founded on a rock for him and his successors through Christ himself whom he has confessed; the Lord himself saying to Peter: "Whatsoever thou shalt bind," etc. Whoever, therefore, resists this power thus ordained by God, resists the ordination of God, unless he makes believe, like the Manichean, that there are two beginnings. This we consider false and heretical, since by the testimony of Moses, not "in the beginnings," but "in the beginning" God created the Heavens and the earth. Indeed we declare, announce and define, that it is altogether necessary to salvation for every human creature to be subject to, the Roman pontiff. The Lateran, Nov. 14, in our 8th year. As a perpetual memorial of this matter.

Medieval Lyric Poetry

Carmina Burana

Perhaps the best-known manuscript of medieval songs was found at the Benedictine monastery of Benediktbeuern, Bavaria, in 1803. The collection includes songs that celebrate spring, drinking, love, and learning in rhymed Latin (and occasionally German) lyrics that are sometimes serious, often satirical, always clever. The songs were presumably the products of the revelries of itinerant students and scholars who gathered in taverns in university towns. Although the original music for the Carmina Burana *has been recorded several times, many of the songs are familiar today mainly through the great rhythmic setting for chorus, orchestra, and dancers by Carl Orff (1895-1982), the Munich composer, conductor, and theorist who was interested in musical education that involved rhythm and movement. The two songs given here are also high points in Orff's* Carmina Burana *(1937), and the translations attempt the difficult task of miming the rhythm of Orff's setting of the colloquial Latin.*

O Fortuna

O how Fortune,
  inopportune,
apes the moon's inconstancy:
  waxing, waning,
  losing, gaining,
life treats us detestably:
  first oppressing
  then caressing
shifts us like pawns in her play:
  destitution,
  restitution,
mixes and melts them away.

  Fate, as vicious
  as capricious,
whirling your merry-go-round:
  evil doings,
  worthless wooings,
crumble away to the ground:

The translations by David Parlett are from *Selections from the Carmina Burana* (New York: Penguin, 1986).

    darkly stealing,
     unrevealing,
working against me you go:
    for your measure
     of foul pleasure
I bare my back to your blow.

    Noble actions,
     true transactions,
no longer fall to my lot:
    powers to make me
     then to break me
all play their part in your plot:
    now seize your time—
     waste no more time,
pluck these poor strings and let go:
    since the strongest
     fall the longest
let the world share in my woe.

In taberna quando sumus

In the tavern when we're drinking,
though the ground be cold and stinking,
down we go and join the action
with the dice and gaming faction.
what goes on inside the salon
where it's strictly cash per gallon
if you'd like to know, sir, well you
shut your mouth and I shall tell you.

Some are drinking, some are playing,
some their vulgar side displaying:
most of those who like to gamble
wind up naked in the scramble;
some emerge attired in new things,
some in bits and bobs and shoestrings:
no one thinks he'll kick the bucket
dicing for a beery ducat.

First to those who pay for wallowing,
then we layabouts toast the following:
next we drink to all held captive,
thirdly drink to those still active,
fourthly drink to the Christian-hearted,
fifthly drink to the dear departed,
sixthly to our free-and-easy sisters,
seventhly to all out-of-work enlisters.

Eighthly drink to friars deconverted,
ninthly, monks from monast'ries diverted,
tenthly, sailors of the oceans,
eleventhly, louts who cause commotions,
twelfthly, those who wear the penitential,
thirteenth, and whose journey is essential—
to this fat pope, to that thin king—
who the hell cares why they're drinking!

Drinking tinker, drinking tailor,
drinking soldier, drinking sailor,
drinking rich man, drinking poor man,
drinking beggarman, thief and lawman,
drinking servant, drinking master,
drinking mistress, drinking pastor,
drinking doctor, drinking layman,
drinking drunkard, drinking drayman:

Drinking rude man, drinking proper,
drinking tiddler, drinking whopper,
drinking scholar, drinking gypsy,
drinking drunk or maudlin tipsy,
drinking father, drinking mother,
drinking sister, drinking brother,
drinking husbands, wives and lovers
and a hundred thousand others—

Half a million pounds would never
pay for all we drink together:
for we drink beyond all measure,
purely for the sake of pleasure:
thus you see us, poor and shoddy,
criticized by everybody—
God grant that they be confounded
when at last the trump is sounded!

King Richard I (1157–1199)

Richard Coeur-de-Lion (reigned 1189–1199) was the son of England's King Henry II and Eleanor of Aquitaine, whose first husband was the king of France. A sometime crusader, Richard was captured in Austria and held for an enormous ransom. This song, in the style of the troubadour music that was all the rage in France in the late twelfth century, is a musical curse upon Richard's friends for letting him rot so long in prison. Although the Robin Hood legends make him heroic next to his brother, the evil King John, he was a weak and absent king. In fact, his mother ruled during his absences, she saw to the gathering of the ransom, and she traveled to Austria to accompany him home.

This translation is by James J. Wilhelm in *Lyrics of the Middle Ages* (New York: Garland, 1990).

"Ja nuls homs pris ne dira sa raison"

1. A man imprisoned can never speak his mind
   As cleverly as those who do not suffer,
   But through his song he can some comfort find.
   I have a host of friends, poor the gifts they offer.
   Shame on them if this ransoming should trail
   Into a second year in jail!

2. This they know well, my barons and my men,
   English, Norman, Gascon, and Poitevin,
   What I'd leave of my property in prison!
   O I'm not saying this to cast derision,
   But still I'm here in jail!

3. Here is a truth I know that can be told:
   Dead men and prisoners have neither parents nor friends,
   No one to offer up their silver and gold.
   It matters to me, but much more to my men.
   For after my death, they'll be bitterly assailed
   Because I'm so long in jail!

4. No wonder if I have a grieving heart
   When I see my land torn by its lord asunder:
   If he'll recall the pact in which we took part
   And remember the pledges we vowed we'd both live under,
   Truly within the year, without a fail,
   I'd be out of jail!

5. This they know, the Angevins and Tourains,
   Those bachelors there who are strong and own a lot,
   While I'm encumbered here in another's hands;
   They loved me lots, but now they don't love a jot;
   Over the plains I don't see a piece of mail
   Although I'm still in jail!

6. I've loved and I love still my companions true,
   The men of Cahiu and the men of Porcherain,
   But tell me, song, if they still love me too,
   For never to them was I double-faced or vain:
   They're villains if my lands they now assail—
   Since I am here in jail!

Contessa de Dia

In twelfth-century France a new way of talking about love swept the country, beginning in the south with the troubadours, and then spreading northward and into Germany. So popular was the intimate, personal style cultivated by these singers—as if, like today's country-and-western singers, they were giving heartfelt expression to the joys and torments of their own experience—that we know the names of some 400 troubadours and the melodies of almost 300 songs have survived. The melodies were mono-phonic and could be sung without accompaniment or could be adapted to a variety of styles, some of them borrowed from Arabic music. Four songs have come down from the Contessa de Dia, about whom we know very little. In this song she tells of her resentment at losing her lover to another woman.

"A chantar m'er de so q'ieu no volria"

I must sing of things I would rather not sing.
So much rancor have I against the man whose sweet friend I am.
For I love him more than anything.
Pity and courtesy are worth nothing to him.
Neither are my beauty or my merit or my good sense.
I'm as trapped and betrayed
as I might have deserved to be, if I hadn't the least charm.

But this consoles me—that I have committed no injury
    against you, dear friend, through any fault of mine.
I love you more than Seguin loved valor.
It gives me pleasure to vanquish you in loving—
since you, dearest friend, are the most valiant of men.
You treat me proudly in words and looks,
while showing gentleness to all the others.

I marvel at your arrogant presence
confronting me; for I have good reason to grieve.
It's unjust that another love tears you from me.
Whatever she may say—however she may welcome you—
remember the beginning
of our love. Please God that I'm not at fault
for this parting of ours!

Both the great prowess that lodges in your heart,
and your striking pride make me unhappy.
For I don't know of any woman, near or far,
who wouldn't be drawn to you—if she were ready for love.
But you, dear friend, are so knowing, that you ought to
    recognize the truest woman.
Remember the verses we exchanged at our parting.

My merit, my high rank, should count for something,
and my beauty, and my faithful heart above all.
And so I'm sending you—there to your great house—
this song that serves as my messenger.

This song is translated by Marcelle Thiébaux in the *Writings of Medieval Women,* 2nd Ed. (New York: Garland, 1994).

I want to know, best and dearest of noble friends,
why you show yourself so fierce, so savage to me.
I don't know if it's arrogance or ill will.

Messenger, I wish you to tell him this besides:
that lofty pride damages many a man

English Songs
"Sumer is icumen in"

This well-known thirteenth-century song, from British Museum MS Harley 978, f. 11v (modernized here by the editor), is the first known example of a canon *(rota, or "round"), and it is also important in the development of* gymel. *A round (like "Row, row, row your boat") was called a canon because a single line of music could be elaborated into a complex piece simply through rules. In the* Sumer-canon, *four voices sing through the whole song, the second, third, and fourth singers each beginning when the previous voice has finished the first line. A fifth and sixth voice sing the two* pes *("foot") lines continuously beneath the melody. The result is a six-part full harmony based on major thirds* (gymel), *the pleasant harmony that is considered natural today but in the Middle Ages was admired only in England. In Europe, medieval harmony was based on Pythagorean ideas that favored the fourth (C-F), fifth (C-G), and octave (C-C)—intervals that sound "hollow" or "medieval" today. In the fifteenth century, parallel thirds (C-E) came to be accepted as non-dissonant throughout Western music, under the influence of English music.*

Sumer is icumen in—	*Spring has come*
lhude sing, cuccu!	*loudly*
Groweth sed and bloweth med	*meadow*
and springth the wde nu.	*woods*
Sing, cuccu!	
Awe bleteth after lomb,	*ewe bleats*
lhouth after calve cu;	*lows, cow*
bulluc sterteth, bucke verteth—	*bull leaps, farts*
murye sing, cuccu!	
Cuccu, cuccu!	
Wel singes thu, cuccu;	
ne swik thu naver nu.	*Cease, never*

pes
Sing, cuccu, nu! Sing, cuccu!
Sing, cuccu! Sing, cuccu, nu!

"Myrie it is"

This Middle English song, from Bodleian Library MS Rawlinson G.22, f. 1v (modernized here by the editor), is, along with the Sumer-canon above, one of only 33 English songs before 1400 which survive with their music intact. It is much more common in medieval Europe for words to have been written down without any notation of the music: people either just "knew" the melody ("to be sung to the tune of Greensleeves*") or they didn't know how to read or write musical notation but wanted to remember the words. This short poem, sung to a wonderful dance melody that doesn't quite match the stark ending of the text, is typical of English lyrics that allow several possible interpretations.*

Myrie it is while sumer ilast	
with fugheles song;	*bird's*
oc nu neheth windes blast	*but, draws near*
and weder strong.	*weather*
Ei, ei! what this niht is long!	*Alas! how long this night is!*
And ich, with wel michel wrong,	*very great*
soregh and murn and fast.	*sorrow*

Geoffrey Chaucer (c.1343–1400)
"Chaucers Wordes Unto Adam, His Owne Scriveyn"

In this lyric poem the English poet Geoffrey Chaucer (c.1343–1400) complains about the bad job his scribe does in copying his works. Because Chaucer must rub and scrape the parchment to make corrections, he curses the scribe to the same fate, rubbing and scraping the dandruff on his head. The text, from Trinity College Cambridge MS R.3.20, is modernized by the editor.

Adam scriveyn, if ever it thee befalle	*scribe*
Boece or Troylus for to wryten newe,	*Boethius' Consolation, Troilus & Criseyde*
Under thy long lokkes thou most have the scalle,	*scales on the scalp*
But after my makyng thow wryte more trewe;	*writing (poems)*
So ofte adaye I mot thy werk renewe,	
It to correcte and eke to rubbe and scrape,	*also*
And al is thorugh thy negligence and rape.	

JACOB VON KÖNIGSHOFEN (1346–1420)
Chronicle

Jacob von Königshofen was an archivist, and his Chronicle *contains an account that reminds us that the twentieth century doesn't have a monopoly on atrocities. In fact, before the Nazi Holocaust in the middle of this century, the worst cases of wholesale slaughter probably occurred in the Middle Ages, the favorite victims being heretical Christians in southern France and Jews.*

In earlier times, Christian doctrine labeled as usury *the collection of any interest on loans. Christians were therefore forbidden to lend money at interest, and Jews became the principal money-lenders, especially on the scale needed to finance the wars of the nobility. It often became convenient for a king, when his debts were particularly large, to find an excuse to banish the Jews, and cancel any debts owed them. Because of the loss of property, the Jews early on learned not to have their own money tied up in real estate, preferring easily portable valuables like jewelry and precious metals.*

The same prejudices which justified the confiscation of property often inflamed more dangerous passions. Jews, conveniently remembered from the gospel accounts as the people who had killed Christ, were resented by some Christians. The rumors spread that Passover rituals required the blood of Christian children, or that water supplies were poisoned by Jews to cause outbreaks of disease and plague. In these cases, unruly mobs committed atrocities like that in Strasbourg on St. Valentine's Day in 1349, during the Black Death. The Strasbourg historian F. Closener was probably an eyewitness to the terrible events, and his account was incorporated by Königshofen into his Chronicle.

[The Cremation of the Strasbourg Jewry]

In the year 1349 there occurred the greatest epidemic that ever happened. Death went from one end of the earth to the other, on that side and this side of the sea, and it was greater among the Saracens than among the Christians. In some lands everyone died so that no one was left. Ships were also found on the sea laden with wares; the crew had all died and no one guided the ship. The bishop of Marseilles and priests and monks and more than half of all the people there died with them. In other kingdoms and cities so many people perished that it would be horrible to describe. The pope at Avignon stopped all sessions of court, locked himself in a room, allowed no one to approach him and had a fire burning before him all the time. [This last was probably intended as some sort of disinfectant.] And from what this epidemic came, all wise teachers and physicians could only say that it was God's will. And as the plague was

---

This document is taken from *The Jew in the Medieval World: A Source Book: 315–1791*, by Jacob R. Marcus (Jewish Publication Society, 1938; rpt. Atheneum, 1969).

now here, so was it in other places, and lasted more than a whole year. This epidemic also came to Strasbourg in the summer of the above-mentioned year, and it is estimated that about sixteen thousand people died.

In the matter of this plague the Jews throughout the world were reviled and accused in all lands of having caused it through poison which they are said to have put into the water and the wells—that is what they were accused of—and for this reason the Jews were burnt all the way from the Mediterranean into Germany, but not in Avignon, for the pope protected them there.

Nevertheless they tortured a number of Jews in Berne and Zofingen [Switzerland] who then admitted that they had put poison into many wells, and they also found the poison in the wells. Thereupon they burnt the Jews in many towns and wrote of this affair to Strasbourg, Freiburg, and Basel in order that they too should burn their Jews. But the leaders in these three cities in whose hands the government lay did not believe anything ought to be done to the Jews. However in Basel the citizens marched to the city hall and compelled the council to take an oath that they would burn the Jews, and that they would allow no Jew to enter the city for the next two hundred years. Thereupon the Jews were arrested in all these places and a conference was arranged to meet at Benfeld [Alsace, February 8, 1349]. The bishop of Strasbourg [Berthold II], all the feudal lords of Alsace, and representatives of the three above-mentioned cities came there. The deputies of the city of Strasbourg were asked what they were going to do with their Jews. They answered and said that they knew no evil of them. Then they asked the Strasbourgers why they had closed the wells and put away the buckets, and there was a great indignation and clamour against the deputies from Strasbourg. So finally the bishop and the lords and the Imperial Cities agreed to do away with the Jews. The result was that they were burnt in many cities, and wherever they were expelled they were caught by the peasants and stabbed to death or drowned. . . .

[The town-council of Strasbourg which wanted to save the Jews was deposed on the 9th/10th of February, and the new council gave in to the mob, who then arrested the Jews on Friday, the 13th.]

On Saturday—that was St. Valentine's Day—they burnt the Jews on a wooden platform in their cemetery. There were about two thousand people of them. Those who wanted to baptize themselves were spared. [Some say that about a thousand accepted baptism.] Many small children were taken out of the fire and baptized against the will of their fathers and mothers. And everything that was owed to the Jews was cancelled, and the Jews had to surrender all pledges and notes that they had taken for debts. The council, however, took the cash that the Jews possessed and divided it among the working-men proportionately. The money was indeed the thing that killed the Jews. If they had been poor and if the feudal lords had not been in debt to them, they would not have been burnt. After this wealth was divided among the artisans some gave their share to the cathedral or to the Church on the advice of their confessors.

Thus were the Jews burnt at Strasbourg, and in the same year in all the cities of the Rhine, whether Free Cities or Imperial Cities or cities belonging to the lords. In some towns they burnt the Jews after a trial, in others, without a trial. In some cities the Jews themselves set fire to their houses and cremated themselves.

It was decided in Strasbourg that no Jew should enter the city for a hundred years, but before twenty years had passed, the council and magistrates agreed that they ought to admit the Jews again into the city for twenty years. And so the Jews came back again to Strasbourg in the year 1368 after the birth of our Lord.

Giovanni Boccaccio (1313–1375)
The Decameron

In spite of his literary bent, Boccaccio's early years were spent in business in Naples, where he also stud-ied canon law. Because of his family's implication in a bankruptcy, he returned to his family home in Florence and began more seriously pursuing his literary interests, troubled by poverty and financial reverses. His early poems (some written in Naples) exploited the romance themes of chivalry and love. Several of them, in fact, are well known to English readers because they were translated, or transformed, by the English poet Geoffrey Chaucer (1343–1400)—Boccaccio's Teseida *became Chaucer's* Knight's Tale, *Boccaccio's* Il Filostrato *became Chaucer's* Troilus and Criseyde, *which in turn became Shakespeare's play* Troilus and Cressida.*

The Black Death, which struck Florence when Boccaccio was there in 1348, became the occasion for his masterpiece, The Decameron. *It is a collection of 100 tales told by a group of 7 young ladies and 3 young men from Florence, who decide to flee to one of their villas outside the city when the plague is at its height. To pass the time, they devise a tale-telling game: every day each of them will tell a tale, the theme for each day being set by the presiding ruler for that day. After ten days, each of them would have chosen the theme for a day, and each would have told ten tales, a hundred in all. Framed thus, Boccaccio's collection provides a remarkable view of medieval preoccupations, expressed through tales of love, treachery, nobility, lust, piety, and idealism. Some of the tales were so scurrilous—like the "Tale of Alibech," naturally included here—that they were excluded from English versions of the* Decameron *until well into our own century. In addition, Boccaccio's introductory account of the plague in Florence is a remarkable social document, providing a unique view of one of the most devas-tating calamities in human history.*

Author's Introduction [The Plague in Florence]

Most gracious ladies, knowing that you are all by nature pitiful, I know that in your judgment this work will seem to have a painful and sad origin. For it brings to mind the unhappy rec-ollection of that late dreadful plague, so pernicious to all who saw or heard of it. But I would not have this frighten you from reading further, as though you were to pass through nothing but sighs and tears in your reading. This dreary opening will be like climbing a steep moun-tain side to a most beautiful and delightful valley, which appears the more pleasant in pro-portion to the difficulty of the ascent. The end of happiness is pain, and in like manner mis-ery ends in unexpected happiness.

Richard Aldington's translation of *The Decameron* was first published by Garden City Publishing Company in 1930.

This brief fatigue (I say brief, because it occupies only a few words) is quickly followed by pleasantness and delight, as I promised you above; which, if I had not promised, you would not expect perhaps from this opening. Indeed, if I could have taken you by any other way than this, which I know to be rough, I would gladly have done so; but since I cannot otherwise tell you how the tales you are about to read came to be told, I am forced by necessity to write in this manner.

In the year 1348 after the fruitful incarnation of the Son of God, that most beautiful of Italian cities, noble Florence, was attacked by deadly plague. It started in the East either through the influence of the heavenly bodies or because God's just anger with our wicked deeds sent it as a punishment to mortal men; and in a few years killed an innumerable quantity of people. Ceaselessly passing from place to place, it extended its miserable length over the West. Against this plague all human wisdom and foresight were vain. Orders had been given to cleanse the city of filth, the entry of any sick person was forbidden, much advice was given for keeping healthy; at the same time humble supplications were made to God by pious persons in processions and otherwise. And yet, in the beginning of the spring of the year mentioned, its horrible results began to appear, and in a miraculous manner. The symptoms were not the same as in the East, where a gush of blood from the nose was the plain sight of inevitable death; but it began both in men and women with certain swellings in the groin and under the armpit. They grew to the size of a small apple or an egg, more or less, and were vulgarly called tumours. In a short space of time these tumours spread from the two parts named all over the body. Soon after this the symptoms changed and black or purple spots appeared on the arms and thighs or any other part of the body, sometimes a few large ones, sometimes many little ones. These spots were a certain sign of death, just as the original tumour had been and still remained.

No doctor's advice, no medicine could overcome or alleviate this disease. An enormous number of ignorant men and women set up as doctors in addition to those who were trained. Either the disease was such that no treatment was possible or the doctors were so ignorant that they did not know what caused it, and consequently could not administer the proper remedy. In any case very few recovered; most people died within about three days of the appearance of the tumours described above, most of them without any fever or other symptoms.

The violence of this disease was such that the sick communicated it to the healthy who came near them, just as a fire catches anything dry or oily near it. And it even went further. To speak to or go near the sick brought infection and common death to the living; and moreover, to touch the clothes or anything else the sick had touched or worn gave the disease to the person touching.

What I am about to tell now is a marvelous thing to hear; and if I and others had not seen it with our own eyes I would not dare to write it, however much I was willing to believe and whatever the good faith of the person from whom I heard it. So violent was the malignancy of this plague that it was communicated, not only from one man to another, but from garments of the sick or dead man to animals of another species, which caught the disease in that way and very quickly died of it. One day among other occasions I saw with my own eyes (as I said just now) the rags left lying in the street of a poor man who had died of the plague; two pigs came along, and as their habit is, turned the clothes over with their snouts and then munched at them, with the result that they both fell dead almost at once on the rags, as if they had been poisoned.

For these and similar or greater occurrences, such fear and fanciful notions took possession of the living that almost all of them adopted the same cruel policy, which was entirely to avoid the sick and everything belonging to them. By so doing, each one thought he would secure his own safety.

Some thought that moderate living and the avoidance of all superfluity would preserve them from the epidemic. They formed small communities, living entirely separate from everybody else. They shut themselves up in houses where there were no sick, eating the finest food and drinking the best wine very temperately, avoiding all excess, allowing no news or discussion of death and sickness, and passing the time in music and suchlike pleasures. Others thought just the opposite. They thought the sure cure for the plague was to drink and be merry, to go about singing and amusing themselves, satisfying every appetite they could, laughing and jesting at what happened. They put their words into practice, spent day and night going from tavern to tavern, drinking immoderately, or went into other people's houses, doing only those things which pleased them. This they could easily do because everyone felt doomed and had abandoned his property, so that most houses became common property and any stranger who went in made use of them as if he had owned them. And with all this bestial behaviour, they avoided the sick as much as possible.

In this suffering and misery of our city, the authority of human and divine laws almost disappeared, for, like other men, the ministers and the executors of the laws were all dead or sick or shut up with their families, so that no duties were carried out. Every man was therefore able to do as he pleased.

Many others adopted a course of life midway between the two just described. They did not restrict their victuals so much as the former, nor allow themselves to be drunken and dissolute like the latter, but satisfied their appetites moderately. They did not shut themselves up, but went about, carrying flowers or scented herbs or perfumes in their hands, in the belief that it was an excellent thing to comfort their brain with such odours; for the whole air was infected with the smell of dead bodies, of sick persons and medicines.

Others again held a still more cruel opinion, which they thought would keep them safe. They said that the only medicine against the plaguestricken was to go right away from them. Men and women, convinced of this and caring about nothing but themselves, abandoned their own city, their own houses, their dwellings, their relatives, their property, and went abroad or at least to the country round Florence, as if God's wrath in punishing men's wickedness with this plague would not follow them but strike only those who remained within the walls of the city, or as if they thought nobody in the city would remain alive and that its last hour had come.

Not everyone who adopted any of these various opinions died, nor did all escape. Some when they were still healthy had set the example of avoiding the sick, and, falling ill themselves, died untended.

One citizen avoided another, hardly any neighbour troubled about others, relatives never or hardly ever visited each other. Moreover, such terror was struck into the hearts of men and women by this calamity, that brother abandoned brother, and the uncle his nephew, and the sister her brother, and very often the wife her husband. What is even worse and nearly incredible is that fathers and mothers refused to see and tend their children, as if they had not been theirs.

Thus, a multitude of sick men and women were left without any care except from the charity of friends (but these were few), or the greed of servants, though not many of these could be had even for high wages. Moreover, most of them were coarse-minded men and women, who did little more than bring the sick what they asked for or watch over them when they were dying. And very often these servants lost their lives and their earnings. Since the sick were thus abandoned by neighbours, relatives and friends, while servants were scarce, a habit sprang up which had never been heard of before. Beautiful and noble women, when they fell sick, did not scruple to take a young or old man-servant, whoever he might be, and with no sort of shame, expose every part of their bodies to these men as if they had been women, for they were compelled by the necessity of their sickness to do so. This, perhaps, was a cause of looser morals in those women who survived.

In this way many people died who might have been saved if they had been looked after. Owing to the lack of attendants for the sick and the violence of the plague, such a multitude of people in the city died day and night that it was stupefying to hear of, let alone to see. From sheer necessity, then, several ancient customs were quite altered among the survivors.

The custom had been (as we still see it today), that women relatives and neighbours should gather at the house of the deceased, and there lament with the family. At the same time the men would gather at the door with the male neighbours and other citizens. Then came the clergy, few or many according to the dead person's rank; the coffin was placed on the shoulders of his friends and carried with funeral pomp of lighted candles and dirges to the church which the deceased had chosen before dying. But as the fury of the plague increased, this custom wholly or nearly disappeared, and new customs arose. Thus, people died, not only without having a number of women near them, but without a single witness. Very few indeed were honoured with the piteous laments and bitter tears of their relatives, who, on the contrary, spent their time in mirth, feasting and jesting. Even the women abandoned womanly pity and adopted this custom for their own safety. Few were they whose bodies were accompanied to church by more than ten or a dozen neighbours. Nor were these grave and honourable citizens but grave-diggers from the lowest of the people who got themselves called sextons, and performed the task for money. They took up the bier and hurried it off, not to the church chosen by the deceased but to the church nearest, preceded by four or six of the clergy with few candles and often none at all. With the aid of the grave-diggers, the clergy huddled the bodies away in any grave they could find, without giving themselves the trouble of a long or solemn burial service.

The plight of the lower and most of the middle classes was even more pitiful to behold. Most of them remained in their houses, either through poverty or in hopes of safety, and fell sick by thousands. Since they received no care and attention, almost all of them died. Many ended their lives in the streets both at night and during the day; and many others who died in their houses were only known to be dead because the neighbours smelled their decaying bodies. Dead bodies filled every corner. Most of them were treated in the same manner by the survivors, who were more concerned to get rid of their rotting bodies than moved by charity towards the dead. With the aid of porters, if they could get them, they carried the bodies out of the houses and laid them at the doors, where every morning quantities of the dead might be seen. They then were laid on biers, or, as these were often lacking, on tables.

Often a single bier carried two or three bodies, and it happened frequently that a husband and wife, two or three brothers, or father and son were taken off on the same bier. It frequently happened that two priests, each carrying a cross, would go out followed by three or four biers carried by porters; and where the priests thought there was one person to bury, there would be six or eight, and often, even more. Nor were these dead honoured by tears and lighted candles and mourners, for things had reached such a pass that people cared no more for dead men than we care for dead goats. Thus it plainly appeared that what the wise had not learned to endure with patience through the few calamities of ordinary life, became a matter of indifference even to the most ignorant people through the greatness of this misfortune.

Such was the multitude of corpses brought to the churches every day and almost every hour that there was not enough consecrated ground to give them burial, especially since they wanted to bury each person in the family grave, according to the old custom. Although the cemeteries were full they were forced to dig huge trenches, where they buried the bodies by hundreds. Here they stowed them away like bales in the hold of a ship and covered them with a little earth, until the whole trench was full.

Not to pry any further into all the details of the miseries which afflicted our city, I shall add that the surrounding country was spared nothing of what befell Florence. The villages on a smaller scale were like the city; in the fields and isolated farms the poor wretched peasants and their families were without doctors and any assistance, and perished in the highways, in their fields and houses, night and day, more like beasts than men. Just as the townsmen became dissolute and indifferent to their work and property, so the peasants, when they saw that death was upon them, entirely neglected the future fruits of their past labours both from the earth and from cattle, and thought only of enjoying what they had. Thus it happened that cows, asses, sheep, goats, pigs, fowls and even dogs, those faithful companions of man, left the farms and wandered at their will through the fields, where the wheat crops stood abandoned, unreaped and ungarnered. Many of these animals seemed endowed with reason, for, after they had pastured all day, they returned to the farms for the night of their own free will, without being driven.

Returning from the country to the city, it may be said that such was the cruelty of Heaven, and perhaps in part of men, that between March and July more than one hundred thousand persons died within the walls of Florence, what between the violence of the plague and the abandonment in which the sick were left by the cowardice of the healthy. And before the plague it was not thought that the whole city held so many people.

Oh, what great palaces, how many fair houses and noble dwellings, once filled with attendants and nobles and ladies, were emptied to the meanest servant! How many famous names and vast possessions and renowned estates were left without an heir! How many gallant men and fair ladies and handsome youths, whom Galen, Hippocrates and AEsculapius themselves would have said were in perfect health, at noon dined with their relatives and friends, and at night supped with their ancestors in the next world!

Third Day, Tenth Tale [Alibech and Rustico]

Most gracious ladies, perhaps you have never heard how the devil is put into hell; and so, without departing far from the theme upon which you have all spoken today, I shall tell you about it. Perhaps when you have learned it, you also will be able to save your souls, and you may also discover that although love prefers to dwell in gay palaces and lovely rooms rather than in poor huts, yet he sometimes makes his power felt among thick woods and rugged mountains and desert caves. Whereby we may well perceive that all us are subject to his power.

Now, to come to my story—in the city of Capsa in Barbery there lived a very rich man who possessed among other children a pretty and charming daughter, named Alibech. She was not a Christian, but she heard many Christians in her native town crying up the Christian Faith and service to God, and one day she asked one of them how a person could most effectively serve God. The reply was that those best serve God who fly furthest from the things of this world, like the hermits who had departed to the solitudes of the Thebaid Desert.

The girl was about fourteen and very simple minded. Urged by a mere childish enthusiasm and not by a well ordered desire, she secretly set out next morning quite alone, without saying a word to anyone, to find the Thebaid Desert. Her enthusiasm lasted several days and enabled her with great fatigue to reach those solitudes. In the distance she saw a little hut with a holy man standing at its entrance. He was amazed to see her there, and asked her what she was seeking. She replied that by God's inspiration she was seeking to serve Him, and begged the hermit to show her the right way to do so. But the holy man saw she was young and pretty, and feared that if he kept her with him he might be tempted of the devil. So he praised her good intentions, gave her some roots and wild apples to eat and some water to drink, and said:

"Daughter, not far from here dwells a holy man who is a far greater master of what you are seeking than I am; go to him."

And so he put her on the way. When she reached him, she was received with much the same words, and passing further on came to the cell of a young hermit named Rustico, to whom she made the same request as to the others. To test his spiritual strength, Rustico did not send her away, but took her into his cell. And when night came, he made her a bed of palm leaves and told her to sleep there.

Almost immediately after this, temptation began the struggle with his spiritual strength, and the hermit found that he had greatly over-estimated his powers of resistance. After a few assaults of the demon he shrugged his shoulders and surrendered. Putting aside holy thoughts and prayers and macerations, he began to think of her beauty and youth, and then pondered how he should proceed with her so that she should not perceive that he obtained what he wanted from her like a dissolute man. First of all he sounded her by certain questions, and discovered that she had never lain with a man and appeared to be very simple minded. He then saw how he could bring her to his desire under pretext of serving God. He began by eloquently showing how the devil is the enemy of the Lord God, and then gave her to understand that the service most pleasing to God it to put the devil back into hell, to which the Lord God has condemned him. The girl asked how this was done, and Rustico replied:

"You shall soon know. Do what you see me do."

He then threw off the few clothes he had and remained stark naked, and the girl imitated him. He kneeled down as if to pray and made her kneel exactly opposite him. As he gazed at her beauty, Rustico's desire became so great that the resurrection of the flesh occurred. Alibech looked at it with amazement, and said:

"Rustico, what is that thing I see sticking out in front of you which I haven't got?"

"My daughter," said Rustico, "that is the devil I spoke of. Do you see? He gives me so much trouble at this moment I can scarcely endure him."

Said the girl:

"Praised be God! I see I am better off than you are, since I haven't such a devil."

"You speak truly," said Rustico, "but instead of this devil you have something else which I haven't."

"What's that?" said Alibech.

"You've got hell," replied Rustico, "and I believe God sent you here for the salvation of my soul, because this devil gives me great trouble, and if you will take pity upon me and let me put him into hell, you will give me the greatest comfort and at the same time will serve God and please Him, since, as you say, you came here for that purpose."

In all good faith the girl replied: "Father, since I have hell in me, let it be whenever you please."

Said Rustico: "Blessings upon you, my daughter. Let us put him in now so that he will afterwards depart from me."

So saying, he took the girl on one of their beds, and showed her how to lie so as to imprison the thing accursed of God. The girl had never before put any devil into her hell and at first felt a little pain, and exclaimed to Rustico:

"O father! This devil must certainly be wicked and the enemy of God, for even when he is put back into hell he hurts it."

"Daughter," said Rustico, "it will not always be so."

To prevent this from happening, Rustico put it into hell six times, before he got off the bed, and so purged the devil's pride that he was glad to rest a little. Thereafter, he returned often and the obedient girl was always glad to take him in; and then the game began to give her pleasure, and she said to Rustico:

"I see that the good men of Capsa spoke the truth when they told me how sweet a thing is the service of God. I certainly do not remember that I ever did anything which gave me so much delight and pleasure as I get from putting the devil into hell. I think that everyone is a fool who does anything but serve God."

Thus it happened that she would often go to Rustico, and say:

"Father, I came here to serve God and not to remain in idleness. Let us put the devil in hell."

And once as they were doing it, she said:

"Rustico, I don't know why the devil ever goes out of hell. If he liked to remain there as much as hell likes to receive and hold him, he would never leave it."

The girl's frequent invitations to Rustico and their mutual pleasures in the service of God so took the stuffing out of his doublet that he now felt chilly where another man would have been in a sweat. So he told the girl that the devil must not be chastened or put into hell except when pride makes him lift his head. "And we," he said, "have so quelled his rage that he prays God to be left in peace." And in this way he silenced the girl for a time. But when she found that Rustico no longer asked her to put the devil in hell, she said one day:

"Rustico, your devil may be chastened and give you no more trouble, but my hell is not. You should therefore quench the raging of my hell with your devil, as I helped you to quell the pride of your devil with my hell."

Rustico, who lived on nothing but roots and water, made a poor response to this invitation. He told her that many devils would be needed to soothe her hell, but that he would do what he could. In this way he satisfied her hell a few times, but so seldom that it was like throwing a bean in a lion's mouth. And the girl, who thought they were not serving God as much as she wanted, kept murmuring.

Now, while there was this debate between the excess of desire in Alibech's hell and the lack of potency in Rustico's devil, a fire broke out in Capsa, and burned Alibech's father with all his children and servants. So Alibech became heir to all his property. A young man named Neerbale, who had spent all his money in riotous living, heard that she was still alive and set out to find her, which he succeeded in doing before the Court took over her father's property as that of a man who had died without heirs. To Rustico's great relief, but against her will, Neerbale brought her back to Capsa and married her, and together they inherited her large patrimony. But before Neerbale had lain with her, certain ladies one day asked her how she had served God in the desert. She replied that her service was to put the devil in hell, and that Neerbale had committed a great sin by taking her away from such service. The ladies asked:

"And how do you put the devil in hell?"

Partly in words and partly in gestures, the girl told them. At this they laughed so much that they are still laughing, and said:

"Be not cast down, my child, they know how to do that here, and Neerbale will serve the Lord God with you in that way."

As they told it up and down the city, it passed into a proverb that the service most pleasing to God is to put the devil into hell. And this proverb crossed the seas and remains until this day.

Therefore, young ladies, when you seek God's favour, learn to put the devil in hell, because this is most pleasing to God and to all parties concerned, and much good may come of it.

Fifth Day, Ninth Tale [Federigo's Generosity]

In the past there was in Florence a young man named Federigo, the son of Messer Filippo Alberighi, renowned above all other young gentlemen of Tuscany for his prowess in arms and his courtesy. Now, as most often happens to gentlemen, he fell in love with a lady named Monna Giovanna, in her time held to be one of the gayest and most beautiful women ever known in Florence. To win her love, he went to jousts and tourneys, made and gave feasts, and spent his money without stint. But she, no less chaste than beautiful, cared nothing for the things he did for her nor for him who did them.

Now as Federigo was spending far beyond his means and getting nothing in, as easily happens, his wealth failed and he remained poor with nothing but a little farm, on whose produce he lived very penuriously, and one falcon which was among the best in the world. More in love than ever, but thinking he would never be able to live in the town any more as he desired, he went to Campi where his farm was. There he spent his time hawking, asked nothing of anybody, and patiently endured his poverty.

Now while Federigo was in this extremity it happened one day that Monna Giovanna's husband fell ill, and seeing death come upon him, made his will. He was a very rich man and left his estate to a son who was already growing up. And then, since he had greatly loved Monna Giovanna, he made her his heir in case his son should die without legitimate children; and so died.

Monna Giovanna was now a widow, and as is customary with our women, she went with her son to spend the year in the country house she had near Federigo's farm. Now the boy happened to strike up a friendship with Federigo, and delighted in dogs and hawks. He often saw Federigo's falcon fly, and took such great delight in it that he very much wanted to have it, but did not dare ask for it, since he saw how much Federigo prized it.

While matters were in this state, the boy fell ill. His mother was very much grieved, as he was her only child and she loved him extremely. She spent the day beside him, trying to help him, and often asked him if there was anything he wanted, begging him to say so, for if it were possible to have it, she would try to get it for him. After she had many times made this offer, the boy said:

"Mother, if you can get me Federigo's falcon, I think I should soon be better."

The lady paused a little at this, and began to think what she should do. She knew that Federigo had loved her for a long time, and yet had never had one glance from her, and she said to herself:

"How can I send or go ask for this falcon, which is, from what I hear, the best that ever flew, and moreover his support in life? How can I be so thoughtless as to take this away from a gentleman who has no other pleasure left in life?"

Although she knew she was certain to have the bird for the asking, she remained in embarrassed thought, not knowing what to say, and did not answer her son. But at length love for her child got the upper hand and she determined that to please him in whatever way it might be, she would not send, but go herself for it and bring it back to him. So she replied:

"Be comforted, my child, and try to get better somehow. I promise you that tomorrow morning I will go for it, and bring it to you."

The child was so delighted that he became a little better that same day. And on the morrow the lady took another woman to accompany her, and as if walking for exercise went to Federigo's cottage, and asked for him. Since it was not the weather for it, he had not been hawking for some days, and was in his garden employed in certain work there. When he heard that Monna Giovanna was asking for him at the door, he was greatly astonished, and ran there happily. When she saw him coming, she got up to greet him with womanly charm, and when Federigo had courteously saluted her, she said:

"How do you do, Federigo? I have come here to make amends for the damage you have suffered through me by loving me more than was needed. And in token of this, I intend to dine today familiarly with you and my companion here."

"Madonna," replied Federigo humbly, "I do not remember ever to have suffered any damage through you, but received so much good that if I was ever worth anything it was owing to your worth and the love I bore it. Your generous visit to me is so precious to me that I could spend again all that I have spent; but you have come to a poor host."

So saying, he modestly took her into his house, and from there to his garden. Since there was nobody else to remain in her company, he said:

"Madonna, since there is nobody else, this good woman, the wife of this workman, will keep you company, while I go to set the table."

Now, although his poverty was extreme, he had never before realised what necessity he had fallen into by his foolish extravagance in spending his wealth. But he repented of it that morning when he could find nothing with which to do honour to the lady, for love of whom he had entertained vast numbers of men in the past. In his anguish he cursed himself and his fortune and ran up and down like a man out his senses, unable to find money or anything to pawn. The hour was late and his desire to honour the lady extreme, yet he would not apply to anyone else, even to his own workman; when suddenly his eye fell upon his falcon, perched on a bar in the sitting room. Having no one to whom he could appeal, he took the bird, and finding it plump, decided it would be food worth such a lady. So, without further thought, he wrung its neck, made his little maid servant quickly pluck and prepare it, and put it on a spit to roast. He spread the table with the whitest napery, of which he had some left, and returned to the lady in the garden with a cheerful face, saying that the meal he had been able to prepare for her was ready.

The lady and her companion arose and went to table, and there together with Federigo, who served it with the greatest devotion, they ate the good falcon, not knowing what it was.

They left the table and spent some time in cheerful conversation, and the lady, thinking the time had now come to say what she had come for, spoke fairly to Federigo as follows:

"Federigo, do you remember your former life and my chastity, which no doubt you considered harshness and cruelty, I have no doubt that you will be surprised at my presumption when you hear what I have come here for chiefly. But if you had children, through whom you could know the power of parental love, I am certain that you would to some extent excuse me."

"But, as you have no child, I have one, and I cannot escape the common laws of mothers. Compelled by their power, I have come to ask you—against my will, and against all good manners and duty—for a gift, which I know is something especially dear to you, and reasonably so, because I know your straitened fortune has left you no other pleasure, no other recreation, no other consolation. This gift is your falcon, which has so fascinated my child that if I do not take it to him, I am afraid his present illness will grow so much worse that I may lose him. Therefore I beg you, not by the love you bear me (which holds you to nothing), but by your own nobleness, which has shown itself so much greater in all courteous usage than is wont in other men, that you will be pleased to give it to me, so that through this gift I may be able to say that I have saved my child's life, and thus be ever under an obligation to you."

When Federigo heard the lady's request and knew that he could not serve her, because he had given her the bird to eat, he began to weep in her presence, for he could not speak a word. The lady at first thought that his grief came from having to part with his good falcon, rather than from anything else, and she was almost on the point of retraction. But she remained firm and waited for Federigo's reply after his lamentation. And he said:

"Madonna, ever since it has pleased God that I should set my love upon you, I have felt that Fortune has been contrary to me in many things, and have grieved for it. But they are all light in comparison with what she has done to me now, and I shall never be at peace with her again when I reflect that you came to my poor house, which you never deigned to visit when I was rich, and asked me for a little gift, and Fortune has so acted that I cannot give it to you. Why this cannot be, I will briefly tell you.

"When I heard that you in your graciousness desired to dine with me and I thought of your excellence and your worthiness, I thought it right and fitting to honour you with the best food I could obtain; so, remembering the falcon you ask me for and its value, I thought it a meal worthy of you, and today you had it roasted on the dish and set forth as best I could. But now I see that you wanted the bird in another form, it is such a grief to me that I cannot serve you that I think I shall never be at peace again."

And after saying this, he showed her the feathers and the feet and the beak of the bird in proof. When the lady heard and saw all this, she first blamed him for having killed such a falcon to make a meal for a woman; and then she inwardly commended his greatness of soul which no poverty could or would be able to abate. But, having lost all hope of obtaining the falcon, and thus perhaps the health of her son, she departed sadly and returned to the child. Now, either from disappointment at not having the falcon or because his sickness must inevitably have led to it, the child died not many days later, to the mother's extreme grief.

Although she spent some time in tears and bitterness, yet, since she had been left very rich and was still young, her brothers often urged her to marry again. She did not want to do so, but as they kept on pressing her, she remembered the worthiness of Federigo and his last act of generosity, in killing such a falcon to do her honour.

"I will gladly submit to marriage when you please," she said to her brothers, "but if you want me to take a husband, I will take no man but Federigo degli Alberighi."

At this her brothers laughed at her, saying:

"Why, what are you talking about, you fool? Why do you want a man who hasn't a penny in the world?"

But she replied:

"Brothers, I know it is as you say, but I would rather have a man who needs money than money which needs a man."

Seeing her determination, the brothers, who knew Federigo's good qualities, did as she wanted, and gave her with all her wealth to him, in spite of his poverty. Federigo, finding that he had such a woman, whom he loved so much, with all her wealth to boot, as his wife, was more prudent with his money in the future, and ended his days happily with her.

Sixth Day, Seventh Tale [Madonna Filippa's Defense]

Most worthy ladies, it is always a good thing to know how to speak well, but I think it is best of all when it is called for by necessity. This was well done by a lady, of whom I intend to tell you, for she not only provided merriment and laughter to those who heard her, but saved herself from the snare of a shameful death, as you shall hear.

In Prato there was once a law, no less blameworthy than harsh, which without any distinction condemned to be burned alive any woman whose husband found her in adultery with a lover, just like a woman who lay with any other man for money.

While this law was in force a beautiful woman, named Madonna Filippa, who was very much in love, was found one night in her room by her husband, Rinaldo de' Pugliesi, in the arms of Lazzarino de' Guazzagliotri, a noble and handsome young man of that country, whom she loved beyond her own self. Rinaldo was exceedingly angry when he saw this, and could scarcely refrain from rushing at them and killing them. And if he had not feared the consequences to himself in following his anger, he would have done so.

He restrained himself from this, but could not refrain from claiming from the law of Prato what was forbidden him to take himself—his wife's life. He produced sufficient evidence, and the next day he brought the accusation against his wife and had her cited before the court, without consulting anyone.

The lady was a great-hearted woman, as usually happens with women who are really in love; and although she was advised against it by her numerous friends and relatives, she determined to appear before the Court and rather die bravely confessing her fault than to live in exile by basely fleeing, and thus showing herself unworthy of such a lover as the man in whose arms she had lain the night before. She appeared before the judge accompanied by many men and women, who urged her to deny the fault; and asked him in a clear voice and with firm countenance what he wanted of her.

The judge looked at her, saw she was beautiful and accomplished, and, as her speech showed, a woman of high spirit. He felt compassion for her, suspecting that she would make the confession which, for his honour's sake, would force him to condemn her to death. But, since he could not avoid putting the question to her, he said:

"Madonna, as you see, here is Rinaldo your husband, and he lays a plaint against you that he has found you in adultery with another man. And therefore he demands that in accordance with the law I punish you for it by death. But this I cannot do unless you confess it, and so beware of what you say in answer, and tell me if your husband's accusation is true."

The lady, without the slightest fear, replied in a pleasant voice:

"Messer, it is true that Rinaldo is my husband, and that last night he found me in the arms of Lazzarino, wherein I have often lain, through the deep and perfect love I have for him. Nor shall I ever deny it. But I am certain you know that the laws should be equal for both sexes and made with the consent of those who are to obey them. That is not so in this case, for it only touches us poor women, who are yet able to satisfy many more than men can; moreover, no woman gave her consent or was even consulted when this law was passed. And so it may reasonably be called an inequitable law.

"If, to the harm of my body and your own soul, you choose to carry out this law, it is for you to do so. But before you proceed to judgment, I ask one little favour of you—ask my husband whether or not I have not always wholly yielded him my body whenever and howsoever often he asked it."

Rinaldo, without awaiting the judge's question, immediately replied that beyond all doubt she had always yielded to his pleasure whenever he required it.

"Then," said the lady swiftly, "I ask you, Messer Judge, if he has always had from me what he needed and pleased, what should and shall I do with what remains over? Should I throw it to the dogs? Is it not far better to give it to a gentleman who loves me beyond himself than to let it spoil or go to waste?"

This case concerning so well known a lady had attracted to the Court almost all the inhabitants of Prato. When they heard this amusing question they laughed heartily, and then almost with one voice shouted that the lady was right and spoke well. Before they separated, with the judge's consent they modified this cruel law, and limited it only to those women who were unfaithful to their husbands for money.

So Rinaldo departed in confusion, and the lady returned home free and happy and in triumph, like one escaped from the flames.

Tenth Day, Tenth Tale [The Story of Griselda]

A long time ago the eldest son of the Marquess of Saluzzo was a young man named Gualtieri. He was wifeless and childless, spent his time hunting and hawking, and never thought about marrying or having children, wherein he was probably very wise. This displeased his subjects, who several times begged him to take a wife, so that he might not die without an heir and leave them without a ruler, offering to find him a wife born of such a father and mother as would give him good hopes of her and content him. To which Gualtieri replied:

"My friends, you urge me to do something I was determined never to do, seeing how hard it is to find a woman of suitable character, and how many of the opposite sort there are, and how wretched is the life of a man who takes a wife unsuitable to him. It is foolishness of you to think you can judge a girl by the characters of her father and mother (from which you argue that you can find me one to please me), for I do not see how you can really know the fathers' or mothers' secrets. And even if you did know them, daughters are often quite different from their fathers and mothers."

"But you want me to take these chains, and I am content to do so. If it turns out badly I want to have no one to complain of but myself, and so I shall choose for myself. And I tell you that if you do not honour the wife I choose as your lady you will find out to your cost how serious a thing it is to have compelled me by your entreaties to take a wife against my will."

They replied that they were content, if only he would take a wife.

For some time Gualtieri had been pleased by the character of a poor girl in a hamlet near his house. He thought her beautiful, and that he might live comfortably enough with her. So he decided that he would marry her without seeking any further, and, having sent for her father, who was a very poor man, arranged to marry her. Having done this, Gualtieri called together all his friends from the surrounding country, and said:

"My friends, it has pleased you to desire that I should marry, and I am ready to do so, more to please you than from any desire I have of taking a wife. You know you promised me that you would honour anyone I chose as your lady. The time has now come for me to keep my promise to you and you to keep yours to me. I have found a girl after my heart quite near here; I intend to marry her and to bring her home in a few days. So take thought to make a handsome marriage feast and how you can honourably receive her, so that I may consider myself content with your promise as you may be with mine."

The good men cheerfully replied that they were glad of it, and that they would consider her their lady and honour her as their lady in all things. After which, they all set about preparing a great and handsome wedding feast, and so did Gualtieri. He prepared a great and fine banquet, and invited many friends and relatives and noblemen and others. Moreover, he had rich and beautiful dresses cut and fitted on a girl, who seemed to him about the same build as the girl he proposed to marry. And he also purchased girdles and rings and a rich and beautiful crown, and everything necessary to a bride.

When the day appointed for the wedding arrived, Gualtieri about the middle of Terce mounted his horse, and so did those who had come to honour him. Everything being arranged, he said:

"Gentlemen, it is time to go for the bride."

Setting out with all his company he came to the hamlet and the house of the girl's father, where he found her drawing water in great haste, so that she could go with the other women to see Gualtieri's bride. And when Gualtieri saw her, he called her by her name, Griselda, and asked where her father was. She blushed and said:

"He is in the house, my lord."

Gualtieri dismounted, told everyone to wait for him, and entered the poor little house where he found the girl's father (who was named Giannucole), and said to him:

"I have come to marry Griselda, but first I want to ask her a few things in your presence."

He then asked her whether, if he married her, she would try to please him, and never be angry at anything he said or did, and if she would be obedient, and several other things, to all of which she said "Yes." Gualtieri then took her by the hand and led her forth. In the presence of all his company he had her stripped naked, and then clothes he had prepared were brought, and she was immediately dressed and shod, and he had a crown put on her hair, all unkempt as it was. Everyone marvelled at this, and he said:

"Gentlemen, I intend to take this girl as my wife, if she will take me as her husband."

He then turned to her, as she stood blushing and irresolute, and said:

"Griselda, will you take me as your husband?"

"Yes, my lord," she replied.

"And I will take you as my wife," said he.

Then in the presence of them all he pledged his faith to her; and they set her on a palfrey and honourably conducted her to his house. The wedding feast was great and handsome, and the rejoicing no less than if he had married the daughter of the King of France.

The girl seemed to have changed her soul and manners with her clothes. As I said, she was beautiful of face and body, and she became so agreeable, so pleasant, so well-behaved that she seemed like the daughter of a nobleman, and not Giannucole's child and a cattle herder; which surprised everyone who had known her before. Moreover, she was so obedient and so ready to serve her husband that he felt himself to be the happiest and best matched man in the world. And she was so gracious and kindly to her husband's subjects that there was not one of them but loved her and gladly honoured her, while all prayed for her good and her prosperity and advancement. Whereas they had said that Gualtieri had showed little wisdom in marrying her, they now said that he was the wisest and shrewdest man in the world, because no one else would have known the lofty virtue hidden under her poor clothes and village garb.

In short, before long she acted so well that not only in the marquisate but everywhere people were talking of her virtues and good actions; and whatever had been said against her husband for having married her was now turned to the opposite. She had not long been with Gualtieri when she became pregnant, and in due time gave birth to a daughter, at which Gualtieri rejoiced greatly.

Soon after this the idea came to him to test her patience with a long trial and intolerable things. He said unkind things to her, seemed to be angry, and said that his subjects were most discontented with her on account of her low birth, and especially when they saw that she bore children. He said they were very angry at the birth of a daughter and did nothing but murmur. When the lady heard these words, she did not change countenance or cheerfulness, but said to him:

"My lord, you may do with me what you think most to your honour and satisfaction. I shall be content, for I know that I am less than they and unworthy of the honour to which you have raised me by your courtesy."

Gualtieri liked this reply and saw that no pride had risen up in her from the honour done her by him and others.

Soon after, he informed his wife in general terms that his subjects could not endure the daughter she had borne. He then gave orders to one of his servants whom he sent to her. The man, with a dolorous visage, said:

"Madonna, if I am to avoid death I must do what my lord bids me. He tells me I am to take your daughter and . . ."

He said no more, but the lady, hearing these words and seeing the servant's face, and remembering what had been said to her, guessed that he had been ordered to kill the child. She went straight to the cradle, kissed and blessed the child, and although she felt great anguish in her heart, put the child in the servant's arms without changing her countenance, and said:

"Do what my lord and yours has ordered you to do. But do not leave her for the birds and animals to devour her body, unless you were ordered to do so."

The servant took the child and told Gualtieri what the lady had said. He marvelled at her constancy, and sent the servant with the child to a relative at Bologna, begging her to bring her up and educate her carefully, but without ever saying whose daughter she was.

After this the lady again became pregnant, and in due time brought forth a male child, which delighted Gualtieri. But what he had already done was not enough for him. He pierced the lady with a worse wound, and one day said to her in pretended anger:

"Since you have borne this male child, I cannot live at peace with my subjects, who complain bitterly that a grandson of Giannucole must be their lord after me. If I am not to be driven out, I fear I must do now as I did before, and in the end abandon you and take another wife."

The lady listened to him patiently, and her only reply was:

"My lord, content yourself and do what is pleasing to you. Do not think about me, for nothing pleases me except as it pleases you."

Not many days afterwards Gualtieri sent for his son in the same way that he had sent for his daughter, and while pretending in the same ways to kill the child, sent it to be brought up in Bologna, as he had sent the girl. And his wife said no more and looked no worse than she had done about the daughter. Gualtieri marvelled at this and said to himself that no other woman could have done what she did; and if he had not seen that she loved her children while she had them, he would have thought she did it to get rid of them whereas he saw it was from obedience to him.

His subjects thought he had killed his children and blamed him severely and thought him a cruel man, while they felt great pity for his wife. And when the women condoled with her on the death of her children, she never said anything except that it was not her wish but the wish of him who begot them.

Several years after his daughter's birth, Gualtieri thought the time had come for the last test of his wife's patience. He kept saying that he could no longer endure to have Griselda as his wife, that he knew he had acted childishly and wrongly when he married her, that he therefore meant to solicit the Pope for dispensation to marry another woman and abandon Griselda; for all of which he was reproved by many good men. But his only reply was that it was fitting this should be done.

Hearing of these things, the lady felt she must expect to return to her father's house and perhaps watch cattle as she had done in the past, and see another woman take the man she loved; at which she grieved deeply. But she prepared herself to endure this with a firm countenance, as she had endured the other wrongs of Fortune.

Not long afterwards Gualtieri received forged letters from Rome, which he showed to his subjects, pretending that the Pope by these letters gave him a dispensation to take another wife and leave Griselda. So, calling her before him, he said to her in the presence of many of his subjects:

"Wife, the Pope has granted me a dispensation to leave you and to take another wife. Now, since my ancestors were great gentlemen and lords of this country while yours were always labourers, I intend that you shall no longer be my wife, but return to Giannucole's house with the dowry you brought me, while I shall bring home another wife I have found more suitable for me."

At these words the lady could only restrain her tears by a great effort, beyond that of women's nature, and replied:

"My lord, I always knew that my lowly rank was in no wise suitable to your nobility; and the rank I have had with you I always recognized as coming from God and you, and never looked upon it as given to me, but only lent. You are pleased to take it back, and it must and does please me to return it to you. Here is the ring with which you wedded me; take it. You tell me to take the dowry I brought you; to do this there is no need for you to pay anything nor shall I need a purse or a sumpter horse, for I have not forgotten that I came to you naked. If you think it right that the body which has borne your children should be seen by everyone, I will go away naked. But in exchange for my virginity, which I brought here, and cannot carry away, I beg you will at least be pleased to let me take away one shift over and above my dowry."

Gualtieri, who was nearer to tears then anyone else present, managed to keep his countenance stern, and said:

"You shall have a shift."

Those who were present urged him to give her a dress, so that she who had been his wife for thirteen years should not be seen to leave his house so poorly and insultingly as it would be for her to leave it in a shift. But their entreaties were vain. So the lady, clad only in her shift, unshod and with nothing on her head, commended him to God, left his house, and returned to her father accompanied by the tears and lamentation of all who saw her.

Giannucole (who had never believed it was true that Gualtieri would keep his daughter as a wife and had always expected this event), had kept the clothes she had taken off the morning when Gualtieri married her. So she took them and put them on, and devoted herself to drudgery in her father's house, enduring the assaults of hostile Fortune with a brave spirit.

After Gualtieri had done this, he told his subjects that he was to marry the daughter of one of the Counts of Panago. He therefore made great preparations for the wedding, and sent for Griselda to come to him; and when she came, he said:

"I am bringing home the lady I have just married, and I intend to do her honour at her arrival. You know there is not a woman in the house who can prepare the rooms and do many other things needed for such a feast. You know everything connected with the house better than anyone, so you must arrange everything that is to be done, and invite all the women you think fit and receive them as if you were mistress of the house. Then, when the marriage feast is over, you can return home."

These words were a dagger in Griselda's heart, for she had not been able to dispense with the love she felt for him as she had her good fortune, but she said:

"My lord, I am ready."

So, in her coarse peasant dress, she entered the house she had left a little before in her shift, and had the rooms cleaned and arranged, put out hangings and carpets in the halls, looked to the kitchen, and set her hand to everything as if she had been a scullery wench of the house. And she never paused until everything was ready and properly arranged.

After this she invited all the ladies of the surrounding country in Gualtieri's name, and then awaited the feast. On the wedding day, dressed in her poor clothes, she received all the ladies with a cheerful visage and a womanly manner.

Gualtieri had had his children carefully brought up in Bologna by his relative, who was married into the family of the Counts of Panago. The daughter was now twelve years old, the most beautiful thing ever seen, and the boy was seven. He sent for her and asked her to come to Saluzzo with his son and daughter, to bring an honourable company with her, and to tell everyone that she was bringing the girl as his wife, and never to let anyone know that the girl was anything else. Her husband did what the Marquess asked, and set out. In a few days he reached Saluzzo about dinner time, with the girl and boy and his noble company; and all the peasants of the country were there to see Gualtieri's new wife.

The girl was received by the ladies and taken to the hall where the tables were spread, and Griselda went cheerfully to meet her, saying:

"Lady, you are welcome."

The ladies had begged Gualtieri, but in vain, to allow Griselda to stay in her room or to lend her one of her own dresses, so that she might not have to meet strangers in such a guise. They all sat down to table and began the meal. Every man looked at the girl and said that Gualtieri had made a good exchange, and Griselda above all praised her and her little brother.

Gualtieri now felt that he had tested his wife's patience as far as he desired. He saw that the strangeness of all this did not alter her and he was certain it was not the result of stupidity, for he knew her to be an intelligent woman. He thought it now time to take her from the bitterness which he felt she must be hiding behind a smiling face. So he called her to him, and in everyone's presence said to her smilingly:

"What do you think of my new wife?"

"My lord," replied Griselda, "I see nothing but good in her. If she is as virtuous as she is beautiful, as I well believe, I have no doubt that you will live with her the happiest lord in the world. But I beg you as earnestly as I can not to give her the wounds you gave the other woman who was your wife. I think she could hardly endure them, because she is younger and because she has been brought up delicately, whereas the other laboured continually from her childhood."

Gualtieri saw that she really believed he was to marry the other, and yet spoke nothing but good of her. He made her sit down beside him, and said:

"Griselda, it is now time that you should reap the reward of your long patience, and that those who have thought me cruel and wicked and brutal should know that what I have done was directed towards a pre-determined end, which was to teach you to be a wife, then how to choose and keep a wife, and to procure me perpetual peace for so long as I live with you. When I came and took you to wife, I greatly feared that this would not happen to me; and so, to test you, I have given you the trials and sufferings you know. I have never perceived that you thwarted my wishes by word or deed, and I think that in you I have the comfort I desire. I mean to give you back now what I deprived you of for a long time, and to heal the wounds I gave you with the greatest delight. Therefore, with a glad spirit, take her whom you think to be my wife and her brother as your children and mine. They are the children whom you and many others have long thought that I had cruelly murdered. And I am your husband, who loves you above all things, believing I can boast that no man exists who can so rejoice in his wife as I in you."

He then embraced and kissed her. She was weeping with happiness. They both arose and went to where their daughter was sitting, quite stupefied by what she had heard, and tenderly embraced her and her brother, thus undeceiving them and many of those present.

The ladies arose merrily from the table and went with Griselda to her room. With better hopes they took off her old clothes and dressed her in one of her noble robes, and brought her back to the hall a lady, which she had looked even in her rags.

They rejoiced over their children, and everyone was glad at what had happened. The feasting and merrymaking were prolonged for several days, and Gualtieri was held to be a wise man, although they thought the testing of his wife harsh and intolerable. But above all they esteemed the virtue of Griselda.

The Count of Panago soon afterwards returned to Bologna. Gualtieri took Giannucole away from his labour and installed him as his father-in-law, so that he ended his days honourably and in great content. He afterwards married off his daughter to a nobleman of great wealth and distinction, and lived long and happily with Griselda, always honouring her as much as he could.

What more is to be said, save that divine souls are sometimes rained down from Heaven into poor houses, while in royal palaces are born those who are better fitted to herd swine than to rule over men? Who but Griselda could have endured with a face not only tearless but cheerful, the stern and unheard-of tests imposed on her by Gualtieri? It would perhaps not have been such a bad thing if he had chosen one of those women who, if she had been driven out of her home in a shift, would have let another man so shake her fur that a new dress would have come from it.